T0216628

Lecture Notes in Artificial Intelligence 5422

Edited by R. Goebel, J. Siekmann, and W. Wahlster

Subseries of Lecture Notes in Computer Science

FoLLI Publications on Logic, Language and Information

Peter Bosch   David Gabelaia
Jérôme Lang (Eds.)

Logic, Language, and Computation

7th International Tbilisi Symposium
on Logic, Language, and Computation, TbiLLC 2007
Tbilisi, Georgia, October 1-5, 2007
Revised Selected Papers

 Springer

Volume Editors

Peter Bosch
Universität Osnabrück
Institut für Kognitionswissenschaft
49069 Osnabrück, Germany
E-mail: pbosch@uos.de

David Gabelaia
Razmadze Mathematical Institute
1 Aleksidze st., 0193, Tbilisi, Georgia
E-mail: gabelaia@gmail.com

Jérôme Lang
LAMSADE, Université Paris-Dauphine
75775 Paris Cedex 16, France
E-mail: lang@lamsade.dauphine.fr

Library of Congress Control Number: Applied for

CR Subject Classification (1998): I.2, F.4.1

LNCS Sublibrary: SL 7 – Artificial Intelligence

ISSN	0302-9743
ISBN-10	3-642-00664-7 Springer Berlin Heidelberg New York
ISBN-13	978-3-642-00664-7 Springer Berlin Heidelberg New York

springer.com

© Springer-Verlag Berlin Heidelberg 2009
Printed in Germany

Typesetting: Camera-ready by author, data conversion by Scientific Publishing Services, Chennai, India
Printed on acid-free paper   SPIN: 12614431   06/3180   5 4 3 2 1 0

Preface

This volume presents a selection of papers presented in Tbilisi on the occasion of the 7th International Tbilisi Symposium on Logic, Language, and Information, jointly organized by the Centre for Language, Logic, and Speech (CLLS) in Tbilisi, the Georgian Academy of Sciences, and the Institute for Logic, Language, and Computation (ILLC) in Amsterdam. The conference and the volume are representative of the aims of the organizing institutes: to promote the integrated study of logic, information, and language. While the conference is open to contributions to any of the three fields, it hopes to promote cross-fertilization by achieving stronger awareness of developments in the other fields, and of work which embraces more than one field or belongs to the interface between fields. The topics and brief characterizations of the contributions in this volume bear witness to these aims.

Conceptual Modeling of Spatial Relations. Rusudan Asatiani proposes that spatial relations as expressed in Georgian preverbs can be captured with the help of the dimensions Point of View (speaker's or teller's position), Geographic Space (various directions and distance dichotomy), and Communicational Space (Ego and Alter Spaces). Point of View, Ego Space, and Distance Dichotomy are flexible: They can be changed according to the speaker's (or teller's) attitude, while abstract relations are stable. Various combinations of the dimensions are represented in Georgian by the preverbs: there are nine simple and seven complex preverbs.

Pragmatics and Game Theory. Anton Benz proposes a game-theoretic account of a subclass of 'relevance' implicatures arising from irrelevant answers. He argues that these phenomena can be explained on the assumption that interlocutors agree on production and interpretation strategies that are robust against small 'trembles' in the speaker's production strategy. Benz argues for a new pragmatic principle which he calls the Principle of Optimal Completion. He also claims that the proposed model provides a parallel account of scalar implicatures which removes some limitations of previous accounts.

Atypical Valency Phenomena. Igor Boguslavsky discusses a set of phenomena arising in cases where arguments (actants) are not, as would typically be the case, directly syntactically subordinated to their predicates. In less typical cases, arguments can syntactically subordinate their predicate (passive valency slots) or may have no immediate syntactic link with it (discontinuous valency slots). These types of valency slots are mostly characteristic of adjectives, adverbs, and nouns. A number of linguistic concepts are related, directly or indirectly, to the notion of actant. However, usually only the typical valency instantiation is taken into account. If one also takes into consideration passive and discontinuous valency slot filling, the area of actant-related phenomena expands greatly and, as Boguslavsky shows, a broader generalization of the notions of diathesis and conversion seems to be called for.

Lexical Typology. Anastasia Bonch-Osmolovskaia, Ekaterina Rakhilina, and Tatiana Reznikova present a study in lexical typology, specifically on the semantic domain of pain or unpleasant bodily sensations. They report on a database they constructed for a sample of 23 languages and the methodology used, and show that the multidimensional classifications implemented in the database permit cross-linguistic generalizations on pain and human body conceptualizations as well as on regularities of semantic shifts in different languages.

Formal Semantics and Experimental Evidence. Peter Bosch argues that experiments on the online processing of linguistic utterances provide information about language processing in the first instance, and only indirectly about linguistic knowledge, while it has been linguistic knowledge, and not linguistic processing, that has been the subject matter of theoretical linguistics. So how can such evidence be relevant to theoretical linguistics? Or how can linguistic theory inform a theory of language processing? Bosch discusses this issue with respect to the processing and the formal semantics of the English definite determiner. He argues that the meaning of the definite determiner, as it shows up in experiments on online comprehension, can actually be accounted for in an incremental variant of current formal semantics.

Exceptional Quantifier Scope. Adrian Brasoveanu and Donka Farkas propose a new solution to the problem of exceptional scope of (in)definites, exemplified by the widest and intermediate scope readings of the sentence 'Every student of mine read every poem that a famous Romanian poet wrote'. They argue that the exceptional scope readings have two sources: (i) discourse anaphora to particular sets of entities and quantificational dependencies between these entities that restrict the domain of quantification of the two universal determiners and the indefinite article; (ii) non-local accommodation of the discourse referent that restricts the quantificational domain of the indefinite article. The proposal is formulated in a compositional dynamic system in classical type logic and relies on two independently motivated assumptions: (a) the discourse context stores not only (sets of) individuals, but also quantificational dependencies between them, and (b) quantifier domains are always contextually restricted. Under this analysis, (in)definites are unambiguous and there is no need for special choice-functional variables to derive exceptional scope readings.

Georgian Focussing Particles. Anna Chutkerashvili describes the uses of the Georgian particles ķi and –c, both rendered in English by 'even'. These particles are similar in meaning and can both have a focusing function. Still, they do not substitute for each other. The central difference is that -c is a bound form while ķi is not. Both particles often occur together. The dominating element in building up the meaning of '-c ķi' is -c, which is stronger in emphasis; -c ķI is used to emphasize something unexpected or surprising.

Polarity and Pragmatics. Regine Eckardt argues that current pragmatic theories of licensing Negative Polarity Items (NPIs) fail to capture the distinction between strong and weak NPIs. She attempts to show that an analysis in terms of covert 'even' alone cannot account for the limited distribution of strong NPIs. Eckardt further investigates the implicatures of 'even' sentences in weak licensing contexts and shows that they give rise to a minimal-achievement implicature which can be used to derive the markedness of strong NPIs in weak licensing contexts.

Dynamics of Belief. Sujata Ghosh and Fernando R. Velazquez-Quesada propose a model for the evolution of the beliefs of multiple agents involved in interactive situations, based on the trust they have in each other. Beliefs are actually evaluated by a neutral agent (the observer) – an event or an agent is ultimately believed if the observer's belief in it stabilises after a certain time point. The model uses a fixpoint theory inspired by Gupta and Belnap's semantics for self-reference.

Learning Theory. Nina Gierasimczuk investigates two types of hypothesis verification (with certainty and in the limit), and similarly, two types of hypothesis identification. Both these procedures are based on induction. She proves two results showing a connection between verifiability and identifiability. She shows how her results can be applied to the verification of monotone quantifiers.

Inquisitive Semantics. Jeroen Groenendijk introduces an inquisitive semantics for a language of propositional logic, where the interpretation of disjunction is the source of inquisitiveness. Indicative conditionals and conditional questions are treated on a par both syntactically and semantically. The semantics comes with a new logical-pragmatical notion which judges and compares the compliance of responses to an initiative in inquisitive dialogue.

Modal Logic. Ali Karatay considers the question of first-order definability of a modal formula motivated by the logic of ability. He offers a decisive solution in the negative, proving that the formula in question expresses an essentially second-order condition on Kripke frames.

Coalgebras. Clemens Kupke provides an alternative, game-theoretic proof of a fundamental result by J. Worrel regarding the finite approximation of a (possibly infinite) behaviour of states in a coalgebra based on a finitary set functor. The proof is based on a novel description of the behavioural equivalence in coalgebras for a finitary set functor in terms of two-player graph games in which at every position a player has only finitely many moves.

Computational Linguistics of Georgian. Paul Meurer presents ongoing work on building a full-scale computational grammar for Georgian in the Lexical Functional Grammar framework and illustrates both practical and theoretical aspects of grammar development. He shows how morphology interfaces with syntax and illustrates how some of the main syntactic constructions of Georgian are implemented in the grammar. Meurer also presents the tools that are used in developing the grammar system: the finite state tool *fst*, the XLE parsing platform, the LFG Parsebanker, and a large searchable corpus of non-fiction and fiction texts.

Type-Logical Grammar and Cross-Serial Dependencies. The paper by Glyn Morrill, Oriol Valentin, and Mario Fadda shows Type-Logical Grammar at work on an interesting linguistic case: the incremental processing of Dutch subordinate clause word order, namely, the so-called cross-serial dependencies. With the help of proof net machinery adapted for the continuous and discontinuous Lambek calculus they are able to account for the increasing unacceptability of cross-serial dependencies with increasingly multiple embeddings.

Non-monotonic Logic. Alexei Muravitsky considers the relation of logical friendliness in propositional logic introduced by D. Makinson. He gives a complete Gentzen-style axiomatization of this relation and obtains the property of strong compactness as a corollary.

Japanese Quantifiers. Sumiyo Nishiguchi argues that Generalized Quantifier Theory does not directly apply to Japanese quantifiers because the number of noun phrase arguments is underspecified and quantities are often expressed by predicative adjectives. Nishiguchi further shows that word order changes quantifier interpretation. Non-split quantifiers, for instance, correspond to definite NPs that are unique in the domain of discourse, while split NPs are wide-scope indefinites. Adjectival quantifiers require a polymorphic type, and continuation-based Combinatory Categorial

Grammar can account, as Nishiguchi demonstrates, for meaning differences between (non)split quantifiers.

Intuitionistic Logic. Tahsin Oner and Dick de Jongh study the structure of rigid frames for Intuitionistic Propositional Calculus (or for the modal logic S4.Grz). They give a full description and classification of all rigid frames of depth 3.

Semantics of Negated Nominals. Anna Pazelskaya discusses Russian event nominals, their negation and their meaning under negation. She claims that there are three ways to combine the negative marker with an event nominal, depending on the meaning of the nominal itself and requirements of the context. This leads to negated stative nominals derived from positive stative nominals, negated stative nominals derived from non-stative telic nominals, and negated non-stative telic nominals derived from non-stative telic nominals. Pazelskaya argues that these three types of negated nominals differ not only aspectually, but also with respect to where the negation is attached and how the denotation of the whole nominal is evaluated.

Word Sense Disambiguation. Ekaterina Rakhilina, Tatiana Reznikova, and Olga Shemanaeva discuss a method of Word Sense Disambiguation, which is applied to polysemous adjectives in the Russian National Corpus. The approach implies formulating rules to select the appropriate sense of the adjective by using co-occurrence restrictions observed in the corpus. The disambiguating filters operate with various kinds of grammatical and semantic information on the adjectives and the nouns modified, and are shown to be effective tools for Word Sense Disambiguation in the Russian National Corpus.

Semantics of Question-Embedding Predicates. Kerstin Schwabe and Robert Fittler investigate the conditions under which German propositional verbs embed interrogatives. They propose necessary and sufficient conditions for *dass* verbs taking *ob* complements. The corresponding verbs they call 'objective'. An objective verb has a wh-form (*F weiß, wer kommt* 'F knows who is coming') if it is consistent with *wissen dass*. A non-objective *dass*-verb does not have an *ob*-form, but it can have a wh-form if it permits a *da-* or *es*-correlate and meets particular consistency conditions which render it factive or cognitive in the presence of the correlate (cf. *bedauern* 'regret' vs. *annehmen* 'assume'). Schwabe and Fittler argue that the meaning of the wh-form of non-objective verbs deviates distinctly from the meaning of the wh-form of objective verbs and they claim that the proposed rules are general and hold without exceptions.

Reciprocals and Computational Complexity. Jakub Szymanik studies the computational complexity of reciprocal sentences with quantified antecedents. He observes a computational dichotomy between different interpretations of reciprocity and discusses consequences for the status of the so-called Strong Meaning Hypothesis.

We would like to express our sincere gratitude to the anonymous reviewers who have helped us in the preparation of this volume and of course to the organizers of the conference. A special thanks goes to Johan van Benthem, Paul Dekker, Frans Groen, Dick de Jong, Ingrid van Loon, and Anne Troelstra for their support in obtaining funding for the conference.

December 2008   Peter Bosch
                                                          David Gabelaia
                                                          Jérôme Lang

Organization

7th International Tbilisi Symposium on Language, Logic and ComputationTbilisi, October 1–5, 2007

Organization

Centre for Language, Logic and Speech at the Tbilisi State University
Georgian Academy of Sciences,
Institute for Logic, Language and Computation of the University of Amsterdam

Organizing Committee

Ingrid van Loon (Chair)
Rusudan Asatiani (Co-chair)
Paul Dekker (Co-chair)

Kata Balogh
Nick Bezhanishvili
Nani Chanishvili
David Gabelaia
Cigdem Gencer
Marina Ivanishvili
Nino Javashvili
Liana Lortkipanidze
Khimuri Rukhaia
Nana Shengelaia
Levan Uridia

Local Organization

Rusudan Asatiani
Nani Chanishvili
George Chikoidze (Chair)

David Gabelaia
Marina Ivanishvili
Nino Javashvili
Liana Lortkipanidze
Khimuri Rukhaia
Nana Shengelaia

Program Committee

Dick de Jongh - Chair	University of Amsterdam
George Chikoidze - Co-chair	Georgian Academy of Sciences
Leo Esakia - Co-chair	Tbilisi State University
Matthias Baaz	University of Vienna
Balder ten Cate	University of Amsterdam
Paul Dekker	University of Amsterdam
Ulle Endriss	University of Amsterdam
Frans Groen	University of Amsterdam
Jost Gippert	University of Frankfurt
Gogi Japaridze	Villanova University, Pennsylvania
Levan Uridia	University of Amsterdam
Barbara Partee	University of Massachusetts

Henk Zeevat   University of Amsterdam
Hedde Zeijlstra   University of Amsterdam
Ede Zimmermann   Johann Wolfgang Goethe Universität
                                         Frankfurt

and all invited speakers

Tutorials

Regine Eckardt (on language)   University of Goettingen
Benedikt Löwe (on logic)   University of Amsterdam
Jérôme Lang (on computation)   CNRS/IRIT, Toulouse

Invited Lectures

Matthias Baaz   University of Technology, Vienna
Guram Bezhanishvili   New Mexico State University
Igor Boguslavsky   Russian Academy of Sciences and
                                         Polytechnical University of Madrid
Peter Bosch   University of Osnabrück
Glyn Morrill   Universitat Politecnica de Catalunya
R. Ramanujam   C.I.T. Campus, Taramani, India
Wolfgang Thomas   RWTH Aachen
Frank Veltman   University of Amsterdam

Table of Contents

A Computational Grammar for Georgian

Paul Meurer

Aksis, UNIFOB, University of Bergen
paul.meurer@uib.no

Abstract. In this paper, I give an overview of an ongoing project which aims at building a full-scale computational grammar for Georgian in the Lexical Functional Grammar framework and try to illustrate both practical and theoretical aspects of grammar development. The rich and complex morphology of the language is a major challenge when building a computational grammar for Georgian that is meant to be more than a toy system. I discuss my treatment of the morphology and show how morphology interfaces with syntax. I then illustrate how some of the main syntactic constructions of the language are implemented in the grammar. Finally, I present the indispensable tools that are used in developing the grammar system: *fst*; the XLE parsing platform, the LFG Parsebanker, and a large searchable corpus of non-fiction and fiction texts.

Keywords: Georgian, Lexical-Functional Grammar, XLE, computational grammar, treebanking.

1 Introduction

In this paper, I give an overview of an ongoing project which aims at building a full-scale computational grammar for Georgian in the Lexical Functional Grammar (LFG) framework [1]. The grammar is part of the international ParGram project ([2], [3], [4]), which coordinates the development of LFG grammars in a parallel manner using the XLE (Xerox Linguistic Environment) grammar development platform developed by the Palo Alto Research Center.[1] In its current state, the grammar has a large lexicon and most of the morphology as well as most basic and some more advanced syntactic constructions are covered.[2]

In the first part, I describe the lexicon and morphology part of the grammar. I then illustrate how some of the main syntactic constructions of the language are implemented in the grammar and also touch upon some issues of theoretical interest. Finally, I present the indispensable tools that are used in developing the grammar system: *fst*; the XLE parsing platform; and the LFG Parsebanker.

---

[1] See http://www.parc.com/research/projects/natural_language/

[2] It is however premature to give coverage figures of the grammar on unrestricted text.

P. Bosch, D. Gabelaia, and J. Lang (Eds.): TbiLLC 2007, LNAI 5422, pp. 1–15, 2009.
© Springer-Verlag Berlin Heidelberg 2009

2   Morphology

The standard tool for morphological analysis with the XLE platform is the Xerox finite state tool (*fst*) [5]. *fst* integrates seamlessly with XLE, and it is very fast. Transducers written in *fst* are reversible, they can be used both for analysis and generation.

The lexical input to the Georgian morphological transducer was taken mainly from a digitized version of Kita Tschenkéli's *Georgisch-deutsches Wörterbuch* [6], which is one of the best Georgian dictionaries, and particularly well-suited as a basis for computational work because of its superb presentation of the verbs. Currently, the base form lexicon of the transducer comprises more than 74,000 nouns and adjectives and 3,800 verb roots.[3]

A prominent feature of Georgian morphology is long-distance dependencies, in the sense that affixes before the verb root license other affixes after the root. Such long-distance dependencies are difficult to model in finite-state calculus, since in the traversal of a finite-state network, no memory is kept of states traversed earlier (i.e. affixes encountered); transitions at a later stage in a traversal cannot be licensed by earlier steps in the traversal. In order to overcome these difficulties and to enlarge the expressiveness of the calculus, *fst* uses a device called *flag diacritics*. Flag diacritics are named flags that can be set, checked and otherwise manipulated in the course of network traversal; they can be used as a memory of encountered earlier stages and thus are well-suited for the treatment of long-distance dependencies. Flag diacritics can be compiled out of the network, yielding a possibly larger, but pure finite state transducer.

The output of an *fst* parse of a given word form is a set of analyses, each consisting of a lexicon entry form, which serves as a lookup key in the LFG grammar's lexicon (see below), plus LFG-relevant morphosyntactic features. Relevant features for nouns include case, number, full vs. reduced case inflection, double declension case and number, animateness, postpositions and various clitics. Features for verbs include tense/mood, person and number marking (encoded as +Subj/+Obj), and verb class. Examples:

(1) *ġvino* 'wine'
    → ġvino+N+Nom+Sg

(2) *gogo-eb-isa-tvis-ac* 'for the girls, too'
    → gogo+N+Anim+Full+Gen+Pl+Tvis+C

(3) *bavšvob-isa-s* 'in childhood'
    → bavšvoba+N+DGen+DSg+Dat+Sg

(4) *da-mi-xaṭ-av-s* 'I apparently painted it'/'he will paint it for me'
    → { da-xaṭva-3569-5+V+Trans+Perf+Subj1Sg+Obj3
      | da-xaṭva-3569-18+V+Trans+Perf+Subj1Sg+Obj3
      | da-xaṭva-3569-18+V+Trans+Fut+Subj3Sg+Obj1Sg }

---

[3] I would like to thank Yolanda Marchev, the co-author of the *Georgisch-Deutsches Wörterbuch*, for kindly allowing me to use the material of the lexicon in this project, and Levan Chkhaidze for giving me access to noun and adjective lists.

3   Morphosyntax

In Lexical-Functional Grammar, each verb is associated with a set of subcategorization frames (argument structures) and a mapping of each of the arguments (thematic roles) in the argument structures to a grammatical function such as subject or object. The argument-to-function mapping is subject to morphosyntactic alternations and hence differs for example between the transitive and the passive form of a verb. Morphosemantic alternations like causativization or formation of the applicative alter the argument structure itself and delete thematic roles or introduce new ones. For example, a basic transitive verb like *ga-v-a-ket-eb* 'I will do it' (Tschenkéli Class T[1], see below) will have argument structure and associated grammatical functions as displayed in (5), whereas its passive alternation *ga-ket-d-eb-a* 'it will be done' (Class P[2]) is described by (6). The mapping of the applicative transitive *ga-v-u-ket-eb* 'I will do it for him/her' (Class T[3]) is given in (7).

$$
\text{(5)} \quad
\begin{array}{cc}
\text{agent} & \text{theme} \\
\downarrow & \downarrow \\
\end{array}
$$
$$
\text{ga-kețeba} < \text{SUBJ}, \ \text{OBJ} >
$$

$$
\text{(6)} \quad
\begin{array}{cc}
\text{agent} & \text{theme} \\
\downarrow & \downarrow \\
\end{array}
$$
$$
\text{ga-kețeba} < \text{NULL}, \ \text{SUBJ} >
$$

$$
\text{(7)} \quad
\begin{array}{ccc}
\text{agent} & \text{benefic} & \text{theme} \\
\downarrow & \downarrow & \downarrow \\
\end{array}
$$
$$
\text{ga-kețeba} < \text{SUBJ}, \text{OBJben}, \ \text{OBJ} >
$$

Verb entries together with argument structure information for the basic alternations are coded in the LFG lexicon, which is consulted by the XLE parser to instantiate the parse chart. The thematic roles themselves that a given verb is associated with are not made explicit in XLE-based LFG grammars; only the grammatical functions they are mapped to are coded in the LFG lexicon. Argument-to-function mappings of morphosyntactic and morphosemantic alternations are derived in the grammar with the help of lexical transformation rules; their application is triggered by morphological features of the surface verb form.

In addition to argument structure, a lexical entry also stores the verb class. In combination with tense information, which is supplied by the tense feature of the morphological analysis, the verb class is needed to determine case alignment and mapping of morphological tense to tense/aspect features. Nouns, adjectives and other word classes are stored in a similar way.

Traditionally, Georgian verbs are classified into four main classes, according to a combination of morphological and case alignment criteria. These criteria can roughly be stated as follows: Verbs in Class I have an ergative subject in the aorist, and they form their future by adding a preverb. Class I verbs are transitive. Class II verbs, too, form their future by the addition of a preverb, but the subject of these verbs is always in the nominative. These verbs are intransitive and mostly passive or unaccusative. Verbs in Class III exhibit the same case alignment as Class I verbs, yet they have no own future forms, but rather recruit their future from related Class I paradigms. These verbs are unergative, or, less often, transitive. The verbs in Class IV are called indirect; their experiencer subject is invariably in the dative. Also this verb class lacks an own future paradigm, it uses forms from related Class II paradigms. (See (15) for details on the alignment patterns of these verb classes.)

The verb classification in Kita Tschenkéli's *Georgisch-deutsches Wörterbuch* follows this classification – the corresponding classes are called T, P (RP), MV (RM) and IV –, yet it is more fine-grained: information about the nature of indirect objects is also coded. Therefore, Tschenkéli's classification could be used directly to automatically derive a preliminary version of the Georgian LFG verb lexicon. For example, Tschenkéli's Class T^3 maps to the argument structure P<SUBJ, OBJ, OBJben>, and RP^1 maps to P<SUBJ, OBJth>, where P is an arbitrary predicate.

In many cases, however, the correct frames are not (easily) deducible from Tschenkéli's classification and have to be added or corrected manually. Examples are:

Verbs taking oblique or genitive arguments:

(8) ča-tvla<SUBJ, OBJ, OBL$_{adv}$>   'to consider sb. to be sth.'
     še-šineba<SUBJ, OBJ$_{gen}$>   'to be afraid of sb./sth.'

Class III verbs: Many of them can be transitive and intransitive (unergative), whereas some are only transitive and others only intransitive. This information is not available in the dictionary. For example:

(9) tamaši<SUBJ, (OBJ)>   'to play (a game)'
     ga-qidva<SUBJ, OBJ>   'to sell sth.'
     ça-svla<SUBJ>   'to go away'

Class II verbs: They can be passives or unaccusatives in the syntactic sense. A passive verb is always related to an active transitive verb via a function-changing lexical transformation; the active and the passive verb have the same set of thematic roles, they merely differ in whether and how the thematic roles are mapped to grammatical functions. Whereas in the active verb, agent and theme (patient) are mapped to SUBJ and OBJ, respectively, in the passive verb, the theme is mapped to SUBJ while the agent is either suppressed or mapped to the oblique function OBL-AG, corresponding to a postpositional phrase with the postposition *mier* 'by' (10). Examples are given in (11) and (12).

$$
\begin{array}{llll}
& active: & \text{agent}\quad\text{theme} & passive: & \text{agent}\quad\text{theme}\\
& & \downarrow\quad\ \downarrow & & \downarrow\qquad\ \downarrow\\
(10) & \text{ga-ḳeteba} < \text{SUBJ, OBJ} > & \longleftrightarrow & \text{ga-ḳeteba} < \text{NULL, SUBJ} > / \\
& & & \text{ga-ḳeteba} < \text{OBL-AG, SUBJ} >
\end{array}
$$

(11) *ga-ḳet-d-eb-a*   *(mtavrob-is   mier).*
      will-be-done.PASS (government.GEN by)

    'It will be done (by the government).'

(12) *mtavroba*   *ga-a-ḳet-eb-s.*
      government.NOM will-do-it.TRANS

    'The government will do it.'

Unaccusatives, on the other hand, have only one thematic argument which is invariably mapped to SUBJ, and there is no suppressed agent which could optionally resurface as an oblique:

      unaccusative: theme
(13)   ↓
      da-bruneba $<$ SUBJ $>$

(14) *da-brun-d-eb-a* *(* ded-is   mier).*
      he-will-return (* mother.NOM by)

    'He will return. (/ * He will be returned by the mother.)'

Since Tschenkéli's classification is primarily a morphological one, it does not explicitly distinguish between passives and unaccusatives of the same morphological shape. The distinction has to be made manually, or could at best be derived from the (non)existence of an active counterpart in the same superparadigm.

For these reasons, the automatically derived lexicon entries had and still have to be refined and corrected later on.

4   Mapping Case and Affixes to Grammatical Functions

Georgian uses both head-marking (mainly 1st and 2nd person affixes) and dependent-marking (case, restricted to 3rd person) to code grammatical functions, where it follows a complex split-ergative scheme that is further complicated due to what is commonly (e.g. in the Relational Grammar literature, [7]) called 'inversion'.

The dependency of the mapping of person/number affix resp. case to grammatical function on the parameters verbal class and tense group can be read off of the following tables:

(15) Three case
      alignment patterns

	SUBJ	OBJ	OBJben
A	ERG	NOM	DAT
B	NOM	DAT	DAT
C	DAT	NOM	*-tvis*

(16) Two person/number affix
      alignment patterns

	SUBJ	OBJ	OBJben
A, B	*v-*	*m-*	*h-*
C	*h-*	*v-*	-

(17) Selection of alignment pattern depending on verb class and tense group

	I	II	III	IV
	trans.	*unacc.*	*unerg.*	*indir.*
present	B	B	B	C
aorist	A	B	A	C
perfect	C	B	C	C

The mapping of verbal affixes to grammatical functions is coded into the morphology transducer, whereas case alignment is treated in the syntax by f-structure equations attached to the verb lexicon entries. Example (18) shows a simplified version of the equation that codes pro-drop and subject case alignment for Class I and III verbs.

(18)   { (↑ SUBJ PRED) = 'pro'
        | @(*ifelse* (↑ _TENSEGROUP) $=_c$ pres
            [(↑ SUBJ CASE) = nom]
            [@(*ifelse* (↑ _TENSEGROUP) $=_c$ aor
                [(↑ SUBJ CASE) = erg]
                [(↑ SUBJ CASE) = dat])]) }.

5   Syntax: An Overview

In the following, I present the most important grammatical features and some selected construction types of Georgian covered by the grammar and point out how they are dealt with in an LFG setting.

5.1   Word Order, Nonconfigurationality and Discourse Functions

Georgian is traditionally taken to be a language with 'free word order.' This is true at the phrase level; there is no VP constituent that would enable one to configurationally distinguish subject position from complement position; the finite verb and other constituents can occur in arbitrary order, or, phrased differently, any permutation of the constituents results in a grammatical sentence. This is what we would expect for a language with full-fledged head- and dependent-marking: since grammatical functions are (mostly unambiguously) coded morphologically, there is no need to repeat the coding of grammatical functions configurationally. Thus one could as a first approximation assume a flat top-level phrase structure:

(19) Initial approximation: S → V, XP*

The Kleene star (∗) means that there can be arbitrarily many XP constituents, and the comma means that V and XP constituents can occur in arbitrary order. XP denotes any maximal projection, i.e. NP, DP, AP, POSSP, etc.

Since syntax plays no role in the coding of grammatical functions, word order is available for expressing discourse functions like TOPIC and FOCUS. Although in Georgian, TOPIC and FOCUS do not seem to be coded exclusively configurationally, there is a strong tendency in the language for configurational coding: The TOPIC is mostly sentence-initial, which is very common cross-linguistically. The constituent bearing the FOCUS function normally occupies the position immediately in front of the inflected verb, or, more exactly, the inflected verb complex, which in addition to the verb may contain a negation particle and other modal particles. Heavy focused constituents tend to follow the verb or occupy sentence-final position. Focused verbs mostly precede their arguments.

In addition to the configurational encoding of the FOCUS function (which may be ambiguous if there are constituents both in front of and following the verb), Georgian also uses rising intonation to mark focus, there are a couple of adverbial clitics (-c, ķi etc.) that can be used to mark focus (and topic), and finally, clefting can be utilized to put a constituent into focus.

The position of question words is fully grammaticalized in Georgian: they invariantly occupy the position immediately in front of the verb complex. Since the position of a focused word often mirrors the position of the question word in a question–answer–scenario/pair, the pre-verbal focus position follows quite naturally.

The apparent configurational significance of the position immediately in front of the inflected verb motivates a revision of the basic phrase structure rule (19): In compliance with the LFG variant of X' theory ([1] p. 98), I assume that I is the category of the inflected verb (24), and that the specifier position of IP, if present, is occupied by question words (22) or by a potentially focused (or topicalized, if it is sentence-initial) constituent (21). Constituents further to the left are recursively adjoined to IP (20), and the complement of I is the exocentric, non-projecting category S that hosts the material right to the verb (23, 25).

(20) IP → XP IP   (22) IP → QP+ I'   (24) I → *Vinfl*

(21) IP → XP I'   (23) I' → I (S)   (25) S → XP+

Some examples that illustrate these rules follow.

(26) *çvim-s.*
rains
'It rains.'

IP
|
I
|
çvims

(27) *bavšv-i   tamaš-ob-s.*
child.NOM   plays
'The child is playing.'

(28) *student-i   çer-s   çeril-s.*
student.NOM   writes   letter.DAT
'The student writes a letter.'

Subordinate phrases with initial *rom* or *tu* etc. or without overt complementizer are complementizer phrases (CP, 29).

(29) CP → (C) IP

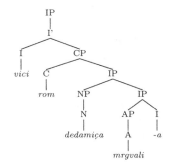

(30) *v-i-c-i   rom   deda-miça   mrgvali-a.*
     I-know   that   mother-earth.NOM   round-is

'I know that the earth is round.'

Noun phrases and the like are normally proper (projective) constituents (e.g., NP → AP N), but modifiers such as relative clauses, adjectives, genitive modifiers and possessive pronouns may be dislocated to the right, that is, they do not need to form a continuous constituent together with the head they modify. An example of a dislocated possessive is (31), whose non-dislocated version is (32).

(31) *gvar-i   ar   v-u-txar-i   čem-i*
     last-name.NOM   not   I.told.it.to-him   my.NOM.

'I did not tell him my last name.'

(32) *čem-i   gvar-i   ar   v-u-txar-i*
     my.NOM   last-name.NOM   not   I.told.it.to-him.

'I did not tell him my last name.'

This example (as well as (34, 35)) illustrates nicely how the separation of c- and f-structure in LFG enables a unified analysis of superficially disparate constructions: Both sentences have the same f-structures, as the analyses in (33) show. In the first c-structure, the dislocated possessive is located below S, which is the normal location of constituents right to the verb. In the c-structure of the non-dislocated version below, the possessive occupies its normal position as a specifier of NP.

It is the annotation of these two nodes which guarantees that both c-structures are mapped to the same f-structure: In the case of the non-dislocated possessive, the straightforward annotation (↑ SPEC POSS)=↓ makes sure that the possessive is mapped to the value of the path SPEC POSS in the f-structure of the noun it modifies. When the possessive is dislocated, the challenge is to find the nominal it modifies. An eventual candidate has to fulfill three conditions: It has to be located to the left of the possessive, its case has to match the case of the possessive, and it has to be a common noun. In addition, the candidate should correspond to a core grammatical function (GF).

(33)

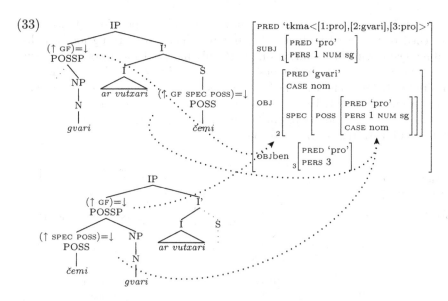

These conditions can be formally stated as equations annotating the POSS node. The main annotation is (↑ GF SPEC POSS)=↓, which states that the possessive should be mapped to the value of SPEC POSS of *some* grammatical function. Similar annotations make sure that the other conditions are met; in particular, the condition stating that cases have to match picks out exactly one grammatical function in most cases (in the example, it is the OBJ function), leading to an unambiguous attachment of the possessive in the f-structure.

5.2 Pro-Drop

Georgian is a pro-drop language: core arguments of the verb are not obligatorily realized as independent morphological words (e.g. personal pronouns) that are syntactic constituents. If an argument is realized, the person/number markers in the verb function as agreement features in the verb, but are providing a pronominal interpretation if the argument is missing ([8]). Dropped pronouns do not figure in the c-structure: the Principle of lexical integrity ([1] p. 92), which formalizes the view that (c-structure) syntax does not have access to word-internal structure, does not allow bound affixes to appear as lexical nodes.[4] It is the functional annotation of the lexicon entries that makes sure that the grammatical functions of the verb are properly instantiated in the case of pro-drop.

5.3 Postpositions as Phrasal Affixes; Double Declension

Postpositions in Georgian affect whole noun phrases including coordinations, they are phrasal/lexical affixes (not clitics proper).[5] My implementational choice

---

[4] Bound clitics are considered syntactic words and are not affected by this principle; see also section 5.3.

[5] See [9] for the distinction between clitics and phrasal affixes.

is not to give independent c-structure status to bound postpositions (those that are attached to the word to their left), but to adhere to a strong form of the Lexical integrity principle, maintaining that only morphological words and true clitics can be c-structure lexical nodes, but not bound phrasal affixes, while free postpositions are lexical nodes. The f-structures for bound and free postpositions, however, are not different. Unlike most case endings, virtually all postpositions have semantic content and are predicates on their own that subcategorize for an OBJ.[6] This is illustrated in (34) and (35).

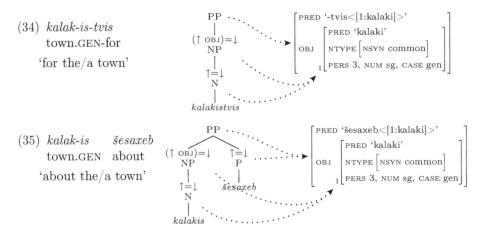

(34) *kalak-is-tvis*
town.GEN-for
'for the/a town'

(35) *kalak-is   šesaxeb*
town.GEN   about
'about the/a town'

The second case affix in double declension forms, i.e. nouns that carry two case markers as the result of ellipsis of the head noun, is treated in a similar way. In forms like *bavšvob-is*.GEN-*a-s*.DAT, 'in childhood', from *bavšvoba* 'childhood', the syntax has access to the inner case, as can be seen from the agreement between possessive pronoun and noun in the phrase (36). This indicates that the second case in a double-case construction has phrasal affix properties.[7]

(36) [*čem-i   bavšvob-isa*]-*s*
     [my.GEN   childhood.GEN].DAT
     'in my childhood'

---

[6] The only exceptions are the postpositions -*tvis*, -*tan* and -*ze*, when they are grammaticalized to mark (oblique) indirect objects in the perfect series. In such constructions, they have no PRED value/semantic content and are treated similarly to case endings.

[7] As to whether case endings in general have clitic- or phrasal affix-like properties, see the discussion in [10], where the distinction between clitics and phrasal affixes is not explicitly drawn. There, Harris shows that case endings are not clitics. But there is at least one peculiar construction where case endings clearly behave like phrasal affixes: In [11], §103, Šanije discusses 'sentence declension' (*cinadadebis bruneba*), by which he denotes the interpretation of a whole phrase or sentence as a cited noun phrase, which as such can be in inflected, case-marked argument position, for example: [*mex-i ḳi da-g-e-c-a*]-*sa-c zed da-a-ṭan-da*. '«May lightning strike you», he would also add.'

5.4 *unda* and *šeijleba*

In this section, I discuss in somewhat more detail the implementation I have chosen for constructions involving *unda* 'must' and *šeijleba* 'possibly', as they have received little and inadequate treatment in the literature.

At first glance, *unda* and *šeijleba* behave like adverbials which put modality restrictions on the verb they are attached to: The verb has to stand in one of the modal tenses (Optative, Pluperfect, Conjunctive Present/Future), but the case syntax of all of the arguments is determined by the (main) verb, as (37) and (38) demonstrate.

(37) *gia-m   çeril-i   unda   da-çer-o-s.*
      Gia.ERG   letter.NOM   must   write.OPT.

  'Gia must write a letter.'

(38) *gia   çeril-eb-s   unda   çer-d-e-s.*
      Gia.NOM   letter.PL.DAT   must   write.CONJ-PRES.

  'Gia must write letters.'

This contrasts to the control constructions (39) and (40) with the homonymous verb form *unda* 'he wants', which clearly require a biclausal analysis.

(39) *gia-s   u-nd-a   rom   çeril-i   da-çer-o-s.*
      Gia.DAT   wants.PRES   that   letter.NOM   write.OPT.

  'Gia wants to write a letter.'

(40) *gia-s   u-nd-a   rom   çeril-eb-s   çer-d-e-s.*
      Gia.DAT   wants.PRES   that   letter.PL.DAT   write.CONJ-PRES.

  'Gia wants to write letters.'

Harris and Campbell [12] analyze the construction with *unda* 'must' (37, 38) as a monoclausal structure with auxiliary and main verb. They interpret the modern construction as the result of a diachronic 'Clause fusion' process, in the course of which the construction with the 3rd person singular verb form *unda* (which is cognate to the inflected verb form *u-nd-a* 'he wants') underwent a semantic shift, followed by clause fusion, and consequently a change in case syntax. As evidence for a synchronic monoclausal analysis, they more or less implicitly state the case syntax of the construction, which is determined by the main (subordinate) verb alone, the invariability of the modal, and the impossibility of a *rom* complementizer, which is obligatory in the parallel control constructions.

There are, however, several constructions involving *unda* and *šeijleba* which indicate that a biclausal analysis is appropriate also here, both at f-structure and c-structure level. One of those constructions is negation: the negation particle *ar* 'not' can be placed either in front of *unda/šeijleba*, or in front of the main verb, or in front of both, as in (41).

(41) *man   ar   šeijleba   ar   i-cod-e-s,   rom   ...*
      he.ERG   not   possible   not   knows.CONJ-PRES,   that   ...

  'It is not possible that he does not know that ...'

The two negation possibilities can be most naturally accounted for in a biclausal analysis: the first *ar* negates the matrix clause, whereas the second *ar* negates the subordinate clause.

A still stronger argument for a biclausal analysis is verb phrase coordination: *unda* and *šeijleba* in front of the first verb normally have scope over both verbs, as in (42):

(42) *unda   ga-gv-i-xar-d-e-s   da   v-i-dǧesasçaul-o-t.*
     must   rejoice.OPT.1PL   and   celebrate.OPT.1PL.

'We should be happy and celebrate.'

We can account for these facts if we treat *unda* and *šeijleba* syntactically as verbs that occupy the I position like normal inflected verbs, but that, in contrast to other verbs taking phrasal arguments, subcategorize for one single argument, namely the subordinate phrase in COMP function (which, at c-structure level, corresponds to a CP node). Analyses of (37) and (41) are given in (43) and (44).

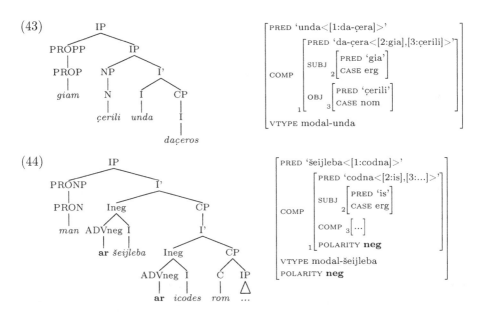

Finally, treatment of *unda* as a syntactic verb allows for an easy explanation of constructions with postponed *unda* as in (45). In such cases, the verb is in IP specifier position and thus focussed.

(45) *sxva   gza   ar   aris,   ga-nadgur-d-e-s   unda   demon-i.*
     other   way.NOM   not   is,   destroy.PASS.FOCUS   must   demon.NOM

'There is no other way, the demon has to be *destroyed.*'

IP tree diagram and f-structure:

```
            IP
          /    \
         V      I'
         |     /  \
   ganadgurdes I   NP
              |     |
            unda    N
                    |
                  demoni
```

$$
\begin{bmatrix}
\text{PRED 'unda<[1:ga-nadgureba]>'} \\[4pt]
\text{COMP}_1 \begin{bmatrix} \text{PRED 'ga-nadgureba<NULL, [2:demoni]>'} \\ \text{SUBJ}_2 \begin{bmatrix} \text{PRED 'demoni'} \\ \text{CASE nom} \end{bmatrix} \end{bmatrix} \\[4pt]
\text{FOCUS} \begin{bmatrix} 1 \end{bmatrix} \\[4pt]
\text{VTYPE modal-unda}
\end{bmatrix}
$$

6 Tools for LFG Grammar Development

In this part, I present the essential tools that are used in the development of the Georgian grammar.[8]

6.1 XLE and *fst*: The Development Environment for LFG Grammars

XLE (Xerox Linguistic Environment) is at the heart of most computational work with LFG grammars. It is a sophisticated development platform for LFG grammars developed by the Palo Alto Research Center with active participation of some of the inventors of LFG. XLE consists of a parser, a generator and a transfer module. These modules can be used both from Emacs via a Tcl/Tk interface that provides powerful viewing and debugging facilities, and as a shared library, which opens up for integrating XLE into custom software. Tokenization and morphological analysis is normally done with the Xerox finite state tool, *fst*.

6.2 XLE-Web: A Web Interface to XLE

XLE-Web is an easy-to-use pedagogical Web interface to XLE for parsing sentences on the fly. I developed it originally as a tool to facilitate the accomodation of the Norwegian ParGram grammar for use in the Norwegian–English machine translation project LOGON.[9] The software is now in use for many of the ParGram grammars. Main features of the system are display of c- and f-structures of LFG analyses, visualization of the mapping from c- to f-structure, and display of compact packed representations of c- and f-structures that combine the c- and f-structures of all analyses of a given parse into one c- and one f-structure graph.

6.3 LFG Parsebanker: Grammar Development and Treebanks

When developing a large grammar, it is essential to be able to run the grammar on a set of sample sentences, to store the parse results, and to rerun successive versions of the grammar on the same sentences, in order to monitor progress, to assess coverage and to compare analyses across different grammar versions.

---

[8] Some of the tools discussed here as well as the Georgian grammar can be tested online at http://www.aksis.uib.no/kartuli

[9] See http://www.emmtee.net/

Eventually, one might want to run the grammar on a larger set of sentences (perhaps chosen from running text), and let the collection of annotated sentences evolve into a treebank in the sense of a linguistic resource. Since sentences of only moderate complexity often are highly ambiguous, and the desired or correct reading is only one of the analyses offered by the grammar, it should be possible to manually disambiguate the parses in an efficient way.

Together with Rosén and de Smedt ([13], [14]) I have been developing a Web-based treebanking toolkit that suits exactly these needs: the LFG Parsebanker. The LFG Parsebanker is a comprehensive and user-friendly treebanking toolkit for manual disambiguation of a parsed corpus. It supports a process flow involving automatic parsing with XLE, sophisticated querying, and, crucially, efficient manual disambiguation by means of discriminants.

One can characterize discriminants roughly as 'any elementary linguistic property of an analysis that is not shared by all analyses' [15]. In LFG grammars, there are often a large number of elementary properties that are not shared by all analyses, such as local c-structure node configurations and labels or f-structure attributes and values. Any such elementary property is a candidate for being a discriminant. In using discriminants, our toolkit is somewhat similar to the Treebanker [15], Alpino [16] and the LinGO Redwoods project's [incr tsdb()] tool [17]. It is, however, specifically designed for LFG grammars. The underlying design and implementation of our LFG discriminants is described in detail in [18].

6.4   A Georgian Corpus of Fiction and Non-fiction Texts

An indispensable resource for research in Georgian syntax is a searchable text corpus of decent size. There are several collections of Georgian texts available on the Internet which can be used to build up such a corpus. One of them is the electronic newspaper archive Opentext. It comprises more than 100 million words and is by far the largest collection of Georgian texts available online. Another important collection of non-fiction is the text archive of the Georgian service of Radio Free Europe/Radio Liberty with around eight million words. The largest archive of fiction (both prose and poetry) is the UNESCO Project digital collection of Georgian classical literature (both prose and poetry) with three million words.[10]

I have harvested the texts of these three archives and imported them into corpus query software based on Corpus Workbench[11] which is being developed at Aksis. Although the corpus is not part-of-speech tagged, the versatile query language of Corpus Workbench allows for sophisticated searches.

7   Conclusion

In this paper, I have presented a project that aims at building a linguistically motivated full-scale computational grammar for Georgian in the LFG framework.

---

[10] See http://www.opentext.org.ge, http://www.tavisupleba.org,
http://www.nplg.gov.ge/gsdl/

[11] See http://www.ims.uni-stuttgart.de/projekte/CorpusWorkbench/

I have given an overview of the major issues that need to be addressed in this type of project, and I have shown how implementing a grammar in a formal linguistic framework can help solving issues in theoretical linguistics.

References

1. Bresnan, J.: Lexical-Functional Syntax. Blackwell Publishers, Oxford (2001)
2. Parallel Grammar Project, http://www2.parc.com/isl/groups/nltt/pargram/
3. Butt, M., Dyvik, H., King, T.H., Masuichi, H., Rohrer, C.: The Parallel Grammar Project. In: Proceedings of the COLING Workshop on Grammar Engineering and Evaluation, Taipei, pp. 1–7 (2002)
4. Butt, M., King, T.H., Niño, M.-E., Segond, F.: A grammar writer's cookbook. CSLI Publications, Stanford (1999)
5. Beesley, K.R., Karttunen, L.: Finite State Morphology. CSLI Publications, Stanford (2003)
6. Tschenkéli, K., Marchev, Y.: Georgisch-Deutsches Wörterbuch. Amirani-Verlag, Zürich (1965–1974)
7. Harris, A.C.: Georgian Syntax. A study in relational grammar. Cambridge University Press, Cambridge (1981)
8. Strunk, J.: Pro-drop in nominal possessive constructions. In: Proceedings of the 10th International LFG Conference. CSLI Publications, Stanford (2005)
9. Halpern, A.: On the placement and morphology of clitics. CSLI Publications, Stanford (1995)
10. Harris, A.C.: Origins of Apparent Violations of the 'No Phrase' Constraint in Modern Georgian. Linguistic Discovery 1(2), 1–25 (2002)
11. Šanije, A.: Kartuli enis gramaṭikis sapujvlebi (in Georgian). Tbilisi University Press, Tbilisi (1973)
12. Harris, A.C., Campbell, L.: Historical syntax in cross-linguistic perspective. Cambridge University Press, Cambridge (1995)
13. Rosén, V., Meurer, P., de Smedt, K.: Constructing a parsed corpus with a large LFG grammar. In: Proceedings of the 10th International LFG Conference. CSLI Publications, Stanford (2005)
14. Rosén, V., Meurer, P., de Smedt, K.: Towards a toolkit linking treebanking to grammar development. In: Proceedings of the Fifth Workshop on Treebanks and Linguistic Theories, Prague, pp. 55–66 (2006)
15. Carter, D.: The TreeBanker. A Tool for Supervised Training of Parsed Corpora. In: Proceedings of the Workshop on Computational Environments for Grammar Development and Linguistic Engineering, Madrid (1997)
16. Bouma, G., van Noord, G., Malouf, R.: Alpino. Wide-Coverage Computational Analysis of Dutch. In: Computational Linguistics in the Netherlands, pp. 45–59. Rodopi, Amsterdam (2001)
17. Oepen, S., Flickinger, D., Toutanova, K., Manning, C.D.: LinGO Redwoods, a rich and dynamic treebank for HPSG. Research on Language & Computation 2(4), 575–596 (2004)
18. Rosén, V., Meurer, P., de Smedt, K.: Designing and Implementing Discriminants for LFG Grammars. In: Proceedings of the 12th International LFG Conference. CSLI Publications, Stanford (2007)

The Structure of Rigid Frames of Depth 3 Only

Tahsin Oner[1,*] and Dick de Jongh[2]

[1] Department of Mathematics, Ege University, Izmir, Turkey
tahsin.oner@ege.edu.tr
[2] Institute for Logic, Language and Computation, Universiteit van Amsterdam
d.h.j.dejongh@uva.nl

1   Introduction

In this paper we classify all rigid rooted **IPC**-frames of depth 3. Among other things we show that these have at most 3 maximal elements. The interest in rigid frames arose from the paper [5]. In this paper *quasi-characterizing inference rules* were discussed. These rules are built on the pattern of Jankov-formulas of finite rooted frames but a Jankov-formula of the form $\varphi \rightarrow p$ is transformed into a quasi-characterizing rule φ/p. Such a rule is called *self-admissible* if it is admissible in the logic generated by the frame corresponding to the rule itself. The important results of [5] are that self-admissible rules are admissible in **IPC** itself, and that such a quasi-characterizing inference rule is self-admissible iff the frame it derives from is not rigid. The classification of rigid frames thus becomes of interest.

The paper [6] depicted the structure of all rigid modal rooted frames of depth 2. Since in general the structure can be very complicated we deal here only with nonstrict partially ordered frames of depth 3 (**IPC**, i.e., intuitionistic, or **S4Grz**-frames). By applying simple reasoning we will be in a position to give a very transparent description of the rigid rooted **IPC**-frames of depth 3. There turn out to be only finitely many. The hope is that our results can be extended to a more general characterization of rigid **IPC**-frames.

2   Preliminary Definitions and Notations

We are assuming the reader to be aware of the basic notations and definitions concerning modal and intermediate (superintuitionistic) logics and Kripke semantics, as well as of algebraic semantics (see, for example, [6] or [2]). Here all frames are **IPC**-frames. We briefly recall notations and certain definitions.

Definition 1. *Let a be an element and X a subset of the basis set of a frame $\Im := (W, R)$ with binary relation R. Then $a^R = \{b \in W : aRb\}$ and $X^R = \{b \in W : \exists c \in X(cRb)\}$.*

---

* This research was supported by Turkish Scientific Technical Research Council (TUBITAK).

P. Bosch, D. Gabelaia, and J. Lang (Eds.): TbiLLC 2007, LNAI 5422, pp. 16–22, 2009.
© Springer-Verlag Berlin Heidelberg 2009

We will now recall the following lemma and definitions about p-morphisms from [4] and [3] that will enable us to decide quickly whether there exists a p-morphism between two finite rooted frames.

Definition 2. *Let* $\Im = (W, R)$ *and* $\Im' = (W', R')$ *be frames. A map* f *from* $\Im$ *into* $\Im'$ *is called a* p-morphism *of* $\Im$ *to* $\Im'$ *if the following conditions hold for every* $a, b \in W$:

(a) aRb *implies* $f(a)R'f(b)$,
(b) $f(a)R'f(b)$ *implies* $(\exists c \in W)(aRc \wedge f(c) = f(b))$.

Lemma 1. *Let* $\Im = (W, R)$ *be a frame.*

(a) Assume $a, b \in W$, *and* a *is the only immediate successor of* b. *Define a map* $f : (W, R) \longrightarrow (W\backslash\{b\}, R)$, $f(w) = w$ *if* $w \neq b$, *and* $f(b) = a$. *Then* f *is a p-morphism and is called an* α-reduction.

(b) Assume $a \neq b \in W$ *and the set of immediate successors of* a *and* b *coincide. Define a map* $f : (W, R) \longrightarrow (W\backslash\{b\}, S)$, *where* $xSy \Leftrightarrow xRy \vee (xRb \wedge y = a)$, $f(w) = w$ *if* $w \neq b$, *and* $f(b) = a$. *Then* f *is a p-morphism and is called a* β-reduction.

The next lemma was in [3]. For a proof, see [1].

Lemma 2. *Let* $\Im = (W, R)$ *and* $\Re = (W', R')$ *be finite frames. Suppose that* $f : W \longrightarrow W'$ *is a p-morphism. Then there exists a sequence* $f_1, \ldots f_n (0 \leq n)$ *of* α- *and* β-reductions such that $f = f_1 \circ \ldots \circ f_n$.

Lemma 2 is used extensively in the proofs of the lemmas that follow.

Definition 3. *We say an element* w *of a frame* $\Im$ *is of* depth n *if there is a chain of* n *points in* $\Im$ *starting with* w *and no chain of more than* n *points starting with* w. *A frame* $\Im$ *is said to have* depth m *if the maximum of the depths of elements in* $\Im$ *is* m.

$Sl_m(\Im)$ *is the set of all elements of depth* m *from* $\Im$. $S_m(\Im)$ *is the set of all elements from* $\Im$ *with depth not more than* m.

A node a *is a* co-cover *of the set of nodes* X *if* X *is the set of immediate successors of* a.

Somewhat improperly we may sometimes call a a co-cover of the set X of all its successors where more properly a should be called a co-cover of $min(X)$.

3   Results

We adapt the definition of rigid frame of [5] to the specific case of **IPC**-frames.

Definition 4. *We say that* $\Im$ *is* rigid *if the following holds. For each nonrooted generated subframe* $\Re$ *of* $\Im$, *if there is a rooted p-morphic image* $\Im_1$ *of a generated subframe of* $\Im$ *such that* $\Re \cong \Im_1\backslash root(\Im_1)$, *then there is a* $c \in \Im$ *such that* c *is a co-cover of* $\Re$.

Theorem 1. *All rooted rigid frames of depth 3 with one maximal element are*

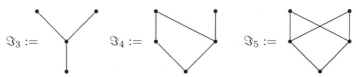

The ones with two maximal elements are

and the ones with three maximal elements are

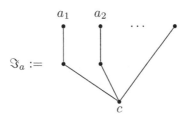

The proof of the main theorem is based on the next group of lemmas.

Lemma 3. *If f is an α- or β-reduction from $\mathfrak{I}_7$ into itself, then $f(\mathfrak{I}_7)$ has ≤ 2 maximal elements.*

Proof. $\mathfrak{I}_7$ allows no α-reduction. The only β-reductions that are possible are ones that identify two of the maximal nodes. This results in a frame with ≤ 2 maximal elements. ⊣

Lemma 4. *A p-morphism of a finite frame can never increase the number of maximal elements.*

Proof. By Lemma 3 it is sufficient to show that α- or β-reductions cannot increase the number of maximal elements. Actually, it is easy to see that the set of maximal elements stays the same in α- or β-reductions unless one has a β-reduction with two maximal elements being 'identified'. In the latter case the number of maximal elements decreases. ⊣

Lemma 5. *If a frame is rigid of depth 3 and has more than one maximal element, then at least one set of more than one element of depth 1 has a co-cover.*

Proof. Assume that the lemma is false and that the following frame $\mathfrak{I}_a$ is a counterexample: only one-element sets of depth 1 in $\mathfrak{I}_a$ have a co-cover.

Consider in $\Im_a$ an arbitrary element d of depth 2. It has only one successor a_i. One can identify d and a_i by an α-reduction. This does not change anything for the other elements of depth 2, so one can keep applying such α-reductions until none of the original elements of depth 2 are left. We only have $a_1, \ldots, a_n$ plus the root c. But $\{a_1, \ldots, a_n\}$ does not have a co-cover in $\Im_a$. Therefore, $\Im_a$ is not rigid. ⊣

Lemma 6. *If a frame $\Im$ is rigid of depth 3, $z \in Sl_2(\Im)$ and $X = S_1(z^R)$, then for any $Y \subseteq S_1(\Im)$ such that $1 < \|Y\| \le \|X\|$ there is a co-cover for Y in $\Im$.*

Proof. Consider a frame like the following.

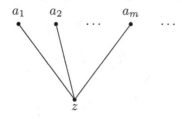

If $n \le m$, then

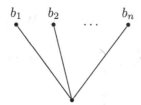

where $n > 1$, is a p-morphic image of z^R. This means that any set of elements $\{b_1, \ldots, b_n\}$ needs a co-cover: the frame cannot be rigid. ⊣

Lemma 7. *If a frame is rigid of depth 3 and has more than two maximal elements, then no singleton set of depth 1 has a co-cover.*

Proof. Suppose that $\Im_c$ is a counterexample and that a_1 in $\Im_c$ has a co-cover. The situation looks as follows.

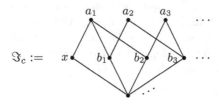

Note that all two-element sets have a co-cover. We contract a_1 and x by an α-reduction. We get

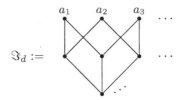

$\Im_d :=$

Then $\Im_c$ is not rigid, since the set of elements of depth 2 in $\Im_d$ does not have a co-cover in $\Im_c$.   ⊣

Lemma 8. *If a rigid frame has depth 3 and has at least 3 maximal elements, then a set of elements of depth 1 can never have more than one co-cover.*

Proof. Suppose that $\{a_1, \ldots, a_k\}$ of depth 1 has two co-covers b_1 and b_2.

$\Im_e :=$

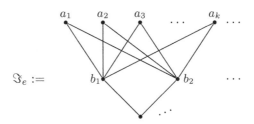

We contract b_1 and b_2 to b_1 by a β-reduction. We get

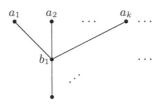

The set of elements in $\Im_e$ of depth 2 minus b_2 does not have a co-cover, $\Im_e$ is not rigid.   ⊣

Lemma 9. *If a frame $\Im$ is rigid of depth 3, then $\Im$ cannot have more than three maximal elements.*

Proof. Assume that $\Im$ has maximal elements $a_1, \ldots, a_n$ where $n > 3$.

We know by Lemmas 6, 7, 8 that the frame consists of a root c plus a number of elements of depth 1 and 2 in such a way that, for some $k \geq 2$, for each cardinality m with $2 \leq m \leq k$ exactly one co-cover $co(X)$ exists of depth 2 for each set X of elements of depth 1 of cardinality m, and there are no other elements of depth 2 than just these co-covers.

Define f as follows:

- $f(a_i) = a_i$ if $i \leq n-1$ and $f(a_n) = a_{n-1}$.
- $f(co(X)) = co(f(X))$ unless $f(X) = \{a_{n-1}\}$. Then $f(co(X)) = a_{n-1}$.
- Let c be the root. Then $f(c) = c$.

This definition is proper since, for the nodes of depth 2, $f(X)$ is always such that $2 \leq |f(X)| \leq k$ unless $f(X) = \{a_{n-1}\}$, and that case has been provided for.

We show that f is a p-morphism. Let xRy. If $x = c$, clearly $f(c) = cRf(y)$. For x of depth 1 it is trivial. If x is of depth 2, then $x = co(X), f(X) = co(f(X))$. Therefore, $f(y) \in f(X)$, so $f(x)Rf(y)$.

Let $f(x)Ry$. Assume $x = co(X)$, the other cases are trivial. Here the only problematic case is that $a_{n-1} \in co(f(X))$, $a_n \notin co(f(X))$. That can only arise if $f(x)Ra_n, f(a_n) = a_{n-1}$. But then xRa_n.

It is clear that the image is a frame with elements of depth 1: $a_1, \ldots, a_{n-1}$ and elements of depth 2: all $co(X)$ with X of a cardinality $2 \leq m \leq k$. Thus $f(\mathfrak{S})\backslash\{f(c)\}$ is a proper generated subframe of $\mathfrak{S}$. But it has no co-cover in $\mathfrak{S}$. $\mathfrak{S}$ is not rigid.   ⊣

Proof of Theorem 1. First one should prove that each of the given frames is rigid. It comes down to checking that the frame $\mathfrak{S}$ has no non-rooted generated subframe $\mathfrak{S}'$ without a co-cover in $\mathfrak{S}$ plus a p-morphism of a generated subframe of $\mathfrak{S}$ to an isomorphic copy of $\mathfrak{S}'$ with a root as co-cover. We leave the check that the given 7 frames are rigid to the reader.

Next one should prove that these 7 frames are the only possibilities. We first note that, by Lemma 9 we can restrict our attention to frames with 3 or less maximal elements. Let us first consider the case of 3 maximal elements. We determine the nodes of depth 2 by establishing which sets of maximal elements they can be the co-cover of. By Lemma 7 each of the nodes of depth 2 co-covers more than one element, and, by Lemma 8 no 2 elements of depth 2 co-cover the same set of maximal elements. By Lemma 6 then all the 2-element sets of maximal elements will be co-covered by exactly one element of depth 2, and possibly the set of all 3 maximal elements will be co-covered by some element of depth 2 as well. This leaves one exactly the two possibilities $\mathfrak{S}_6$ and $\mathfrak{S}_7$.

Next, let us consider the case of an $\mathfrak{S}$ with one maximal element. Let us suppose that there are 3 or more elements of depth 2 in $\mathfrak{S}$. Then we can obtain $\mathfrak{S}_2$ as a p-morphic image, but the two elements of depth 2 of $\mathfrak{S}_2$ do not have a co-cover in $\mathfrak{S}$. So, $\mathfrak{S}$ is not rigid.

Finally, let us consider the case of an $\mathfrak{S}$ with two maximal elements. Once we see that 3 elements of depth 2 is in this case an impossibility the rest is elementary. That 3 elements of depth 2 is an impossibility follows from considerations similar to the ones in Lemmas 7 and 8.   ⊣

Acknowledgement. We would like to thank V.V. Rybakov for giving ideas for the solution of the problem of this paper. We thank an unknown referee for a number of helpful remarks, and we thank the editors for considerable help and Nina Gierasimczuk for technical assistance.

References

1. Bezhanishvili, N.: Lattices of Intermediate and Cylindric Modal Logics, PhD thesis, ILLC, Universiteit van Amsterdam (2006)
2. Chagrov, A., Zakharyaschev, M.: Modal Logic, p. 605. Clarendon Press, Oxford (1997)
3. de Jongh, D.: Investigations on the Intuitionistic Propositional Calculus, PhD thesis, University of Wisconsin (1968)
4. de Jongh, D., Troelstra, A.: On the connection of partially ordered sets with some pseudo-Boolean algebras. Indagationes Mathematicae 28, 317–329 (1966)
5. Rybakov, V.V., Terziler, M., Gencer, C.: Description of Self-Admissible Quasi-Characterizing Inference Rules. Studia Logica 65, 417–428 (2000)
6. Rybakov, V.V., Oner, T.: The Structure of the Rigid Frames of Restricted Depth 2. Bulletin Section Logic 27(4), 172–181 (1998)
7. Rybakov, V.V.: Admissibility of Logical Inference Rules, Studies in Logic and Foundations of Mathematics, vol. 136, p. 617. Elsevier, Amsterdam (1997)

Three Kinds of Event Nominal Negation in Russian[*]

Anna Pazelskaya

ABBYY Production, Kasatkina 11/1
129301 Moscow, Russia
avis39@mail.ru

Abstract. This paper is about Russian event nominals, their negation and their meaning under negation. The paper shows that there are three ways to (semantically) combine negative marker with an event nominal, depending on the meaning of the nominal itself and requirements of the context. The main factors driving these differences can be shown to be of an aspectual nature; both aspectual characteristics of the initial nominal and the (contextually-driven) properties of the resulting nominal are important. As for the range of possibilities, one can find negated stative nominals derived from positive stative nominals, negated stative nominals derived from non-stative telic nominals, and negated non-stative telic nominals derived from non-stative telic nominals. These three types of negated nominals differ not only aspectually, but also with respect to where the negation is attached and how the denotation of the whole nominal is evaluated.

Keywords: Event nominals, negation, telicity, stativeness, behaviour under negation.

1 Preliminaries

Most of the classic works about negation (e.g. Horn 1989, Haegeman 1995, Kim & Sag 2002, Zeijlstra 2007) study verbal, or rather predicative negation, when the negation both syntactically and semantically refers to the whole predication. However, in a number of languages there is also a way to negate other types of expressions, cf. English negated adjectives (*unlikely*) or nominals (*non-ability*). There is some evidence that predicative and non-predicative negation differ not only in form, but also in the semantics of the expression (see discussion in Horn 1989: 53-55). Given this, it is worth looking at the negation of expressions of intermediate nature, namely, of event nominals, in order to see if their negation is closer to the predicative or to the non-predicative one. This is exactly what is done in this paper with respect to the Russian event nominals.

The rest of this paper is organized as follows: Section 2 defines two key notions of this paper, namely, what I will consider as event nominals here, and how they can be

---

[*] I am grateful to Elena Paducheva, Sergey Tatevosov and Igor Yanovich, whose discussions and observations on the matters addressed here have been very useful. I would like as well to thank the symposium and the proceedings volume reviewers for their profitable comments.

P. Bosch, D. Gabelaia, and J. Lang (Eds.): TbiLLC 2007, LNAI 5422, pp. 23–37, 2009.

negated. Section 3 presents three semantic types of negated event nominals which can be found in Russian, with a special discussion of cases of shifts from one semantic type to another (section 3.4). Section 4 treats aspectual distinctions among the attested types of negated nominals. Section 5 concludes the paper.

2 Event Nominals and Their Negation

2.1 Event Nominals

The term "event nominal" is due to Jane Grimshaw (1990), who uses it to refer to all the deverbal nominals which can denote situations. In this book a distinction between simple event nominals (SENs) and complex event nominals (CENs) is introduced: CENs are derived from transitive verbs and inherit the aspectual and argument structure from the verb they are derived from, whereas SENs are derived mostly from intransitive verbs and lack aspectual and argument structure.

In this paper I will use the term "event nominal" more broadly than in Grimshaw 1990, and this broadening goes in two ways. First, I will discuss not only deverbal situation-denoting nominals, but also deadjectival and non-derived ones, since the argumental structure of the nominal and its inheritance from the initial verb is irrelevant here. Second, I will apply this term not only to names of events, i.e. telic dynamic eventualities, but also to names of processes (atelic dynamic eventualities) and states (atelic static eventualities).[1] Some examples of event nominals are presented in (1).

(1)   *vypolnenie* 'fulfilment'   *uspex* 'success'

       priezd 'coming'   *napadenie* 'aggression'

       znanie 'knowing'   *sootvetstvie* 'conformity, accordance'

Grimshaw's distinction of simple event nominals (SENs) and complex event nominals (CENs) is also irrelevant for our purposes and will be ignored here. Aspectual properties of event nominals, when needed, will be established by independent tests applicable to event nominals, without referring to the verbs they are derived from and possible inheritance of the aspectual structure from them.[2]

To summarize, in this paper I will call an event nominal every nominal which can refer to a situation, no matter if the nominal is derived from some verb or not, if it has some arguments of its own, and if the situation is telic or atelic, dynamic or static.

---

[1] I realize that using the term "event nominal" for stative atelic situation-denoting nouns can evoke some misunderstanding, but I will still do it for a lack of better words. Its use can be justified as referring not to "event", but to "eventuality" (in the sense of Bach 1981, 1986). When speaking about dynamicity and telicity in the sense of e.g. Krifka 1998, 2001, I will use these explicit terms, or the tern "eventive" to refer to telic eventualities ("events proper"). The use of word "event" here has nothing to do with the fact-proposition-event distinction (cf. Zucchi 1993, Vendler 1968, Peterson 1997).

[2] Besides, as has been shown (see A. Alexiadou 2002, 2004), SENs, as well as CENs, also have aspectual structure. Russian deverbal nominals derived from transitive verbs, from intransitive ones and underived situation-denoting nominals share a lot of properties, and behaviour under negation is one of them.

2.2 Negation

Almost every event nominal can be negated by attaching negative prefix *ne-*[3], as is shown in (2)[4]

(2) *nevypolnenie* 'non-fulfilment'
   neuspex 'failure, lack of success'
   nepriezd 'non-coming, failure to come'
   nenapadenie 'non-aggression'
   neznanie 'not knowing, ignorance'
   nesootvetstvie 'discrepancy'

Negative prefix in Russian is a distinctive feature of nonverbal parts of speech, namely, nouns (even those that do not denote situations, e.g. 3a), adjectives (3b), and adverbs (3c):

(3) a. **ne-***drug* 'enemy'   b. **ne-***vysokij* 'not high'   c. **ne-***xorosho* 'badly'
       NEG-friend   NEG-high   NEG-well

However, some quite idiomatic cases excluded, neither finite verbs, nor infinitives or adverbial participles can attach the negation prefix (4abc) and a negative particle should be used instead (4def):

(4) a. *Petja **ne-**priexal.
       Peter   NEG-come

   (intended) *Peter has not come.*

b. *Petja xochet **ne-**priexat'.
      Peter wants   NEG-come.INF

   (intended) *Peter wants to not to come.*

c. *Petja, **ne-**priexav,   rasstroil nas.
      Peter   NEG-come.ADV upset   we.ACC

   (intended) *Peter, having not come, upset us.*

d. Petja   **ne**   priexal.
      Peter   not   come

   Peter has not come.

e. Petja xochet **ne**   priexat'.
      Peter wants   not   come.INF

   Peter wants to not to come.

f. Petja,   **ne**   priexav,   rasstroil nas.
      Peter   not   come.ADV   upset   we.ACC

Peter, having not come, upset us.

This negative verbal particle, however homophonous with the nominal negative prefix, has clearly distinctive morphosyntactic features, their distinction being not just an

---

[3] Cf. its English counterparts discussed, a.m.o., in Zucchi 1993: 23-25, 184-187, Baeuerle 1987, Higginbotham 1996, Stockwell, Schachter & Partee 1973, Horn 1989, Polish ones in Przepiórkowski 1999.

[4] Constituent negation is beyond the scope of this paper. What will be considered is phrasal negation for verbs and what is natural to view as its counterpart in other parts of speech, namely, the negation which is marked most closely at the negated element and negates its own content, not the whole sentence with focus on this element, as is usually the case with constituent negation.

orthographical convention. First, verbal *ne* is distinctive from prefixed *ne-* intonationally in that it bears secondary stress and can be even focused in emphatic contexts. Second, and even more important, it can be easily shown that the negation expressed by the preverbal *ne* is in fact relevant for the whole situation denoted by the sentence, infinitival or participle clause — i.e., it is not verbal, it is sentential negation. For instance, negative particle in emphatic constructions can be linearly separated from the verb by other material (5):

(5)	Eto	**ne**	Petja	priexal,	eto	Masha	uezzhaet.
	it	not	Peter	come	it	Maria	leave

It is not the case that Peter has come, it is the case that Masha is leaving.

This is not the case with the nonverbal negation illustrated in (3) above. The negative prefix modifies only the denotation of the adjective, nominal or adverb it attaches to, without its arguments. E.g. an NP with a relational noun *Petin nedrug* 'Peter's enemy' refers to someone who is evil to Peter, and cannot denote a person who is kind to someone else: it is the denotation of the word *drug* 'friend' which is negated, and not the whole situation 'X is a friend of Y'. And in no case the nonverbal prefixed negation can be detached from the word it applies to.

The negative prefix we find in deverbal nominals, like the one in nouns, adjectives and adverbs, cannot be separated from the nominal by anything else. What we see in (6a) is in no case an instance of such a separation, since it is not synonymous to (6b):

(6) a.	Eto	**ne**	Petin	priezd,	eto	Mashin
	it	not	Peter.POSS	arrival	it	Maria.POSS

	otjezd	menja	rasstroil.
	departure	me.ACC	disappoint

It is not Peter's arrival, it is Masha's departure that disappointed me.

b.	Eto	Petin	**ne**-priezd	menja	rasstroil.
	it	Peter.POSS	NEG-arrival	me.ACC	disappoint

It is Peter's non-arrival that disappointed me.

Crucially, (6a), unlike (5) above, does ̇not convey that Peter did not come, rather it says that Peter has arrived, but it is not the thing that disappointed the speaker. On the contrary, (6b) says that Peter did not arrive, and that this disappointed the person uttering the sentence. Unlike (6b), (6a) is an instance of sentential negation with a special focus on the NP *Petin priezd*, and the *ne* in this sentence is attached at the clausal level. This can be proved by the fact that the two types of negation, clausal and event nominal one, can cooccur in one sentence (6c):

(6) c.	Eto	**ne**	Petin	**ne**-priezd,	eto	Mashin
	it	not	Peter.POSS	NEG-arrival	it	Maria.POSS

	otjezd	menja	rasstroil.
	departure	me.ACC	disappoint

It is not Peter's non-arrival, it is Masha's departure that disappointed me.

One more crucial distinction is the distinction between contrary and contradictory negation (Geach 1969, cf. the notion *idiomatic* in Boguslavsky 1985). The negation we find on nonverbal parts of speech is generally contrary: it denotes the opposite value on some scale introduced by the noun, adjective or adverb. Verbal negation is contradictory: it refers to lacking some property, non-occurrence of some (expected) situation, etc.

All the facts above show that the negation the verbs in Russian bear on them is merged in the syntax, while the nonverbal negation attaches in the lexicon, and therefore cannot be separated from the negated item and negates only its denotation, not the whole situation behind it.

An interesting question is, however, if the difference between verbal and event nominal negation (and between verbal and nominal negation, too) supports the hypothesis that prefixed *ne-* and verbal cliticized *ne* are two different phenomena, or, alternatively, one and the same negative marker comes in different shapes when it is used to negate different things.

Now we are in the position to formulate the main questions addressed in the paper: what are the differences between verbal and event nominal negation? What can they tell us about the difference between verbal and non-verbal (nominal, adjectival, etc) negation? Is event nominal negation close to the verbal or to the nonverbal one?

What we have seen above suggests that the morphosyntactic behaviour of the event nominal negation is of the nominal type. In the rest of this paper we will look at the semantics of the negated event nominals and at the contribution of the negative prefix in order to understand what underlies these surface differences and affinities.

3 Semantics of Negation and Aspectual Properties of the Nominals

The first thing that can be noticed when looking at the semantics of the negated nominals in (2) above, is that not all the six instances of negation are of the same kind. Namely, one can attest three types of negated nominals with respect to the aspectual properties of the positive and negative nominal and to how the negation combines with the meaning of the nominal:

(i) stative negative nominals ('negative state'): *neznanie* 'not knowing, ignorance', *nesootvetstvie* 'discrepancy';
(ii) eventive negative nominals ('failure to'): *nevypolnenie* 'non-fulfilment', *nepriezd* 'non-coming, failure to come', *neuspex* 'failure, lack of success';
(iii) existential negative nominals ('no occurrence of the event on some long interval'): *nenapadenie* 'non-aggression'.

In the following three sections we will discuss these three types of negated event nominals in more detail and see what are the semantic differences between them, from what types of nominals they are derived, and in what contexts they can occur.

3.1 Stative Negative Nominals (i)

Stative negative nominals, like *neznanie* 'ignorance' and *nesootvetstvie* 'discrepancy', are derived from names of states. Negated nominals of this type denote a state of affairs in which some other state, namely, the state denoted by the positive nominal does not hold. Indeed, *neznanie* 'ignorance' is the state of a person when (s)he does not know some relevant information, and *nesootvetstvie* 'discrepancy' is a state of two (or more) entities which holds when they have different or incompatible properties.

Semantically, the negation in these cases can be contrary, as well as contradictory. Contrary negation inverts the properties of the state denoted by the initial positive nominal, therefore creating a new state referred to by the negative nominal which describes an opposite value on the scale introduced by the adjective (7a). Contradictory negation denotes lacking the property the original state referred to (7b,c):

(7) a. *zavisimost'* 'dependence' — ***ne**zavisimost'* 'independence'

   b. *naxozhdenie* 'being (at some place)'
             — ***ne**naxozhdenie* 'not being (at some place)'

   c. *prinadlezhnost'* 'membership, affiliation'
             — ***ne**prinadlezhnost'* 'non-membership'

Note that negation of this kind applies to names of individual-level states (*neznanie* 'ignorance') and to stage-level states (*nenaxozhdenie* 'not being (at some place)') — see Carlson 1977 about this distinction. The derived negative nominal preserves this characteristic: individual-level positive nominals derive individual-level negative nominals, and vice versa.

As for the typical context of use, stative negative nominals have no special preferences and are used in fairly the same contexts as all the other (stative) event nominals, e.g. they can be verbal arguments (8):

(8)
Prinadlezhnost'	ili	**ne-prinadlezhnost'**	grazhdan	k
membership	or	**NEG-membership**	citizen.GEN.PL	to
obshchestvennym		objedinenijam	ne	mozhet
social		institution.DAT.PL	not	can
sluzhit'	osnovaniem	dlja	ogranichenija	ix	prav
serve	ground.INSTR	for	limitation	their	right.PL
i	svobod.				
and	liberty.PL				

Citizens' membership or non-membership in social institutions cannot be a ground for limiting their rights and liberties.

Stative negative nominals have no plural form (9ab) and are incompatible with adjectives of repetition (like *mnogokratnyj* 'repeated', 9c). Only adjectives referring to time periods (e.g. *mnogoletnij* 'lasting for many years', *dlitel'nyj* 'long-lasting') are possible (9de).

(9) a. ne-znanie   —   *ne-znanija
      NEG-knowing.SG   NEG-knowing.PL

not knowing, ignorance   Int. *instances of (showing) ignorance*

   b. ne-zavisimost'   —   *ne-zavisimosti
      NEG-dependence.SG   NEG-dependence.PL'

independence   Int. *instances of independence*

c. *mnogokratnaya ne-milost'
    repeated   NEG-favour

Int. *repeated disfavour*

d. mnogo-let-nee ne-sootvetstvie
    many-year-ADJ NEG-accordance

discrepancy which holds for many years

e. dlitel'naya   ne-milost'
    long.term   NEG-favour

long lasting disfavour

Aspectual consequences of these properties of stative negative nominals (i.e. of their failure to pluralize and to occur with adjectives of repetition) will be discussed below in section 4.

3.2 Eventive Negative Nominals (ii)

The second semantic group of negated event nominals are event nominals with properly eventive meaning, such as *nevypolnenie* 'non-fulfilment', *nepriezd* 'non-coming, failure to come', *neuspex* 'failure, lack of success'. They are derived from telic event nominals, that is, in this case, like in the case of stative negative nominals discussed above, the aspectual characteristic of the nominal is preserved under negation.

Nominals of the eventive negative type denote an event consisting in that the expected event denoted by the positive nominal fails to take place. For agentive predicates this either means refusal of the agent to perform the action, or a failed attempt. Here the negation is contradictory and close to the verbal one in that the negative nominal tells us that the event denoted by the initial positive nominal failed to take place. The negation in this case is always contradictory, the negated nominal denoting absence of the event, without any scalar operations:

(10) *javka* 'appearance' — *nejavka* 'failure to appear, no-show'

    vyplata 'payment' — *nevyplata* 'non-payment'

    popadanie (v cel') 'hitting (the target)' — *nepopadanie* 'missing (the target)'

Eventive negative nominals are frequently used in conditional adjuncts with PP *v sluchae...* 'in case of' (11a) or with preposition *pri* 'by, in case of' (11b), as well as in other non-assertive contexts.

(11) a. v   sluchae **ne-javki**   sportsmenu   grozit
      in   case   **NEG-appearance** sportsman.DAT threaten

      prinuditelnyj   privod.
      compulsory   bringing.on.the.spot

In case of no-show the sportsman may be compulsorily brought to the spot.

b. Pri   **ne-dostizhenii**   soglashenija   zainteresovannoe
   by   **NEG-achievement.PREP** agreement.GEN   concerned

   lico   vprave   obratit'sja   v   sud.
   person has.a.right   address   to   court

In case of failure to reach an agreement the person concerned has the right to apply to court.

Eventive negative nominals easily pluralize, a nominal in plural refers to many instances when the event was expected but failed to take place (12ab), e.g. *nejavki* 'failures to appear' denotes several points of time when the person was expected to come somewhere but didn't. Eventive negative nominals, unlike stative negative nominals, cooccur with adjectives of repetition (12cd), but not with adjectives of time period (12e).

(12) a. *nejavka* 'failure to appear' — *nejavki* 'failures to appear'

   b. *nevyplata* 'non-payment' — *nevyplaty* 'non-payments'

   c. *reguljarnoe nesobljudenie instrukcii*
      'regular non-observance of the instruction'

   d. *mnogokratnoe nevypolnenie sluzhebnyx objazannostej*
      'repeated non-fulfilment of office duties'

   e.#*mnogoletnee nesobljudenie instrukcii*
      'regular non-observance of the instruction (as a matter of policy, or by habit)'

The noun phrase in (12e) with an adjective *mnogoletnij* 'lasting for many years' which refers to a long time period is in fact possible, but the nominal shifts its meaning into existential negative (type iii).[5]

Another important difference between stative negative nominals and eventive negative nominals is that in the former the state of affairs denoted by the positive nominal is negated without its participants, while in the latter with its participants. This is proved by the fact that eventive negative nominals and stative negative nominals show different meaning when they are used with quantifying adjective *vsjakij* 'any, every', cf. (13ab):

(13) a. Ego   razdrazhalo   vsjakoe ne-znanie,
       he.ACC   irritate.PST   every   NEG-knowing

       osobenno   ego   sobstvennoe.
       especially   his   own

He was irritated by every ignorance, especially by his own.

   b.[??]Ego   razdrazhala   vsjakaja ne-javka,
       he.ACC   irritate.PST   every   NEG-appearance

       osobenno   ego   sobstvennaja.
       especially   his   own

Int.: *He was irritated by every no-show, especially by his own.*

---

[5] We will see more instances of meaning shifts between different types of negated nominals in section 3.4.

Sentence (13a) with stative negative nominal *neznanie* 'ignorance' is found on the Internet and a little modified, but is still a good Russian sentence. While (13b) with eventive negative nominal *nejavka* 'no-show' in the same place is very odd, if not totally out, the quantification in (13b) being possible only by some other parameters than the subject, e.g. by manner or time. The reason for this is presumably that in eventive negative nominals the subject argument is under negation and therefore inaccessible for quantification by *vsjakij* 'every', while in stative negative nominals it is merged after the negation and can undergo quantification.

3.3 Existential Negative Nominals (iii)

Existential negative nominals (e.g. *nenapadenie* 'non-aggression', *nevmeshatel'stvo* 'non-interference'), like eventive negative nominals, are derived from telic event nominals. They refer to a long time interval during which there exists no moment *t* when the event denoted by its positive counterpart takes place. Negation of this type, like the negation in eventive negative nominals, is always contradictory.

Semantically it is the most complicated type, as nominals of this type denote a sort of "generic state" (Vendler 1967), a generic abstraction from different instances of non-occurrence of the event denoted by the initial nominal (see Smith 1975):

(14) *vmeshatel'stvo* 'interference' — *nevmeshatel'stvo* 'non-interference'

   rasprostranenie 'proliferation' — *nerasprostranenie* 'non-proliferation'

   razglashenie 'disclosure' — *nerazglashenie* 'non-disclosure'

Existential negative nominals are usually used to describe long-term agreements, general attitudes, or policies (15). They can easily be found in official documents, diplomatic speech or political newspaper articles.

(15)
Poxozhe,	chto	politika	**ne-vmeshatel'stva**	v
look.like	that	policy	**NEG-interference.GEN**	into
dela	sosednej	strany,	kotoruju Rossija	nachala
affair.PL	neighbour	country	which Russia	begin.PST
provodit',	prinosit	plody.		
follow.INF	bring.PRS	benefit.PL		

It looks as if the policy of non-interference with the neighbour country's business which Russia began to follow brings benefits.

Existential negative nominals don't pluralize (16ab). They easily cooccur with adjectives of time period (16cd), but not with those of repetitivity (16e).

(16) a. *nevmeshatel'stvo* 'non-interference'
                    — **nevmeshatel'stva* int. 'non-interferences'

   b. *nerasprostranenie* 'non-proliferation'
                    — ** nerasprostranenija* int. 'non-proliferations'

   c. *mnogoletnee nerasprostranenie*
   'non-proliferation lasting for many years'

d. *dlitel'noe nevmeshatel'stvo*   e. **mnogokratnoe nerasprostranenie*
   'long-lasting non-interference'   Int. 'repeated non-proliferation'

Preference for adjectives of time period and incompatibility with adjectives of repetition clearly denies the hypothesis that existential negative nominals could denote a set of telic eventualities of the same kind as those referred to by eventive negative nominals. Although they are derived from names of telic events, they are more like stative negative nominals, since both existential negative nominals and stative negative nominals cannot pluralize and cooccur with adjectives of repetitivity, but are admissible with time period adjectives.

As for the *vsjakij* 'every' quantification test, the existential negative nominals pattern together with eventive negative nominals, and not with stative negative nominals (17):

(17) ??Ego   razdrazhalo   vsjakoe ne-vmeshatel'stvo,
      he.ACC   irritate.PST   every   NEG-interference

      osobenno   ego   sobstvennoe.
      especially   his   own

He was irritated by every non-interference, especially by his own.

This behaviour of existential negative nominals shows that in these nominals the content of the positive negated nominal is negated as a whole, together with its arguments, in the same way as in eventive negative nominals, and unlike what we see in the stative negative nominals.

3.4   Contextual Modifications

The distinction between eventive negative nominals and existential negative nominals is not so impenetrable: they are formed from the same class of telic nominals; therefore one and the same positive nominal can potentially derive negative nominals of any of the two types. In other words, nouns of any of the two types can be attested in both "eventive" (17) and "existential" (18) contexts.

(17) a. v   sluchae ne-vypolneni-ja   plan-a
       in   case   NEG-fulfilment-GEN   plan-GEN

   in case the plan fails to be fulfiled

   b. v   sluchae ne-razglasheni-ja   shpion-om   tain-y
      in   case   NEG-disclosure-GEN   spy-INSTR   secret-GEN

   in case the spy fails to disclose the secret

(18) a. Ja   podgovor-il   ego   na   sistematicheskoe
        I   incite-PST   he.ACC to   systematic

     ne-vypolneni-e   plan-a.
     NEG-fulfilment-ACC   plan-GEN

   I incited him to systematical non-fulfilment of the plan.

  b. My   dogovorilis'   o
     we   come.to.agreement-PST   about

  ne-razglasheni-i   tain-y.
  non-disclosure-PREP   secret-GEN

we came to an agreement about non-disclosure of the secret.

Our classifications above reflect only statistically more common usages. It is not surprising, e.g., that the nominal *nevmeshatel'stvo* 'non-interference' which belongs to the official diplomatic language is largely attested in existential contexts, whereas e.g. *nepopadanie* 'missing (the target)' with its associations with sports competitions is usually found in episodic eventive negative contexts.

What really distinguishes eventive negative nominals from existential negative nominals, and what is relevant in the contexts above, is the aspectual distinction between episodic use (for eventive negative nominals) and habitual use (for existential negative nominals).

In order to better understand this distinction and to see how it is derived, let us turn now to the aspectual properties of the negative nominals, of the nominals they are derived from, and of the contexts in which they are used.

4 Aspectual Properties

As has been already partly shown, main differences among the three attested types of negative nominals lie in the lexical aspectual domain, i.e. in the domain of actionality: they differ with respect to the aspectual properties of the negative and the initial positive nominals. Let us summarize one more time all the above mentioned information about the aspectual properties of the three types of negative event nominals.

Stative negative nominals (i) are stative themselves and are derived from stative nominals. This is proved by their lexical meaning and by their inability to pluralize[6] and to cooccur with adjectives of repetition.

Eventive negative nominals (ii) are telic and ascend to names of telic events as well: they and the nominals they are derived from can pluralize and cooccur with adjectives of repetitivity. For the negative nominals this has been shown above in (12), and the nominals they are derived from in plural form are presented in (19):

(19) *vypolnenie* 'fulfilment' — *vypolnenija* 'fulfilments, instances of fulfilment'

     javka 'appearance' — *javk-i* 'appearances, different instances of appearance'

Existential negative nominals (iii) are similar to stative negative nominals in that they are also stative (as their incompatibility with adjectives of repetitivity shows), but they share with the eventive negative nominals the property of being derived from a telic source (20).

(20) *razglashenie* 'disclosure'
         — *razglashenija* 'disclosures, different instances of disclosure'.

---

[6] This criterion, however rough, can be used as a first approximation; see e.g. Esau 1973 for the same phenomenon in German, Brinton 1995 for English.

The difference between eventive negative nominals (ii) and existential negative nominals (iii) consists in the interval of evaluation: the former are evaluated immediately when the expected event fails to take place, whereas the latter requires a long-term interval to be evaluated. The property of being evaluated on an extensive period of time is shared by existential negative nominals and stative negative nominals, which are also compatible with adjectives referring to (long) time intervals.

This difference in interval of evaluation resembles that of individual-level vs. stage-level predicates (see Carlson 1977, Krifka et al. 1995): eventive negative nominals that denote individual events are counterparts of stage-level predicates in the verbal domain, while existential negative nominals that are evaluated on long time intervals correspond to individual-level predicates.

Indeed, eventive negative nominals describe an instance, a moment of time when the event was expected and was probable to occur but failed to. Such a nominal, like a sentence with a stage-level predicate, is evaluated against the state of affairs at this time point, at this very moment.

Existential negative nominals, by contrast, like individual-level predicates, refer to a characteristic of the person or object involved in the situation and do not need to be exemplified by an occurrence when the person/object in fact doesn't perform the negated action.

Among stative negative nominals, as has been noted, there are those which are evaluated on long intervals and those which are relevant in timepoints, depending on the properties of the positive nominal they are derived from.

5 Conclusions

We have discussed event nominals, their negation, and their meaning under negation. As our Russian data suggest, there are three ways to combine the negative marker with an event nominal semantically, depending on the meaning of the nominal itself and requirements of the context:

(1) stative negative nominals, denoting a state that is characterized by the fact that some other state denoted by the positive nominal does not hold: *neznanie* 'not knowing, ignorance';

(2) eventive negative nominals, denoting an event (that consists of the non-occurrence of some other event which is denoted by the positive nominal and which is probably expected) fails to occur: *nevypolnenie* 'non-fulfilment';

(3) existential negative nominals, denoting a long time interval during which there exists no moment *t* when the event denoted by the positive nominal occurs: *nenapadenie* 'non-aggression'.

These differences are driven by aspectual factors, i.e. by aspectual properties of the initial positive noun and the requirements of the context the negative is built into. Properties of the three types of negative event nominals are summarized in Table 1.

Table 1. Properties of negative event nominals

Type of nominal	Derived from	Type of negation	Compatible with adjectives of	Plural	Evaluated on	Scope of negation
stative negative	states	contrary or contradictory	time period	no	timepoints or long intervals	without arguments
eventive negative	events	contradictory	repetition	yes	timepoints	with arguments
existential negative	events	contradictory	time period	no	long intervals	with arguments

As for the nature of the negation of event nominals, it seems that it is different for various types of negative event nominals. Stative negative nominals with their ability to accept contrary negation and to preserve the aspectual properties of the positive nominal are fairly close to adjectives, adverbs, and non-event nominals (relational nouns, names of physical objects, qualities, etc.). The most natural way of treating them is to assume that their formation follows the same principles, that is that if the nominal under negation introduces some scalable property, the negated nominal will refer to the opposite value on the scale involved (therefore contrary negation), and if the property is unscalable, the negated nominal will denote absence of the property (and the negation will be contradictory).

The other two types of negative event nominals, eventive negative nominals and existential negative nominals, are semantically similar to verbs with negation. The negative marker semantically denies not the lexical component of the meaning of the nominal, but the event it denotes in the given sentence and the use of this sentence. Therefore, as well as for the verbs, the negation should be attached at the stage of the derivation where the event is already constituted. This is also proved by the fact that in the eventual negative nominals and the existential negative nominals the eventuality is negated as a whole, with its arguments, as the *vsjakij* 'every' quantification test shows.

All these facts lead to a hypothesis that stative negative nominals, like negative "object" nominals, adjectives and adverbs, are formed in the lexicon, while the eventive negative nominals and existential negative nominals attach their negation in the process of syntactic derivation, and relatively late, after the constitution of the event. It is for this reason that stative negative nominals preserve a maximum of the properties of the positive nominal (interval of evaluation, stativeness, relation to a scale) and are negated without arguments, while event negative nominals and existential negative nominals are more dependent on the context they are used in: they can be individual-level, as well as stage-level, they are negated together with their arguments, and the scales introduced by their positive counterparts (if any) are invisible for them.

However, as we have seen above as well, attaching the negation in the lexicon or in the syntax gives more or less the same result on the surface, since stative negative nominals and eventive negative nominals look alike. They both have the prefix *ne-* as a marker of negativity, which is inseparable from the nominal.

Taking seriously the hypothesis that the negation in stative event nominals is the same as nominal negation, and the negation in event negative nominals is the same as the verbal one, the identity of surface realization of the stative nominal and eventive nominal negation leads us to a stipulation that verbal and nominal negation can themselves be of the same nature, the observable differences being due to (i) the stage of the derivation at which the negation is attached, and (ii) to the diversity in the morphosyntax of the constituents they attach to. Reason (i) primarily accounts for the semantic dissimilarity between the verbal negation and negation of non-stative event nominals, on the one hand, and all the other nominals, adjectives and adverbs, on the other hand. Reason (ii), i.e., morphosyntactic diversity of the negated phrases, underlies the superficially observed differences between verbal negation and the negation of all the other types of expressions.

References

Alexiadou, A.: Functional Structure in Nominals. John Benjamins, Amsterdam (2002)

Alexiadou, A.: Argument structure in nominals. Ms., Universität Stuttgart (2004)

Bach, E.: On time, tense, and aspect: An essay in English metaphysics. In: Cole, P. (ed.) Radical Pragmatics. Academic Press, New York (1981)

Bach, E.: The algebra of events. Linguistics and Philosophy 9 (1986)

Baeuerle, R.: Ereignisse und Repraesentationen. Habilitationschrift, Universitaet Konstanz (1987)

Barwise, J., Perry, J.: Situations and attitudes. MIT Press, Cambridge (1983)

Boguslavsky, I.M.: Issledovanija po sintaksicheskoj semantike: sfery dejstvija logicheskix slov (Essays on syntactic semantics: scopes of logical words). Moscow (1985) (in Russian)

Brinton, L.J.: The aktionsart of deverbal nouns in English. In: Bertinetto, P.M., Bianchi, V., Dahl, Ö., Squartini, M. (eds.) Temporal Reference, Aspect, and Actionality, Torino, vol. 1, pp. 27–42 (1995)

Carlson, G.N.: Reference to kinds in English. Ph.D. dissertation. Amherst University (1977)

Cresswell, M.J.: Interval semantics for Some Event Expressions. In: Baeuerle, R., Egli, U., von Stechow, A. (eds.) Semantics from different points of views, pp. 90–116. Springer, Berlin (1979)

Esau, H.: Nominalization and Complementation in Modern German, Amsterdam, London, New York (1973)

Geach, P.T.: Contradictories and Contraries. Analysis 29(6), 187–190 (1969)

Grimshaw, J.: Argument Structure. MIT Press, Cambridge (1990)

Haegeman, Liliane, M.V.: The Syntax of Negation. Cambridge University Press, Cambridge (1995)

Higginbotham, J.: On events in linguistic semantics, version of 25 June 1997. Oxford University Press, Oxford (1996) (unpublished manuscript)

Horn, L.R.: A Natural History of Negation. University of Chicago Press, Chicago (1989)

Kim, J.-B., Sag, I.A.: Negation without Head-Movement. Natural Language & Linguistic Theory 20(2) (2002)

Krifka, M.: The origins of telicity. In: Rothstein, S. (ed.) Events and Grammar. Kluwer Academic Publishers, Dordrecht (1998)

Krifka, M.: The mereological approach to aspectual composition. In: Perspectives on Aspect, Uil-OTS, University of Utrecht (2001)

Krifka, M., Pelletier, F.J., Carlson, G.N., ter Meulen, A., Link, G., Chierchia, G.: Genericity: An Introduction. In: Carlson, G.N., Pelletier, F.J. (eds.) The generic book. University of Chicago Press, Chicago (1995)

Lewis, D.: Events. In: Lewis, D. (ed.) Philosophical Papers, vol. II, pp. 241–269. Oxford UP, New York (1986)

Parsons, T.: Events in the semantics of English. MIT Press, Cambridge (1990)

Peterson, P.L.: Facts, Propositions, Events. Kluwer AP, Dordrecht (1997)

Przepiorkowski, A.: On negative eventualities, negative concord, and negative yes/no questions. In: Matthews, T., Strolovitch, D. (eds.) Proceeding of Semantics and Linguistic Theory, vol. 9, pp. 237–254. CLC Publications, Ithaca (1999)

Smith, N.: On Generics. Transactions of the Philological Society (1975)

Stockwell, R., Schachter, P., Partee, B.H.: The major syntactic structures of English. Holt Rinehart and Winston, New York (1973)

Vendler, Z.: Linguistics in Philosophy. Cornell University Press, Cornell (1967)

Vendler, Z.: Adjectives and Nominalizations, Paris (1968)

Zeijlstra, H.H.: Negation in Natural language: on the Form and Meaning of Negative Elements. Language and Linguistics Compass 1, 498–518 (2007)

Zucchi, A.: The Language of Propositions and Events: issues in the syntax and the semantics of nominalization. Kluwer AP, Dordrecht (1993)

A Dynamic Conceptual Model for the Linguistic Structuring of Space: Georgian Preverbs

Rusudan Asatiani

Institute for Oriental Studies, Georgian Academy of Science
Acad, G. tsereteli str.3, Tbilisi 0162, Georgia
r_asatiani@hotmail.com

Abstract. For structuring of space relations in the Georgian language three dimensions are valuable: 1. Point of View (speaker's or teller's position); 2. Geographic Space (various directions and distance dichotomy); 3. Communicational Space (Ego and Alter Spaces). 'Point of View', 'Ego space' and 'Distance dichotomy' are flexible: They can be changed according to the speaker's (or teller's) attitude, while abstract relations of 'Geographic Space' are stable. Various combinations of the dimensions are represented in Georgian by the preverbs: There are 9 simple and 7 complex preverbs. The paper proposes a dynamic conceptual model of space structuring for Modern Standard Georgian and examines the possibilities of its linguistic representation.

1 Introduction: The Structure of the Georgian Verb

The Georgian verb forms represent various grammatical categories. The principle of agglutination along with inflexion builds a string of morphemes and morphology mirrors the system of very complex and complicated verb categories. Structurally a Georgian verb may incorporate the following elements:

(1) Preverb(s)
(2) S/O agreement prefix (-*v*-/-*m*-/-*g*-/-*gv*-/-*h*-,-*s*-,-*0*-)
(3) Version vowel (-*a*-/-*i*-/-*u*-/-*e*-)
(4) Root
(5) Passive formant (-*d*-) or causative suffix (-*in*-/-*evin*-)
(6) Thematic suffix (-*eb*-/-*ob*-/-*av*-/-*am*-/-*op*-/-*i*-/*0*)
(7) Imperfect marker (-*d*-/-*od*-)
(8) Tense/mood vowel (-*a*-/-*i*-/-*o*-/-*e*-)
(9) S 3rd person agreement suffix (-*s*-/-*a*-/-*o*-/-*en*-/-*an*/-*n*/-*nen*/-*es*)
(10) Plural suffix (-*t*)

E.g.   *da – g – a – c'er – in – eb – d – e – s*
         prev – O.2– vers. – write – cause – them – imp. – mood – S.3

         da – g – a – c'er – in – eb – d – a – t
         prev – O.2 – vers. –write – cause – them – imp. – S.3 – pl(O)

Although for a theoretically possible string of morphemes in the structural formula for one verb root there are maximally 10 positions (3 for prefixes and 6 for suffixes), the verb form can consist of not more than 9 morphemes. There are some implicational and/or restrictive rules:

P. Bosch, D. Gabelaia, and J. Lang (Eds.): TbiLLC 2007, LNAI 5422, pp. 38–46, 2009.

1. Imperfect Marker (7) implies the existence of Thematic Markers (6);
2. Plural Suffix (10) phonetically excludes the appearance of the S 3rd person suffix *-s* (9); it can co-occur only with the S 3rd person suffixes: *-a* or *-o* (9);
3. The S 3rd person suffixes (*-a* or *-o*) phonetically exclude the appearance of Tense-Mood vowel suffixes (8).

Rules 2 and 3 can be generalized as they reflect a more universal phonetic tendency: No vowel or consonant clustering at morpheme boundaries.

Thus, the allowed combinations are either (8)-(10) or (9)-(10) and the string (8)-(9)-(10) is excluded. All other combinations of positions are possible and a concrete verb form is defined by the various combinations of verb categories.

2 Georgian Preverbs

Preverbs, which occupy the first position in the structural formula of the Georgian verb forms originally indicate direction (Shanidze 1973). There are 9 simple and 7 complex preverbs. Simple preverbs (SP) show different directions of an action: *a-* 'from down to up', *cha-* 'from up to down', *ga-* 'from inside to outside', *she-* 'from outside to inside', *gada-* 'crossing some obstacles', *mi-* 'from speaker and listener', *mo-* 'to speaker and listener', *c'a-* 'from something or somebody' and *da-* 'above some space'. The simple preverb *mo-* may be added to other simple preverbs for indicating the 'hitherness'. As a result complex preverbs (CP) arise: *a+mo-* 'up to us', *cha+mo-* 'down to us', *ga+mo-* 'out to us', and so on. As *da-* denotes movement over a path without marked directionality, the combination *da+mo-* is logically excluded[1].

Preverbs have additional functions of grammaticalization of perfective [+Prev]: imperfective [-Prev] aspect and future tense [+Prev]. They often combine the root to change the overall meaning of the verb as well (compare with the prepositional elements in English – look up/back/down/at/into etc.).

3 Conceptual Representation of Space Structuring in Georgian

Semantic and pragmatic analysis of preverbs make clear that for the structuring of space in Georgian it is important to distinguish between the Geographic Space (GS) and the Communicational Space (CS). GS is structured due to the abstract relations that have concrete interpretation only on the basis of the Point of View (PV) of a 'teller'. The 'teller' usually coincides with the speaker, but this is not always the case: Sometimes the 'teller' differs from the speaker and the space is structured according to the teller's and not the speaker's PV; E. g. "Nino says that she is going up". Although the place where Nino is going to could not be "up" for the speaker, who is located geographically higher than Nino, the speaker can still structure the space according to the teller's, i.e., Nino's, point of view.

Abstract geographic relations are represented in the linguistic structures of the Georgian language by the so-called simple preverbs (SP). The relations can be described by the following conceptual structures:

---

[1] The sequence /da+mo-/ can be found in some frozen Participle or Masdar forms (e.g.: /damo=k'id-eb-ul-i/ "dependant"), implying that it was logically possible at an earlier stage of the language, but in Modern Standard Georgian it is not productive and does not exist in verb forms.

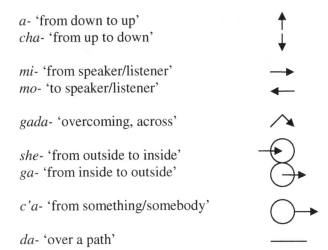

a- 'from down to up'
cha- 'from up to down'

mi- 'from speaker/listener'
mo- 'to speaker/listener'

gada- 'overcoming, across'

she- 'from outside to inside'
ga- 'from inside to outside'

c'a- 'from something/somebody'

da- 'over a path'

Communicational Space (CS) is further divided into 'Ego Space' and 'Alter Space'. Differences between ES and AS are represented in linguistic structures of Georgian by the formal opposition Complex Preverbs ([SP + *mo-*]) : Simple Preverbs (all SP except *mo-*). The opposition distinguishes the orientation of an action according to the dichotomy: 1st/2nd person [action directed/oriented to 1st/2nd person (ES)]: 3rd person [action directed/oriented to 3rd person (AS)]. Thus, the addition of *mo-* changes the orientation of an action.

It is a peculiarity of the Georgian language that 2nd person is included into ES, e.g.:

(1) *šen-tan*   *xval*   *gamo-v-ivli*
     2.DAT-at   tomorrow   PR:FUT-S.1-come:FUT(S.1.SG)
     'I'll come to you tomorrow'

(2) *Mosk'ov-ši*   *amo-v-(v)al*
     Moscow[DAT]-in   PR:FUT-S.1-come:FUT(S.1.SG)
     'I'll arrive (to you) in Moscow'

The examples describe a situation where the speaker's ES is definitely different from the listener's CS, but, yet the forms with *mo-* representing the orientation to ES are used. The examples are not exceptional ones and represent the regularity of the usages of *mo-*. Thus, we have to conclude that ES in Georgian includes 2nd person as well.

It must be mentioned that the orientation to the space, which belongs to speaker and/or listener, is not always regarded by the speaker/teller as included into ES; e.g.:

(3) *saxl-ši*   *gvian*   *mi-v-(v)ed-i*
     house[DAT]-in   late   PR:PRF-S.1-come-AOR(S.1.SG)
     'I came home late'

(4) *šen-tan,   mosk'ov-ši,*   *a-v-(v)al*
     2.DAT-at Moscow[DAT]-in   PR:FUT-S.1-come:FUT(S.1.SG)
     'I'll arrive to Moscow'

Sentence (3) reflects the following situation: The speaker, A, is referring to his or her own home and is in conversation with somebody, B, who is not at A's home; still A includes B in ES and, consequently, has to exclude A's home from ES, despite the fact that it is the speaker's, A's, own home. – Compare with the sentence: *saxl-ši gvian mo-v-(v)ed-i*, which reflects a situation where both the speaker's home and the addressee are included in ES; Presumably, either they live together or the addressee is a neighbor or the owner of the house; etc.

Sentence (4) mirrors the following situation: The speaker, A, will arrive in Moscow; A knows that the addressee, B, lives in Moscow, but A also knows that B will not be in Moscow by the time of A's arrival. – Compare with the (2), which shows the speaker's presupposition that the addressee will be in Moscow when the speaker arrives or is going to visit Moscow when the addressee will be in Moscow.)

These examples argue once more that in the structuring of space geographic relations and their inclusion in ES are not decisive in the interpretation of space relations: Structuring of CS mainly depends on the speaker's attitude.

On the basis of the ES:AS opposition the dynamic conceptual model of SP can be represented by the diagram in Figure 1.

Ego Space   Alter Space

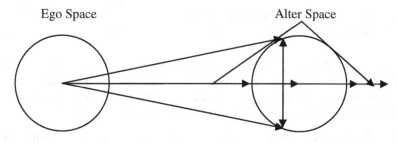

Fig. 1.

Depending on the speaker's attitude, ES can be either compressed or expended and it can include AS. This is the case when a CP with *mo-* arises:

ES

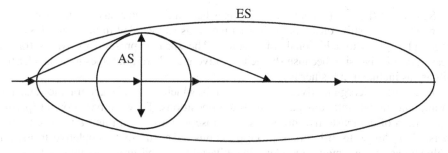

Fig. 2.

ES does not always conform to the semantics of 'Proximate':'Distal', which is an important feature for structuring of GS according to the concept of 'distance'. The 'distance', like the ES, is relative and is defined by the speaker's or teller's attitude, which is different from the opposition ES:AS. Objects near to us are not obligatorily included into ES and vice versa: 'Near' does not always mean 'to us' and 'Far' does not always mean 'from us'. All logically possible cases can be represented by the following figures:

(5) *ak mo-vid-a* 'S/he came to us(1st/2nd pers.) here'
     here PR-come-AOR.S.3.SG

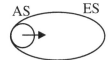

(6) *ik mo-vid-a* 'S/he came to us(1st/2nd pers) there'
     there PR-come-AOR.S.3.SG

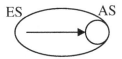

(7) *ak mi-vid-a* 'S/he came to 3rd pers here'
     here PR-come-AOR.S.3.SG

(8) *ik mi-vid-a* 'S/he came to 3rd pers there'
     there PR-come-AOR.S.3.SG

In Georgian all these possibilities can be realized in linguistic structures and the most 'unexpected' situatons, i.e., (6) and (7) can be illustrated by the sentences (9)-(10). The situations corresponding to the cases (6) and (7) are very specific, of course, and, consequently, the sentences like (9) and (10) are rare as well.

(9) *ik,   tbilis-ši,   bevr-i   xalx-i   mo-di-s   xolme   mit'ing-eb-ze*
     thereTbilisi[DAT]-in many-NOM people-NOM PR-come-PRS.S.3. SG PTC(usually) meeting-PL[DAT]-on
     'There, in Tbilisi, a lot of people are coming to meetings'

(10) *ak st'undent'-eb-i xšir-ad a-di-an xolme me>sam<e sartul-ze bibliotek'a-ši*
     here student-PL-NOM   often-ADV PR: up-go-PRS.S.3.PL(usually) third[DAT] floor[DAT]-on library[DAT]-i
     'Here students often go up to the third floor into the library'

Sentence (9) corresponds to a situation, where the speaker has a conversation far from Tbilisi but still considers the Tbilisi meetings as included in his or her ES. Sentence (10) gives us additional information: The speaker presumably works (or, at least, is) in University, because she/he uses adverb *ak* 'here', but does not consider the library as included in his/her ES.

In general, Georgian adverbs and pronouns which represent geographic (and not communicational) relations build tripartite oppositions. They are based on a tripartite opposition of demonstrative pronouns: *es* 'close to 1st person, this'*: eg* 'close to 2nd person'*: is* 'close to 3rd person'. The pronouns have different, suppletive forms for oblique cases: *am : mag : im.* Consequently, adverbs and pronouns mostly have demonstrative function and distinguish the following space relations: Close to 1st person (forms with vowel *a-*); Close to 2nd person (forms beginning with syllable *ma(g)*); and Close to 3nd person (forms with vowel *i-*):

(11) *amdeni : magdeni : imdeni* – 'Quantity'
  aseti : maseti : iseti – 'Quality'
  amnairi : magnairi : imnairi – 'Quality'(*dialectal*)
  ak : mand : ik – 'Place'
  ase : mase : ise – 'Manner'
  amit'om : magit'om : imit'om – 'Reason'
  amdenad : magdenad : imdenad – 'Quantity of manner' and so on.

Semantic and pragmatic analysis of these forms make clear that geographic feature 'distance' and not the persons' factual inclusion in CS plays an important role in their usages. (See above discussion concerning the adverbs *ak : ik.*)

4 The Main Dimensions of Space Structuring and Their Various Combinations

Due to our analysis, the main dimensions for space structuring in Georgian are the following:

1. Point of View (speaker's or teller's);
2. Geographic Space (various directions and distance dichotomy);
3. Communicational Space (Ego and Alter Spaces).

'Point of View', 'Ego Space' and 'Distance' are relative while abstract relations of 'Geographic Space' are stable. The speaker's or the teller's PVs are not always the same (cf. Section 3). Moreover, speaker's PV is not defined according to his or her position or geographic location and it can be changed for the speaker as well. There are various possibilities: (1) PV conforms with the speaker's position (SP); (2) PV is above the SP; (3) PV is downward from the SP:

When I am on the fourth floor and my friend is going to the third floor. I can say:

  My friend is going up to the third floor. (3)
  My friend is going down to the third floor. (2) or (1)

When I am on the fourth floor and my friend is going to the sixth floor. I can say:

  My friend is going up to the sixth floor. (3) or (1)
  My friend is going down to the sixth floor. (2)

If during the structuring 'my friend's space' is regarded as included in ES, a more complex situation arises and the meaning 'to me/you' is also added. Such a situation in Georgian is represented by CP. In general, if ES is somehow included during the structuring of a space, CP always becomes relevant.

5 Preverbs and Exceptional Ditransitive Verb Forms in Georgian

Some ditransitive verbs like 'to give' show recipient person suppletion that is a typologically well known phenomenon for some languages. In Georgian such verbs have a specific paradigm where distribution of the preverbs *mi-* and *mo-* is the basis for the suppletion. Polypersonal verb forms in Georgian incorporate subject markers as well as object markers. A 1st or 2nd person recipient is represented by the object markers. As the semantics of the verb 'to give' (*micema*) implies the meaning of direction, preverbs *mo-* or *mi-* are obligatory and their distribution is in accordance with their conceptual interpretation: *mo-* is used in cases of 1st/2nd person recipients and *mi-* in cases of 3rd person recipients. Thus, we have an exceptional suppletive paradigm for this verb; cf (12).

(12) *mi-v-eci*   (I gave to him/her)
      mi-eci   (You gave to him/her)
      mi-s-c-a   (S/he gave to him/her)
      mo-m-c-a   (S/he gave to me)
      mo-g-c-a   (S/he gave to you-sg)
      mo-gv-c-a   (S/he gave to us)
      mo-g-c-a-t   (S/he gave to you-pl)

The forms *mi-m-c-a* 'S/he gave me to him/her', *mi-g-c-a* 'S/he gave you to him/her' have different glossing: 1st/2nd person markers refer here to the patient or DO and never to the recipient or IO[2].

The same suppletion according to the preverbs *mi-* and *mo-* is characteristic also for other ditransitive verbs (actually for any of them which semantics allow for differences in orientation): *mic'odeba* 'to send', *mipurtxeba* 'to spit to', *mipereba* 'to caress', *mikiraveba* 'to hire out', *mitxoveba* 'to marry to' and so on.

Some such ditransitive verbs allow the form *mi-ac'oda* 'S/he gave it to smb.' as well as the form *mo-ac'oda* 'S/he gave it to smb.'. This happens when verb semantics permits the 3rd person recipient to be included in ES. But the forms *mi-m-ac'oda*, and *mi-g-ac'oda* where *-m-*, *-g-* could be the markers of 1st/2nd person recipient are absolutely excluded.

6 Cognitive Interpretation of Semantic Roles: Conceptual Structures of EDV

To understand the peculiarities of such exceptional ditransitive verbs it might be helpful, first of all, to consider the conceptual structure of the semantic roles. There are various semantic features according to which the roles are defined, but none of them is the decisive one. We are proposing a comprehensive representation for them, which defines all other features and helps us to understand the process of the creation of verb forms (Asatiani 2003).

Every concept has its own space within which 'it stays with itself'. Conceptual space usually is defined according to many features. For the conceptual spaces of the semantic roles the most relevant are the features which characterize the noun in relation to the action which is represented by the verb.

---

[2] /mo=s-ca/ was perfectly acceptable in Old Georgian , but such forms are excluded in Modern Standard Georgian.

In the course of the action described, the referents of nouns can: (1) cross the space; (2) approach the space; (3) stay within the space. The three possibilities seem to be decisive for distinguishing between Ag, P, and Ad. The Agent (as far as it is active, telic, volitional, dynamic, high in potency, etc) is the referent which crosses (its own or something/somebody else's) space. The Patient (as it is inactive, atelic, non-volitional, static, low in potency) is the referent which stays within its own space; it allows the space to be crossed but never crosses the space itself. The Addressee is the role which receives something, can be reached but does not allow the space to be crossed. Schematically:

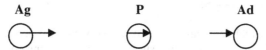

Different combinations of these features construct the conceptual structures which mirror the process of the linguistic structuring of the extra-linguistic situations respective to the concrete verb semantics. Some examples:

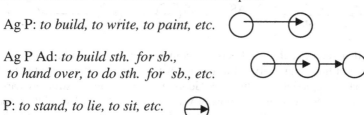

Ag P: *to build, to write, to paint, etc.*

Ag P Ad: *to build sth. for sb.,*
to hand over, to do sth. for sb., etc.

P: *to stand, to lie, to sit, etc.*

Ag: *to live, to dance, to think, etc.*

The strategy of structuring can differ: If the situation implies simple space relations between the nouns, only one conceptual structure is constructed. Universally, each linguistic-cognitive system provides for the same conceptual model for the structuring of the simple relations, i.e., all languages map nouns onto the semantic roles similarly; E.g. *to build* in almost all languages is structured as follows:

But: If the situation allows for different interpretations, then languages choose their own specific strategies for the linguistic structuring. According to these strategies languages differ in the way of structuring and provide different linguistic structures (Asatiani 2003).

The specific semantics of the ditransitive verb 'to give' *'micema'* can be represented by the following conceptual structure:

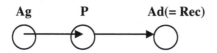

The preverbs *mo-* and *mi-*, as was mentioned above, are elements of the linguistic realization of spatial relations in Georgian, where two dimensions are relevant: 'Ego Space' and 'Alter Space'. The opposition of the preverbs *mo-* : *mi-* is the linguistic representation of the cognitive opposition ES:AS. Thus, *mo-* marks a situation where an action is directed/oriented to the 1st or 2nd person (ES), whereas *mi-* is the formal representation of a situation with an action directed/oriented to the 3rd person. According to this opposition the conceptual relations involved can be represented by the following schemes:

1st and 2nd person recipients are included in ES, while 3rd person recipients are excluded. If we match the two conceptual structures, the following complex structures arise:

We suppose that such matching reflects the complex cognitive process of the linguistic structuring of the 'to give'-type ditransitive verb concepts. It clarifies the basis of the 'exceptional', suppletive paradigms in Georgian: The linguistic structures arise in accordance with the conceptual meanings of verb and preverbs, and yield their specific paradigm absolutely logically. Thus, they need not any more be qualified as being outside the language system and in any way 'exceptional'.

References

1. Asatiani, R.: Semantics and Typology of Dative Subject (on the Georgian Data). In: Dekker, P., van Rooy, R. (eds.) Proceedings of the 14th Amsterdam Colloquium 2003, pp. 69–75. Amsterdam Uni. press, Amsterdam (2003a)
2. Asatiani, R.: Conceptual Representation of the Verb Form creation (on the Georgian Data). In: Proceedings of the Fifth Tbilisi Symposium on LLC, pp. 21–29. Grafisch Centrum Amsterdam, Amsterdam (2003b)
3. Chanishvili, N.: Structuring of Space in Georgian. In: Proceedings of the Fifth Tbilisi Symposium on LLC, pp. 51–59. Grafisch Centrum Amsterdam, Amsterdam (2003)
4. Gärdenfors, P.: Conceptual Spaces: The Geometry of Thoughts. In: A Bradford Book. The MIT press, Cambridge (2000)
5. Givon, T.: On Understanding Grammar. Acad. Press, New York (1979)
6. Shanidze, A.: Kartuli enis gramat'ik'is sapudzvlebi (Principles of the Georgian Language Grammar). Mecniereba, Tbilisi (1973)

even in Horn Space

Regine Eckardt

Göttingen University, Germany
regine.eckardt@phil.uni-goettingen.de

Abstract. In the first part of the paper, I argue that current pragmatic theories of NPI licensing fail to capture the distinction between strong and weak NPIs. Specifically, I will show that an analysis in terms of covert *even* alone can not account for the limited distribution of strong NPIs. In the second part, I investigate the implicatures of *even* sentences in weak licensing contexts. I show that they give rise to a minimal-achievement implicature which can be used to derive the markedness of strong NPIs in weak licensing contexts.

1 Introduction

The aim of this paper is to develop an analysis of the weak-strong distinction for NPIs in terms of scale-based NPI licensing. More modestly, I will be concerned with an analysis of the following range of examples.

(1)   *Few students had any idea about syntax.*

(2)   *Few students even carried a pen.*

(3)   **Few students lifted a finger in this class.*

(4)   *Few students at least carried a pen.*

(5)   *Tom at least carried a pen.*

Sentence (1) shows the use of NPI *any* in the scope of *few* where licensing clearly is independent of negation. According to Zwarts (1998) and van der Wouden (2007), contexts like the scope of *few* are characterized by being downward-entailing but not antimorphic. I will call such contexts *weak* contexts in the following. Sentence (2) offers an example of *even* in the scope of *few*. We seem to understand *carry a pen* as a minimal type of intellectual involvement in class, on a scale like *carry a pen, read the paper, understand the paper*. The sentence is grammatical and coherent. Moreover it strongly suggests that 'some students just carried a pen to class and did nothing else'. Sentence (3) shows the typical textbook ungrammaticality of strong NPIs in weak licensing contexts. Whatever the reason, this is one of the diagnoses that the NPI *lift a finger* is a strong NPI. Sentence (4) seems to convey practically the same message as sentence (2). The adverbial *at least* like *even* signals that the degree of involvement signalled by *carry a pen* is minimal. Strangely, the sentence in (4) does not share the note of exasperation we feel in (2). The scalar situation, however, appears

P. Bosch, D. Gabelaia, and J. Lang (Eds.): TbiLLC 2007, LNAI 5422, pp. 47–61, 2009.

to be the same. Sentence (5) finally illustrates that *at least*, unlike *even*, is not polarity sensitive. This shows that scalar particles need not be polarity sensitive per se. This is acknowledged by the major theories of scalar NPI licensing. Yet, scale-based licensing is sometimes erroneously connected to the prediction that "anything scalar is polarity sensitive". I therefore want to compare the analyses of *even* and *at least* at the end of the paper.

2   Logic and Ladusaw

In our set of examples, the two NPIs by themselves do not pose any particular problem for the classical logical approach to NPI licensing. This is how the approach would analyse those data.

We assume that *few* means *at most few* or *few, perhaps none*. Let me use $few_\le$ as a shorthand to explicate this assumption. Now, $few_\le$ is downward entailing in both arguments. E.g. $few_\le$ S do P entails $few_\le$ S do P* for P* $\subset P$. Therefore, $few_\le$ licenses NPIs in both arguments. However, $few_\le$ is not antimorphic in either argument. Therefore, strong NPIs are not licensed in the arguments of $few_\le$.

This argument follows the analyses by Ladusaw (1979), Zwarts (1998), and van der Wouden (2007). In recent years, this approach to NPI licensing has been criticized because it cannot handle phenomena like subtriggering, locality effects, licensing in non-DE contexts and others. However, the approach did well for the two NPI examples in our set, which are the type of examples it was designed for.

3   Scalar Theories

Fauconnier (1975) initiated a strand of research which considers NPI licensing as a pragmatic effect. Two main families of analyses are currently entertained. The *strengthening analysis* relies on the idea that NPIs invite us to think about alternative possible utterances / propositions and to compare their logical strength with that of the actual utterance. An NPI is licensed iff the actual utterance is logically stronger than all its alternatives. This idea is implemented in Kadmon and Landman (1993), Krifka (1995; first half), and Chierchia (2004).

The *hidden 'even' analysis* is based on the idea that the proposition expressed is compared to alternatives by an explicit or covert *even*. The use of *even* presupposes that the alternatives are ordered on a scale, and that the utterance denotes a proposition at the top end of this scale. Most accounts assume scales of likelihood / surprisingness where being likely among the alternatives commonly is modelled as being logically weak among the alternatives. This is the guiding idea in Krifka (1995; second half) as well as Chierchia (2006), Lahiri (1998) and the examples in Eckardt (2005), (2007). An early predecessor of this idea can be found in Heim (1984) where, interestingly, contentful scales rather than logical scales are assumed to play a role. Israel (1996 and later) can be read as proposing 'independent scales' although he is often not very explicit about the nature of his scales.

Interestingly, scale-based theories of NPI licensing are often presented as covering some, but not all instances of NPI licensing. Guerzoni (2004) assumes that *even*-based licensing in questions is responsible for the rhetorical quality of questions with strong NPIs. Likewise, Krifka (1995) assumes that the restricted use of strong NPIs is due to the fact that they are licensed by **emphatic.assert** (tantamount to hidden *even*). Heim (1984) also points out that hidden *even* should explain the limited acceptability of strong NPIs in the restrictor of universal quantifiers (including conditionals). Other authors like Chierchia (2006) remain open in this respect; the proposals in Eckardt (2005), (2007) are in line with Chierchia in that no extra restrictions are expected to arise from scale-based licensing. I think that I have been careful for good reason.

To my knowledge, there are no other attempts to distinguish strong and weak NPIs in a scale- or alternative-based theory of licensing. Guerzoni (2006) implicitly adopts the view that strong NPIs are licensed by a covert *even* whereas weak NPIs are licensed in the syntax by a feature-checking mechanism. Once again it is scalar licensing that accounts for the limited contexts of strong NPIs. In the next section, I will argue that this can't be true.

4   Hidden *even* Doesn't Make You Strong

The argument that, I think, strikingly stands against the equation that *strong NPI = covert even* is the fact that overt *even* (positive and negative) is perfectly acceptable in weak contexts. Consider example (2), repeated below.

(6)   Few students even carried a pen.

This example illustrates all the properties that have been proposed to characterize NPIs, except for the fact that *carry a pen* is a lexically neutral VP which can be used in positive contexts. However, in the most natural scenario for (6), *carry a pen* denotes a property which is presented as a minimal way of involvement in class. This property includes several more narrow properties like *read the paper*, *understand the paper* which (so the sentence suggests) come along with carrying a pen but go beyond it. In short, *carry a pen* in (6) works like the NPI *lift a finger* in (3), the only difference being that the former is a transparent property and not a fixed expression.

If there were anything logically defective about the scalar assertion in example (3), we would expect exactly the same logical or pragmatic deficiencies to hold for (6) as well. Given that (6) is a perfectly well-formed sentence, we can conclude that a covert *even* analysis for (3) can not straightforwardly explain why the sentence is marked.

Is it possible that covert *even* has different properties than overt *even*? None of the available analyses ever suggest anything beyond the semantic contribution of overt *even*. Some explicitly characterize the operator as hidden *even*. Notice that if we insert an overt *even*, the situation in (3) does not improve.

(7)   *Few students even lifted a finger in this class.

According to several native speakers that I consulted, sentence (7) is as ill-formed as (3). Therefore I will assume that overt *even* is not able to license strong NPIs in weak contexts. Given that overt *even* can license other scalar minimizing expressions (see (4)), this is surprising. Most pragmatic theories formulate licensing in terms of the logical and pragmatic properties of the utterance without recurring to specific syntactic ties between licensor and NPI. Hence, on most of these theories it should not make a difference whether we use explicit or tacit *even*. The only exception is Chierchia (2006) who proposes that licensors as well as NPIs carry syntactic features that allow a checking mechanism. He could postulate that hidden *even* but not ouvert *even* is able to check the relevant features. However, his tacit *even* operator EC does not show any differences to overt *even* either. Therefore, the logics and pragmatics of examples (2) and (3) should again be the same. Finally, note that Chierchia (2006) seems to assume that *any* as a domain widener is also licensed by hidden *even*. Once again, we may ask why, then, licensing in example (1) is possible whereas licensing in example (3) (=(6)) fails.

In the present paper, I will propose a way to exclude strong NPIs from weak contexts in terms of a scalar theory of licensing. The core assumption of the account will be, that strong NPIs are antiveridical in a sense to be made precise below. Informally, antiveridical properties P are such that no sentence should suggest (implicate, state) that some x did P-and-nothing-else. Strong NPIs denote properties that are antiveridical in this sense. They should therefore not be used in sentences that implicate that someone did P-and-nothing-else. In the next sections, I will explicate this idea and defend the following points:

1. Previous analyses fail to acknowledge the implicature that 'some S do P-and-no-more'.
2. NPIs are licensed in the scope of *few* by covert *even* in the same way as scalar expressions are licensed by overt *even* in the scope of *few*.
3. Strong NPIs are excluded from weak contexts by an additional antiveridicality condition. I will use a combination of ideas by Krifka/Chierchia/Lahiri on one side and Giannakidou (2001) on the other side to account for the strong-weak distinction.

5   *even* in Horn Space

In this section, I will discuss the implicatures and meaning of *even* in the scope of *few* and similar quantifiers. I will first empirically establish what I call the minimal achievement implicature. Next, I derive this implicature on the basis of the (otherwise rarely exploited) maxim of relevance. In the final part of this section, I will discuss, and ultimately reject, several alternatives. Throughout, I will assume a scopal theory of *even*: *even* makes the same scalar contribution in negative and positive sentences (Wilkinson 1996, Lahiri 2006). Consider once again the following example.

(8)   Few students even carried a pen.

By uttering (8), a speaker can convey the following side messages.

- existence: Some students DID carry a pen.
- scale: Not many students carried a pen.
- minimal achievement: Some students carried a pen and that was all they contributed.

The determiner *few* is usually analysed in terms of *at most k, perhaps even zero*. Under this analysis, the scale information follows as logical entailment from the sentence. Moreover, *few* competes with *no* on a Horn scale where *no* leads to a stronger proposition. The existential proposition therefore follows as a scalar implicature. The origin of the minimal achievement implicature is less obvious.

Let me first compare sentences with and without *even*. The minimal pairs illustrate that *even* + focus are necessary to create minimal achievement implicatures, and that it does not arise readily in sentences without *even*.

(9) a. Few Germans know Larry Gonink.

   b. Few Germans even KNOW Larry Gonink.

Consider the following two possible continuations. Both are, of course, possible in both (9.a) and (9.b). However, (10.a) is more natural after (9.a) than after (9.b). In contrast, (10.b) is a natural follow-up for (9.b). The sentence pairs in (11) and (12) show the same pattern.

(10) a. But those who do all love his books.

   b. ... let alone have read his comic *History of the Universe*

(11) a. a. Few people believe in God.

   b. Few people even BELIEVE in God.

(12) a. a. But those who do pray regularly.

   b. ... let alone know where the nearest church might be

If a speaker asserts that *few N do P* and evokes a contrast between *P* and more specific properties *P'* we understand that *P* is the most specific (or 'the best') that can be asserted of even a small amount of entities. If we utter (9.a) and continue by (10.a), we state that there is a small but eager Larry Gonink community in Germany. Uttering (9.b) conveys the expectation that 'knowing Larry Gonink' is already uncommon among Germans, and that all more specific attitudes towards Larry Gonink are even rarer. This is a good start for (10.b). The continuation in (10.a) contradicts the expectation that all more specific attitudes are rarer, and therefore sounds slightly incoherent. Similar observations hold for (11). The impression is confirmed by a brief Web survey for German analogous *wenige ... auch nur* examples. The following hit is typical:

(13) Unwissenheit war damals wirklich groß, wenige vollendeten auch-nur
   Ignorance   was then   really   huge, few   completed   even
   die Volksschule,   viele blieben Analphabeten.
   the elementary-school, many stayed analphabets

   'Ignorance was really pervalent at that time, few even completed elementary school, many stayed illiterate'

The topic of the passage is the general ignorance of people. Once more, the passage does not create the impression that all those who finished elementary school went on to higher education. Clearly, the suggestion is that at least some of those who finished elementary school never learned anything beyond that; it is even unclear whether some people that finished elementary school might be illiterate.

Note that I am not attempting to make claims about collocational restrictions. One might find continuations of the *let alone* type in corpora for the a. examples above as well as for b. examples. These continuations however require a pitch accent on an appropriate place in the first sentence, e.g. *know* in (9.a). Given that a focus accent brings forth alternatives, this prosody triggers an interpretation as an emphatic assertion (cf. Krifka 1995).

(14)   Few Germans KNOW Larry Gonink
       ... let alone have read his comic History of the Universe.

The empirical finding, in sum, is this: An emphatic focus in the scope of *few*, with or without *even*, gives rise to alternative properties. These range from less to more specific properties, where more specific properties are usually also more desirable or "better". One of the inferences triggered by sentence such as (9.b) is that the speaker lacks evidence to assert that *few N have P* for "better" properties P'. Hence, we can infer that at least some of those few entities referred to in the utterance exhibit the property P (*know LG*) but none of its alternatives (*love LG, have read the History of the Universe, ...*). The sentence conveys the additional information that the Minimal Achievement reported in the sentence is all that can truthfully asserted in the given sentence context, i.e., with the quantifier *few*.

Let us now attempt to derive Minimal Achievement as an implicature of a scalar *few* sentence. It won't be easy.

6   The Minimal Achievement Implicature

In what follows, we will keep in mind that (8) gives rise to two different sets of alternatives. First, the quantifier *few* belongs to the Horn Scale *no ... few*. Note that *many ... all* do not compete with $few_{<}$ because they are semantically incompatible. Second, focus on the VP and *even* trigger alternatives to the VP. These are logically stronger: 'read the paper' entails (by world knowledge) 'carry a pen', and 'understand the paper' entails 'read the paper'. I will use P, P', P'' to abbreviate these properties with the notational convention that $P'' \subset P' \subset P$. We get the following entailments.

$$few_{\leq} \text{ S do P}$$
$$\rightarrow few_{\leq} \text{ S do P'}$$
$$\rightarrow few_{\leq} \text{ S do P''}$$

The utterance is the logically strongest alternative, hence the least likely one (for this connection, I refer the reader to Krifka 1995). Therefore, according to the standard analysis of *even*, the scalar presupposition is coherent here.

Let us turn to the proposition that *some student carried a pen and no more*. This proposition is not logically entailed by the sentence. We noted above that the implicature arises only when we face alternative properties P, P', ... Therefore the implicature should derive somehow from the comparison of

$few_\leq$ S do P
$few_\leq$ S do P'
$few_\leq$ S do P"

However, the first proposition above is the logically strongest alternative and therefore, we can get no scalar implicatures at this point.

We could try to compare possible alternative utterances with implicatures, instead of propositions simpliciter. While this type of competition is not part of the classical Gricean account, it is implemented in (Chierchia 2004) and we could use his procedure here. Consider then the alternative utterances *Few students read the paper* and *Few students understood the paper*. All these utterances carry an existential implicature. Alternatives plus implicatures are listed here.

$few_\leq$ S do P $\wedge$ some S do P
$few_\leq$ do P' $\wedge$ some S do P'
$few_\leq$ S do P" $\wedge$ some S do P"

This, at first sight, seems to bring us closer to home: Can we claim that the speaker avoided the utterance *Few students read the paper* because she could not committ herself to the implicature that some students did read the paper? In that case we could conclude that some students carried a pen and nothing more, which is what we seek to derive. Unfortunately, the logical relations between the alternatives do not warrant this implicature. In the above conjunctions, the first conjuncts entail each other from top to down. The second conjuncts entail each other bottom to top. Therefore, the lower conjunctions do not entail the upper ones. Indeed, we can check that there are situations where

(15) $P' \subset P$
       $few_\leq$ S do P $\wedge$ some S do P is false
       $few_\leq$ S do P' $\wedge$ some S do P' is true

(16) $P = GERMANS$, $P' = FEMALE\text{-}GERMANS$, $S = GROW\text{-}A\text{-}BEARD$
       Under real-world conditions, 'few Germans grow beards' (in the sense that they have the potential to grow one) is false because the whole male population has this potential. However, 'few female Germans grow beards, but some actually do' is true.

Therefore, we can not exclude alternative utterances on the basis of their scalar implicatures simply because they do not convey stronger alternative propositions.

I propose that the minimal achievement implicature arises from the interaction of the maxims of relevance and quality. Consider the alternative utterances in (17).

(17)   a. Few students carried a pen
        b. Few students read the paper.

The example in (a.) is logically stronger than (b.) in literal meaning.[1] If we compute the two meanings plus implicatures, the examples are logically incomparable. However, it seems fair to say that for the more restricted properties P', P' would be more *relevant* in comparison to the minimal achievement in (a.). Hence, the hearer expects that if the speaker had evidence in favour of an alternative like (17.b) he would have been required to utter this alternative because it would have been relevant[2].

Let us briefly check that this proposal makes the correct predictions about the different behaviour of *a few* and *few* with respect to *even*. Compare the examples in (18) and (19).

(18)   Few students even carried a pen. (= this is something minimal)

(19)   A few students even carried a pen. (= sounds like a true achievement)

The determiner *a few* in (19) is traditionally analysed as 'at least few, perhaps more' and strengthened to 'few but not many' by scalar implicature. The determiner is upward-entailing in its scope. The following entailment relations illustrate this behaviour where I will assume that 'read the paper' is more restricted 'than carry a pen', and 'be physically present' is most comprehensive.

(20)   A few students read the paper
        → A few students carried a pen
        → A few students were physically present.

The use of *even* presupposes that the proposition expressed is the least probable among the salient alternatives. Therefore, *even* in the scope of *a few* can only trigger less specific alternatives (e.g. 'be physically present'), not stronger ones. Given that all alternatives are less demanding than the assertion, we can derive why *carry a pen* sounds like a true achievement in (19). Note that these are well known textbook examples which are repeated here in order

- to make sure that the present analysis extends to *even* in the scope of *a few*
- to show that we need no syntactic features in order to derive different scales associated with *even* in different contexts
- to show why attempts to derive the minimality implicature as a logical implicature on the basis of a new analysis of *few* are most likely bound to fail (if *few* and *a few* are too similar in meaning, it will be hard to account for the contrast in (18)/(19)).

---

[1] Keep in mind that 'read the paper' entails 'carry a pen' in this context, even though the two properties are logically independent.

[2] In fact, the example bears close resemblance to Grice's original example of a letter of recommendation which mentions the clear handwriting, but fails to state anything about a person's professional achievements.

Note that the analysis in many places hinges on the fact that *even* associates with literal meanings of sentences and not meanings+implicatures. This argues against the recursive implicature computation as advocated in (Chierchia 2004).

7   Antiveridicality: Strong NPIs in a Scalar World

At this point, we have clarified several issues. Firstly, in a wide scope construal *even* can be combined with *few* to make a statement about minimal achievements. Secondly, such statements come along with a minimal achievement implicature. Let us now turn these ingredients into a general account of NPI licensing by covert *even*, concentrating on the different behaviour of strong and weak NPIs in weak contexts.

(21)   Few students had read any of the assigned papers.

I will follow the standard assumption that *any* is an existential quantifier and makes alternative DPs salient, as below.

(22)   Alt(any N) = { some N, some N', some N", ... }
       where N', N", ... are salient more narrow alternatives to N.

In the present case, the alternatives could be more specific kinds of papers, for instance hard papers, technical papers etc. Note that the alternatives can be very limited in number; we need not consider just any subset in N, only some salient ones. (This difference is important in some licensing contexts like in the scope of *only* or superlatives). Under the hidden *even* analysis, *any* is licensed in a sentence iff the proposition that is denoted by the sentence with *some N* is more striking, less probable than the propositions expressed by the corresponding sentences with N, N etc.

I will not make any assumptions about the prosody of examples like (21). According to my intuitions, *any* as well as *few* are pitch-accented in these examples. This accent has no direct pragmatic impact (or else, we would contrast quantifiers with other quantifiers); note however that Krifka (1995) reports the intuition that stressed *any* behaves like a strong NPI, i.e., should not be licensed in (21). He treats stressed *any* on a par with *any ... whatsoever*. For the latter NPI, I would agree that it is not allowed in a context like (21) and will now turn to a proposal why that is so. Let me start with the NPI *lift a finger* and consider the following example.

(23)   *Few students (even) lifted a finger in class.

As in all earlier cases, I will assume that the denotation of the NPI is one of the alternatives.

(24)   Alt('lift a finger') = { 'lift a finger', 'read some papers', 'discuss in class', 'listen', ... } with N, N', ... linearly ordered by set inclusion.

I assume that expressions like *lift a finger* indeed have a denotation. In the present example, *lift a finger* denotes activities that arise as part of some more substantial way of taking part in class. I have called such activities subminimal activities elsewhere. The particular set of activities will be context-dependent. It is conceivable that among the same group of students none lifted a finger in the course of intellectual achievements but many lifted fingers literally and non-literally when, say, sending text messages under the table. The overall content of the sentence suggests an appropriate range of activities where *lift a finger* denotes the smallest possible ones. The notion of a subminimal activity as such has been explored in more detail in Eckardt (2007).

At this point, the minimal achievement implicature becomes crucial. I argued that structurally similar examples with *even* in association with a "proper" activity description P give rise to the implicature that some students did P and no more. We get the same implicature for (23).

(25) Some students lifted a finger-and-no-more.

According to our world knowledge, this is impossible. The activities in the extension of *lift a finger* can never occur without other activities higher on the scale. The NPI is abused to make an utterance that carries a contradictory implicature. I propose that there is an antiveridicality constraint on strong NPI.

(26) If a sentence with an NPI gives rise to contradictory implicatures on basis of the NPI, the NPI is not licensed in this context.

The condition in (26) is tailored for NPIs like *give a damn*, *bat an eyelash*, or *(own a) red cent*. It can, however, easily be extended to expressions like *budge an inch* which are not literally impossible. At least since the discovery of millimeters or nanometers we would agree that moving 1 inch is a movement large scale. In these cases, antiveridicality has to be ensured by a lexical convention on NPI interpretation which mimics the subminimal denotations of *lift a finger*, or *bat an eyelash*.

(27) Strong NPIs are subject to the lexical convention that their denotation is subminimal in the denotations of the contextual alternatives.

By making this assumption, we can apply the antiveridicality constraint to more strong NPIs. Note that the assumption, even though perhaps no longer part of our conceptualization of the world, is historically motivated in these cases. Let me turn to NPIs which are maximizers (see Krifka 1995 as one of the few who mention and treat this type of polarity-sensitive item), like the proverbial 10 horses.[3]

---

[3] An aside on the possible German translations of *even*. To my knowledge, *even* with low scope is *sogar* while *even* with high scope over negative operators has two NPI translations in German: *auch nur* and *einmal*. These two show the bagel NPI distribution that has been described in Pereltsvaig (2003). In direct combination with *nicht*, we have to use *einmal* (*nicht einmal* vs **nicht auch nur*). In all other cases, *auch nur* is used. I will not address the general problem that *auch nur/einmal* in German translates *even*-in-high-scope in English. The German data suggest that in this language, at least, we need to adopt an ambiguity analysis of *even1/even2* ,i.e., *sogar/auch nur*.

(28)   Da   bringen mich keine zehn Pferde rein.
      there bring   me   no   ten   horses inside
      I will not enter even if ten horses would pull me

Once again, it is easy to see why the implicatures that would arise in *few*-type contexts are funny, to say the least.

(29)   *In diese Kneipe brachten mich selten (auch-nur) zehn Pferde rein.
      in   this   pub   brought me   rarely (even)   ten   horses in
      *Rarely could even ten horses pull me into this pub

Like in our previous examples, it is possible to derive an implicature that there were actually some occasions where the speaker was dragged into the pub by ten horses. Apart from the difficulty of making the connection between an *even* statement and a maximal power (one needs to assess an was sufficiently strong to ... interpretation), I am sure that it is the grotesqueness of this implicature that rules out (29). The example in (30) shows that the management of the scales alone would not be a problem. I made it one horse, which allows for a literal interpretation and plausibly contrasts to pushing, dragging with 5 men, wheelchair, and so on. The same example would work, more dramatically, with ten horses.

(30)   Jones (was so fat, he) could not be moved even with a HORSE.

Let us now turn to most-general-property NPIs like *any ... whatsoever* and its German counterpart *ein wie auch immer geartetes N* (an N of any kind whatever), *in IRGENDeiner Weise* (in any form whatever), *IRGENDeine Art von* and others. I will first restrict attention to *whatsoever* and then take a look at the German cases.

(31)   *Few students had read any paper whatsoever.

At this point, we can take advantage of the specific implementation of the domain widening mechanism on which *even* is supposed to operate. Several mechanisms and theories of domain widening have been proposed in the literature, some making domains wider and some making them smaller. Kadmon and Landmann (1993) were the first to propose domain widening, literally meaning "widening" in the sense of "normally, the extension of N is restricted in some sense but here, we are supposed to refer to the extension of N in the widest possible sense". Their main example, plausibly, contrasts *potatoes* (...edible, unspoiled, of a certain size) to *any potatoes* (... including the inedible, mouldy, small ones). Krifka (1995) points out that some nouns do not support the distinction between "normal" and "any" so readily. The noun *prime number*, for instance, has a clearly defined content which is not further subdividable into "marginally prime" and "prototypical prime". Therefore, he suggested to contrast N with more narrow properties N', N'' and use these in drawing comparisons about the logical strength of alternatives. Chierchia (2004, 2006) returns to domain widening, pointing out that all logical conditions that can be formulated for the upward theory (domain widening) can also be formulated for the downward theory (narrower domains). In the present proposal, I have adopted the downward version. We are now at a point to take advantage of this decision. I assume that *N-whatsoever* indeed denotes a widened domain around *N*, as suggested by its etymology. Intuitively, no real object ever can be an *N-whatsoever* object. For example, whenever we think about papers, we can not conceive of a *paper whatsoever*; any actual paper will be a paper of a specific kind. It is crucial that *whatsoever* does not introduce domain widening on the basis of a grey area around the extension of paper-proper (e.g. squibs, handwritten notes, half-finished drafts are not what distinguishes *papers-whatsoever* from *papers*). I assume that it refers to something like an abstract paper *per se* which has all and only those properties that all real papers share. In our given case, the paper-*per-se* has an author, a title (even if the title says "sans title"), some content, etc. but no specific person is actually the author of the paper-*per-se*, no specific content is actually its content, no title is its title, and so on. You could think of paper-*per-se* as a kind of paper frame; but abstract objects of this kind also have a long and reputable tradition in philosophy.

(32)   [[N-whatsoever]] := { m ; m is a fictitious abstract object which has all
and only the properties that all objects in [[N]] share }
Alt(any N-whatsoever) = { some N-whatsoever, some N, some N' ... }
N, N', ... are linearly ordered by set inclusion

With these assumptions, the properties of whatsoever follow again from the minimality implicature. Sentence (31) implicates that for some students, none of the more relevant alternatives *few students read some paper, few students read a hard paper, few students read a paper on formal syntax* etc. can truthfully be asserted. Therefore, we can conclude that one or two students read a *whatsoever-paper* which was not a paper, a hard paper or a paper on formal syntax. The hearer will then conclude that these students read one of the abstract papers *per se* in the set difference between N and N-whatsoever. As for all other nonlicensed strong NPIs in weak contexts, it is this minimal achievement implicature that makes the sentence marked.

I want to close this section with a side remark on strong NPIs in German. Some native speakers (linguists and other) insist that they do not have a problem with sentences like in (33).

(33)   Wenige Hooligans haben auch-nur eine IRGENDWIE geartete
Few   Hooligans have   even   a   anyhow   shaped
Entschuldigung geäußert.
excuse   uttered

few hooligans offered any excuse whatsoever

These speakers conceive *irgendwie geartet* as a domain widening operator in the Kadmon and Landmann sense. In the present example, this amounts to the inclusion of a low "sorry", uttered while the Hooligan was staring into the opposite corner of the room, into the range of possible excuses whereas in its usual sense, an "excuse" needs to be more explicit than that. In contrast, German speakers who consider (33) as bad as the corresponding *any* examples interpret *irgendwie geartet* as extending the denoted domain by objects-per-se and and thus triggering the same contradictory implicatures as *any* does in this context.

8   Other Scalar Particles

Let me end by taking a brief look at the minimizer *at least* in (34), and propose a first analysis of this item. As a starting point, consider the sentences in (34) and (35) which are nearly synonymous. Both sentences contain a scalar particle, and both sentences convey that the achievement 'carry a pen' is low on a scale of alternatives. However, while *even* is a polarity sensitive item, *at least* is neutral and allows for uses in positive contexts. This might lead to the misconception that they are synonyms which only differ in sensitivity. If 'synonym' were more-over understood as 'having the same semantic entry in the lexicon' then one could derive an argument in favour of a syntactic feature NPI. This is what I want to argue against.

(34)   Few students at least carry a pen.

(35)   Few students even carry a pen.

According to my analysis in Section 3, *even* takes high scope over the subject in the most salient reading of the example in (35). It associates with an element that gives rise to alternatives, and it triggers the presupposition that the proposition expressed is the least expected on the scale of possible alternative propositions. The expression *at least* is the dual of *even*. I propose the following semantic analysis.

(36)   *at least p*
        associates with alternative propositions Alt(p) = { p, p', p'', } derived by focus in the scope of *at least*
        presupposition: the proposition expressed is the most likely on the scale of alternatives
        assertion: p

Clearly, *even* and *at least* can not both have the same scope in this example. Remember the alternatives that were available for high scope *even*.

(37)   a. Few students carried a pen
        b. Few students read the paper.

(a.) is logically stronger than (b.) in its literal meaning. This offered the basis to apply *even*: logical strength correlates with low probability. But if (a.) is stronger than (b.) then *at least* can not operate on these two propositions because it would require the opposite probability ranking. However, *at least* could scope below the subject and combine with a VP with free variable x:

(38)   *at least* $+ \exists y(CARRY(x,y) \wedge PEN(y))$

The range of alternatives raised by *carry a pen* still comprises *carry a pen, read the paper, understand the paper*. But now the logical and probabilistic directions are reversed, no matter which individual instantiates x. The following propositions are ordered in decreasing likelihood for an arbitrary x.

(39) $\lambda w \exists y (CARRY(x,y) \wedge PEN(y))$
$\lambda w \exists y (READ(x,y) \wedge PAPER(y))$
$\lambda w \exists y (UNDERSTAND(x,y) \wedge PAPER(y))$

Thus, the presuppositions of *at least* are satisfied for arbitrary values for x. We can now combine this part of the clause with the subject and get that few students were such that they at least carried a pen. Again, we will understand that at least some of them did not do anything beyond that (minimality) due to the salience of more relevant alternative assertions. The same kind of semantic derivation will also work in positive episodic sentences like 'Tom at least carried a pen'. Hence, the analysis correctly predicts that *at least* is not polarity sensitive. The near-synonymy of the two example sentences comes about by semantic composition. It is not due to a synonymy of the two particles involved. The scale-based hidden *even* licensing of polarity sensitive items does not predict indirectly that all scalar particles create polarity sensitivity.

9 Summary

In the present paper, I proposed an analysis of the weak-strong distinction in terms of a scalar (covert *even*) analysis of NPIs. The distinction has so far been neglected in this type of theory, and those accounts that address the difference at all are provably insufficient. An implicit or explicit assumption in the literature has been that 'hidden-*even*' is responsible for the restriction to strong licensing contexts. I have shown that this is not so.

I proposed a theory of the weak-strong distinction that relies on two ingredients. Firstly, I argued that the crucial examples give rise to the minimal achievement implicature in addition to the widely acknowledged existential implicature. Secondly, I proposed that this implicature gives rise to a contradiction in the case of strong NPIs. I suggested that these NPIs have to obey an antiveridicality condition and have shown how this antiveridicality condition can be derived for a typical range of examples of strong NPIs.

References

1. Chierchia, G.: Scalar Implicatures, Polarity Phenomena, and the Syntax / Pragmatics Interface. In: Belletti, A. (ed.) Structure and Beyond: The Cartography of Syntactic Structures, vol. 3, pp. 39–103. Oxford University Press, Oxford (2004)
2. Chierchia, G.: Broaden your Views. Linguistic Inquiry 13, 535–590 (2006)
3. Eckardt, R.: Too poor to mention. In: Maienborn, C., Wöllstein-Leisten, A. (eds.) Events in Grammar. Tübingen, Niemeyer (2005)

4. Eckardt, R.: The lower part of event ontology. In: Löwe, B. (ed.) Algebra, Logic, Set Theory. A Festschrift for Ulrich Felgner. Studies in Logic Series, pp. 85–102. Kings College, London (2007)

5. Fauconnier, G.: Pragmatic Scales and Logical Structure. Linguistic Inquiry 6, 353–375 (1975)

6. Giannakidou, A.: The Meaning of Free Choice. Linguistics and Philosophy 24, 659–735 (2001)

7. Guerzoni, E.: Even-NPIs in yes-no questions. Natural Language Semantics 12, 319–343 (2004)

8. Guerzoni, E.: Intervention effects on NPIs and feature movement. Natural Language Semantics 14, 359–398 (2006)

9. Heim, I.: A Note on Negative Polarity and Downward Entailingness. Proceedings of NELS 14, 98–107 (1984)

10. Israel, M.: Polarity Sensitivity as lexical semantics. Linguistics and Philosophy 19, 619–666 (1996)

11. Israel, M.: The Rhetoric of Grammar. PhD. Diss, University of California at San Diego. Cambridge University Press, Cambridge (2005) (1998[2005])

12. Israel, M.: The pragmatics of Polarity. In: Horn, L., Ward, G. (eds.) The Handbook of Pragmatics, pp. 701–723. Blackwell, Malden (2004)

13. Kadmon, N., Landman, F.: Any. Linguistics and Philosophy 15, 353–422 (1993)

14. Krifka, M.: The semantics and pragmatics of polarity items. Linguistic Analysis 25, 209–257 (1995)

15. Ladusaw, W. (1979): Polarity Sensitivity as Inherent Scope Relations. Ph.D. dissertation. The University of Texas at Austin. Garland, New York (in print, 1980)

16. Ladusaw, W.: Negation and Polarity Items. In: Lappin, S. (ed.) The Handbook of Contemporary Semantic Theory, pp. 321–341. Blackwell, Oxford (1996)

17. Lahiri, U.: Focus and Negative Polarity in Hindi. Natural Language Semantics 6(1), 57–123 (1998)

18. van der Wouden, T.: Negative Contexts - Collocation, Polarity and Multiple Negation. Routledge, London (2007)

19. Wilkinson, K.: The scope of even. In: Natural Language Semantics, pp. 193–215 (1996)

20. Zwarts, F.: Three types of Polarity. In: Hamm, F., Hinrichs, E. (eds.) Plurality and Quantification, pp. 177–228. Kluwer, Dordrecht (1998)

On -c and ḳi Particles in Georgian

Anna Chutkerashvili

Shavgulidze st. 7a, flat 61, Tbilisi, Georgia, 0183
annamushu@hotmail.com

Abstract. This paper considers the Georgian particles *ḳi* and *-c*. These particles
are frequently used, separately as well as together. They have different meanings, but both of them can have a focusing function: emphasizing a word or a
phrase they are attached to. In spite of having similar or even the same semantic
features, the particles *ḳi* and *-c* cannot substitute for each other. One reason for
this is that *-c* is a bound form and *ḳi* is not. They never substitute for each other
but they very often occur together and they are much more emphatic when they
are used together. The dominating element in building up the meaning of *-c ḳi* is
-c, which is stronger in emphasis. *-c ḳi* is used to emphasize something unexpected or surprising. These particles are rendered in English by 'even'.

Keywords: Pragmatics of particles, emphasis, focus-related phenomena.

1 The Particles –c and ḳi

This paper presents an analysis of the particles *ḳi* and *-c*. These particles are widely
used and very often occur together (*-c ḳi*). Also, they are constituents of some other
particles (*ḳidec*). It is interesting to see what semantic features they have in common
and in what features they differ. Both particles are often used to emphasize a phrase or
a word they are attached to. We will try to characterize the positioning and semantics
of *-c* and *ḳi* and their variations separately and together.

The meaning and function of these particles are firstly studied in their co-
occurrence with nouns, and then with verbs.

1.1 Basic Meanings of –c and ḳi

1.1.1 ḳi

(i). The main meaning of *ḳi* in Georgian is to show confirmation, *ḳi* in Georgian
means 'yes'. *ḳi* shows that the speaker agrees to what is just mentioned, confirms
what has been said before. E.g.,

vašli	ginda?	ḳi	minda
an apple	want[you]	yes	want[I]

Do you want an apple? Yes, I do

A subgroup of the confirmation uses of *ḳi* can be distinguished where it is emphatic
while the main meaning is neutral. In this case its function is focusing, e.g.,

P. Bosch, D. Gabelaia, and J. Lang (Eds.): TbiLLC 2007, LNAI 5422, pp. 62–68, 2009.
© Springer-Verlag Berlin Heidelberg 2009

me	ķi	minda	magram…
I	yes	want[I]	but…

I do want, but…

(ii) A very important meaning of *ķi* is to show a contrast between the parts of a statement. *ķi* introduces a contrasting meaning that is not related to the whole phrase. *ķi* has a phrase-final position, it marks the last item of a set of homogenous members in coordination. E.g.,

me	šensķen	šen	ķi	ešmaķebisķen
I	on your side	you	as for	on the devil's side

I am on your side, as for you, you are on the devil's side.

1.1.2 –c

We distinguish four meanings of the particle -c.. Different from *ķi* the particle -c doesn't occur separately. It's a bound form and is always used with another form.

(i). -c turns question words into relative words, e.g.,

vin ‖ vinc	ra ‖ rac
who ‖ who/that	what ‖ which/that

(ii) The additive meaning of -c is close to the meaning of 'also' or 'too' in English. E.g.,

mec	minda	misi	naxva
I too	want[I]	him	to see

I want to see him too
I too want to see him

(iii) The emphatic (focusing) meaning of -c underlines the word it applies to. In the case of coordinated homogenous members in the sentence -c makes the statement emphatic and is added to each homogenous member separately (except for the verb, in which case the particle '*ķidec*' is used). E.g.,

zoop'arķši	mgelic	vnaxe	da	iremic
in the zoo	a wolf too	saw[I]	and	a deer too

I saw a wolf and a deer too at the zoo

ķidec	ceķvavs	ķidec	mɣeris
also	dances[he]	also	sings[he]

He does dance and does sing too.

(iv) Expresses an unwilling agreement to someone's demands under some circumstances. The referent of the noun that -c attaches to is persuaded to give in as a result of some strong influence, as, e.g., in

qurebi	gamoučeda	rčevebvit	da	isic	datanxmda
ears	[she]filled[him]up	with advices	and	he too	agreed

She was so persistent in her advices that he had to agree.

So far, we have given some examples to see the meanings of these particles in affirmative, interrogative, and negative sentences.

1.2 Different Positions of –c and ķi

1.2.1 -c

Also the position of the particle is important because sometimes the meaning of a sentence or a phrase depends on it.

Consider

agrilda	da	çvimac	çamovida
it got cooler	and	rain too	started[it]

It got cooler and the rain started too.

In this sentence -c is attached to a noun and has the additive meaning. The second part of the sentence 'çvimac çamovida' means that something has happened earlier, probably something causing the rain. The particle -c points to the conjunction 'and' that proposes a naturally expected event; so -c implies the existence of one, or more than one element of the sentence before the conjunction 'and', which could be explicit or not. This meaning of -c isn't emphatic. E.g.,

zghvazec	çavalt?
to the sea too	go[we]?

Shall we go to the sea too?

In this sentence -c expresses that we have already been or we shall go to other places that to the sea. -c has here an additive meaning.

In affirmative and interrogative sentences –c is rendered in English by 'too'. Unlike the particle -c, which is a bound form and is always attached to a word, 'too' in English mostly occurs in the sentence final position. Cf.

georgic	ar	mosula	(a)	
George too	not	came[he]		(I)
arc	giorgi	mosula	(b)	
not too	George	came[he]		

Neither George has come.

Negative sentences are very interesting. There are two cases: Either -c is added to a semantically related word, or it is added to the negative particle 'ar' . As we have already mentioned -c occurs only with nouns and not with verbs. But in negative statements when -c is added to the negative particle 'ar' it is placed immediately before the verb, and the verb is negated. In that case the order of words, the position of 'arc' is semantically significant. Cf.

georgi	arc	mosula…	
George	even not	came[he]…	(II)

George hasn't even come…

English does not use the particle 'too' in this case, but uses 'neither…nor' instead.

1.2.2 ķi

Consider

bavšvi	ķi	midioda		da	mgheroda
a child	as for	was walking[he]		and	singing[he]

As for child, he was walking and singing

The particle *ķi* (cf.. above: -c) contrasts the parts of the sentence. In this example *ķi* shows that something was happening after which the child's walking and singing was unexpected and unnatural. At the same time *ķi* can emphasize that despite of hardship or inadequacy of the situation the child was still walking and singing, as in

mas	ķi	unda?
He	as for	wants[he][it]?

As for him, does he want it?

This sentence is actually ambiguous: He does not want something that someone else does want. Here the particle *ķi* has a contrastive meaning. In the second version someone doesn't want it, and probably 'he' doesn't want it either. Using *ķi* in an interrogative sentence, the speaker shows his own emotional attitude - anger, irony, doubt, etc. E.g.,

bavšvi	ķi	ara	mxecia
a child	yes	not	a beast is [he]

Not a child but a beast is he!

Here *ķi* that precedes the negation 'ara' is emphatic. As the sentence is negative the confirmative meaning of *ķi* is cancelled by the negative particle 'ar'. Here *ķi* stresses that the child is really a beast. At the same time the contrast between the two objects or qualities of the opposite meanings (here a child vs. a beast) is emphasized. *ķi ara* also stresses the quantitative difference between the objects or qualities of the same character, as in

bavšvi	ķi	ara,	angelozia
child	yes	not	an angel is [he]

He is not a child he is an angel

2 ķi and ķidec in the Pre-verb Position

We now turn to the semantic functioning of *ķi* and the variant of *-c* (*ķidec*) in the pre-verb position.

2.1. ķidec

Consider

ķidec	ceķvavs	ķidec	mgheris
also	dances[he]	also	sings[he]

He does dance and does sing too.

ķidec is emphatic and has additive meaning. The speaker stresses that somebody is able to dance as well as sing. *ķidec* here is equal in its meaning to -*c*.

icinis	ķidec?
laughs [he]	also?

And he dares to laugh?

This sentence is emphatic. The speaker is indignant, because someone who has probably done something wrong (in the opinion of the speaker), behaves improperly. The interrogative form of the sentence strengthens the emphasis:

ķidec	ar	migabrdzanos	akedan!
also	not	[he]throw [you]away	from here

He can even easily throw you away.

This sentence is emphatic too. The particles *ķidec* and *ar* together are stronger than either of them separately. And also the verb *migabrdzanos* is emphatic in itself because it's an honorific form used ironically in this context. The speaker warns or threatens the listener, and tells the listener that he – the listener – isn't able to evaluate the situation properly.

2.2 ķi

Consider

ķi	mgheris	magram	ver	ceķvavs
yes	sings[she]	but	can not	dances[she]

Yes, she can sing for sure, but she can't dance.

In this sentence *ķi* has confirmative meaning, it isn't emphatic. *ķi* confirms that someone is really able to sing. In the following sentence,

šesdzlebs	ķi?
could [he]do[it]	for sure?

Could he do it for sure?

ķi is emphatic and focusing. The speaker expresses his doubt about someone's abilities. In this case *ķi* is rendered in English by 'for sure'.

In the following

ķi	ar	mgheris	čxavis
yes	not	sings[she]	croaks[she]

As for her she doesn't sing she does croak.

ķi has confirmative meaning. The sentence is emphatic, which is results not only from the particle *ķi*, but also from the negation (*ķi ar*) and the semantic character of the verb 'čxavis', which is used when we want to say that someone has highly unpleasant voice. In English the emphasis is brought about by the auxiliary.

In the following sentence,

mgheris	ḳi	ara	is
sings [she]	yes	no	that/what

What she does isn't singing!

ḳi is confirmative and emphatic too. *ḳi* underlines 'ara' (negation). The speaker mentions ironically that he/she isn't able to sing or he doesn't believe that he/she is singing at the moment of communication.

3 -c ḳi

Consider

moulodnelad	gaçvimda	seṭqva-c ḳi	çamovida
suddenly	it rained	hail even	fell

Suddenly it started raining, even hail fell.

Here, *-c ḳi* expresses extremity; it means that some event or object is much stronger or rarer than was expected. The rain wasn't expected, but the hail was already too much. In this example *-c ḳi* is emphatic and also has additive meaning. In this construction (*-c ḳi*) *-c* is semantically dominant.

In

cxovelebisa-c ḳi	esmis?
Animals even	understands [he]

-c ḳi has additive meaning. The speaker is astonished that the person he is speaking about has many strange abilities; he is even able to understand animals.

In

saxli	ar	mosçons	samsaxurita-c ḳi	ar	aris	ḳmaqopili
a house	not	likes[she]	a job even	not	is	satisfied

She doesn't like her house; even with her job she isn't satisfied.

-c ḳi has additive meaning and makes the sentence emphatic. The speaker couldn't imagine why the person referred to shouldn't like her job which in speaker's opinion is not bad. The speaker thinks that she is very capricious.

The following sentence is ambiguous:

es	bavšvma-c ḳi	icis
that	a child even	knows[he]

Even a child knows that.

In the first meaning the particle is emphatic and has contrastive meaning, *ḳi* is dominant. The speaker stresses that the thing he doesn't know is in fact something very simple. The speaker is surprised or ironic. In the second meaning someone knows the mentioned fact too, but the speaker wants to say that it is not a reason for boasting.

4 Summary

To summarize, we can say that the particles *-c* and *ḳidec* are in contrastive distribution; *-c* occurs only with nouns except in the case when it is added to the negation *ar-c.* In that case it can also be used with verbs.. In affirmative and interrogative sentences with verbs the particle *ķidec* is used instead. *ķidec* is also used in negative statements with verbs. The particles *–c* and *ķidec* have basically a focusing function, whereas *ķi* can have both a focusing and topicalizing function. These different discourse functions are reflected in their positioning.

The particle *ķi* is freer in distribution. *ķi* can be placed in a sentence-initial position as well as in front of the verb, as a contrast that focuses one element of the contrast set. *ķi* occurs with nouns and also with verbs. It is not used as a variation of *–c*, though both of them have a focusing function for a phrase or a sentence. They never substitute for each other.

The combination of the discourse clitics *–c* and *ķi* (*-c ķi*) has the features of both *– c* plus *ķi*. Their simultaneous occurrence is much stronger and clearer in focusing than one or the other separately. The positioning of *–c ķi* is the same positioning as that of *–c*. In spite of having the meanings of *ķi*, *-c ķi* never occurs with verbs. *–c* and *ķi* convey modal meanings too; such as surprise, indignance, anger, or doubt as seen above.

References

1. Erteschik-shir, N.: Information structure. The Syntax-Discourse Interface. Oxford University Press, Oxford (2007)
2. Shanidze, A.: The works in XII volumes. The Basis of Georgian Grammar, Tbilisi, vol. III (1980) (in Georgian)

Dealing with Polysemy in Russian National Corpus: The Case of Adjectives

Ekaterina V. Rakhilina[1], Tatiana I. Reznikova[2], and Olga Yu. Shemanaeva[3]

[1] Institute of Russian Language, RAS, Moscow
[2] Dept. of Linguistic Studies, VINITI, RAS, Moscow
[3] Institute of Linguistics, Russian State University for Humanities, Moscow
rakhilina@gmail.com, tanja_reznikova@mail.ru,
shemanaeva@yandex.ru

Abstract. The paper describes a research carried out in the Russian National Corpus project (www.ruscorpora.ru). We discuss a method of word sense disambiguation, which is now being applied to polysemous adjectives in the RNC. The approach implies formulating rules to select the appropriate sense of the adjective by using co-occurrence restrictions observed in the corpus. The disambiguating filters operate with various kinds of grammatical and semantic information on the adjectives and the nouns modified. Our results demonstrate that the semantic filters are effective for WSD.

Keywords: Corpus linguistics, word sense disambiguation, semantic annotation, Construction Grammar, Russian.

1 Introduction

In our work we discuss a method for word sense disambiguation, which is now being applied to the annotation system of the Russian National Corpus. Unlike most of the existing strategies that rely on statistical and machine learning methods (cf. the overview in [1]), our technique combines statistics with a rule-based approach. Disambiguation rules are formulated based on the statistical analysis of co-occurrence restrictions that can be observed in the corpus data. We claim that this approach reveals important generalizations, which are of high relevance for theoretical linguistics.

This paper presents the domain of adjectives denoting physical characteristics (such as temperature, colour, size, form, time, speed, etc.) or human properties (cf. 'courageous', 'intelligent', 'honest', etc.). Dealing with these data we will discuss the application of our method and its perspectives.

The study is based on the theoretical framework of Construction Grammar (cf. [2], [3], [4]). The Construction Grammar theory assumes that constructions – i.e. conventionalized pairings of form and meaning – are the basic units of language. All the constituents in a construction are bound into the whole entity; they are co-dependent and influence one another, which means that the change of any constituent leads to the change in the meaning of the whole pattern. In regard of this, polysemy can be viewed not as an independent property of a lexeme, but instead as its ability to

P. Bosch, D. Gabelaia, and J. Lang (Eds.): TbiLLC 2007, LNAI 5422, pp. 69–79, 2009.

be *coerced* by particular constructions into having other meanings, cf. the notion of "coercion" in the works of R. Jackendoff [5], J. Pustejovsky [6], B. Partee [7].

Within Construction Grammar, the practical task of word sense disambiguation takes the following form: given a polysemous word, we have to formulate constitutive properties for each construction that can have this word as its part. Since different constructions are associated with different meanings, these properties can be used for context identification and accordingly for sense determination[1].

The structure of the paper is as follows: Section 2 outlines the principles of semantic annotation in RNC. Section 3 illustrates the functioning of the rule-based system. Finally, the theoretical relevance of the approach is discussed in Section 4.

2   Semantic Annotation in RNC

The present research is carried out within the larger Russian National Corpus (RNC) project (www.ruscorpora.ru). The RNC currently contains over 140 mln. words and provides different kinds of annotation, particularly POS-tagging (with information on parts of speech and morphological features)[2]. What is unique for a large corpus of this kind is its semantic annotation (cf. [10]).

Semantic tags in the RNC correspond to conceptual categories assigned on the basis of vocabulary classification. The principles of lexical classification are derived from the project "Lexicograph" (http://www.lexicograph.ru) supervised by E. Paducheva and E. Rakhilina. The project aims at establishing a comprehensive database on the lexical semantics of Russian (up to the present moment, the study has mainly been focused on verbs and object nouns, for the theoretical ideas behind the project, see [11], [12], [13]). For the needs of the Russian National Corpus, the classification was revised and extended to cover all content words.

The classification follows the multi-faceted principle: there are several parameters (some of them hierarchical) independent of one another. At present, six classifications are involved in the annotation:

Category (e.g. "concrete nouns": *stol* 'table', *sneg* 'snow'; "abstract nouns": *ljubov'* 'love', *žara* 'heat'; "proper nouns": *Moskva* 'Moscow', *Ivan*; "qualitative adjectives": *tverdyj* 'hard'; "relational adjectives": *kamennyj* 'stony, made of stone'; "possessive adjectives": *papin* 'father's'; "invariable adjectives": *bež* 'beige');

Taxonomy (e.g. "weapon": *puška* 'cannon', *ruž'e* 'gun'; "device": *gradusnik* 'thermometer', *telefon* 'phone'; "space&place": *gorod* 'town', *pole* 'field'; "perception": *sluh* 'hearing', *vzgljad* 'look'; "emotion": *pečal'* 'sorrow', *udovol'stvie* 'delight'; "physical properties:form": *krivoj* 'curved', *kruglyj* 'round'; "size:large": *vysokij* 'high, tall', *dlinnyj* 'long'; "behaviour": *krivljatsja*: 'to make faces', *skandalit'* 'to brawl');

Mereology (e.g. "building parts": *dver'* 'door', *arka* 'arch'; "sets and aggregates": *mebel'* 'furniture', *trava* 'grass'; "quanta and portions of stuff": *kusoček* 'lump', *volna* 'wave');

---

[1] For the interaction of corpus linguistics and Construction Grammar cf. [8].

[2] The RNC includes also a corpus of syntactically annotated texts; see [9].

Topology (e.g. "container": *stakan* 'glass', *dom* 'house'; "holes": *okno* 'window', pora 'pore'; "ropes": *tsep'* 'chain', *nitka* 'thread');

Evaluation (e.g. "positive": *aromat* 'odor', *četkij* 'precise'; "negative": *man'jak* 'maniac', *preslovutyi* 'notorious');

Derivational classes (e.g. "diminutives": *knižečka* 'little book', "adjectives derived from nouns": *sosnovyj* 'piny').

The term Category refers to prime lexical divisions that determine main semantic and morphological features. Nouns are divided into abstract, concrete, and proper, while adjectives have four classes of qualitative, relational, possessive, and invariable. Relational adjectives differ from qualitative adjectives in that they are not gradable and cannot form comparatives.

The system of taxonomic classes is rather elaborated. It includes size, distance, quantity, time, physical and human properties for adjectives; people, animals, plants, buildings, devices, stuff, texts, food and drinks for concrete nouns; first and last names, patronymic names and toponyms for proper nouns; classes of abstract nouns are inherited mainly from verb and adjective hierarchies and include movement, impact, speech, human properties, colour, temperature, diseases, sports, parameters, etc.

Mereological annotation is applied to concrete nouns only. It provides a distinction between parts of the body, parts of instruments, clothes and other things as well as quanta & portions of stuff and phases of processes. The feature of sets and aggregates are used for such words as 'set', 'bunch', 'furniture', 'mankind'. Nouns like 'animal', 'fruit', 'instrument', 'name' that denote categories of the world belong to the "names of classes" group.

The notion of topological types was put forward by L. Talmy [14], who has demonstrated their significance for the understanding of linguistic structures that describe space and shape as well as undoubted cross-linguistic relevance of geometric features. Names of physical objects associated with such topological types as "horizontal spaces", "containers", "holes", "juts", "ropes", etc. appear to be sensitive to space operators, such as adjectives of form and size, prepositions, verbs and nouns which refer to form, location, and motion.

Lexical meanings that have positive or negative connotations form two classes in the category of Evaluation. Finally, derivational classes include words in which semantic components are introduced by a certain prefix or suffix or words derived from other parts of speech and what is more, from a particular semantic class of a particular POS (e.g. nouns derived from verbs; adjectives derived from names of substance).

Each content word in the vocabulary is classified along with all applicable parameters, the results are stored in the semantic dictionary of the corpus. For instance, the words *nora* 'burrow' and *naselenie* 'population' have the following attributes:

nora 'burrow'
    category: "concrete", taxonomy: "space", toponymy: container
naselenie 'population'
    category: "concrete", mereology: "aggregate of persons", derivational class: "derived
        from verbs".

In case of a polysemous word, attributes are defined separately for each sense, cf. for the word *tihij*:

*tihij*₁ 'low (about sounds)'
    category: "qualitative", taxonomy: "sound";
*tihij*₂ 'quiet'
    category: "qualitative", taxonomy: "human property";
*tihij*₃ 'faint'
    category: "qualitative", taxonomy: "degree:minimal";
*tihij*₄ 'slow'
    category: "qualitative", taxonomy: "speed:minimal".

The semantic dictionary is then applied to the corpus. During the annotation process each content word in the RNC is automatically assigned all the tags that it has in the semantic dictionary. This in particular means that polysemous words are not disambiguated, that is, for instance, each occurrence of the word *tihij* receives four tags from the taxonomic classification: "sound" / "human property" / "degree" / "speed".

On the part of the user, this means that the search for semantic characteristics of words returns many irrelevant results, e.g. the query for adjectives of "form" yields, among others, word combinations like ***tupoj*** *čelovek* '<u>stupid</u> person' and ***tupaja bol'*** '<u>dull</u> pain', as one of the meanings of the adjective *tupoj* refers to form, cf. ***tupoj*** *ugol* '<u>obtuse</u> angle', or *botinki s* ***tupym*** *noskom* '<u>square-tipped</u> shoes'.

Thus, our goal is to distinguish the different meanings of adjectives and to provide the users of the Russian National Corpus with the semantically disambiguated texts. As a result, they could easily use them without any inconveniences such as finding inappropriate homonyms alongside with the needed word.

In order to achieve this goal, i.e. to avoid the polysemy of adjectives in RNC, we formulate rules (filters), which assign the only meaning to the adjective in the corresponding construction. Once the filter has been applied, all meanings of the target adjective that are inappropriate for the construction are deleted. The disambiguated adjectives are marked with the following features: 1) SEM (for a tag set that characterizes the first meaning listed in the dictionary), 2) SEM2 (for tag sets associated with other meanings) and 3) SEMF (for tag set(s) of disambiguated meanings). Thus, the subsequent queries in the corpus may focus only on the first meanings of the words, or on the disambiguated meanings.

3   The Rule-Based Approach to Disambiguation

The disambiguating rules are formulated manually on the database of 2- and 3-word clusters with associated frequency, POS, and semantic tags. The filters operate with the following information about the target adjective and the neighbour noun:

Morphosyntactic information

- grammatical features of the adjective ("long" vs. "short" form[3]; case, number; comparative, superlative)
- grammatical features of the neighbour noun (animate vs. non-animate[4], case, number)

---

[3] Russian adjectives may appear in two forms: the long form, which has case, number, gender features, and the short form, which has number and gender features only. The latter can be used only predicatively.

[4] This in principle semantic category has morphologic realizations in Russian, unlike in English, and that is why it is treated under grammatical properties.

- syntactic pattern of the adjective-noun construction
- stable prepositional collocations

Semantic information

- category of the neighbour noun (concrete vs. abstract)
- taxonomic class of the neighbour noun (e.g. "motion", "time", "sound", "colour", "place", "emotions", "natural phenomena", "hair", "animals", "plants", "texts", "food and drinks", "relatives", "professions", "stuff")
- mereological information (e.g. "parts of the body", "quanta & portions of stuff")
- topological information (e.g. "containers", "horizontal spaces")

Below we will illustrate how each type of information mentioned above is relevant for the filters (for each adjective below, not *all* the rules are given but those that illustrate the importance of the types of information discussed; in other words, we provide a fragment of the filter set for each word).

3.1 Grammatical Form of the Adjective: "Long" vs. "Short"

According to standard Russian dictionaries [15] and [16], the adjective *celyj* has two meanings: (a) 'whole, entire' and (b) 'safe, intact'. The corpus data reveal that in the so-called "short" form the adjective is not ambiguous and has the only meaning (b) 'safe, intact'. Thus, we can formulate the following filter:

celyj & short form ⇨ *celyj* 'safe, intact' (cf. *cel, cela, celo, cely*)

The resulting disambiguated tag is shown in the table below:

target word	conditions	WSD
celyj	short form	SEM=category: "qualitative", taxomomy: "physical property"

3.2 Grammatical Form of the Noun

The lexico-grammatical category of a n i m a c y crucially affects the meaning of attributive adjective construction. Consider the example of the adjective *tolstyj*, which has the meaning 'fat' when co-occurring with an animate noun (cf. *tolstyj čelovek* 'fat man'), and the meaning 'thick' in connection with a non-animate noun (cf. *tolstaja kniga* 'thick book'):

target word	conditions	WSD
tolstyj	+ "animate"	SEM2=category: "qualitative", taxomomy: "appearance", evaluation: "negative"
tolstyj	+ "non-animate"	SEM=category: "qualitative", taxomomy: "size:maximal"

The adjective *pokojnyj* 'deceased/comfortable' provides a further example for the relevance of animacy for sense disambiguation (cf. *pokojnyj otec* 'deceased father' vs. *pokojnyj divan* 'comfortable sofa'):

target word	conditions	WSD
pokojnyj	+ "animate"	SEM2=category: "relational"
pokojnyj	+ "non-animate"	SEM=category: "qualitative"

Another grammatical parameter used in the context filters is the c a s e of the neighbour noun. This kind of rules relies on the fact that some Russian adjectives govern certain cases (cf. also 3.3 below). Interestingly, there is a strong tendency in our data that polysemous adjectives show this property only in one of their meanings, thus, the corresponding uses can be filtered out. The adjective *polnyj* can exemplify this type of rule. There are four different senses associated with this word, cf. *vanna polnaja šampanskogo* '<u>full</u> tub <u>of</u> Champaign', *polnyj čelovek* 'fat person', *opisat' polnyj krug* 'make a <u>complete</u> cycle', *polnyj durak* '<u>absolute</u> idiot'. However, if *polnyj* governs genitive it can convey only the 'full of' meaning. The filter is applied to all genitive noun constructions apart from those which include the genitive form of the target adjective, since two genitive forms may stand in a syntactic relation of agreement, not of government, and then the target adjective may express any of four relevant senses.

target word	conditions	WSD
polnyj	!GEN + S&GEN	SEM=category: "qualitative", taxonomy: "content"

3.3 Syntactic Pattern

Almost all filters take into account the syntactic relation between the target adjective and the neighbour noun. Basic syntactic patterns used for filters are summarized below (A stands for adjective, S for noun, PR for preposition):

(1) A + S (agreement), cf. *slabyj veter* ('<u>weak</u>' + 'wind': 'light wind');
(2) A + S (government without preposition), cf. *slabyj glazami* ('<u>weak</u>' + 'eye'-INSTR: 'weak-eyed');
(3) A + PR + S (government with preposition), cf. *slabyj na golovu* ('<u>weak</u>' + 'on' + 'head'-ACC: 'thin in the upper crust');
(4) PR + A + S (prepositional phrase), cf. *v slaboj stepeni* ('in' + '<u>weak</u>'-PRAEP + 'degree'-PRAEP: 'to a small degree').

In most cases, the syntactic information is used alongside with the conditions on morphological and semantic properties of the context. However, sometimes the syntactic pattern alone is sufficient to disambiguate the target adjective. This is mainly the case with the patterns (2) and (3).

Filters that match the pattern (2) operate with the case of the governed noun; an example of such a rule was discussed above (see 3.2, the word *polnyj*). Pattern (3) is applied to those adjectives which in some contexts require the use of a certain preposition. For such adjectives, the preposition has disambiguating power – it signals that the target word can be interpreted unambiguously. The adjective *gluhoj* illustrates this kind of rules. Among its meanings are 'deaf' (cf. *gluhoj mal'čik* '<u>deaf</u> boy'), 'dull' (of sound, cf. *gluhoj zvuk* '<u>dull</u> sound'), 'lonely/remote' (cf. *gluhaja derevnja* '<u>lonely/remote</u> village'), 'impervious' (cf. *gluh k dovodam* '<u>impervious</u> to argument'. Data analysis reveals that only the latter sense can be conveyed by the construction with the preposition *k* 'to':

target word	conditions	WSD
gluhoj	+ *k*	SEM2= category: "qualitative", taxonomy: "human property", evaluation: "negative"

3.4 Stable Collocations

When used in stable collocations, words often exhibit specific semantic properties. Such expressions are treated as a special kind of disambiguating contexts. They are represented as syntactic patterns with fixed lexical items. For instance, consider the adjective *černyj* 'black' in the collocations like *černyj hod* '<u>back</u> entrance', *černaja magija* '<u>black</u> magic', *na černyj den'* 'for a <u>rainy</u> day', etc.:

target word	conditions	WSD
černyj	+ *hod*	"multiword expression", SEM2=category: "relational", taxonomy: "species"
černyj	+ *magija*	"multiword expression", SEM2=category: "relational", taxonomy: "species"
černyj	*na + .. + den'*	"multiword expression", SEM2=category: "qualitative", evaluation: "negative"

3.5 Category of the Neighbour Noun

This parameter specifies whether the adjacent noun is concrete or abstract. The relevance of this division for the disambiguation task can be evidenced, e.g., by the adjective *legkij*, which means 'light' (of weight) when occurring with a concrete noun, and 'easy' or 'faint' when referring to an abstract noun (further differentiation is possible based on the taxonomic class of the abstract noun).

target word	conditions	WSD
legkij	+ "concrete"	SEM= category: "qualitative", taxonomy: "physical property: weight"

3.6 Taxonomic Class of the Noun

Taxonomy is undoubtedly the most frequently used parameter to discriminate between the different senses of an adjective. The word *golyj* provides an example of taxonomic differentiation within the domain of concrete nouns, whereas *holodnyj* illustrates the same issue with abstract nouns.

The adjective *golyj* has among its meanings 'nude', cf. *golyj čelovek* '<u>nude</u> person', 'bare', cf. *na golom polu* 'on the <u>bare</u> floor', and 'pure', cf. *golyj spirt* '<u>pure</u> alcohol', each of them imposing restrictions on the taxonomic affiliation of the following noun:

target word	conditions	WSD
golyj	+ "human"	SEM=category: "qualitative", taxonomy: "physical state"
golyj	+ "space"	SEM2=category: "qualitative", taxonomy: "appearance"
golyj	+ "stuff"	SEM2=category: "qualitative", taxonomy: "physical property"

The word *holodnyj* occurs, among others, in the following senses: 'cold', cf. *holodnyj veter* '<u>cold</u> wind', 'cold (of colour)', cf. *holodnye cveta* '<u>cold</u> colours', and 'cold/stony', cf. *holodnyj vzgljad* '<u>cold</u> look'. Within the domain of abstract nouns we can draw the following contextual distinctions:

target word	conditions	WSD
holodnyj	+ "weather" + "time"	SEM=category: "qualitative", taxonomy: "physical property: temperature"
holodnyj	+ "colour"	SEM2=category: "qualitative", taxonomy: "physical property: colour"
holodnyj	+ "mental sphere" + "emotions" + "psychological states" + "human qualities" + "human behaviour"	SEM2=category: "qualitative", taxonomy: "human property"

3.7 Mereological Class of the Noun

The parameter of taxonomic class, however efficient, cannot account for all relevant semantic properties of the noun. Thus, the adjective *redkij* can show two different senses when used with nouns of the same taxonomic class, cf. *redkaja trava* '<u>sparse</u> grass' and *redkoe rastenie* '<u>rare</u> plant' (both nouns represent the class "plants"). In such cases, the mereological categorization may prove its usefulness for sense disambiguation. In the example above, for instance, the feature "aggregate", which is characteristic of the word *trava* 'grass', is crucial for distinguishing between the two senses of the adjective *redkij*.

target word	conditions	WSD
redkij	+ "plant" & "aggregate"	SEM=category: "relational", taxonomy: "physical property"

3.8 Topological Class of the Noun

Topology, i.e. geometric features of the object referred to by a noun, is a further parameter which may be of use when the taxonomic classification fails to differentiate between senses. The adjective *tugoj* illustrates the case in question. When used with a noun of object, it usually means 'tight', cf. *tugoj uzel* '<u>tight</u> knot'. An exception to this is objects associated to the topological type of "containers", cf. *tugoj košelek* '<u>fat</u> purse'.

target word	conditions	WSD
tugoj	+ "containers"	SEM2=category: "qualitative", taxonomy: "size:maximal"
tugoj	+ "concrete"	SEM=category: "qualitative", taxonomy: "physical property"

4 Conclusion: Theoretical Extensions of the Research

There is a total amount of about 300 frequently used polysemous adjectives denoting qualities in RNC (those that occur more than 2000 times per 140 mln words). Presently 240 of them are supplied with disambiguating filters. The results obtained show that the method discussed above is highly efficient in those contexts where an adjective is adjacent to the modified noun. However, non-adjacent uses of adjectives, in particular predicative adjectives, are more problematic for the current version of the rules. In other words, we achieve a high precision rate (93%), but a lower recall rate (47%). As a next step, we plan to develop rules which would account for non-adjacent positions of adjectives.

Due to the method applied, the practical task of WSD may have theoretical extensions, which concern the nature of polysemy and the principles of semantic evolution.

– The procedure of a rule-based approach helps to specify the linguistically relevant classes of nouns for word-sense disambiguation. The classes which have proven to be the most useful for meaning differentiation are 'animate' (including 'human') vs. 'non-animate', and 'abstract' vs. 'concrete'. The change between these classes always leads to a shift in meaning of a modifying adjective. However, the question is, what *other* classes may be of any relevance for changing the meaning of a word. The fact that a taxonomic class is used in filters proves that it is cognitively relevant.

– The analysis done for the filters makes it possible to identify the regular patterns of semantic shifts in adjective meaning (cf. adjectives with the basic meaning of physical property combined with a noun of the taxonomic class 'human' regularly obtain the sense of the non-physical property of a person: *mjagkij divan* '<u>soft</u> sofa'– *mjagkij čelovek* '<u>tender</u> person', *legkij čemodan* '<u>light</u> bag'– *legkij čelovek* '<u>easy</u> person <u>to get along with</u>').

– The important characteristic of a semantic shift is not only the initial and the final meanings of an adjective, but the nature of the shift itself. The two main types of shifts are metaphor and metonymy. We have seen some examples of metaphorical shifts above; regular metonymy can be instantiated by the application of a human property to body parts (cf. *dobryj čelovek* '<u>kind</u> person' – *dobrye glaza* '<u>kind</u> eyes'). Russian adjectives offer a fertile ground for research on the so far less studied domain of metonymy occurring through parts of speech (cf. [17]): many adjectives are metonymically associated with the adverbs derived from them (cf.

redkij 'thin-growing, sparse': ***redkaja** boroda* '<u>thin</u> beard' – *derev'ya **redko** rastut* 'the trees grow <u>sparsely</u>'). The cataloguing of the semantic shifts of adjectives can contribute to the general theory of metaphor and metonymy and can extend the list of known metaphoric and metonymic patterns (cf. [18]).

- The reasons for the dissimilar behavior of synonyms and antonyms should be thoroughly examined. Although synonymic and antonymic pairs sometimes reveal similar meaning shifts (cf. *sil'ny čelovek – sil'ny harakter – sil'ny učenik* '<u>strong</u> man' – '<u>strong</u> character' – '<u>strong</u> pupil', and *slaby čelovek – slaby harakter – slaby učenik* – '<u>weak</u> man' – '<u>weak</u> character' – '<u>weak</u> pupil'), they are not always symmetric: consider, for example, the antonymic adjectives *dikij* 'wild' and *domašnij* 'domestic'. The first of them, beside its main meaning 'living in the wild, not cultivated', develops such senses as the human property 'strange' (*dikiy rebenok* '<u>strange</u> child'), negative 'odd, strange' (*dikaja vyhodka* '<u>odd</u> action'), and high degree 'wild' (*dikij vostorg* '<u>wild</u> gaiety'). The antonym of *dikij* – the adjective *domašnij* – has only the meaning that corresponds to the idea of house (*domašn'aja rabota* 'homework', *domašnije tapočki* '<u>house</u> slippers' and so on.

- Gaining an evaluational polarity (positive / negative) or a change in polarity constitutes a further type of adjective meaning shifts. Several constraints on possible transitions can be observed. Thus, for instance, we have not encountered so far any case of an adjective that has changed from negative to positive polarity.

So the practical problem of word sense disambiguation turns to be a challenge to theoretical semantics and lexicology. The more language data is involved in the analysis, the better we can observe the systematic character of the lexicon organization and the regularity of the models of semantic evolution.

Acknowledgments

The present research is supported by RFBR foundation (ref. 08-06-00197). We would like to thank two anonymous reviewers for their constructive comments that helped to improve the manuscript.

References

1. Agirre, E., Edmonds, P.: Introduction. In: Agirre, E., Edmonds, P. (eds.) Word Sense Disambiguation: Algorithms and Applications, pp. 1–28. Springer, Heidelberg (2006)
2. Fillmore, C.J., Kay, P., O'Connor, K.T.: Regularity and Idiomaticity in Grammatical Constructions: The Case of LET ALONE. Language 64, 501–538 (1988)
3. Goldberg, A.E.: Constructions: A Construction Grammar Approach to Argument Structure. Chicago University Press, Chicago (1995)
4. Jackendoff, R.: Twistin' the night away. Language 73, 534–559 (1997)
5. Jackendoff, R.: Semantic Structures. MIT Press, Cambridge (1990)
6. Pustejovsky, J.: Type Coercion and Lexical Selection. In: Pustejovsky, J. (ed.) Semantics and the Lexicon, pp. 73–94. Kluwer Academic Publishers, Dordrecht (1993)
7. Partee, B.H.: Compositionality and Coercion in Semantics: The Dynamics of Adjective Meaning. In: Bouma, G., Kraemer, I., Zwarts, J. (eds.) Cognitive Foundations of Interpretation, pp. 145–161. Royal Netherlands Academy of Arts and Sciences, Amsterdam (2007)

8. Lashevskaja, O.: Corpus-aided Construction Grammar: Semantic Tools in the Russian National Corpus. In: Proceedings of the Second International Conference of the German Cognitive Linguistics Association, Munich, October 5-7 (2006)

9. Apresjan, Y.D., Boguslavskij, I.M., Iomdin, B.L., Iomdin, L.L., Sannikov, A.V., Sannikov, V.Z., Sizov, V.G., Tsinman, L.L.: Sintaksicheski i semanticheski annotirovannyj korpus russkogo jazyka: sovremennoe sostojanie i perspektivy (in Russian). In: Natsionalnyj korpus russkogo jazyka: 2003—2005, pp. 193–214. Indrik, Moscow (2003)

10. Rakhilina, E.V., Kobritsov, B.P., Kustova, G.I., Shemanaeva, O.Y.: Mnogoznachnost' kak prikladnaja problema: Leksiko-semanticheskaja razmetka v NKRJa (in Russian). In: Laufer, N.I., Narinjani, A.S., Selegej, V.P. (eds.) Kompjuternaja lingvistika i intellektual'nye tehnologii: Trudy mezhdunarodnoj konferencii «Dialog 2006», pp. 445–450. Izd-vo RGGU, Moscow (2006)

11. Rakhilina, E.V.: Kognitivnyj analiz predmetnyx imen: semantika i sočetaemost' (in Russian). Russkie slovari, Moscow (2000)

12. Paducheva, E.V.: Dinamičeskie modeli v semantike leksiki (in Russian). Jazyki slavjanskoj kul'tury, Moscow (2004)

13. Kustova, G.I.: Tipy proizvodnyx značenij i mexanizmy jazykovogo rasširenija (in Russian). Jazyki slavjanskoj kul'tury, Moscow (2004)

14. Talmy, L.: How language structures space. In: Pick, H., Acredolo, L. (eds.) Spatial Orientation: Theory, Research, and Application, pp. 225–282. Plenum Press, New York (1983)

15. Ozhegov, S.I., Shvedova, N.J.: Tolkovyj slovar' russkogo jazyka (in Russian). Russkij jazyk, Moscow (1992)

16. Evgen'eva, A.P. (ed.): Slovar' russkogo jazyka (in Russian), vol. 1-4. Russkij jazyk, Moscow (1999)

17. Radden, G., Kövecses, Z.: Towards a Theory of Metonymy. In: Panther, K.-U., Radden, G. (eds.) Metonymy in language and thought, pp. 17–59. Benjamins, Amsterdam (1999)

18. Lakoff, G.: Women, Fire, and Dangerous Things: What Categories Reveal about the Mind. University of Chicago Press, Chicago (1987)

Inquisitive Semantics:
Two Possibilities for Disjunction

Jeroen Groenendijk[*]

ILLC/Department of Philosophy
University of Amsterdam
j.a.g.groenendijk@uva.nl

Abstract. We introduce an inquisitive semantics for a language of propositional logic, where the interpretation of disjunction is the source of inquisitiveness. Indicative conditionals and conditional questions are treated on a par both syntactically and semantically. The semantics comes with a new logical-pragmatical notion which judges and compares the compliance of responses to an initiative in inquisitive dialogue.

1   Introduction

In this paper we introduce an *inquisitive semantics* for a language of propositional logic. In inquisitive semantics, the semantic content of a sentence is not identified with its informative content. Sentences are interpreted in such a way that they can embody both data and issues.

The propositional language for which we define the semantics is a hybrid inquisitive language. By this we mean that there is no distinction in the syntax of the logical language between declarative and interrogative sentences, but questions and assertions can be characterized in semantic terms, next to hybrid sentences, which are both informative and inquisitive. Plain contingent disjunctions will count as such.

The language will enable us not only to express simple polar questions such as: "Will Bea go to the party?", but also conditional questions like: "If Alf goes to the party, will Bea go as well?", and alternative questions like: "Will Alf go to the party, or Bea?".

The natural use of an inquisitive language lies in dialogues that have the purpose of raising and resolving issues. We will introduce a logical notion that

---

[*] I presented material related to this paper at several occasions in the past two years, including my Semantics and Pragmatics classes. I thank everyone involved in these events, especially my students, for helping me to get clearer about things. I owe special thanks to Floris Roelofsen for his many comments on many earlier drafts; to Frank Veltman, who insisted on improving the selling points; to Kata Balogh, who works with me on inquisitive pragmatic matters; and, last but not least, my close companion in this project, Salvador Mascarenhas, who discovered the inquisitive behavior of disjunction in an older version of the semantics. I am also grateful to the two anonymous referees for their helpful comments, and apologize for not having been able to respond more adequately to their remarks.

P. Bosch, D. Gabelaia, and J. Lang (Eds.): TbiLLC 2007, LNAI 5422, pp. 80–94, 2009.

judges whether a sentence φ *is compliant to* a sentence ψ. We look upon φ as a response to an initiative ψ, and require φ to be strictly and obediently related to ψ. Compliance is a very demanding notion of dialogue coherence.[1]

2 Two Possibilities for Disjunction

The present paper explores an inquisitive logic for the simple artificial language of propositional logic. Hence, the logical notion of compliance that the semantics gives rise to applies to artificial inquisitive dialogues within this toy language. Nevertheless, such a logical semantical enterprise would be idle if we cannot make *some* connection with dialogue coherence relations in natural language.

I will discuss a small set of examples where I hope to illustrate that not only interrogatives, but also certain indicative sentences, in particular disjunctions, can be inquisitive. The empirical support for this comes from observations concerning compliant responses to such sentences.[2]

If an utterance is inquisitive and embodies an issue, a most compliant response to it is an utterrance that resolves the issue. If an indicative sentence allows for responses that are like answers to a question, are like typical responses to an interrogative sentence, I take this to indicate that the sentence has inquisitive semantic content.

To be able to contrast inquisitive with non-inquisitive sentences, with purely informative sentences, I also have to make certain assumptions about characteristic reponses to non-inquisitive sentences. I take it that if an utterance is purely informative, a response to it may typically be preceded by an interjection that reports the attitude of the responder to the information that was provided. We can take the function of that to establish the status of the information in relation to the common ground.

Consider the simple disjunction in (1), and the interrogative in (2).

(1) Alf or Bea will go to the party.

(2) Will Alf or Bea go to the party?

It is generally acknowledged that the interrogative in (2) has different intonation patterns. On one pattern, the two responses in (3) are the most compliant ones.

(3) a. Yes. Alf or Bea will go to the party.

     b. No. Neither of them will go.

---

[1] In Groenendijk (1999), I defined a similar notion which I called 'licensing'. I switched to the term 'compliance', because it has a negative ring to it, and thus communicates more clearly that being non-compliant can easily be a virtue rather than a vice.

[2] A difficulty I have to face is that in discussing examples I have to rely on intuitions about what counts as a compliant response to an initiative in a dialogue, just as much as in declarative semantics we have to rely on intuitions about entailment relations. The latter have been shaped and sharpened by the practices of the semanticist community. As for intuitions about compliance, I can only hope that you can share mine to at least some extent.

Of course, though not answers in this case, these are equally good responses to the indicative sentence in (1), confirming and rejecting what (1) says, respectively, with opposite effects on the common ground status of the information provided by (1).

On another intonation pattern, perhaps the more common one, (2) is not a yes/no-question, but has an alternative question interpretation, which has two *different* most compliant responses, one of which is (4).

(4) Bea will go.

The crucial thing to note is that the indicative disjunction in (1) *also* has an intonation pattern, on which (4) and its alternative are fully compliant responses. That is not to say that something that *amounts to* (4) could not be given as a reaction to (1), when it has the intonation pattern where the responses in (3) are the most expected ones, but the most 'appropriate' way to do it, would then be by means of (5) rather than (4).

(5) Yes. (In fact,) Bea will go.

First (1) as such is confirmed, establishing that the information it provides can enter the common ground, which sort of clears the way to elaborate on this by stating one of the disjuncts of (1), thus addressing a further issue, not embodied by (1) as such. Much the same holds for (5) in response to (2) on its yes/no-reading.

Subtle as it may be, I take this to be evidence that like the interrogative in (2) is semantically ambiguous between a yes/no-reading and an alternative question reading, the indicative in (1) is semantically ambiguous between a purely informative reading, and a hybrid reading under which (1) is inquisitive as well. The ambiguity of the question in (2) can then be traced back to an underlying inquisitiveness ambiguity of disjunction as such.

The two readings, which can be set apart by intonation, have different effects on what counts as a compliant response, just as much as in declarative semantics different readings of a sentence can have different effects on entailment relations.

I will argue in the final section of the paper, that a hybrid disjunction and the corresponding alternative question also implicate that not both disjuncts hold, and that the logical notion of compliance can offer an explanation for that.

3   Hybrid Propositional Syntax

The syntax of our propositional language is stated in a reasonably standard way.

Definition 1 (Hybrid Propositional Syntax). *Let $\wp$ be a finite set of propositional variables.[3] The set of sentences of $L_\wp$ is the smallest set such that:*

---

[3] The assumption that the set of atoms is finite only plays a marginal role in this paper, but is of importance, e.g., for proving functional completeness. See footnote 8.

1. *If $p \in \wp$, then $p \in L_\wp$*
2. $\perp \in L_\wp$
3. *If $\varphi \in L_\wp$ and $\psi \in L_\wp$, then $(\varphi \rightarrow \psi) \in L_\wp$*
4. *If $\varphi \in L_\wp$ and $\psi \in L_\wp$, then $(\varphi \wedge \psi) \in L_\wp$*
5. *If $\varphi \in L_\wp$ and $\psi \in L_\wp$, then $(\varphi \vee \psi) \in L_\wp$*

The non-standard nature of the language, the fact that it is a hybrid inquisitive language, becomes apparent in the last two items in the following small list of notation conventions.

Definition 2 (Notation Conventions)

1. $\neg\varphi := \varphi \rightarrow \perp$ 2. $\top := \neg\perp$ 3. $!\varphi := \neg\neg\varphi$ 4. $?\varphi := (\varphi \vee \neg\varphi)$

The interpretation of negation, which is standardly defined in terms of implication and the falsum, will be such that $\neg\varphi$ is never inquisitive, is always an assertion. Hence, whether φ is inquisitive or not, $!\varphi$ will be non-inquisitive and will only be equivalent with φ, if φ is an assertion.

The interpretation of disjunction will be such that although $\varphi \vee \neg\varphi$ is never informative, $\varphi \vee \neg\varphi$ is inquisitive as soon as φ is contingent. This means that $\varphi \vee \neg\varphi$ and $\top$ are not equivalent, since given the way in which $\top$ is defined, it is not only non-informative but also non-inquisitive. Since $\varphi \vee \neg\varphi$ can only be inquisitive it makes sense to mark it as the question $?\varphi$.

Another non-standard feature of the language is that unlike in classical propositional logic, conjunction, disjunction and implication are not interdefinable in the usual way with the aid of negation.[4]

There is no perfect match between our toy logical language and natural language. For example, the logical syntax allows for the negation of questions, questions occurring as the antecedent of conditional sentences, and disjunctions of questions. I will not discuss such disputable features of the logic in the present paper.

4   Inquisitive Semantics

We state the semantics for a language $L_\wp$ relative to a set $W_\wp$ of *suitable possible worlds for* $L_\wp$, where a world $w \in W_\wp$ is a valuation function with the set of propositional variables $\wp$ as its domain and the two values $\{1, 0\}$ as its range.[5]

For a declarative language, a standard way to define the interpretation of the sentences of the language is by the notion $w \models \varphi$, which can be read as: w confirms the information provided by φ. This will not suffice to interpret our hybrid inquisitive language, where sentences may not only provide information, but may also embody issues.

---

[4] In its non-standard features, inquisitive logic bears resemblances to intuitionistic logic. Inquisitive logic is a so-called intermediate logic. Except for one more footnote, I will not address the matter. See Mascarenhas (2008).

[5] We will often suppress the subscript $\wp$ on L and W.

The minimal way to deal with this is to evaluate sentences relative to pairs of worlds, and define the interpretation of the language in terms of the notion $(w, v) \models \varphi$, which we read as w *and* v *agree upon* φ. We take this to mean that both w and v confirm the information provided by φ, and that if φ embodies an issue the answer to it can be the same in w and v. In case of $(w, w) \models \varphi$ this boils down to w confirms the information provided by φ.[6]

Definition 3 (Inquisitive Semantics). *Let* $\varphi \in L_\varphi$, *and* $w, v \in W_\varphi$.

1. $(w, v) \models p$ *iff* $w(p) = 1$ *and* $v(p) = 1$
2. $(w, v) \not\models \bot$
3. $(w, v) \models (\varphi \vee \psi)$ *iff* $(w, v) \models \varphi$ *or* $(w, v) \models \psi$
4. $(w, v) \models (\varphi \wedge \psi)$ *iff* $(w, v) \models \varphi$ *and* $(w, v) \models \psi$
5. $(w, v) \models (\varphi \rightarrow \psi)$ *iff for all pairs* π *in* $\{w, v\}^2$: *if* $\pi \models \varphi$, *then* $\pi \models \psi$

The definition has pretty familiar looks,[7] except for the clause for implication, which quantifies over the four pairs $(w, v), (v, w), (v, v)$, and (v, v). It can easily be read from the other clauses that to consider (v, w) next to (w, v) is redundant.

We will discuss implication more extensively later, but note that to inspect whether (w, v) agree upon $\varphi \rightarrow \psi$, we not only check whether if (w, v) *agree* on φ, (w, v) agree upon ψ as well. Also in case (w, v) do *not agree* upon φ, because w confirms the information provided by φ whereas v does not (or the other way around), we still keep on checking in that case, whether w (or v) also confirms the information provided by ψ.

Although, as I announced in the introduction, we will see later that the semantics gives rise to a new logical notion of compliance that rules the use of the inquisitive language in dialogue, an orthodox notion of entailment in terms of agreement suggests itself as well.

Definition 4 (Entailment)

$\varphi_1, \ldots, \varphi_n \models \psi$ *iff*
    $\forall w, v \in W$: *if* $(w, v) \models \varphi_1$ *&* $\ldots$ *&* $(w, v) \models \varphi_n$, *then* $(w, v) \models \psi$.

The notion of entailment is well-behaved and has interesting properties. To note one, from the way in which implication is defined, it immediately follows that under the inquisitive interpretation of the language the following fact holds.

---

[6] The present format of the semantics was suggested to me by Balder ten Cate. The semantics can also be generalized by stating the interpretation relative to sets of possible worlds of arbitrary size. The resulting semantics is richer, and the logic is closer to intuitionistic logic.

[7] The clause for disjunction may also look familiar to you if (like Robert van Rooij, thanks) you have read David Lewis' paper: *'Whether' report* (Lewis (1982)). There, Lewis considers to treat *whether A or B* clauses as *wheth A or wheth B* along the following lines: $\models_{i,j}$ *whether A or B* iff $\models_{i,j}$ *wheth A* or $\models_{i,j}$ *wheth B*, where $\models_{i,j}$ *wheth A* iff $\models_i A$ and $\models_j A$. The notion $\models_{i,j}$ is conceived of as an application of the technique of double indexing.

Fact 1. $\varphi \models \psi$ *iff* $\models \varphi \rightarrow \psi$

Logical equivalence of two formulas is defined as usual as mutual entailment.

Definition 5 (Equivalence). $\varphi \Leftrightarrow \psi$ *iff* $\varphi \models \psi \ \& \ \psi \models \varphi$

With these logical notions in place, we turn to the discussion of the semantics.

4.1   Informativeness and Inquisitiveness

The first clause in Def. 3 implies that a propositional variable p does not embody an issue. The definition says that to see whether w and v agree upon p, it is sufficient to see whether $w(p) = v(p) = 1$. We have that $(w, v) \models p$ iff $(w, w) \models p$ and $(v, v) \models p$.

This is different for a disjunction like $p \vee q$. There we can have that $(w, w) \models p \vee q$ and $(v, v) \models p \vee q$, whereas $(w, v) \not\models p \vee q$, as can be shown as follows.

Let w be a world where $w(p) = 1 \ \& \ w(q) = 0$, and v a world where $v(p) = 0$ $\& \ v(q) = 1$. Then we have that $(w, w) \models p$ and $(v, v) \models q$, and hence, according to clause 3 of Def. 3, both $(w, w) \models p \vee q$ and $(v, v) \models p \vee q$.

At the same time we have that $(w, v) \not\models p$, because $v(p) = 0$; and $(w, v) \not\models q$, since $w(q) = 0$. According to the definition, this means that $(w, v) \not\models p \vee q$. So, we have shown that, unlike in the case of atomic sentences, there are worlds w and v such that $(w, w) \models p \vee q$ and $(v, v) \models p \vee q$, whereas $(w, v) \not\models p \vee q$.

Two such worlds w and v do not agree upon $p \vee q$, because although w and v both confirm the information provided by $p \vee q$, the answer to the issue that $p \vee q$ embodies, the issue whether p or q, is different in w and v, in w the answer is p, in v it is q.

We have just shown that an atomic sentence p is not inquisitive, and that a disjunction like $p \vee q$ is inquisitive, according to the following definition:

Definition 6 (Consistency, Informativeness, and Inquisitiveness)

1. φ is consistent *iff* $\exists w \in W \colon (w, w) \models \varphi$.
2. φ is informative *iff* $\exists w \in W \colon (w, w) \not\models \varphi$.
3. φ is inquisitive *iff* $\exists w, v \in W \colon (w, w) \models \varphi \ \& \ (v, v) \models \varphi \ \& \ (w, v) \not\models \varphi$.

   We also define:

   (a) φ is hybrid *iff* φ is informative and φ is inquisitive.

   (b) φ is contingent *iff* φ is consistent, and φ is inquisitive or informative.

What inquisitiveness of φ requires is that there are pairs of worlds that satisfy the information provided by φ (which implies that φ is consistent), but where the two worlds differ in their answer to an issue embodied by φ, which implies that φ indeed does embody an issue, otherwise two such worlds could not be found.

As we have seen, informativeness and inquisitiveness do not exclude each other, $p \vee q$ is both informative and inquisitive, and hence semantically hybrid.

Given the way the interpretation of $\bot$ is defined, $\bot$ is not contingent, since it is inconsistent. And $\top$ is not contingent either, because $\bot$ is neither inquisitive nor informative.

4.2 Negations and Assertions

Before we turn to negation, we note that on the basis of the informal description of $(w, v) \models \varphi$ in terms of agreement, we may expect the following to hold, which indeed it does, given the way the semantics is defined:

Fact 2 (Symmetry and Reflexive Closure of Agreement)

1. $\forall w, v \in W : (w, v) \models \varphi \Rightarrow (v, w) \models \varphi$.
2. $\forall w, v \in W : (w, v) \models \varphi \Rightarrow (w, w) \models \varphi \ \& \ (v, v) \models \varphi$.

The proof runs by induction on the complexity of φ.[8]

From the definition of inquisitiveness and the last item in Fact 2, the following follows immediately.

Fact 3 (Non-Inquisitiveness)

   φ *is not inquisitive iff* $\forall w, v \in W : (w, v) \models \varphi \Leftrightarrow (w, w) \models \varphi \ \& \ (v, v) \models \varphi$.

Let us now consider $\neg \varphi$ which abbreviates $\varphi \rightarrow \bot$. Clause 5 of Def. 3 tells us that for w and v to agree upon $\varphi \rightarrow \bot$, it should hold for the four pairs (w, v), (v, w), (w, w), and (v, v), that if such a pair agrees on φ it agrees on $\bot$. The interpretation of $\bot$ tells us that no pair agrees on $\bot$. Hence, For w and v to agree upon $\varphi \rightarrow \bot$, it should hold that $(w, v) \not\models \varphi$, $(v, w) \not\models \varphi$, $(w, w) \not\models \varphi$, and $(v, v) \not\models \varphi$. Given Fact 2 and the way negation is introduced in the language, this boils down to:

Fact 4 ($\neg$Negation). $(w, v) \models \neg \varphi$ *iff* $(w, w) \not\models \varphi \ \& \ (v, v) \not\models \varphi$.

Two worlds agree upon a negation as soon as neither of the two confirms the information provided by φ. As we saw to be the case for atomic sentences, negations embody no issue. From Facts 1 and 2 it immediately follows that:

Fact 5 (Negation). $\neg \varphi$ *is not inquisitive.*

That negations are never inquisitive, is of course behind the fact that disjunction, conjunction and implication are not interdefinable in the usual way with the aid of negation. Disjunction is the indispensable source of inquisitiveness in the language. And if we were to define implication and conjunction in terms of disjunction and negation we do not in general obtain the interpretation now assigned by the semantics to formulas of these forms.

---

[8] In inquisitive *update semantics*, a *state* σ *for* $L_\wp$ is defined as a reflexive and symmetric relation on a subset of $W_\wp$. In the semantics we recursively define the effect of updating σ with φ, $\sigma[\varphi]$. The relation with the present semantics is given by: $\sigma[\varphi] = \{(w, v) \in \sigma \mid (w, v) \models \varphi\}$. Salvador Mascarenhas proved a Functional Completeness Theorem, which says that for any two states σ and σ', $\sigma' \subseteq \sigma \subseteq W_\wp^2$: there is a finite sequence of sentences $\varphi_1, \ldots, \varphi_n \in L_\wp$ such that $\sigma[\varphi_1] \ldots [\varphi_n] = \sigma'$. We don't need the full language to achieve this, $\{\neg, \vee\}$ suffices. Since conjunction corresponds to sequencing, if we add $\wedge$, we can move from any state to any of its substates with a single formula of the language. The assumption we made that $\wp$ is finite, is essential for the functional completeness proof. (See Mascarenhas (2008).)

Since $!\varphi$ is defined as double negation, $!\varphi$ is not inquisitive. And we can write:

Fact 6 (!Assertion). $(w, v) \models \,!\varphi$ *iff* $(w, w) \models \varphi$ *&* $(v, v) \models \varphi$.

This means that for any formula φ, $!\varphi$ delivers its interpretation in classical logic. From Facts 3 and 6 it follows that every non-inquisitive sentence can be written as an assertion:

Fact 7 (Assertion). $!\varphi \Leftrightarrow \varphi$ *iff* φ *is not inquisitive.*

Given this fact, we will often refer to non-inquisitive sentences as *assertions*.

Note that Fact 7 tells us that the law of triple negation holds. Since negation is not inquisitive, $!\neg\varphi \Leftrightarrow \neg\varphi$. And iteration of $!$ is superfluous: $!!\varphi \Leftrightarrow !\varphi$.

Also, since $!(p \vee q)$ is not inquisitive, it is not equivalent with the hybrid disjunction $p \vee q$. The assertion $!(p \vee q)$ embodies no issue, $!(p \vee q)$ just embodies the truthconditional content of disjunction in classical logic.

Remember the discussion in Section 2, where we observed that the English indicative disjunction (1), like its interrogative sister (2), is prosodically ambiguous between a yes/no-interpretation, and an alternative interpretation. As for the latter, for both (1) and (2), the hybrid disjunction $p \vee q$ suggests itself as a proper translation. As for the yes/no-interpretation of the indicative (1), the assertion $!(p \vee q)$ seems to cover its meaning. And if we take the disjunction $!(p \vee q) \vee \neg(p \vee q)$, i.e., $?!(p \vee q)$ we get a polar question that suits (2) on its yes/no-reading. This brings us to questions.

4.3 Questions

Consider the atomic question $?p$, which abbreviates $p \vee \neg p$. The interpretation of disjunction tells us that $(w, v) \models p \vee \neg p$ iff $(w, v) \models p$ or $(w, v) \models \neg p$, both worlds agree upon p or both worlds agree upon $\neg p$. This means that $(w, v) \models \,?p$ iff $w(p) = v(p) = 1$ or $w(p) = v(p) = 0$. From this it is clear that $?p$ is not informative, and is inquisitive, $p \vee \neg p$ is contingent, it is an inquisitive question.

Given the interpretation of disjunction and the interpretation of negation given in Fact 4, we can write:

Fact 8 (?Questions). $(w, v) \models \,?\varphi$ *iff* $(w, v) \models \varphi$ *or* $(w, w) \not\models \varphi$ *&* $(v, v) \not\models \varphi$.

If we consider $(w, w) \models \,?\varphi$, we get that $(w, w) \models \,?\varphi$ iff $(w, w) \models \varphi$ or $(w, w) \not\models \varphi$, which trivially holds, hence $\forall w \colon (w, w) \models \,?\varphi$. Given how informativeness is defined, the first item in the next fact holds, from which the second item immediately follows.

Fact 9 (Questions). $?\varphi$ *is not informative* *&* $?\varphi \Leftrightarrow \varphi$ *iff* φ *is not informative.*

Given this fact, we will often refer to non-informative sentences as *questions*. (Note that since $\top$ is neither informative nor inquisitive, it counts both as a (non-informative) assertion, and as a (non-inquisitive) question.)

The last item in Fact 9 implies that iteration of $?$ is superfluous: $??\varphi \Leftrightarrow \,?\varphi$. The fact that iteration of both $!$ and $?$ are superfluous, makes it easy to state things in general about assertions and questions.

4.4 Conditionals: Divide and Conquer

The two specific cases of conditionals with a question, and conditionals with an assertion as consequent, behave more standardly than the clause for implication in Def. 3 might suggest.[9]

Fact 10 (Conditional Questions and Conditional Assertions)

 1. $(w, v) \models \varphi \rightarrow ?\psi$ *iff* $(w, v) \models \varphi \Rightarrow (w, v) \models ?\psi$
 2. $(w, v) \models \varphi \rightarrow !\psi$ *iff* $(w, w) \models \varphi \rightarrow \psi$ *and* $(v, v) \models \varphi \rightarrow \psi$

Clause 5 in Def. 3 requires for $(w, v) \models \varphi \rightarrow \psi$ that it holds for each of the pairs π we can form from w and v, i.e., (w, v), (v, w), (w, w), and (v, v) that: if $\pi \models \varphi$, then $\pi \models \psi$. Given symmetry of agreement (Fact 2), among those four, we can dismiss (v, w).

Furthermore, since $?\psi$ is not informative, i.e., $\forall w \colon (w, w) \models ?\psi$, in evaluating $\varphi \rightarrow ?\psi$, we can dismiss the two identity pairs as well. This also means that if ψ is not informative, then neither is $\varphi \rightarrow \psi$.

Conversely, since $!\psi$ is not inquisitive, i.e., $(w, v) \models \psi$ iff $(w, w) \models \psi$ & $(v, v) \models \psi$ (Fact 3), in evaluating $\varphi \rightarrow !\psi$, we only have to consider the two identity pairs. This also means that if ψ is not inquisitive, $\varphi \rightarrow \psi$ is not inquisitive either, and behaves like classical material implication:

Fact 11 (Non-Inquisitive Conditionals). $\varphi \rightarrow !\psi \Leftrightarrow !(\varphi \rightarrow \psi)$

So, we have seen how the two specific cases of conditionals with non-inquisitive and non-informative consequents behave more standardly than the clause for implication in Def. 3 might suggest. But we can actually show that any conditional reduces to a combination of these two simple cases.

The following fact tells us that every sentence φ can be divided in a *theme* $?\varphi$ and a *rheme* $!\varphi$.

Fact 12 (Division). $\varphi \Leftrightarrow ?\varphi \wedge !\varphi$

From this it immediately follows that every conditional $\varphi \rightarrow \psi$ can be written as $\varphi \rightarrow (?\psi \wedge !\psi)$. Next, we use the following distribution fact.

Fact 13 (Distribution 1). $\varphi \rightarrow (\psi \wedge \chi) \Leftrightarrow (\varphi \rightarrow \psi) \wedge (\varphi \rightarrow \chi)$

This allows us to rewrite the conditional $\varphi \rightarrow (?\psi \wedge !\psi)$ as the conjunction of conditionals $(\varphi \rightarrow ?\psi) \wedge (\varphi \rightarrow !\psi)$. Finally, applying the equivalence in Fact 11 to the second conjunct, we arrive at the following fact.

Fact 14 (Conditional Division). $\varphi \rightarrow \psi \Leftrightarrow (\varphi \rightarrow ?\psi) \wedge !(\varphi \rightarrow \psi)$

---

[9] The semantics of conditional questions presented here is similar to the one proposed in Velissaratou (2000). What is new is that in our hybrid inquisitive language we have a single uniform interpretation of implication that deals both with conditional questions and conditional assertions.

Any conditional can be rewritten as the conjunction of a conditional question and a classical material implication.[10]

4.5 Disjunctive Antecedents

Consider the simplest example $p \to ?q$ of a conditional question. We get that $(w, v) \models p \to ?q$ iff $w(p) = v(p) = 1 \Rightarrow w(q) = v(q)$. I.e., either $w(p) = v(p) = 1 \Rightarrow w(q) = v(q) = 1$ or $v(p) = w(p) = 1 \Rightarrow w(q) = v(q) = 0$. Which means that $p \to ?q$ is equivalent with the disjunction $(p \to q) \vee (p \to \neg q)$. This is a special instance of the following equivalence:[11]

Fact 15 (Mascarenhas Equivalence). $!\varphi \to (\psi \vee \chi) \Leftrightarrow (!\varphi \to \psi) \vee (!\varphi \to \chi)$

This equivalence does not hold generally also in case of inquisitive antecedents. The following pair of examples is a case in point: $(p \vee q) \to ?r \nLeftrightarrow !(p \vee q) \to ?r$. With the Mascarenhas Equivalence, $!(p \vee q) \to ?r$ corresponds to a disjunction of two assertions: $((p \vee q) \to r) \vee ((p \vee q) \to \neg r)$. We will show that $(p \vee q) \to ?r$ corresponds to a longer disjunction of four assertions.

First we note another distribution fact.

Fact 16 (Distribution 2). $(\varphi \vee \psi) \to \chi \Leftrightarrow (\varphi \to \chi) \wedge (\psi \to \chi)$

This means that $(p \vee q) \to ?r$ is equivalent to $(p \to ?r) \wedge (q \to ?r)$, which is Mascarenhas-equivalent to $((p \to r) \vee (p \to \neg r)) \wedge ((q \to r) \vee (q \to \neg r))$, to which we apply the (last) distribution fact:

Fact 17 (Distribution 3)

$$(\varphi \vee \psi) \wedge (\chi \vee \theta) \Leftrightarrow (\varphi \wedge \chi) \vee (\varphi \wedge \theta) \vee (\psi \wedge \chi) \vee (\psi \wedge \theta)$$

This gives us four disjuncts, two of which are $(p \to r) \wedge (q \to r)$ and $(p \to \neg r) \wedge (q \to \neg r)$, which by Fact 16 reduce to the first two of the following four disjuncts, which together are equivalent with $(p \vee q) \to ?r$:

---

[10] Actually, we may take this to mean that the theme of a plain conditional, the question on the background, is the corresponding conditional question (rather than the corresponding questioned conditional). Thus, inquisitive semantics may be taken to give a logical explanation for the idea ventured in the first sentence of Ramsey's famous footnote, known as the Ramsey Test: (Ramsey (1931))

> If two people are arguing "If p will q?" and are both in doubt as to p, they are adding p hypothetically to their stock of knowledge and arguing on that basis about q; so that in a sense "If p, q" and "If p, $\neg q$" are contradictories.

These two 'contradictories' are the two answers to the conditional question that we just found to be the theme of a conditional. See also Grice's paper on 'Indicative Conditionals' in Grice (1989).

[11] The hard part of this equivalence, from left to right (and with $\neg \varphi$ instead of $!\varphi$), is known as the Kreisel-Putnam Axiom and corresponds to an admissible rule in intuitionistic propositional logic. Salvador Mascarenhas has proved that it is also valid in inquisitive propositional logic. This result is crucial in obtaining a disjunctive normal form. (See footnote 14.)

$((p \lor q) \to r) \lor ((p \lor q) \to \neg r) \lor ((p \to r) \land (q \to \neg r)) \lor ((p \to \neg r) \land (q \to r))$.
What we have arrived at, is that there are, as we will call them, four *possibilities* for the sentence $(p \lor q) \to ?r$. In this case, since the sentence is an inquisitive question, the four possibilities correspond to four possible answers.[12]

4.6   Possibilities

Given the properties of $(w, v) \models \varphi$, as stated in Fact 2, the relation between worlds of 'to agree upon a sentence φ', corresponds to a set of sets of worlds.[13]

Definition 7 (Possibilities). *Let $\varphi \in L_\wp$. P is a possibility for φ in $W_\wp$ iff*

1. *$P \subseteq W_\wp$ & $\forall w, v \in P : (w, v) \models \varphi$; and*
2. *$\forall P' \subseteq W_\wp$: if $P \subseteq P'$ & $\forall w, v \in P' : (w, v) \models \varphi$, then $P' = P$.*

A possibility for a sentence φ is a largest set P of worlds (a proposition), such that for any two worlds $w, v \in P$: w and v agree upon φ.[14]

A sentence φ is inquisitive iff there is more than one possibility for φ; φ is not inquisitive iff there is a single possibility for φ. The set of possibilities for $\bot$ in W is $\{\emptyset\}$. The set of possibilities for $\top$ is $\{W\}$. A sentence φ is informative iff the union of the set of possibilities for φ does not equal W.

If there is more than one possibility for a sentence φ, then each possibility corresponds to a proposition that fully resolves the issue embodied by φ. Unions of (some but not all) possibilities for φ correspond to propositions that partially resolve the issue embodied by φ.

5   Inquisitive Logic

If we ask ourselves what the natural purpose of an inquisitive language is, the obvious answer is: to raise and resolve issues; a purpose best suited in dialogue.

---

[12] We discovered this nice feature of the semantics by surprise. Tikitu de Jager programmed the semantics. The program spits out the possibilities (see below) that a formula gives rise to. This is particularly helpful for formulas with more than two propositional variables, which are hard to picture. We ran the program on $(p \lor q) \to ?r$, expecting to get out the two possibilities for $!(p \lor q) \to ?r$. Panic struck when the program predicted four possibilities. But after analyzing what came out, the program — and the semantics — turned out to be right. There is a reading of the question: "If Alf or Bea goes to the party, will Chris go as well?", that has the four possible answers that Tikitu's program came up with.

[13] In terms of the notion of the possibilities for a sentence, we can also more accurately describe $(w, v) \models \varphi$ as w and v agree upon φ iff there is a possibility for φ to which both w and v belong.

[14] Salvador Mascarenhas has proved that the set of possibilities for a sentence φ can be syntactically characterized as a disjunction of assertions, where each assertion characterizes a possibility. Any sentence can be transformed into its Inquisitive Disjunctive Normal Form, which has this property. (Mascarenhas (2008))

Then a natural task for a logic that comes with inquisitive semantics is to address moves in a dialogue concerned with cooperatively raising and resolving issues.

Following the lead of the 'normative' status of the logical notion of entailment in judging validity of argumentation, we can take inquisitive logical notions to judge 'correctness', or 'coherence', or 'compliance' of a response to an initiative in a cooperative inquisitive dialogue.

Here we can draw from general insights in dialogue studies.[15] Two fundamental dialogue coherence relations for a response to an initiative are the following:

Two Dialogue Coherence Relations

(i) Answer an issue raised by an initiative *(informative relation)*; or

(ii) Replace the issue by an easier to answer subissue *(inquisitive relation)*.

The inquisitive option is second choice, a cooperative responder takes recourse to it only if he lacks the information for even a partial fulfilment of the first option. And note that if the initiative is a question, we may assume that the initiator certainly has no full answer to it, but she just may have a bit of a partial answer to her own question. Hence, it can make sense for the responder to ask a counter question, if only because when *that bit* of the issue were resolved, it may become possible for him to provide a full(er) answer to the initial question.[16]

Of course, the less inquisitive such a counter question is, the better the chances are that this bit of the original bigger issue, turns out not to be an issue for the initiator.

If we go from here, then one can take it to be the case, that the general direction an inquisitive dialogue strives for, is to move from *less informed* to *more informed* situations, and from *more inquisitive* to *less inquisitive* situations.

If we look at entailment from this perspective, we see that more informativeness of φ as compared to ψ is measured by $\varphi \models \psi$, whereas less inquisitiveness of φ as compared to ψ runs in the opposite direction, and is measured by $\psi \models \varphi$.

It is not too difficult to design a logical relation that measures informativeness and inquisitiveness in these opposite direction in one go. We call it homogeneity.

Definition 8 (Homogeneity). *φ is at least as homogeneous as ψ, $\varphi \succeq \psi$ iff*

1. For all $w \in W$: if $(w,w) \models \varphi$, then $(w,w) \models \psi$, and

2. For all $w,v \in W$: if $(w,w) \models \varphi$ & $(v,v) \models \varphi$ & $(w,v) \not\models \varphi$, then $(w,v) \not\models \psi$.

The second clause holds trivially for assertions, since the antecedent can never be the case. The first clause holds trivially for questions. The most essential

---

[15] See, e.g., Asher & Lascarides (1998), Hulstijn (2000), and Roberts (1996).

[16] For similar reasons, it may also be sensible not to respond with a subissue, but with an objectively speaking unrelated question, which subjectively, for the responder, is related to the issue posed by the initiator.

features of homogeneity, and its hybrid relation to entailment, are listed below:

Fact 18 (Homogeneity)

1. If $\varphi \succeq \psi$, then $!\varphi \models !\psi$
2. $!\varphi \succeq !\psi$ iff $!\varphi \models !\psi$
3. If $!\varphi \Leftrightarrow !\psi$, then $\varphi \succeq \psi$ iff $?\psi \models ?\varphi$
4. $?\varphi \succeq ?\psi$ iff $?\psi \models ?\varphi$
5. $!\varphi \succeq ?\psi$
6. $\bot \succeq \varphi$
7. $\top \succeq ?\varphi$

Although homogeneity gives the *general* direction an inquisitive dialogue strives for, as is particularly clear from the fact that *any* assertion is at least as homogeneous as *any* question (item 5 in the list), we need some more specific directions that tell us, e.g., *which* assertions are proper responses to *which* questions. The logical notion of relatedness, defined in terms of possibilities, does that.

Definition 9 (Relatedness). φ is related to ψ, $\varphi \propto \psi$ iff
every possibility for φ is the union of a subset of the set of possibilities for ψ.

Relatedness is defined generally for all kinds of sentences, but if φ is an assertion, for which there is only a single possibility P, relatedness of φ to ψ requires that P is the union of a subset of the set of possibilities for ψ, which, in case ψ is inquisitive, is as close as you can logically expect to get, in characterizing partially resolving the issue raised by an initiative ψ.

By homogeneity we can measure whether the information contained in one sentence more fully resolves an issue, than the information contained in another sentence. Were it not for the borderline case of non-contingent $\bot$, which is more homogeneous than any contingent sentence, and is also related to every sentence, we could equate the most homogeneous related responses to an inquisitive initiative ψ with those sentences φ that completely resolve the issue ψ embodies.

In other words, under the general constraint of contingency of a response, relatedness, combined with homogeneity, tells us how well a sentence does in resolving an issue. This concerns the informative dialogue coherence relation.

Concerning the inquisitive dialogue coherence relation, we get a similar story. First of all, if a question $?\varphi$ is related to and at least as homogeneous as a question $?\psi$, it is indeed guaranteed that $?\varphi$ is at least as easy to answer as $?\psi$.

Secondly, by homogeneity we can measure whether one question is a more minimal subissue of some issue, than another question is. Were it not for the borderline case of non-contingent $\top$, which is the most homogeneous 'question', and is also related to every question, we could equate the most homogeneous related questions to some question ψ? with the minimal subquestions of ψ?.

In other words, under the general constraint tof contingency of a response, relatedness, combined with homogeneity, tells us how well a question does in replacing an issue by an easier to answer subissue. This concerns the inquisitive dialogue coherence relation.

We put our findings together in the following definition of compliance that deals with both dialogue coherence relations.

Definition 10 (Compliance). φ is a compliant response to ψ *iff*

1. *φ is contingent; and*
2. *φ is related to ψ; and*
3. *φ is at least as homogeneous as ψ.*

This qualitative notion of compliance embodies a comparative quantitative notion as well: among contingent sentences which are related to an initiative, homogeneity prefers more informative sentences, and among two equally informative sentences, it prefers less inquisitive sentences.

These are the borderline cases:

Fact 19 (Ultimate Compliance). *Let ψ be a contingent initiative.*

1. *φ is a least compliant response to ψ iff φ is equivalent to ψ.*
2. *φ is a most compliant response to ψ iff there is a single possibilty P for φ, such that P is a possibility for ψ as well.*
3. *If ψ is a question, φ is a most compliant non-informative response to ψ iff φ is a polar subquestion of ψ.*

Note that in case the initiative is a polar question, the most compliant non-informative responses coincide with the least compliant responses. If the responder has no answer to a polar question, there is no significant move to make.

Similarly, in case the initiative is a contingent assertion, the least and most compliant responses coincide: repeating the initiative, at most rephrasing it a bit, is the only compliant move to make.

This is why we characterized compliance informally as strict and obedient relatedness. Compliance as such does not allow for critical responses. Logically speaking, it is just a small step to allow for critical responses: also permit compliance to the *theme* $?\psi$ of an initiative ψ. Emotionally, though, say for a parent with a maturing child, this may be a big step. But that's another story.

6   Conclusion: Inquisitive Pragmatics

It will not have escaped your attention that the way the logical notion of compliance is defined bears resemblances to the Gricean Cooperation Principle and its Maxims of Quality, Relation and Quantity. This may give rise to the expectation that implicatures are around the corner.

Consider the example of a hybrid disjunction $p \vee q$ as an initiative. There are, up to equivalence, only two most compliant responses: p and q. In particular, the more homogeneous sentence $p \wedge q$ is blocked, because it is not related to $p \vee q$. Apparently, according to the initiator, it does not count.

How can that be? We have taken it to be the case that a cooperative dialogue strives for more homogeneous situations. In principle, the initiator should be interested in obtaining the information whether $p \wedge q$ on top of the information that p (or q). By blocking $p \wedge q$ as a response, the initiator *suggests* that: not both p and q. And by responding with just p to $p \vee q$, the responder signals that he goes along with that suggestion. Hence, his answer p *implicates* that $\neg q$. Cooperatively, initiator and responder have agreed upon exclusive disjunction.

Of course, the responder may have reasons for not following the exclusiveness suggestion made by the initiator, just as he may have reasons not to accept the informative content, which excludes that neither p nor q. In both cases, the responder opts for not being compliant. In such situations, the appropriate way to do this, is not to bluntly reject the information provided, with: "Neither p nor q!"; or to protest against the suggestion being made with: "Both p and q!". Compliant non-compliant responses are rather: "Well, actually, neither p nor q"; and: "Well, in fact, both p and q.", thus explicitly signalling awareness of the non-compliance of one's response. (See also the examples in Section 2.)

References

Aloni, M., Butler, A., Dekker, P. (eds.): Questions in Dynamic Semantics. Elsevier, Oxford (2007)

Asher, N., Lascarides, A.: Questions in Dialogue. Linguistics and Philosophy 21, 237–309 (1998)

Grice, H.P.: Studies in the Ways of Words. Harvard University Press, Cambridge (1989)

Groenendijk, J.: The Logic of Interrogation. In: Matthews, T., Strolovitch, D.L. (eds.) The Proceedings of the Ninth Conference on Semantics and Linguistic Theory, pp. 109–126. CLC Publications, Ithaca (1999); Also in: Aloni, Butler, and Dekker (2007)

Hulstijn, J.: Dialogue Models for Inquiry and Transaction, Ph.D. thesis, University of Twente (2000)

Lewis, D.: 'Whether' Report', in his: Papers in Philosophical logic, pp. 45–56. Cambridge University Press, Cambridge (1982)

Mascarenhas, S.: Inquisitive Logic, MSc in Logic thesis, ILLC, University of Amsterdam (2008)

Ramsey, F.P.: General Propositions and Causality. In: Braithwaite, R.B. (ed.) The Foundations of Mathematics and other Logical Essays, pp. 237–255. Kegan Paul, Trench & Trubner, London (1931)

Roberts, C.: Information Structure in Discourse. In: Yoon, J.H., Kathol, A. (eds.) Working Papers in Linguistics, vol. 49, pp. 91–136. The Ohio State University (1996)

Velissaratou, S.: Conditional Questions and Which-Interrogatives, MSc in Logic thesis, ILLC, University of Amsterdam (2000)

Implicatures of Irrelevant Answers and the Principle of Optimal Completion

Anton Benz

Center for General Linguistics, Schützenstrasse 18, 10117 Berlin, Germany
benz@zas.gwz-berlin.de

Abstract. In this paper, we present a game–theoretic account of a sub-class of '*relevance*' implicatures arising from *irrelevant* answers. We show that these phenomena can be explained if we assume that interlocutors agree on production and interpretation strategies that are robust against small 'trembles' in the speaker's production strategy. In this context, we argue for a new pragmatic principle which we call the *principle of optimal completion*. We also show that our model provides a parallel account of scalar implicatures which removes some limitations of previous accounts.

Keywords: Implicatures, relevance, optimal completion, question answering, game theory.

1   Introduction

The pragmatic appropriateness of answers and their implicatures in decision contexts has been a major topic in the field of game–theoretic pragmatics, see, e.g., [6, 8, 9]. In [3], a uniform account was given for scalar and relevance implicatures arising in decision contexts. This account was based on the *optimal–answer* (OA) model [1]. In this paper, we address some open problems which arise in connection with apparently irrelevant answers. This will lead to a major revision and improvement of the OA framework. The crucial examples are derived from the classical *Out-of-Petrol* Example [4]:

(1) *H* is standing by an obviously immobilized car and is approached by *S*, after which the following exchange takes place:

    H: I am out of petrol.
    S: There is a garage round the corner. (*G*)
    +> The garage is open. (*I*)

In the OA approach, the implicature is explained by the presumed optimality of the answer *G*. If $\neg I$, the answer *G* would not be useful, hence the hearer can infer that *I*. This reasoning presupposes that the speaker knows that the pure propositional content of answer *G* will induce the hearer to go to the garage. In this paper, we are interested in examples where the analogous presupposition is not met, as in the following example:

P. Bosch, D. Gabelaia, and J. Lang (Eds.): TbiLLC 2007, LNAI 5422, pp. 95–109, 2009.

(2) An email was sent to all employees that bus tickets for a joint excursion have been bought and are ready to be picked up. By mistake, no contact person was named. Hence, H asks one of the secretaries:

H: Where can I get the bus tickets for the excursion?
S: Ms. Müller is sitting in office 2.07. (M)
$+>$ Bus tickets are available from Ms. Müller. (I)

In contrast to Example (1), it can not be assumed that the pure content of M will induce the inquirer to perform an optimal action. The difference between the answer G in (1) and M in (2) can be illustrated as follows: Assume in (1) that H finds a map with all petrol stations in town and notices that (G) *there is a garage round the corner*. This will be sufficient information to induce him to go to this garage. Now assume that, in (2), H finds a list with all office numbers of all employees, and reads there that (M) *Ms. Müller is sitting in office 2.07*. If there is no a priori link between M and Ms. Müller having bus tickets, i.e., if the two events are probabilistically independent, then what he reads will not induce H to go to office 2.07. For any reasonable definition of *relevance*, the answer M in (2) is *irrelevant* to the decision problem of H. It follows that the OA model, and the other mentioned models, cannot explain this example.

We will introduce a new pragmatic principle in order to explain the implicatures in examples like (2). We call it the *Principle of Optimal Completion*. The OA model tells us which answers a rational speaker can choose in accordance with his preferences and knowledge. Hence, if the speaker chooses a non–optimal answer, then either he is deviating from the pragmatic principles incorporated in the OA model or he is making a *mistake*. The core of our solution proceeds from the assumption that the hearer's interpretation strategy must be robust against small mistakes by the speaker. Being robust means that the hearer is able to repair these small mistakes and to *complete* under–informative sentences like M to sentences which would be optimal answers in the sense of the OA model.

In (2), we can assume that the optimal answer that S should have given is *Ms. Müller has the tickets. She is sitting in office 2.07* (F). The actual answer M is a part of F. If the speaker follows the best strategy, then the OA model predicts that he can not answer M. Seen from within the model, using M is a *mistake*. Hence, in accordance with our core idea, we have to say what it means that a hearer strategy is robust against speaker's strategies which mix choosing M and F. If there is no other possibly optimal form F' such that M could be completed to F', then the hearer is safe to interprete M as a short form of F. Along these lines, we show that, from the assumption that the hearer's strategy is robust against small mistakes, it follows that there is only one way to interpret M, namely, as meaning F. This entails that the speaker can take advantage and produce, by intention or not, less costly answers, including apparently irrelevant answers. Thus the example can be explained.

In order to turn this sketch into a theory, we first of all have to spell out what we mean by *small* mistake and by a strategy being *robust* against them. As already mentioned, we model question–answering situations by the OA model [1], which concentrates on the pragmatically relevant parameters of the more general signalling games [5]. We derive a concept of robust interpretation strategies by (a strong) modification of the game–theoretic notion of *trembling hand perfect* equilibria [10]. A strategy pair (s, h) is a trembling hand perfect equilibrium if each of the two strategies not only is a best response to the other one but also remains a best response if we add a small amount of noise to the other strategy. Our modification will refer i.a. to the kind of trembles that we allow.

The paper divides into two sections. In the first section, we introduce the OA model, which tells us how to calculate optimal answers and their implicatures. In the second section, we introduce the Principle of Optimal Completion. We will show that our model is able to handle scalar implicatures as well as the above mentioned relevance implicatures. In [3], the scalar implicature from *some* to *not all* can only be explained if *some but not all* has a higher a priori probability than *all*. The improved model will also predict the implicature in cases where *all* has the higher a priori probability.

2   The Optimal–Answer Model

It takes two for tango, and it takes two for a conversation. Conversation is characteristically a *cooperative effort* [4, p. 26]. Our contributions are not isolated sentences but normally subordinated to a joint purpose. In the Out-of-Petrol Example (1), the joint purpose is to solve the decision problem of where to go and look for petrol. In this paper, we will always assume that questioning and answering is embedded in a decision problem in which the inquirer has to make a choice between a given set of actions. His choice of action depends on his preferences regarding their outcomes and his knowledge about the world. The answer helps the inquirer in making his choice. The quality of an answer depends on the action to which it will lead. The answer is optimal if it induces the inquirer to choose an optimal action. We model answering situations as two–player games. We call the player who answers the *expert S*, and the player who receives the answer the *inquirer H*. In game theory, the behaviour of agents is represented by *strategies*, i.e., functions that select actions for each of their possible knowledge states. The expert's action will always be an answer, the inquirer's action may, e.g., be a decision about how to classify a a certain event, or, in the case of (1), where to look for petrol.

For Grice, the information communicated by an answer divides into two parts, the semantic meaning of the answer and its implicated meaning. In our definition of *implicature*, which we provide later, we closely follow Grice's original idea that implicatures arise from the additional information that an utterance provides about the state of the speaker:

> "... what is implicated is what it is required that one assume a speaker to think in order to preserve the assumption that he is observing the Co-operative Principle (and perhaps some conversational maxims as well), ..." [4, p. 86]

In a game–theoretic model, what the speaker utters is determined by his strategy s. If the inquirer receives answer F, then he knows that the expert must have been in a state K which is an element of $s^{-1}(F) = \{K \mid s(K) = F\}$, i.e., the set of all states which are mapped to F by s. Lewis [5, p. 144] calls this the *indicated* meaning of a signal F. We identify the implicature of an utterance with this indicated information. This identification implies that, once we know s, the implicatures can be calculated. Hence, all depends on how we can know the speaker's strategy s. This knowledge will be provided by the Optimal–Answer (OA) Model and its later modifications.

2.1   Optimal Answers

The OA model tells us which answer a rational language user will choose given the inquirer's decision problem and his own knowledge about the world. Instead of introducing full signalling games [5], we reduce our models to the cognitively relevant parameters of an answering situation. We call these simplified models *support problems*. They consist of the inquirer's decision problem and the answering expert's expectations about the world. They incorporate the *Cooperative Principle*, the maxim of *Quality*, and a method for finding optimal strategies which replaces the maxims of *Quantity* and *Relevance*. In this section, we ignore the maxim of *Manner*.

A decision problem consists of a set Ω of the possible states of the world, the decision maker's expectations about the world, a set of actions $\mathcal{A}$ he can choose from, and his preferences regarding their outcomes. We always assume that Ω is finite. We represent an agent's expectations about the world by a probability distribution over Ω, i.e., a real–valued function $P : \Omega \to \mathbb{R}$ with the following properties: (1) $P(v) \geq 0$ for all $v \in \Omega$ and (2) $\sum_{v \in \Omega} P(v) = 1$. For sets $A \subseteq \Omega$ we set $P(A) = \sum_{v \in A} P(v)$. The pair (Ω, P) is called a finite *probability space*. An agent's preferences regarding outcomes of actions are represented by a real–valued function over action–world pairs. We collect these elements in the following structure:

Definition 1. *A* decision problem *is a triple* $\langle (\Omega, P), \mathcal{A}, u \rangle$ *such that* (Ω, P) *is a finite probability space,* $\mathcal{A}$ *a finite, non–empty set and* $u : \mathcal{A} \times \Omega \to \mathbb{R}$ *a function.* $\mathcal{A}$ *is called the* action *set, and its elements* actions; u *is called a* payoff *or* utility *function.*

In the following, a decision problem $\langle (\Omega, P), \mathcal{A}, u \rangle$ represents the inquirer's situation before receiving information from an answering expert. We will assume that this problem is common knowledge. How to find a solution to a decision problem? It is standard to assume that rational agents try to maximise their expected utilities. The *expected utility* of an action a is defined by:

$$EU(a) = \sum_{v \in \Omega} P(v) \times u(a, v). \tag{2.1}$$

The expected utility of actions may change if the decision maker learns new information. To determine this change of expected utility, we first have to know how learning new information affects the inquirer's beliefs. In probability theory the result of learning a proposition A is modelled by *conditional probabilities*. Let H be any proposition and A the newly learned proposition. Then, the probability of H *given* A, written $P(H|A)$, is defined as $P(H|A) := P(H \cap A)/P(A)$ for $P(A) \neq 0$. In terms of this conditional probability function, the *expected utility after learning* A is defined as $EU(a|A) = \sum_{v \in \Omega} P(v|A) \times u(a, v)$. H will choose the action which maximises his expected utilities after learning A, i.e., he will only choose actions a where $EU(a|A)$ is maximal. We assume that H's decision does not depend on what he believes that the answering expert believes. We denote the set of actions with maximal expected utility by $\mathcal{B}(A)$, i.e.:

$$\mathcal{B}(A) := \{a \in \mathcal{A} \mid \forall b \in \mathcal{A} \ EU_H(b|A) \leq EU_H(a|A)\}. \tag{2.2}$$

The decision problem represents the inquirer's situation. In order to get a model of the questioning and answering situation, we have to add a representation of the answering expert's information state. We identify it with a probability distribution P_S that represents his expectations about the world:

Definition 2. *A five–tuple $\sigma = \langle \Omega, P_S, P_H, \mathcal{A}, u \rangle$ is a support problem if (Ω, P_S) is a finite probability space and $D_\sigma = \langle (\Omega, P_H), \mathcal{A}, u \rangle$ a decision problem such that:*

$$\forall X \subseteq \Omega \ P_S(X) = P_H(X|K) \ \text{for} \ K = \{v \in \Omega \mid P_S(v) > 0\}. \tag{2.3}$$

Condition (2.3) implies that the expert's beliefs cannot contradict the inquirer's expectations, i.e., for $A, B \subseteq \Omega$: $P_S(A) = 1 \Rightarrow P_H(A) > 0$.

The expert S's task is to provide information that is optimally suited to support H in his decision problem. Hence, we find two successive decision problems, in which the first problem is S's problem to choose an answers. The utility of the answer depends on how it influences H's final choice:

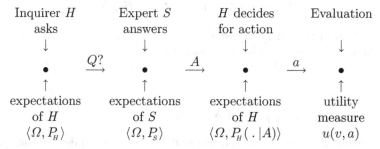

Inquirer H asks		Expert S answers		H decides for action		Evaluation
$\downarrow$		$\downarrow$		$\downarrow$		$\downarrow$
$\bullet$	$\xrightarrow{Q?}$	$\bullet$	$\xrightarrow{A}$	$\bullet$	$\xrightarrow{a}$	$\bullet$
$\uparrow$		$\uparrow$		$\uparrow$		$\uparrow$
expectations of H		expectations of S		expectations of H		utility measure
$\langle \Omega, P_H \rangle$		$\langle \Omega, P_S \rangle$		$\langle \Omega, P_H(\,.\,|A) \rangle$		$u(v, a)$

We assume that S is fully cooperative and wants to maximise H's final success; i.e., S's payoff, is identical with H's. This is our representation of Grice's *Cooperative Principle*. S has to choose an answer that induces H to choose an action that maximises their common payoff. In general, there may exist several equally optimal actions $a \in \mathcal{B}(A)$ which H may choose. Hence, the expected utility of an answer depends on the probability with which H will choose the different actions. We can assume that this probability is given by a probability measure $h(.|A)$ on $\mathcal{A}$. If h is known, the expected utility of an answer A is defined by $EU_s(A) := \sum_{a \in \mathcal{B}(A)} h(a|A) \times EU_s(a)$.

We add here a further Gricean maxim, the maxim of *Quality*. We call an answer A *admissible* if $P_s(A) = 1$, i.e., if S believes A to be *true*. The maxim of Quality is represented by the assumption that the expert S does only give admissible answers. For a support problem $\sigma = \langle \Omega, P_s, P_H, \mathcal{A}, u \rangle$ we set $Adm_\sigma := \{A \subseteq \Omega \mid P_s(A) = 1\}$. Hence, the set of optimal answers in σ is given by:

$$Op_\sigma := \{A \in Adm_\sigma \mid \forall B \in Adm_\sigma \; EU_S(B) \le EU_S(A)\}. \qquad (2.4)$$

We write Op_σ^h if we want to make the dependency of Op on h explicit. In general, the solution to a support problem is not uniquely defined. Therefore, we introduce the notion of the *canonical* solution to a support problem.

Definition 3. *Let* $\sigma = \langle \Omega, P_s, P_H, \mathcal{A}, u \rangle$ *be a support problem. A* (mixed) strategy pair *for* σ *is a pair* (s, h) *such that* s *is a probability distribution over* $\mathcal{P}(\Omega)$ *and* h *a family of probability distributions* $h(.|A)$ *over* $\mathcal{A}$. *The* canonical solution *to* σ *is a pair* (S, H) *of mixed strategies which satisfy:*

$$S(A) = \begin{cases} |Op_\sigma|^{-1}, & A \in Op_\sigma \\ 0 & otherwise \end{cases} , \quad H(a|A) = \begin{cases} |\mathcal{B}(A)|^{-1}, & a \in \mathcal{B}(A) \\ 0 & otherwise \end{cases} . \qquad (2.5)$$

We write $S(\,.\,|\sigma)$ if S is the function that maps each $\sigma \in \mathcal{S}$ to the speaker's canonical strategy, and $H(\,.\,|D_\sigma)$ if H is the function that maps the associated decision problem D_σ to the hearer's canonical strategy.

The expert may always answer everything he knows, i.e., he may answer $K := \{v \in \Omega \mid P_s(v) > 0\}$. From condition (2.3) it trivially follows that $\mathcal{B}(K) = \{a \in \mathcal{A} \mid \forall b \in \mathcal{A} \; EU_s(b) \le EU_s(a)\}$. If expert and inquirer follow the canonical solution, then it is easy to see that:

$$Op_\sigma = \{A \in Adm_\sigma \mid \mathcal{B}(A) \subseteq \mathcal{B}(K)\}; \qquad (2.6)$$

We can call an answer A *misleading* if $\mathcal{B}(A) \not\subseteq \mathcal{B}(K)$; hence, (2.6) implies that Op_σ is the set of all non–misleading answers.

From now on, we will always assume that speaker and hearer follow the canonical solution.

2.2   Implicatures of Optimal Answers

An implicature of an utterance is a proposition which is implied by the assumption that the speaker is cooperative and observes the conversational maxims. More precisely, Grice linked implicatures to what the hearer learns from the utterance about the speaker's knowledge. The speaker's canonical solution maps his possible information states to utterances. Hence, the hearer can use this strategy to calculate what the speaker must have known when making his utterance. As the canonical solution is a solution, it also incorporates the information that the speaker is cooperative and follows the maxims.

We treat all implicatures as particularised implicatures, i.e., as implicatures that follow immediately from the maxims and the particular circumstances of the utterance context. The answering expert knows a proposition I in a situation σ iff $P_S^\sigma(I) = 1$. Hence, if the inquirer wants to know what the speaker knew when answering that A, he can check all his epistemically possible support problems for what the speaker believes. If σ is the support problem which represents the actual answering situation, then all support problems $\hat{\sigma}$ with the same decision problem D_σ are indiscernible for the inquirer. Hence, the inquirer knows that the speaker believed that I when making his utterance A, iff the speaker believes that I in all support problems which are indiscernible and in which A is an optimal answer. This leads to the following definition:

Definition 4 (Implicature). *Let S be a set of support problems and $\sigma \in S$. Let $A, I \subseteq \Omega$ be two propositions with $A \in \mathrm{Op}_\sigma$. Then we set:*

$$A +> I \Leftrightarrow \forall \hat{\sigma} \in [\sigma]_S \, (A \in \mathrm{Op}_{\hat{\sigma}} \rightarrow P_S^{\hat{\sigma}}(I) = 1), \tag{2.7}$$

with $[\sigma]_S := \{\hat{\sigma} \in S \mid D_\sigma = D_{\hat{\sigma}}\}$. If $A +> I$, then we say that the utterance of A implicates that I in σ.

As the hearer has to check all support problems in $[\sigma]_S$, it follows that we find the more implicatures the smaller S is. We are especially interested in cases in which the speaker is a real expert. Let $O(a)$ be the set of all worlds in which a is an optimal action:

$$O(a) := \{w \in \Omega \mid \forall b \in A \, u(w, a) \geq u(w, b)\}. \tag{2.8}$$

Then, we can say that the answering person is a real expert for a decision problem if he knows an action that is best in all possible worlds. We represent this information in S and arrive at the following criterion for implicatures:

Proposition 5. *Let S be a set of support problems such that $\forall \sigma \in S \, \exists a \in A \, P_S^\sigma(O(a)) = 1$. Let $\sigma \in S$ and $A, I \subseteq \Omega$ be two propositions with $A \in \mathrm{Op}_\sigma$. Then, with $A^* := \{v \in \Omega \mid P_H(v) > 0\}$, it holds that:*

$$A +> I \text{ iff } \bigcap_{a \in \mathcal{B}(A)} O(a) \cap A^* \subseteq I. \tag{2.9}$$

For a proof see [2]. We use this criterion in the following examples.

2.3   Examples

We consider three examples: the Out–of–Petrol example, the Bus Ticket example, and scalar implicatures. For more examples, we refer to [3]. We start with the Out–of–Petrol example (1). We distinguish three worlds $\{w_1, w_2, w_3\}$ and two actions $\{\text{go-to-g}, \text{search}\}$. G is the answer "*There is a garage round the corner,*" and I the implicature "*The garage is open.*" The utilities and worlds are defined by the following table:

Ω	G	I	go-to-g	search
w_1	$+$	$+$	1	ε
w_2	$+$	$-$	0	ε
w_3	$-$	$-$	0	ε

The expert knows that he is in w_1. We assume that P_H and ε are such that $EU_H(\text{go-to-g}|G) > \varepsilon$, i.e., the inquirer thinks that the expected utility of going to that garage is higher than doing a random search in the town. Hence $\mathcal{B}(G) = \{\text{go-to-g}\}$. We see that $O(\text{go-to-g}) = \{w_1\} = I$. Hence, by Lem. 5, it follows that $G +> I$.

Now, we compare this situation with the slightly different Bus Ticket example (2). The possible worlds in Ω differ according to whom the tickets can be picked up from, and according to the office number of this person. To simplify the model, we only consider four worlds and two actions. In the following table I stands for '*Bus tickets are available from Ms. Müller*', M for '*Ms. Müller is sitting in office 2.07*'. We assume that there are exactly two staff from whom bus tickets may be available, Ms. Müller and Mr. Schmidt, and that they are available from Ms. Müller iff they are not available from Mr. Schmidt. Furthermore, we assume that either staff is sitting in office 2.07 or 3.11, and that the one is sitting in office 2.07 iff the other one is sitting in 3.11. We assume that all possibilities are equally probable:

Ω	I	M	go-to-2.07	go-to-3.11
w_1	+	+	1	0
w_2	+	−	0	1
w_3	−	+	0	1
w_4	−	−	1	0

The expected utility of either action before learning anything is $\frac{1}{2}$, and after learning M the expected utilities still are $\frac{1}{2}$. Especially, if S knows that w_1, then M is not an optimal answer, and no implicatures are defined for it.

As a third example, we consider scalar implicatures. In (3), it has to be explained why $F_\exists$ implicates that not $F_\forall$:

(3) a) All of the boys came to the party. ($F_\forall$)
     b) Some of the boys came to the party. ($F_\exists$)

We assume that Ω contains three worlds w_1, w_2, w_3. In w_1 all boys came, in w_2 some but not all, and in w_3 none came. The hearer's task is to find out what the actual world is. We only distinguish between success and failure. Hence we can identify the hearer's actions with the worlds w_i, and the expected utility of choosing w_i after learning proposition X with $P_H(w_i|X)$. If the hearer learns that $F_\exists$ and if $P_H(w_2) > P_H(w_1)$, then the set $\mathcal{B}(F_\exists)$ of optimal responses to $F_\exists$ is $\{w_2\}$. As $\{w_2\} \subseteq F_\exists \setminus F_\forall$, it follows with Lem. 5 that $F_\exists +> \neg F_\forall$. But if $P_H(w_2) < P_H(w_1)$, then it would follow that $F_\exists +> F_\forall$, which is contra-intuitive. We will see, that the Principle of Optimal Completion will make the implicature $F_\exists +> \neg F_\forall$ independent of the hearer's expectations P_H.

3   The Principle of Optimal Completion

As mentioned in the introduction, we introduce a new pragmatic principle in order to explain examples like (2). This principle is motivated by the assumption that hearer's interpretation strategies must be robust against small mistakes by the speaker. In this context, we call any utterance a *mistake* if it is not predicted by the OA model. Obviously, it would not be reasonable to assume that the hearer can repair *any* mistake by the speaker. We only consider mistakes which consist in the production of *incomplete* utterances. An utterance is incomplete if the speaker had an optimal proposition in mind but only asserted a part of it. It is then left to the addressees to infer the full proposition, i.e., to complete the utterance to an optimal answer.

The general explanation of implicatures remains unchanged. We will especially not alter condition (2.7) in the previous definition of implicatures. The effect of optimal completion is a shift from the canonical hearer strategy H to a robust strategy $\bar{H}$, which in turn changes the set of optimal answers from which the speaker can make his choice. Hence, the shift from H to $\bar{H}$ will also lead to a shift from the canonical strategy S to a new speaker strategy $\bar{S}$. Implicatures are then calculated by using condition (2.7) relative to $(\bar{S}, \bar{H})$.

3.1   Optimal Completion and Efficient Clarification Requests

In the following, we need representations of answering situations which include explicit representations of linguistic forms and their meanings. We denote the set of forms by $\mathcal{F}$, and assume that there is a fixed semantic interpretation function $[\![\,.\,]\!]$ which maps forms F to propositions. Furthermore, we add a function $c : \mathcal{F} \to \mathbb{R}^+ \setminus \{0\}$ that measures the costs of producing forms. We call a tuple $\langle \Omega, P_s, P_H, \mathcal{F}, \mathcal{A}, u, c, [\![\,.\,]\!] \rangle$ an *interpreted support problem with nominal costs* if $\langle \Omega, P_s, P_H, \mathcal{A}, u \rangle$ is a support problem which satisfies for all $F, H \in \mathcal{F}$: $EU_S([\![F]\!]) < EU_S([\![H]\!]) \Rightarrow EU_S([\![F]\!]) < EU_S([\![H]\!]) - c(H)$. That the costs of forms are *nominal* means that they are positive but very small, so small that they are always smaller than the positive differences of the expected utilities of the propositions expressed. This ensures that the answering expert will always choose an answer which expresses an optimal proposition.

Before introducing optimal completion, we make an addition to the basic optimal answer model which is crucial if optimal completion should not only explain implicatures of irrelevant answers but should also explain the scalar implicatures in (3). Let us consider an example similar to (2). Assume that a bike messenger H approaches the secretary S with a parcel and asks where to deliver it, and the secretary answers thereupon: *'It is for Ms. Müller.'* This information will not be sufficient if there are many offices and H doesn't know the building. The natural response of the messenger is a clarification request

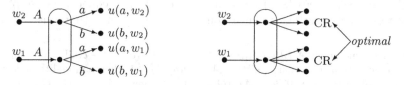

Fig. 1. Left: Without CR risky choice between a and b

CR asking for the office of Ms. Müller. The request CR will lead to an answer which allows H to choose an optimal action a afterwards. In order to capture this possibility, we will add what we call an *efficient clarification request* CR to the hearer's action set. *Efficient* means here that its costs are nominal and its payoff high.[1] This has dramatic effects on the previous models due to backward induction. In a situation in which the speaker gives an answer $A = \{w_1, w_2\}$ which does not determine a unique optimal action, see Figure 1, the hearer has to make a risky choice. The existence of efficient clarification requests means that the hearer will always avoid this decision. Our previous models implicitly assumed that making clarification requests is not an option. If the hearer makes a clarification request, the answering expert has to produce an extra utterance. This leads to production costs which are higher than the cost of immediately producing an optimal answer. Hence, the speaker has an incentive to preempt the possibility of clarification requests. We show the effects on the basic OA model in our discussion of examples in Section 3.3.

Our definition of Implicatures in (2.7) implies that only optimal answers can have implicatures. As the definition of *optimal answer* depends on the hearer's strategy H, a change from the canonical strategy H to a robust strategy $\bar{H}$ will also change the set of utterances for which implicatures are predicted. If the speaker utters E, and E is a proper part of an optimal answer F, then the principle of optimal completion says that the hearer will complete E to F, i.e., interpret utterance E as an indicator of the speaker's intention to utter F. Let us write $E \lhd F$ for *utterance E is a proper part of F*. We assume that $\lhd$ is an undefined, primitive relation. There are obvious constraints that must be satisfied if the success of the principle of optimal completion is to be guaranteed. The triggering of the completion process must be unambiguous. This entails that the incomplete utterance must not be an optimal answer itself. For example, $E =$ '*all of the boys*' is a sub-form of $F =$ '*almost all of the boys,*' but an utterance of E should not trigger a completion to F. Furthermore, there must only be one optimal proposition to which the utterance can be completed. For example, in (2) there are many answers of which "*Ms. Müller is sitting in office 2.07*" is a sub–form. Not only "*Ms. Müller has the tickets. She is sitting in office 2.07*" but also, e.g., of "*I don't know. Last time it was Ms. Müller who had the bus tickets. She is sitting in office 2.07.*" But these answers are optimal in different contexts. If it is common knowledge that the speaker knows the actual state of the world, then the last answer is ruled out as non-optimal.

The concept that guides our game–theoretic interpretation of the principle of optimal completion is the *trembling hand perfect* equilibrium, e.g., [7, Def. 248.1]. In the context of support problems, a trembling hand prefect equilibrium is a pair of mixed strategies (s, h) such that there exists a sequence $(s^k, h^k)_{k=0}^{\infty}$ of completely mixed strategies which converge to (s, h) such that s is a best

---

[1] This means that for all A $EU_H(\mathrm{CR}|A) = \sum_w P_H(w|A)u(a_w, w) - c(\mathrm{CR})$ with $a_w \in \{a \mid \forall b\, u(a, w) \geq u(b, w)\}$. Hence, if $\forall a \in A\, P_H(O(a)|A) < 1$, then nominality of costs entails that $\mathcal{B}(A) = \{\mathrm{CR}\}$. If $\exists a \in A\, P_H(O(a)|A) = 1$, then $\mathcal{B}(A) = \{a \mid P_H(O(a)|A) = 1\}$ and $O(\mathrm{CR}) = \emptyset$ because $P_H(O(a)|A) = 1 \Rightarrow EU_H(\mathrm{CR}|A) = EU_H(a|A) - c(\mathrm{CR})$.

responses to each h^k and h to each s^k. A strategy is *completely mixed* if it chooses every possible action with positive probability. That (s, h) is robust against *small* mistakes is captured by the condition that s and h need only to be best responses if h^k and s^k come close to h and s.

The criterion of trembling hand perfection asks of strategies to be robust against all kind of mistakes. We are interested in this robustness as an ability to repair mistakes which result from the production of sub–parts of optimal utterances. Hence, we will restrict *trembles* to sub-forms of optimal forms. We take into account the effect of clarification requests in the definition of *unique optimal completability* in Def. 7. There, we implicitly assume that the inquirer reacts to an ambiguous answer with a clarification request.

3.2   The Game–Theoretic Model

We first define what it means that a form E is optimally completable to a form F. First, E must be a sub-form of F, both must be admissible, i.e., $P_s^\sigma([\![E]\!]) = P_s^\sigma([\![F]\!]) = 1$, and only F must be optimal. Furthermore, F has to be a minimal optimal form to which E can be completed. *Minimality* is here meant relative to a primitive sub–form relation $\lhd$. In the following definition, we denote by $\min_\lhd M$ the $\lhd$–minimal elements of M.

Definition 6 (Optimal Completion). *We say that, for a support problem σ, a form E can be* optimally completed *to form F, $oc(\sigma, E, F)$, iff $E \in Adm_\sigma \setminus Op_\sigma$ and $F \in \min_\lhd \{F \in Op_\sigma \mid E \lhd F\}$.*

This does not yet include the uniqueness condition. As the hearer does not know the support problem σ but only his decision problem D_σ, it must be excluded that E can be optimally completed to several different forms in support problems with the same associated decision problem D_σ.

Definition 7 (Unique Optimal Completion). *Let S be a given set of support problems with a joint decision problem. We say that E can be* uniquely optimally completed *to F, $uoc(E, F)$, if (1) $\exists \sigma \in S \ oc(\sigma, E, F)$ and (2) for all $\sigma' \in S$: $E \notin Op_{\sigma'} \land \forall F' \in \mathcal{F}(oc(\sigma', E, F')) \Rightarrow F = F')$.*

The uniqueness condition guarantees that the optimal super-form is recoverable from the non-optimal sub-form. As explained before, we only consider speaker's mistakes that are restricted to sub-forms which can be uniquely completed to optimal forms. Inspired by trembling hand perfection, we represent the possibility of speaker's mistakes by noisy strategies s^ϵ which approximate the canonical strategy s. If F is an optimal form for σ, and if the set of uniquely optimally completable sub–forms of F is not empty, then a speaker who follows s^ϵ will choose one of these sub–forms with probability ϵ. If F doesn't have such sub–forms, then the probability of choosing F is the same for s^ϵ and s.

Definition 8. *Let S be a given set of support problems with a joint decision problem. Let $\sigma \in S$, $F \in Op_\sigma$, and n the cardinality of $\{E' \in \mathcal{F} \mid uoc(E', F)\}$. An* epsilon sub-form approximation *of a mixed speaker strategy $s(.|\sigma)$ is a probability* *distribution* $s^\epsilon(\, . \,|\sigma)$ *on* $\mathcal{F}$ *such that (1) if* $n = 0$, *then* $s^\epsilon(F|\sigma) = s(F|\sigma)$, *and* (2) *if* $n > 0$ *and if* E *is such that* $uoc(E, F)$, *we set:*

1. $s^\epsilon(F|\sigma) = (1 - \epsilon)s(F|\sigma)$,
2. $s^\epsilon(E|\sigma) = \epsilon \, n^{-1} \, s(F|\sigma)$,

For all other forms E, $s^\epsilon(E|\sigma) = 0$.

Hence, $s^\epsilon(E|\sigma) > 0$ iff $E \in \mathrm{Op}_\sigma \vee \exists F \in \mathrm{Op}_\sigma \, uoc(E, F)$. Due to the uniqueness condition, the hearer's best response $\bar{H}$ to these noisy speaker strategies can easily be found. We call it the *sub-form extension* of the canonical solution H:

Definition 9. *Let* $\mathcal{S}$ *be a given set of support problems with a joint decision problem* $\langle(\Omega, P_H), \mathcal{A}, u\rangle$. *Let* (S, H) *be the canonical solution to* $\sigma \in \mathcal{S}$. *Then, the sub-form extension* $\bar{H}$ *of* H *is defined as follows:*

1. *If* $F \in \bigcup_{\sigma \in \mathcal{S}} \mathrm{Op}_\sigma$, *then* $\bar{H}(a|F) = H(a|F)$.
2. *If* E, F *are such that* $uoc(E, F)$, *then* $\bar{H}(a|E) = H(a|F)$.

To all forms E *for which there is no* $F \in \bigcup_\sigma \mathrm{Op}_\sigma$ *such that* $E = F$ *or* $uoc(E, F)$, *we assume that the hearer reacts with a clarification request.*

The following lemma shows that the sub-form extension $\bar{H}$ provides a choice of action for all answers which the speaker may choose with positive probability, and that all the choices are optimal. This holds for the ϵ sub-form approximations s^ϵ, as well as for the canonical strategy s itself.

Proposition 10. *Let* $\mathcal{S}$ *be a given set of support problems with a joint decision problem* $\langle(\Omega, P_H), \mathcal{A}, u\rangle$. *Let* (S, H) *be the canonical solution to* $\mathcal{S}$ *and* $\bar{H}$ *the sub-form extension of* H. *For* $\sigma \in \mathcal{S}$ *let* $K_\sigma := \{v \in \Omega \mid P^\sigma_S(v) > 0\}$. *Then, it holds for all* ϵ *and all forms* E *with* $s^\epsilon(E|\sigma) > 0$ *that (1)* $\exists a \in \mathcal{A} \, \bar{H}(a|E) > 0$, *and (2)* $\forall a \in \mathcal{A} \, (\bar{H}(a|E) > 0 \Rightarrow a \in \mathcal{B}(K_\sigma))$.

Proof: The first proposition holds by definition of $\bar{H}$. Let $\sigma \in \mathcal{S}$. Let $\bar{H}(a|E) > 0$ and $s^\epsilon(E|\sigma) > 0$. Then, $E \in \mathrm{Op}^H_\sigma$ or there exists $F \in \mathrm{Op}^H_\sigma$ such that $uoc(E, F)$. If $E \in \mathrm{Op}^H_\sigma$, then $\bar{H}(a|E) = H(a|E)$, hence $a \in \mathcal{B}(K_\sigma)$ by (2.5) and (2.6). If there exists $F \in \mathrm{Op}_\sigma$ such that $uoc(E, F)$, then $\bar{H}(a|E) = H(a|F)$, therefore again $\bar{H}(a|E) > 0 \Rightarrow a \in \mathcal{B}(K_\sigma)$.   ∎

As $s^\epsilon(E|\sigma) > 0$ iff $E \in \mathcal{F}_\sigma = \{E \mid \exists F \in \mathrm{Op}_\sigma(E = F \vee uoc(E, F))\}$, it follows that $s^\epsilon(E|\sigma) > 0$ implies that E is a non-misleading answer, see (2.6), hence, the speaker can optimise his strategy by choosing answers from $\mathcal{F}_\sigma$ which have minimal costs. If we assume that the speaker prefers forms which are minimal relative to the sub-form relation $\lhd$, then the set of speaker–optimal answers relative to $\bar{H}$ is the set of $\lhd$-minimal elements of $\mathcal{F}_\sigma$, which we denote by $\mathrm{Op}^{\bar{H}}_\sigma$. Let $\bar{S}$ be the speaker strategy which chooses the elements of $\mathrm{Op}^{\bar{H}}_\sigma$ with equal probability. We call it the *sub-form extension* of the canonical strategy S. Disregarding nominal costs of forms, it is clear by construction that $(\bar{S}, \bar{H})$ and all $(s^\epsilon, \bar{H})$ are (weakly) dominating all other solutions.

With these preparations, we now can represent the *Principle of Optimal Completion*. It just means that speaker and hearer follow the sub-form extension $(\bar{S}, \bar{H})$ of the canonical solution (S, H). The definition of implicatures remains unchanged. If $\mathcal{S}$ is a set of interpreted support problems with a common decision problem, then, by adjusting (2.7) to $(\bar{S}, \bar{H})$, we arrive at:

$$A +> I \Leftrightarrow \forall \sigma \in \mathcal{S} \, (A \in \mathrm{Op}_\sigma^{\bar{H}} \Rightarrow P_S^\sigma(I) = 1). \tag{3.10}$$

3.3 Examples

We again consider the examples from Section 2.3 and provide models that explain their implicatures using the principle of optimal completion. We start with the standard scalar implicatures:

(4) a) All of the boys came to the party. ($F_\forall$)
  b) Some of the boys came to the party. ($F_\exists$)
    +> Some but not all of the boys came to the party. ($F_{\exists \neg \forall}$)

As in our discussion of Example 3, we assume that Ω contains two worlds w_1, w_2. In w_1, all boys came, and in w_2 some but not all. Here, and in the following examples, we assume that $P_H(w_i) > 0$ for $i = 1, 2$. The hearer's task is to find out what the actual world is. We again only distinguish between success and failure and identify the hearer's actions with the worlds w_i. Hence, the expected utility of choosing w_i after learning proposition X is $P_H(w_i|X)$. Let the hearer's decision problem $\langle (\Omega, P_H), \mathcal{A}, u \rangle$ be any decision problem that satisfies these conditions.

We saw in Section 2.3 that $P_H(w_2) \leq P_H(w_1)$ entails that $F_\exists$ does not implicate $F_{\exists \neg \forall}$. We show now that the principle of optimal completion implies that the implicature becomes independent of $P_H(w_1)$. For this, we have to assume common knowledge of the fact that the answering expert S knows the actual world w_i. We encode common knowledge in the background set $\mathcal{S}$ of possible support problems. Therefore, we assume that $\mathcal{S}$ contains exactly two support problems σ_1 and σ_2 with $P_S^{\sigma_i}(w_i) = 1$. For defining the full interpreted support problems $\langle \Omega, P_s, P_H, \mathcal{F}, \mathcal{A}, u, c, [\![\, . \,]\!] \rangle$, it remains to define the speaker's set of forms $\mathcal{F}$, their meanings and the cost function. Let $\mathcal{F} = \{F_\forall, F_{\exists \neg \forall}, F_\exists\}$ and $[\![F_\forall]\!] = \{w_1\}$, $[\![F_{\exists \neg \forall}]\!] = \{w_2\}$, and $[\![F_\exists]\!] = \{w_1, w_2\}$. We assume that the costs reflect the sub-form relation $\lhd = \{\langle F_\exists, F_{\exists \neg \forall} \rangle\}$. The following tables show the optimal answers for i) $P_H(w_1) < P_H(w_2)$, ii) $P_H(w_1) = P_H(w_2)$, and iii) $P_H(w_1) > P_H(w_2)$. Op_{σ_i} is the set of optimal answers which we derive from the basic OA model in Section 2.1; $\mathrm{Op}_{\sigma_i}^+$ is the set of optimal answer which we get if we add efficient clarification requests to the model; and $\mathrm{Op}_{\sigma_i}^{++}$ shows the effect of optimal completion. As $\mathrm{Op}_{\sigma_i}^+$ and $\mathrm{Op}_{\sigma_i}^{++}$ are identical for all three cases, we depict them only once.

i) σ_i	Op_σ	$\mathrm{Op}_{\sigma_i}^+$	$\mathrm{Op}_{\sigma_i}^{++}$	ii) σ_i	Op_σ	iii) σ_i	Op_σ
w_1	$\{F_\forall\}$	$\{F_\forall\}$	$\{F_\forall\}$	w_1	$\{F_\forall\}$	w_1	$\{F_\forall, F_\exists\}$
w_2	$\{F_\exists, F_{\exists \neg \forall}\}$	$\{F_{\exists \neg \forall}\}$	$\{F_\exists\}$	w_2	$\{F_{\exists \neg \forall}\}$	w_2	$\{F_{\exists \neg \forall}\}$

In case i), $F_{\exists \neg \forall}$ is in Op_σ only if we ignore the speaker's preferences for short forms. If we include them, then only $F_\exists$ is optimal. In both cases, however,

$F_\exists \in Op_\sigma$, as we have seen in Section 2.3. But this holds only if efficient clarification requests are not available as by assumption $EU_H(w_i|\llbracket F_\exists \rrbracket) = P_H(w_i) < 1 - c(\text{CR}) = EU_H(\text{CR}|\llbracket F_\exists \rrbracket)$. Hence, only $F_{\exists\neg\forall}$ is optimal once we take efficient clarification requests into account. Their availability results in the same optimal answers Op_σ^+ in all three cases i)–iii). Clearly, in all cases, $F_\exists \in Adm_{\sigma_2} \setminus Op_{\sigma_2}^+$, $F_\exists \lhd F_{\exists\neg\forall}$, and for all $i \neq 2$: $F_\exists \notin Op_{\sigma_i}^+$ and $\neg\exists F' \in Op_{\sigma_i}^+ \, oc(\sigma_i, F_\exists, F')$. Hence, the uniqueness conditions, Def. 7, are satisfied, therefore $uoc(F_\exists, F_{\exists\neg\forall})$. By definition, it follows that $\bar{H}(w_i|F_\exists) = \bar{H}(w_i|F_{\exists\neg\forall})$. Hence, the addressee will choose w_2 after receiving $F_\exists$ which shows that $F_\exists \in Op_\sigma^{++}$. By definition of $\bar{S}$, $\bar{S}(F_\exists|\sigma_2) = S(F_{\exists\neg\forall}|\sigma_2) = 1$. As $\bar{S}(F_\exists|\sigma_1) = S(F_\exists|\sigma_1) = 0$, it follows that $\bar{S}(F_\exists|\sigma_i) > 0 \Rightarrow P_S^{\sigma_i}(w_2) = 1$. Hence, $F_\exists$ implicates that not all boys came to the party.

We now turn to the Bus Ticket example (2). We consider the same model as in Section 2.3 where we assumed that there are exactly two staff from whom bus tickets may be available, Ms. Müller and Mr. Schmidt, that they are available from Ms. Müller iff they are not available from Mr. Schmidt, and that one of them is sitting in office 2.07 iff the other one is sitting in 3.11. With the sentence frames $A(i, n) = $ 'i is sitting in office n,' and $B(i) = $ 'Bus tickets are available from i', we can describe the speaker's set of forms $\mathcal{F}$ from which he can choose as the set of sentences of the form $B(i)$, $A(i, n)$, or $B(i) \wedge A(i, n)$, with their meaning defined in the usual way. With $i = 0$ for Ms. Müller, and $i = 1$ for Mr. Schmidt, the possible worlds and payoffs can be read off from the first columns of the following table.

Ω	$B(0)$	$A(0, 2.07)$	go-to-2.07	go-to-3.11	$Op_{w_j} \; (= Op_{w_j}^+)$
w_1	$+$	$+$	1	0	$B(0) \wedge A(0, 2.07)$
w_2	$+$	$-$	0	1	$B(0) \wedge A(0, 3.11)$
w_3	$-$	$+$	0	1	$B(1) \wedge A(1, 3.11)$
w_4	$-$	$-$	1	0	$B(1) \wedge A(1, 2.07)$

The sub-form relation $\lhd$ is defined in the obvious way. Again, we have to assume that the answering expert knows the actual state of the world. In the scenario of (2), w_1 is the actual world. The optimal answers can be seen in the last column of the table.

$M := A(0, 2.07)$ is a sub-form of the optimal answer $B(0) \wedge A(0, 2.07) =: I \wedge M$. In w_1, S believes both to be true, and there is no other world w_j where these conditions are satisfied for M. This means that $uoc(M, I \wedge M)$. It follows with Def. 9 that $\bar{H}(\text{go-to-2.07}|M) = 1$ and that $M \in Op_{\sigma_i}^{\bar{H}}$ implies $i = 1$ and $P_S^{\sigma_i}(I) = 1$. Hence, by (3.10), $M +> I$. This proves the claim.

Finally, we turn to the *Out-of-petrol* example (1) and reconsider the model of Section 2.3. If we add efficient clarification requests to the model, then answer G is not optimal any more. To see this, we have to add some more detail to the model. We assume that there are two garages g_1 and g_2, and define Ω, actions, and propositions as in the table below. Let's assume that G_1 corresponds to the assertion "*There is a garage round the corner to the left,*" and G_2 to "*There is a garage round the corner to the right.*" In (1), it is implicitly assumed that it is common knowledge that the speaker knows the actual world. With this assumption, it follows from $EU_H(\text{go-to-g}_i|G_i) = P_H(G_i \wedge I_i) < 1 - c(\text{CR}) = EU_H(\text{CR}|G_i)$ that $G_i \notin \text{Op}^+_{w_j}$. In the table below, $G_i \wedge I_i$ is an element of Op_{w_j} and $\text{Op}^{++}_{w_j}$ only if we do not take into account the speaker's preferences regarding forms. G_1 can be optimally completed to $G_1 \wedge I_1$ in w_1, w_2, and w_3 but not in w_4 and w_5, see $\text{Op}^+_{w_j}$. By definition, $\bar{S}(G_1|w_j) > 0$ iff $j \in \{1, 2, 3\}$, and therefore $G_1 +> I_1$.

Ω	G_1	I_1	G_2	I_2	g-t-g$_1$	g-t-g$_2$	srch	Op_{w_j}	$\text{Op}^+_{w_j}$	$\text{Op}^{++}_{w_j}$
w_1	+	+	+	+	1	1	ε	$\{G_i, G_i \wedge I_i\}$	$\{G_i \wedge I_i\}$	$\{G_i, G_i \wedge I_i\}$
w_2	+	+	+	−	1	0	ε	$\{G_1, G_1 \wedge I_1\}$	$\{G_1 \wedge I_1\}$	$\{G_1, G_1 \wedge I_1\}$
w_3	+	+	−	−	1	0	ε	$\{G_1, G_1 \wedge I_1\}$	$\{G_1 \wedge I_1\}$	$\{G_1, G_1 \wedge I_1\}$
w_4	+	−	+	+	0	1	ε	$\{G_2, G_2 \wedge I_2\}$	$\{G_2 \wedge I_2\}$	$\{G_2, G_2 \wedge I_2\}$
w_5	−	−	+	+	0	1	ε	$\{G_2, G_2 \wedge I_2\}$	$\{G_2 \wedge I_2\}$	$\{G_2, G_2 \wedge I_2\}$

References

[1] Benz, A.: Utility and Relevance of Answers. In: Benz, A., Jäger, G., van Rooij, R. (eds.) Game Theory and Pragmatics, pp. 195–219. Mcmillan, Palgrave (2006)

[2] Benz, A.: How to Set Up Normal Optimal Answer Models. ms. ZAS Berlin (2008)

[3] Benz, A., van Rooij, R.: Optimal assertions and what they implicate: a uniform game theoretic approach. Topoi - an International Review of Philosophy 27(1), 63–78 (2007)

[4] Grice, H.P.: Studies in the Way of Words. Harvard University Press, Cambridge (1989)

[5] Lewis, D.: Convention. first published by Harvard University Press 1969; reissued by Blackwell Publishers Ltd., Oxford (2002)

[6] Merin, A.: Information, Relevance, and Social Decisionmaking: Some Principles and Results of Decision-Theoretic Semantics. In: Moss, L.S., Ginzburg, J., de Rijke, M. (eds.) Logic, Language, and Information, vol. 2, pp. 179–221 (1999)

[7] Osborne, M.J., Rubinstein, A.: A Course in Game Theory. The MIT Press, Cambridge (1994)

[8] Parikh, P.: The Use of Language. CSLI Lecture Notes, Stanford (2001)

[9] van Rooij, R.: Utility of Mention-Some Questions. Research on Language and Computation 4(3), 401–416 (2004)

[10] Selten, R.: Reexamination of the Perfectness Concept for Equilibrium Points in Extensive Games. International Journal of Game Theory 4, 25–55 (1975)

Conceptualization of Pain:
A Database for Lexical Typology

Anastassia Bonch-Osmolovskaya[1], Ekaterina Rakhilina[2], and Tatiana Reznikova[3]

[1] Moscow State University
[2] Institute of Russian Language, RAS, Moscow
[3] Dept. of Linguistic Studies, VINITI, RAS, Moscow
{abonch,rakhilina,tanja.reznikova}@gmail.com

Abstract. The paper presents a study in lexical typology. We focus on the semantic domain of pain as one of the most universal and complex areas of human experience. The predicates of unpleasant bodily sensations are compared in a sample of 23 languages. The collected material demonstrates that the use of pain verbs is dependent on the range of factors of different nature. This data heterogeneity poses the problem of cross-linguistic comparability of pain predicates. As a way to overcome this problem, we propose the construction of a typological database. The multidimensional classifications implemented in the database allow for various cross-linguistic generalizations on pain and human body conceptualizations as well as on regularities of semantic shifts in different languages.

Keywords: Lexical typology, semantics, typological database, pain.

1 Introduction

Over the last several decades, typology has undoubtedly become one of the central fields of linguistic research. There have been considerable advances in the study of cross-linguistic variation in different areas of morphology, syntax, and phonology. However, the domain of vocabulary is still rarely studied from a typological point of view. This is quite understandable: the lexical typology differs from phonological and grammatical typologies as the latter use limited sets of features and their parameters while the former deals with an infinite diversity of lexical systems and implicit parameters of their distribution (cf. [1], [2]). That is why a lexical-typological study should start with an attempt to solve a "pre-typological" problem: how to reveal the domain of systematic lexical relations and to define the set of parameters that structure this domain. It is not accidental, therefore, that the first works on lexical typology were devoted to the best-structured taxonomies of color and kinship terms (see [3], [4], [5]).

As for more complicated lexical domains, the categorization of lexical units has to be carried out using different dimensions. Indeed, a lexical item is associated with certain types of situations. The comparison of these situational types reveals the relevant parameters of linguistic variation within the domain. As far as these parameters can be of different nature, this poses the problem of data comparability. In

P. Bosch, D. Gabelaia, and J. Lang (Eds.): TbiLLC 2007, LNAI 5422, pp. 110–123, 2009.

order to make generalizations about the entire conceptual domain and, in particular, to identify restrictions on its cross-linguistic variation, we need an efficient tool to visualize and analyze typological data.

The present article discusses the construction of a database as a technique for comparative lexical studies. Nowadays, electronic databases are increasingly popular tools in typological research (see for instance the database for word prosodic systems StressTyp, cf. [6], or the typological database of agreement, cf. [7]). In this paper we will demonstrate a lexical-typological database used for the formalization of the conceptual domain of pain.

The paper is organized as follows. Section 2 outlines the peculiarities of the semantic domain in question. Section 3 describes the data and methodology used for data collection. This is followed by a discussion of the database architecture and parameters relevant to the cross-linguistic analysis of pain in Section 4.

2 The Conceptual Domain of Pain

We have chosen the conceptual zone of pain as a target domain for our research. This fact imposes a challenge both for lexical typological studies and for linguistic analyses in general. This is due to several peculiarities of the pain domain and its linguistic conceptualization.

Firstly, pain has a specific ontological status, which accounts for the popularity of the subject in philosophy (cf. classical work by Wittgenstein [8]). pain is universal, in the sense that all human beings have experienced it, and, as such, it provides a fertile ground for cross-linguistic comparisons. At the same time, pain is highly individual and subjective, it cannot be directly observed or shared with others in an objective way. Our access to other people's pain is always mediated through language, i.e. the physiological experience of different people is subject to comparison only on the basis of their verbal descriptions. The verbalization of pain is of crucial importance, since it substantially contributes to healing. Indeed, pain reports are usually aimed at its relief. The more precisely pain is determined, the better it can be diagnosed, and, consequently, the more successfully it can be treated. This implies that a natural language needs to have means for describing and differentiating a great variety of painful sensations. This, again, renders the pain domain very promising for lexical investigation.

However, the non-observability of pain complicates the process of language data elicitation and their subsequent classification. Unlike some previous studies in lexical typology, our research cannot rely on visual stimuli in data collection (cf. cross-linguistic work on the cutting-breaking domain [9]). The domain under examination does not impose any method for data structuring. This raises the question of how to compare data across languages, which is the most essential issue for lexical typology in general. It is due to the problem of data comparability that lexical typology still occupies only a marginal position within the general field of cross-linguistic studies. Thus, an advance in comparative analysis of pain expressions could be a considerable step forward in establishing lexical typology as a research domain.

Secondly, the pain domain seems to be unique with regard to its lexical structure. Languages normally have few lexemes of pain *per se* (among predicative units we have encountered one to four pain-specific verbs in the languages studied so far, cf.

English *hurt*, *ache*; German *schmerzen*, *weh tun*; Russian *bolet'*). The major part of the domain is constituted by lexical units drawn from other semantic fields, which are metaphorically applied to pain (thus, rich systems reveal up to 50 metaphoric pain predicates). In this respect, pain is, in particular, opposed to other non-observable conceptual domains like e.g. 'mental states' or 'emotions' (cf. a wide range of inherently mental predicates in modern English *think*, *know*, *believe*, *consider*, *decide*, *suppose*, *understand*, etc.).

Due to the high rate of metaphoricity, the pain domain offers a new approach to cross-linguistic research on the derived meanings. Up to now comparative studies on metaphors have dealt mainly with the units associated with a unique source of metaphorical shifts and with the routes of their successive semantic derivations (consider the research on 'aqua-motion' [10]). By contrast, in the case of pain, the study is to focus on the goal of metaphors and on the exploration of the semantic shifts of basic meanings in relation to the meaning of pain[1]. This complicates the task of typological comparison: considering different languages, we come across heterogeneous sets of lexical units whose source meanings show great diversity. Indeed, how can we compare the Russian verb *gudet'* 'to hoot' (describes a painful sensation in one's head or legs) and the Serbian verb *burgijati* 'to drill' (describes a painful sensation in one's head or ears)?

As it will be shown below, the database technique used in the current research accounts for the problems of this kind. But before we turn to the description of the database, let us briefly outline the data used in the study and the methodology for its elicitation.

3 Data and Methodology

The data in focus comprises verbs and predicates that denote unpleasant physiological sensations. We favor lexical units with the meaning of inner sensations but not those of well observed external symptom (burning skin vs. reddening skin).

The research was based on the data of 23 languages, including those genetically related (Slavic – Russian, Ukrainian, Bulgarian, Serbian, Polish, Czech; Germanic – English, German; Romance – French, Spanish, Italian; Finno-Ugric – Hungarian, Estonian, Erzya (Mordvin)); a group of areally close languages (Caucasian – Georgian, Balkar (Turkic), Agul (Daghestanian)); and some others (Lithuanian, Hindi, Arabian, Japanese, Chinese, and Khmer). Interestingly, the comparison of closely related languages often shows amazing discrepancies and allows revealing some fine-grained parameters of semantic variation (see [13], [14] for similar remarks).

The specificity of the pain domain described above determines the complexities of data collecting.

Firstly, the non-observability of pain makes impossible the use of visual stimuli. Secondly, the metaphorical pain meaning is rarely enregistered in dictionaries and vocabularies. Therefore the main method of data collection is elicitation.

---

[1] Though there are several studies on source domains available for conceptualizing a certain target domain (see the analysis of anger in [11], the study of linguistic action in [12]), all of them have been done within one language. To our knowledge, no research of this kind deals with comparative data.

We have developed two data elicitation tools for the purposes of this research: a situational and a frame questionnaire. The situational questionnaire comprises a set of stimulus situations, that lead to painful sensations of their participant. A fragment of this questionnaire is shown below in Table 1.

Table 1. Situational questionnaire

1. The person was bound for two hours. What did he feel while being in such a state? What did he feel after he was unbound? What sensations did he get it his head, chest, back, arms, hands?
2. A small girl has a high temperature due to a cold. What are the sensations she has in her head, forehead, eyes, throat, nose, ears?

The frame questionnaire reflects the preliminary classification of five functional physical violation types that lead to pain sensations:

1) Skin sensations (e.g., *my face is stinging*);
2) Loss of functionality (refers to a body part, which is unable to move (back, neck, extremities) or unable to let fluids pass through (nose, ears, extremities), e.g., *my arm is numb*);
3) Volume extension (i.e., all kinds of swellings and tumors, e.g., *my left knee is swelled up*);
4) Anomalism of function (i.e., unpleasant sensations described in terms of the abnormal functioning of a body part, e.g. *my stomach is churning*);
5) Pain sensations *per se* (i.e., inner sensations that are due to systemic bodily disturbances (diseases), e.g., *my head is throbbing*).

Table 2. Frame questionnaire

Part 2. Loss of functionality
    1. Mobile body parts – loss of mobility
        External affect
• cold water (affected body part: hands, legs, fingers, teeth)
• frost (affected body part: hands, legs, fingers)
• poison (affected body part: hands, legs, tongue)
• narcosis (affected body part: hands, legs, tongue, lip)
 	
        Internal affect
• long stay in the same posture (sit, stand, lie; affected body part: hands, legs)
• paralysis (affected body part: hands, legs)
• fatigue (affected body part: hands, legs)
• senility (affected body part: legs)
• strain (affected body part: hands, legs)
    2. Immobile body parts, body cavities – loss of functionality because of filling with extrinsic substances
• flu (affected body part: nose, breast)
• plain, mountains (affected body parts: ears)

The subtypes of each type are distinguished by a difference of stimuli, which can be connected with an external affect (i.e., bright light, smoke, unpleasant scent) or with inner reasons.

At the same time there seems to be a conceptual opposition of affected body parts. For example, the type (2) – loss of functionality – consists of two subtypes, associated with different types of body parts – 1) mobile body parts: loss of mobility 2) immobile body parts: filling with extrinsic substances. Consider a fragment of the frame questionnaire in Table 2:

For some languages the data were gathered by experts on these languages. The data collected by questioning were then checked and supplemented by corpus data (if available).

The semantic analysis of the dataset helped to reveal the relevant parameters of cross-linguistic variations in the lexical domain of pain, which were then used in the database elaboration.

4 Pain Predicates: Parameters for a Typology

4.1 Metaphorical Source

As was mentioned above, the conceptual space of pain is mainly expressed by metaphors. The semantic domains of metaphoric sources show significant similarity among the language sample. There is a limited set of taxonomic verbal classes that can serve as sources for the development of metaphorical pain meaning. That is

- FIRE: verbs meaning 'burn', 'bake', etc., cf. *My throat is **burning***, Serbian *zub tinja* lit. 'tooth is smoldering';
- SOUND: verbs meaning 'hoot', 'buzz', 'ring', etc., cf. *My head **throbs***, Russian *nogi **gudjat*** lit. 'legs are hooting';
- MECHANICAL DESTRUCTION/DEFORMATION, which can be further subdivided into several groups:
  - AGENTIVE, including the following subtypes
    - o INSTRUMENTAL: verbs meaning 'cut', 'prick', etc., cf. Balkar *bašym čančady* lit. 'my head pricked', Hindi *mUh kaT rahaa hai* lit. 'mouth is being cut';
    - o QUASI-INSTRUMENTAL (using teeth, claws, and alike): verbs meaning 'bite', 'scratch', etc., cf. Lithuanian ***graužia*** *akis* lit. 'it gnaws my eyes';
    - o NON-INSTRUMENTAL
      - DESTRUCTION: verbs meaning 'break', 'tear', etc., cf. French *j'ai le dos **rompu*** lit. 'I have the back broken';
      - DEFORMATION: verbs meaning 'pull', 'press', etc., cf. Serbian ***pritiska*** *me u grudima* 'it presses me in the breast';
  - NON-AGENTIVE: verbs meaning 'burst', 'explode', etc., cf. Agul lit. *fun čurq.aa* 'the stomach is bursting';
- MOTION: verbs meaning 'twist', 'spin', etc., cf. English *my stomach is **churning***, Russian *golova **kružitsja*** lit. 'my head is spinning';
- ANTROPOMORPHIC: NEGATIVE EMOTION: verbs meaning 'hate', 'be upset', cf. English *My stomach **hates** me*.

The classes above differ in the consistency of their occurrence within the pain domain. For example the verbs of burning can convey the pain meaning in all languages of our sample, while the anthropomorphic class is rarely instantiated. Interestingly, this parameter can be different in genetically close languages. The sound class of pain sensation counts about 14 verbs in German but only 4 in English.

We consider the loss of functionality concept as a specific development of the pain domain, though it may not be associated with painful sensations, cf. *my arm's **gone to sleep***. In this case other metaphorical sources are employed. Interestingly, they are in some way reverse to the basic pain metaphorical list, as

- "sound" {PAIN} vs. "loss of sound-producing and perception possibility" {FUNCTIONALITY LOSS} (cf. Russian *nemet'* 'become mute', German *taub werden* 'become deaf');
- "movement" {PAIN} vs. "movement impediment" {FUNCTIONALITY LOSS} (cf. English *trap*, *lock*, Spanish *dormirse* 'go to sleep'),
- "destruction" {PAIN} vs. "stiffening" {FUNCTIONALITY LOSS} (cf. English *stiffen*, Spanish. *envararse* lit. 'become stick-like').

The cross-linguistic consistence of semantic sources for pain metaphors provides evidence for their cognitive relevance in the pain domain. Another perspective of the study is to consider the semantic evolution of separate lexical meanings within the same metaphorical class. For example, what kinds of sounds can develop pain meaning and what kind of painful sensations do they correlate with? The important point here is to define the sound verb properly, i.e., to understand precisely what kind of sounds it can denote. This sort of information can rarely be found in the dictionaries but the list of prototypical sound sources could be a good help in this case. It means that not only verbs but their prototypical subjects and objects should be taken into account. If language X does not distinguish the destruction of soft and solid objects, but language Y does, would the corresponding verbs behave differently if used in the pain domain?

So, the first parameter of typological lexical comparison of the pain domain could be sources of metaphorically used verbs, classified as taxonomic classes or analyzed as concrete lexical meanings.

4.2 The Stimulus Situation of Pain

The second parameter is based on the classification of the goal domain, i.e. classification of pain sensations that can be lexicalized in a language.

Anyone who has ever experienced painful sensations would agree that there can be very different kinds of pain. That means that pain can be categorized. The task of pain differentiation is carried out just by the use of particular metaphors. It is not accidental that the famous McGill Pain Questionnaire and its variants, widely applied in medical diagnostics, are based mainly on metaphorical notions (cf. [15]).

We suppose that a good way for pain categorization is to correlate painful sensations with stimulus situation types that can cause pain. Such situations include external events affecting the experiencer (e.g., getting soap in one's eyes, or cold water on one's aching tooth) as well as wide-spread diseases with distinct symptoms. We assume that the same stimulus causes similar physiological reactions of different people, and it gets a conventionalized expression in a language (e.g, in Hungarian the sensation caused by spicy food is expressed with the phrase *ügeti a nyelvemet* lit. 'my tongue (Acc) burns', in Russian the feeling of tiredness in the legs is described with the help of the verb to hoot: *nogi gudjat* lit. 'feet are hooting').

The comparative analysis of pain predicates focused on the stimulus situations is aimed at investigating the typological problem of meaning distribution between language units: what sensations would be commonly expressed by one lexical expression and what sensations are consistently denoted in a different way (cf. the grammatical typology of morpheme semantics). Thus, feelings due to fever and to sun exposure are described with the same predicate in some languages of our sample, cf. German *glühen* 'glow': *mein Kopf glüht* lit. 'my head is glowing', while it is lexically distinguished in the others: cf. Russian. *golova/lob gorit* lit. 'head is burning' (of fever) vs. *golovu pečet* lit. 'it bakes my head (acc)'. The sensations caused by an extremely bright light or an unpleasant scent are usually expressed by different lexemes in most of the languages of our sample, cf. Russian. *glaza režet* lit. 'it cuts my eyes' and *v nosu sverbit* lit. 'it itches in my nose'. Still we can find some examples of these two stimulus situation combined in one pain metaphor, cf. Ukrainian. *oči riže* lit. 'it cuts my eyes', *v nosi riže* lit. 'it cuts my nose'.

4.3 Pain Localization

The next parameter which characterizes the pain domain is the localization of a painful sensation in a distinct body part. Pain is perceived differently in different body parts. This is reflected in the differentiation of language conceptualizations. A sensation caused by one stimulus situation can be expressed differently depending on the body part to which it is applied. For example the painful sensation caused by smoke exposure on the eyes is described in Russian by the verb *ščipat'* 'pinch' (cf. *glaza ščipit* 'it pinches my eyes'), while the same effect on the nose is usually denoted by the verb *sverbet'* 'itch' (cf. *v nosu sverbit* lit. 'it itches in my nose'). Thus, the choice of a pain verb is determined, among other factors, by the body part, where the painful sensation is located.

The data shows that most of the lexical units denoting pain can function only within a limited set of body parts. Therefore the crucial parameter for comparison of pain-denoting predicates is their compatibility with different body parts. The compatibility constraints can be analyzed as a result of interaction between basic (non-metaphoric) verbal meaning and conceptual characteristics of the body part.

The most relevant conceptual properties of a body part can be described as follows:

a) <u>Solid structure vs. soft tissue.</u> The basic semantics of verbs which belong to the taxonomic class of mechanical destruction/deformation usually involves an idea of the specificity of the patient's physical properties. Consider the Georgian verb *texa* 'break' where the patient should be solid vs. the German verb *kneifen* 'pinch' that denotes an idea of temporary change in the object's configuration without destroying its inner structure. If a metaphorical shift into the pain domain takes place, the body part – location of the pain sensation – is conceptualized as a patient of the transitive destruction verb. In this case the conceptual properties of the body part should agree with the object properties of the basic verbal meaning. For example the Georgian verb *texa* 'break' is used to denote pain in joints (cf.

saxsrebši **mtexavs** lit. 'it breaks me in my joints'), but cannot be combined with "soft-tissue" body parts such as the stomach. By contrast, the German verb *kneifen* can be combined with 'stomach' (cf. *es* **kneift** *im Bauch* lit. 'it pinches in the belly') but cannot describe pain in "solid structure" body parts.

b) Topological features. Combinational properties of pain predicates can rely on the notion of the geometrical characteristics of the body parts conceptualized in a language. Thus the view of a body–part as a container seems to be extremely relevant for the pain-domain. The unpleasant physical sensations related to this kind of body parts can be described with a specific subgroup within the verbs of functionality loss, namely, with verbs that denote filling with external substance that impedes normal functioning of the body part, cf. Japanese *hana ga* **cumaru** lit. 'the nose is filled'. Another topological type is surface (skin and outer body parts – forehead, cheeks, feet).

c) Functional characteristics. Another type of compatibility limitations is connected with the idea of the functional properties of the body part. If we consider the verbs of sound, we can see that there are two types of constructions they are involved in: 1) they describe painful reactions accompanied with sound, i.e., the body part should exhibit functional possibilities to emit the sound (and this sound could be heard by an external observer), cf. Agul *ze fun* **raXaa** lit. 'my belly is talking', English *My joints crack*; 2) they refer to a sound that exists only in the consciousness of the experiencer, in this case they combine with the body parts that are functionally related with sound perception – mostly ears and head, cf. Bulgarian *ušite* **piščjat** lit. 'the ears are cheeping', French *J'ai la tête qui* **hurle** lit. 'I have the head that howls'.

It is important to point out that the body part classification is not universal. First of all, the anatomical conceptualization can be different in different languages. Secondly, even within one language a body part can show different properties, thus referring to different categories. For example in Russian the noun "arms" demonstrates an ambivalent behaviour. On the one hand, it can be combined with the verb *lomit'* (cognate with the verb *lomat'* 'break') which is used with solid structure objects:

(1)   *Segodnja noč'ju podnjalas' temperatura 37,3, ruki, nogi* **lomit**. [Online-magazine mama.ru]

   'Last night I got a fever of 37,3, I feel an aching pain in my arms and legs (lit. "it breaks my arms and legs")'.

On the other hand, the painful sensation in the arms can be described by the verb *tjanut'* 'pull/draw', which implies a soft-tissue object:

(2)   *Posle trenirovok u menja 2-3 dnja nabljudajutsja krome bolej naprjaženie v myšcax, ešče i sil'no* **tjanet** *ruki, osobenno po nočam*. [Bodybuilding and Powerlifting Forum]

   'For 2 or 3 days after a training session, aside from the pain, I feel muscle tension, and my arms hurt (lit. "it pulls my arms")'.

The fact is that the conceptual idea of an arm involves both solid structure (bones) and soft tissue (muscles). In (1) the focus is on the bone-like structure, that can be affected with painful sensations due to fever, while in (2) the context indicates pain in the muscles. If the solid structure is expressed explicitly, the use of the verb 'pull' is unacceptable: *[?]sil'no* **tjanet** *kosti ruk* lit. 'it pulls the bones of the arms'.

The compatibility limitations can attenuate as a result of consistent bleaching of the basic verbal meaning. The extreme case is unlimited combinability of the metaphorical verb with all the body parts as in the case of the Russian verb *nyt'* 'whimper', which can describe a background non-intensive pain sensation of almost every body part. Native speakers usually do not associate the pain usage of this verb with any sound.

The specific conceptualization of body parts in a language is manifested also in the syntactic marking of the body part participant in pain expression.

4.4 Syntactic Constructions

A standard pain situation involves two main participants – a Body-part and a pain Experiencer. Also a Reason of pain can be relevant for some kinds of situations (cf. the Frame Perception_body in the FrameNet model). As our investigation of the language sample shows, verbs whose basic meaning is 'ache' can imply a different syntactic coding for the two semantic roles.

- The Body-part can be interpreted as (a) the Location (of the pain) and then coded with a locative construction cf. Czech *Boli mi v krku*, lit. '(it) hurts me in the neck'; (b) the Theme, i.e., the only argument of a one-place predicate, thus getting a subject or direct object marking (= affected with pain) cf. Russian *U menia bolit noga* lit. 'at me hurts leg (nom)' (c) the Stimulus (= initiator of the pain situation) – has the syntactic marking of a subject of a transitive verb, cf. Bulgarian: *Sărceto me zaboljava* lit. 'heart me (acc) hurts'.
- The Experiencer can get (a) Experiential dative marking, cf. German. *mir schmerzt der Kopf* lit. 'me (dat) hurts the head (nom)'; (b) the Possessor (of the body part) – in this case a possessive pronoun or an oblique object is used, cf. *my leg hurts*; (c) the Patient – coded as a direct object, cf. the Bulgarian example above.
- Finally, the Reason can be interpreted as (a) the Causer (of the pain situation) being marked as a subject, cf. French *la lumiure me fait mal aux yeux* lit. 'the light me hurts in the eyes', or as (b) its Source, marked as an oblique object, cf. Russian. *glaza boljat ot sveta* lit. 'eyes ache from light'.

The subject of the investigation is the syntactic structure of metaphorically used verbs. The matters to be taken into account are the basic semantic and syntactic (transitive/intransitive) properties of the verb.

Intransitive verbs (for instance, sound verbs) act in a most predictable way. The Body-part (BP) is marked as subject, or there can be no overtly marked subject with BP marked as a locative phrase. The Experiencer gets a dative or possessive marking. The reason, if expressed, is marked as oblique object, see Table 3.

Let's provide some examples of the constructions above:

(3) Russian
     Ot   ustalosti   *u menja*   *kružitsja*   *golova*
     From   tiredness   at me (poss.)   spin   head (Nom)

(4) Serbian
     Mi   *pišti*   *u*   *ušima,*
     me-dat whistle   in   ears

Table 3. Source verb: Intransitive

$V_{intr-physical}$ ex..<make noise>			X_s		
$V_{intr-pain}$	1	REASON$_{\varnothing/OBL}$	BP_s	EXP$_{DAT/POSS}$	
	2	REASON$_{\varnothing/OBL}$		EXP$_{DAT/POSS}$	BP$_{LOC}$

Transitive verbs used metaphorically demonstrate two types of syntactic constructions: transitive and intransitive.

In a transitive pain construction, formed by a transitive source verb (with core arguments X_S and Y_O), the Body part or Reason may get subject marking, the direct object position can be filled by the Body Part or the Experiencer. As in the case of intransitive source-verbs, subjectless constructions are also possible, see Table 4.

Table 4. Source verb: Transitive, derived verb: Transitive

$V_{tr-physical}$ ex.<cut>			X_A	Y_O	
$V_{tr-pain}$	1	REASON$_{\varnothing/OBL}$	BP_A	EXP$_O$	
	2		REASON$_A$	BP$_O$	EXP$_{DAT/POSS}$
	3	REASON$_{\varnothing/OBL}$		BP$_O$	EXP$_{DAT/POSS}$
	4	REASON$_{\varnothing/OBL}$		EXP$_O$	BP$_{LOC}$

The constructions are exemplified below:

(5)   Bulgarian:
    Gărbăt   *me*   *bode.*
    def.back (nom)   me(acc) prick

(6)   Russian
    Svet   *mne*   *režet*   *glaza*
    Light(nom) me(dat)   cut   eyes(acc)

(7)   Balkar
    Belimi   *tartady.*
    Back-my (acc)   pull

(8)   Bulgarian
    Bode   *me*   *v* *grădite*
    Prick   me(acc)   in def.chest

The most remarkable change of syntactic structure concerns the cases when a basically transitive verb forms an intransitive syntactic construction. This derived construction can be subjectless or can have an overt subject. In this case it is the Body part that gets subject marking, see Table 5.

Table 5. Source verb: Transitive; derived verb: Intransitive

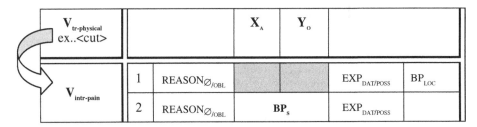

$V_{tr\text{-}physical}$ ex..<cut>			X_A	Y_O	
$V_{intr\text{-}pain}$	1	REASON$_{\varnothing/OBL}$			EXP$_{DAT/POSS}$	BP$_{LOC}$
	2	REASON$_{\varnothing/OBL}$	BP$_s$		EXP$_{DAT/POSS}$	

Here are examples of the defined constructions:

(9)   German
       Es   beißt   mir   in   den   Augen
       It   bite   me (dat) in   def.dat eyes

(10)   Russian
       Včera   večerom   u menja   ochen'   bok   kolol.
       Yesterday evening   at me (poss) very   side(nom) prick

We suppose that the formation of the second construction could be regarded as a result of the basic pain construction influence. In fact the argument structure here copies precisely the syntactic properties of the verb 'ache' (*bolet'*).

4.5   Emotion Viewed as Pain

A number of pain verbs combined with some specific body parts act as secondary metaphorical sources, being used to express emotional states. This fact triggers a range of typological questions. Some of them will be briefly outlined below.

– What body parts can be viewed as the location/source of an emotional state in a language? For example, as one might expect, in all the languages of the sample a pain construction with the heart as a Body part can get an emotional interpretation, cf. English *my heart tightens up*, Agul *jurk' ugaa* lit. 'heart burns' = 'anxiety'. Furthermore, a frequent source of emotional constructions are phrases with 'head' and 'stomach', cf. French *j'ai la tête qui explose* lit. 'I have the head that explodes' = 'stress', Hungarian *felfordul a gyomrom* lit. 'stomach turns round' = 'disgust'. A less frequent example is the emotional interpretation of expressions with 'liver', cf. Hindi *kaleje mE jalan hai* lit. 'in my liver there is burning'. A special task is to analyze what body parts localize particular emotions.

– If a certain body part in a language can be associated with a certain emotional state, does it concern all pain verbs which can be used with the corresponding noun? Are there any pain verbs that never express an emotional state?

– If a certain construction can be used both to denote physical pain and an emotional state, are there any language means to distinguish them? For example in the German sentence *Wenn ich an dich denke, sticht mein Herz* 'When I think of you, my heart <lit.> pricks' the pain is viewed as a complex psycho-physiological event which may or may not include a real physical sensation: the difference here is not reflected in a language expression. At the same time the nominalization construction with the same verb denotes only physical pain: *ich verspüre ein Stechen im Herz* lit. 'I feel a pricking in my heart'.

We have presented a range of parameters that can be relevant for the typological study of the pain domain. In the last section we are going to show how these parameters can be incorporated in a database constructed for the study of a conceptual domain in a typological perspective.

5 Database for the Typology of Pain Predicates

One entry in the database corresponds to one possible combination "predicate + body part", including its syntactic structure in a language. The entry contains all syntactic information about the phrase. If a combination demonstrates variations of the syntactic coding, then each possible syntactic structure will be entered as a separate entry. The database presents the following types of linguistic information:

LANGUAGE. The field is used to show the language of the entry. Currently there is data on 23 languages in the database. The number of languages is to be increased in future.

METTYPE. The field is used to relate the entry to one of the metaphorical classes, described in 4.1 (FIRE, SOUND, INSTRUMENTAL DESTRUCTION, etc.). If the predicate is not a metaphor then the value of the field will be "specific pain verb".

PREDICATE. Contains the basic form of the predicate.

MEANING. The field presents a translation of the predicate into English.

BASIC ARGUMENTS TR. The field is used to determine the basic (= non-pain) meaning of the lexeme, and it is filled only if the verb in its first sense is transitive. Here the prototypical agents and objects are assigned. For example, Russian verb *žeč'* 'burn (tr)' has 'human' as a prototypical agent and 'paper' as an object; English *sting* has 'bee' as an agent, and 'human skin' as an object.

BASIC ARGUMENTS INTR. The field functions similarly to the previous one, but it is filled if the basic verb in its first (= non-pain) sense is intransitive. Here the prototypical subject is assigned (for example, sound sources for sound verbs, cf. 'bell' for the verb *ring*, objects of inchoative destruction, cf. 'baloon'/'soap bubble' for German *platzen*, etc.). Generally only one of the two fields (Basic arguments tr / Basic arguments intr) is chosen depending on the syntactic properties of the verb in its basic meaning. In the case of labile verbs, it is difficult to define which syntactic structure has been the source for the metaphoric usage, so both fields are filled.

EXAMPLE BASIC TR. The field is used to illustrate the function of the predicate in its basic non-metaphorical meaning, cf. Russian verb *žeč'*: *On sžeg starye pis'ma* 'He burned old letters'.

EXAMPLE BASIC INTR. The field functions similarly to the previous one: the usage of the basic intransitive verb is exemplified here, cf. for English verb *ring*: *The bell is ringing.*

BODY PART. Contains information about the body part engaged in the construction of the entry (see Section 4.3).

STIMULUS. Contains information on possible stimulus situations that may cause the pain sensation denoted by the construction of the entry (see Section 4.2).

PAIN SYNTACTIC PATTERN. The field presents schematic information on the syntactic coding of the arguments within the pain construction of the entry. So, for example, the English sentence *My eyes sting* corresponds to the schematic description EXP:POSS BP:S, (the Experiencer is expressed as a possessive pronoun, and the Body Part as a subject). Note that this field does not duplicate the information on transitivity found under BASIC ARGUMENTS TR/ BASIC ARGUMENTS INTR. Whereas the transitivity feature refers to the source (non-pain) meaning of a verb, the argument structure described here is characteristic of its pain uses.

EXAMPLE PAIN. Contains an example of a sentence with a pain construction.

EMOTIVE. This is a Boolean parameter. It is true when the construction of the entry can have an emotional interpretation, and it is false when no emotional state can be denoted.

In this paper, the parameters of the cross-linguistic variations of pain denoting predicates have been described. This list of parameters has been a result of an analysis of data on 23 languages. These parameters have been used to construct a lexical-typological database, which makes it possible to recover information on the various aspects of pain conceptualization and can serve as a good basis for future investigations.

Acknowledgments

We would like to express our sincere gratitude to all our informants and experts on individual languages who made this research possible: Ju. Adaskina (Erzya), K. Böröczki (Hungarian), R. Camus (French), S. Gedzhieva (Balkar), M. Geise, D. Marzo, V. Rube, B. Umbreit (German), L. Khokhlova, E. Kozlova (Hindi), A. Kostyrkin, A. Panina (Japanese), M. Kozlova (Spain), S. Kupp, A. Lammas (Estonian), S. Merdanova (Agul), P. Novichkov (English), Ju. Pakeris, D. Šileikaitė, V. Žemantene (Lithuanian), E. & S. Sanikidze (Georgian), M. Serafimova (Bulgarian), E. Yakushkina (Serbian). We also thank two anonymous reviewers for their helpful comments on a previous version of this manuscript.

The research is supported by INTAS (Ref. Nr 05-1000008-7917) and the Russian Foundation for the Humanities (Ref. Nr 06-04-91403a).

References

1. Rakhilina, E.V., Plungian, V.A.: O leksičeskoj tipologii [On lexical typology] (in Russian). In: Maisak, T., Rakhilina, E. (eds.) Tipologija glagolov dviženija v vode [Typology of AQUA-motion verbs], pp. 9–26. Indrik, Moscow (2007)

2. Koptjevskaya-Tamm, M.: Approaching lexical typology. In: Vanhove, M. (ed.) From Polysemy to Semantic Change: Towards a Typology of Lexical Semantic Associations. Benjamins, Amsterdam (forthc.)
3. Berlin, B., Kay, P.: Basic Color Terms: Their Universality and Evolution. University of California Press, Berkeley (1969)
4. Nerlove, S., Romney, A.K.: Sibling terminology and cross-sex behavior. American Anthropologist 69, 179–187 (1967)
5. Greenberg, J.: Universals of kinship terminology. In: Maquet, J. (ed.) On Linguistic Anthropology: Essays in Honor of Harry Hojer, Undena, Malibu, pp. 9–32 (1980)
6. Goedemans, R.W.N., van der Hulst, H.G., Visch, E.A.M.: StressTyp: A Database for Word Prosodic Systems. Glot International 2(1/2), 21–23 (1996)
7. Tiberius, C., Brown, D., Corbett, G.: A Typological Database of Agreement. In: Proceedings of LREC 2002, the Third International Conference on Language Resources and Evaluation, Las Palmas, Spain, pp. 1843–1846 (2002)
8. Wittgenstein, L.: Philosophical Investigations. Blackwell Publishing, Oxford (1953)
9. Majid, A., Bowerman, M.: Cutting and breaking events: A crosslinguistic perspective. Special issue of Cognitive Linguistics 18(2) (2007)
10. Maisak, T.A., Rakhilina, E.V. (eds.): Tipologija glagolov dviženija v vode [Typology of AQUA-motion verbs]. Indrik, Moscow (2007)
11. Lakoff, G.: Women, Fire, and Dangerous Things: What Categories Reveal about the Mind. University of Chicago Press, Chicago (1987)
12. Goossens, L. (ed.): By word of mouth: Metaphor, metonymy, and linguistic action in a cognitive perspective. Benjamins, Amsterdam (2005)
13. Comrie, B.: Language universals and linguistic typology. Sprachtypologie und Universalienforschung 46, 3–14 (1993)
14. Croft, W.: Typology and universals, 2nd edn. Cambridge University Press, Cambridge (2003)
15. Melzak, R.: The McGill Pain Questionnaire: Major properties and scoring methods. Pain 1, 277–299 (1975)

Expressing Belief Flow in Assertion Networks

Sujata Ghosh[1,2] and Fernando R. Velázquez-Quesada[3]

[1] Department of Mathematics, Visva-Bharati, Santiniketan, West Bengal, India
[2] Center for Soft Computing Research, Indian Statistical Institute,
Kolkata, West Bengal, India
[3] Institute for Logic, Language and Computation, Universiteit van Amsterdam
Plantage Muidergracht 24, 1018 TV, Amsterdam, The Netherlands
{S.Ghosh,F.R.VelazquezQuesada}@uva.nl

Abstract. In the line of some earlier work done on belief dynamics, we propose an abstract model of belief propagation on a graph based on the methodology of the revision theory of truth. A set of postulates is proposed, a dynamic language is developed for portraying the behavior of this model, and its expressiveness is discussed. We compare the proposal of this model with some of the existing frameworks for modelling communication situations.

Keywords: Assertion network, belief flow, belief merging, stability.

1 Introduction

Self-reference is a tricky and complicated issue in logic. Ordinary propositional logic formulas can be expressed by trees, whereas there we have to resort to cyclic graphs (cf. [1]). In both cases, truth propagates backwards along the edges of finite trees or graphs. While this flow of truth stops in case of finite trees, giving a resultant truth value, it goes into a loop in case of cyclic graphs. Consider the *liar* statement *"this sentence is false"*. Graphically, it can be represented as

Gaifman's *pointer semantics* [2,3] and the *revision theory of truth* developed by Herzberger, Gupta and Belnap [4,5] provide semantics for sets of sentences with self-reference by looking at stable patterns among their truth values. Under these semantics, the value of the *liar* sentence never becomes stable as it oscillates between 1 and 0. On the other hand, for the *nested liars* sentences,

"The next sentence is false. The previous sentence is false."

which can be represented by the graph

there are two assignments, 1,0 and 0,1, that generate stable patterns under subsequent revisions of truth values. The main features of theories are the *backward*

P. Bosch, D. Gabelaia, and J. Lang (Eds.): TbiLLC 2007, LNAI 5422, pp. 124–138, 2009.
© Springer-Verlag Berlin Heidelberg 2009

propagation of truth values along the edges (which correspond to the "revisions"), and the recognition of stable patterns.

In [6], the authors provide a formal model of real life communication situations using graphs where both *forward* and *backward* propagation of values are considered, which represents belief flow of a *reasoning agent*. This reasoning agent, also called the *observer*, wants to decide whether to believe or disbelieve certain facts, based on her and other agents' opinion about events/facts as well as agents. The observer's initial beliefs about the agents and facts are *revised* through an *iteration function* against the *merging* of rest of the information. A belief semantics via stability is defined, keeping the spirit of revision semantics mentioned earlier. [6] also provides a concrete model for such communication situations based on an infinite set of belief-values (a closed interval of real numbers). This gives rise to difficulties when segregating those values in terms of their interpretation and then studying their inter-dependence.

In order to overcome such difficulties and facilitate our formal modelling, we consider a finite set of belief-values here. Such finite sets play a significant role in better understanding of the underlying subtleties of the mutually conflicting opinions of the agents involved. We propose a set of postulates that a concrete model of the situations should satisfy.

To provide a sound formal foundation to our proposed model, we introduce a logical language to describe the revision process carried out. Instead of describing the outcome of the whole process (the general tradition of the logical approaches), we focus on the small-step dynamics of such situations, resembling the connectionist viewpoint. One of the main drawbacks of these approaches is the difficulty to provide an explanation of the underlying reasoning mechanism, viz. a *logical* description of the process, though attempts have been made to overcome it ([7,8,9,10]).

The main significance of this work lies in the fact that, though our model follow the connectionist framework, we have been able to provide a logical framework also so as to give a strong formal foundation to the proposed model. The search for an iteration function (the revision function which forms an integral part of the model) that conforms to our intuitions is largely an empirical question. Still, our postulates impose basic restrictions on what this function should satisfy. They describe the way the observer's beliefs at a given stage will influence her beliefs after one step in the merging process.

The paper is organized as follows. In § 2, we recall the formal definition of the *Assertion Network Semantics* from [6] and propose several postulates stating properties the iteration function should satisfy. Then, we provide a concrete definition of such functions, and compare them with the postulates. We support our work with the aid of a software tool called *Assertion Network Toolkit*, which has been introduced in [6]. A dynamic logic of belief flow through this communication networks is proposed in § 3. Finally, § 4 focuses on comparison with some related works, with § 5 providing pointers towards future work.

2 Belief Networks: A Concrete Model

In real life communication situations, we deal not only with sources of information with opinions about the facts/events, but also with opinions about each other. We can get information about the weather from a radio broadcasting, a webpage or a friend, and it is not strange to hear our friend saying *"you should not trust in those guys from the radio"*. Putting all this information together is not an easy task, but as highlighted in [6], the revision theoretic framework of Herzberger, Gupta, and Belnap [5,4] suggests a methodology that can be well applied in dealing with these rather complicated situations.

These situations can be represented by directed labelled graphs (DLG) with vertices representing facts and agents and edges representing agents' opinions. An edge labelled with "+" ("−") from a vertex n_1 to a vertex n_2 indicates that the agent represented by n_1 has positive (negative) opinion about the agent/fact represented by n_2. Although, in order to keep the model as simple as possible, we assign nodes to represent both *agents* and *facts*, we do differentiate them: agents are represented only with non-terminal nodes and facts with terminal ones. Agents with no opinions do not appear in the model.

An *external observer* reasons about the communication situations represented by the DLG. While the agents' opinions are represented by edges in the graph, the observer's beliefs are represented in the following way. Vertices are given values from a non-empty finite set Λ to indicate the states of belief of the observer regarding those agents and facts. As mentioned before, this is a departure from the models in [6], where the value set is a continuous interval, not the discrete set assumed here. We will see how this approach eventually aids in the understanding of the situation in a much more illuminating way and also provides a better insight into the language and logic of these networks.

Thinking of vertices of the graph as agents and facts rather than just sentences, leads from an analysis of truth as done in [4,5] to an analysis of a belief network. Consider the following example, given in [6].

> Suppose the observer is sitting in an office without windows. Next to her is her colleague (C), inside the same office. The observer is simultaneously talking on the phone to her friend (F), who is sitting in a street café.
>
> F: *"Everything your colleague says is false; the sun is shining!"*
> C: *"Everything your friend says is false; it is raining!"*

The information the observer has gathered can be described by the following graph where S is interpreted as *"the sun is shining"* and, while edges F $\xrightarrow{+}$ S and C $\xrightarrow{-}$ S represent the opinions the friend and the colleague have about S, edges F $\xrightarrow{-}$ C and C $\xrightarrow{-}$ F represent the opinions they have about each other.

Although there are two consistent truth value assignments, one of them is intuitively preferred, as the observer's friend has first hand experience of the weather in the street café. Based on this preference, the observer's beliefs *flow* through the graph: the contextually based stronger belief in F leads her to believe in S, but at the same time to disbelieve in C, since it is in conflict with F. Her disbelief in C in turn makes her belief in S stronger, which influences her belief in F once again. Both *forward* and *backward* propagation of beliefs are encountered.

This example shows both *backward* and *forward* propagation of beliefs. If a trusted source has some positive opinion about a certain proposition φ, the belief of the observer over φ will influence her belief on the trusted source, as well as the belief on the trusted source would have some effect over the observer's belief in φ. In the following, we try to base all these ideas on a more concrete level.

2.1   Assertion Network Semantics

An *Assertion Network Model* M is a tuple $M = (\mathcal{G}, \Psi)$, where

- $\mathcal{G} = (\mathcal{V}, \mathcal{E}, \ell)$ is a directed labelled graph, with $\mathcal{V}$ the set of vertices, $\mathcal{E} \subseteq \mathcal{V} \times \mathcal{V}$ the set of edges and $\ell : \mathcal{E} \to \{+, -\}$ the labelling function.
- $\Psi : \Lambda^{\mathcal{V}} \to \Lambda^{\mathcal{V}}$ is the *iteration function*, with Λ the **set of values**.

Vertices represent agents and facts; edges represent agents' opinions.

The observer's beliefs are represented in a different way. We assume a function $H : \mathcal{V} \to \Lambda$, called an *hypothesis*, assigning to every vertex of $\mathcal{G}$ a value in Λ. The value $H(v)$ is interpreted as the state of belief the observer has about v.

The iteration function Ψ comes into play to combine forward and backward propagation, defining a **revision sequence** of the observer's beliefs. Given an initial hypothesis H, we define the sequence of functions $\langle H_i \,;\, i \in \omega \rangle$ as

$$H_0 := H, \qquad H_{i+1} := \Psi(H_i)$$

Inspired by the stability concept of revision theory, we can now define a partial stability semantics for our labelled graph. Let H be an initial hypothesis, v be a vertex in $\mathcal{V}$ and λ be a value in Λ. We say that λ **is the stable value of** v **starting from** H if there is $n \in \omega$ such that $H_i(v) = \lambda$ for all $i \geq n$. The **assertion network semantics** A_H is defined in this way:

$$A_H(v) := \begin{cases} \lambda & \text{if } \lambda \text{ is the stable value of } v \text{ starting from } H \\ \text{undefined} & \text{if } \langle H_i(v) \,;\, i \in \omega \rangle \text{ oscillates.} \end{cases}$$

Following Theorem 1 and Theorem 2 in the section 2 of [6], it is pretty straightforward that,

Theorem 1. *The stable truth predicate of revision semantics is a special case of assertion network semantics, i.e., for every set of clauses Σ there is a labelled graph G and there are evaluation functions such that A_H coincides with the (partial) stable truth predicate on Σ.*[1]

---

[1] Here, we refer to a propositional language with *clauses* as described in [11], with the partial stable truth predicate defined in the proof of Theorem 2 in [6].

2.2   Postulates for the Iteration Function

As mentioned in the introduction, we will consider a finite set of belief-values for building up the *Assertion Network* model. We define the set as $\Lambda := \{-1, 0, 1\}$, where '-1' stands for disbelief, '0' for no opinion and '1' for belief.

The iteration function is the key of this model; it defines how the beliefs of the observer will be in the next stage, given her beliefs in the current one. Let us first make a brief analysis of what should be taken into account when deciding the next state of beliefs.

The case of facts is the simple one. To get her beliefs about some fact (represented by $v \in \mathcal{V}$) at stage $k+1$ ($H_{k+1}(v)$), the observer should take into account her current beliefs about the fact ($H_k(v)$) and her current beliefs about agents having an opinion (positive or negative) about the fact ($H_k(u)$ for every $u \in \mathcal{V}$ s.t. $\langle u, v \rangle \in \mathcal{E}$). This is nothing but *forward propagation* of beliefs.

The case of an agent i (represented by $v \in \mathcal{V}$) is a more involved one. Besides her current beliefs about the agent ($H_k(v)$) and her current beliefs about agents having an opinion about i ($H_k(u)$ for every $u \in \mathcal{V}$ s.t. $\langle u, v \rangle \in \mathcal{E}$; again, *forward propagation*), the observer should take into account the beliefs she has regarding agents and facts *about which i has an opinion* ($H_k(u)$ for every $u \in \mathcal{V}$ such that $\langle v, u \rangle \in \mathcal{E}$: *backward propagation*). All these will influence her next state of belief regarding the agent under consideration.

In the following, we propose some postulates for *rational iteration functions*. They reflect intuitive restrictions on how the belief state of the observer about some agent/fact should be modified during her introspection process.

Let $v \in \mathcal{V}$ be a terminal node (a fact) of the Assertion Network.

1. If **(a)** $H_k(u) = 1$ for every $u \in \mathcal{V}$ s.t. $\langle u, v \rangle \in \mathcal{E}$ with $\ell\langle u, v \rangle = $ "+", and **(b)** $H_k(u) = -1$ for every $u \in \mathcal{V}$ s.t. $\langle u, v \rangle \in \mathcal{E}$ with $\ell\langle u, v \rangle = $ "−", then $\Psi(H_k(v)) = H_{k+1}(v) = 1$ (the *positive enforcement of facts* postulate).
2. If **(a)** $H_k(u) = 1$ for every $u \in \mathcal{V}$ s.t. $\langle u, v \rangle \in \mathcal{E}$ with $\ell\langle u, v \rangle = $ "−", and **(b)** $H_k(u) = -1$ for every $u \in \mathcal{V}$ s.t. $\langle u, v \rangle \in \mathcal{E}$ with $\ell\langle u, v \rangle = $ "+", then $\Psi(H_k(v)) = H_{k+1}(v) = -1$ (the *negative enforcement of facts* postulate).
3. If **(a)** $H_k(u) = 0$ for every $u \in \mathcal{V}$ s.t. $\langle u, v \rangle \in \mathcal{E}$, then $\Psi(H_k(v)) = H_{k+1}(v) = H_k(v)$ (the *persistence of facts* postulate).

Now let $v \in \mathcal{V}$ be a non-terminal node (an agent).

1. If we have **(a)** and **(b)** from 1 of the terminal node case, plus **(c)** $H_k(u) = 1$ for every $u \in \mathcal{V}$ s.t. $\langle v, u \rangle \in \mathcal{E}$ with $\ell\langle u, v \rangle = $ "+", and **(d)** $H_k(u) = -1$ for every $u \in \mathcal{V}$ s.t. $\langle v, u \rangle \in \mathcal{E}$ with $\ell\langle u, v \rangle = $ "−", then $\Psi(H_k(v)) = H_{k+1}(v) = 1$ (the *positive enforcement of agents* postulate).
2. If we have **(a)** and **(b)** from 2 of the terminal node case, plus **(c)** $H_k(u) = 1$ for every $u \in \mathcal{V}$ s.t. $\langle v, u \rangle \in \mathcal{E}$ with $\ell\langle u, v \rangle = $ "−", and **(d)** $H_k(u) = -1$ for every $u \in \mathcal{V}$ s.t. $\langle v, u \rangle \in \mathcal{E}$ with $\ell\langle u, v \rangle = $ "+", then $\Psi(H_k(v)) = H_{k+1}(v) = -1$ (the *negative enforcement of agents* postulate).
3. If we have **(a)** from 3 of the terminal node case, plus **(b)** $H_k(u) = 0$ for every $u \in \mathcal{V}$ s.t. $\langle v, u \rangle \in \mathcal{E}$, then $\Psi(H_k(v)) = H_{k+1}(v) = H_k(v)$ (the *persistence of agents* postulate).

2.3   Concrete Model

We provide a concrete definition of the iteration function, describing the change in observer's beliefs about an agent/fact depending on those of related ones.

Let $M = (\mathcal{G}, \Psi)$ be an *Assertion Network Model* with $\mathcal{G} = (\mathcal{V}, \mathcal{E}, \ell)$. For a vertex $v \in \mathcal{V}$, define

$$\mathrm{In}^+(v) := \{w \in \mathcal{V} \,;\, \ell\langle w,v\rangle = \text{"}+\text{"}\}, \qquad \mathrm{In}^-(v) := \{w \in \mathcal{V} \,;\, \ell\langle w,v\rangle = \text{"}-\text{"}\},$$
$$\mathrm{Out}^+(v) := \{w \in \mathcal{V} \,;\, \ell\langle v,w\rangle = \text{"}+\text{"}\}, \qquad \mathrm{Out}^-(v) := \{w \in \mathcal{V} \,;\, \ell\langle v,w\rangle = \text{"}-\text{"}\}$$

The set $\mathrm{In}(v) := \mathrm{In}^+(v) \cup \mathrm{In}^-(v)$ consists of the vertices that *can reach* v. The set $\mathrm{Out}(v) := \mathrm{Out}^+(v) \cup \mathrm{Out}^-(v)$ consists of the vertices that *can be reached from* v. The set of terminal vertices of $\mathcal{G}$ can be defined as $\mathcal{T}_\mathcal{G} := \{v \in \mathcal{V} \,;\, \mathrm{Out}(v) = \emptyset\}$.

Let H be an hypothesis. For every $w \in \mathrm{In}(v)$, define s_w^v as the H-value of w with sign according to the label of the edge that links it with v; for every $w \in \mathrm{Out}(v)$, define t_w^v as the H-value of w with sign according to the label of the edge that links v to it. Formally,

$$s_w^v := \begin{cases} H(w) & \text{if } w \in \mathrm{In}^+(v) \\ -H(w) & \text{if } w \in \mathrm{In}^-(v) \end{cases} \qquad t_w^v := \begin{cases} H(w) & \text{if } w \in \mathrm{Out}^+(v) \\ -H(w) & \text{if } w \in \mathrm{Out}^-(v) \end{cases}$$

For each value $\lambda \in \Lambda$, define S_λ^v as the set of vertices $w \in \mathrm{In}(v)$ such that $s_w^v = \lambda$; similarly, define T_λ^v as the set of vertices in $w \in \mathrm{Out}(v)$ such that $t_w^v = \lambda$.

$$S_\lambda^v := \{w \in \mathrm{In}(v) \,;\, s_w^v = \lambda\} \qquad\qquad T_\lambda^v := \{w \in \mathrm{Out}(v) \,;\, t_w^v = \lambda\}$$

For a terminal vertex $v \in \mathcal{T}_\mathcal{G}$, its $\Psi(H)$-value depends on the H-values of v itself and on those of the vertices in $\mathrm{In}(v)$. Here is our particular definition.

$$\Psi(H)(v) := \begin{cases} 1 & \text{if } |S_1^v| > |S_{-1}^v| \\ -1 & \text{if } |S_1^v| < |S_{-1}^v| \\ H(v) & \text{otherwise.} \end{cases}$$

For a non-terminal vertex $v \in \mathcal{V} \setminus \mathcal{T}_\mathcal{G}$, the definition is a bit more complicated. Unlike the terminal ones, in addition to the current value of v we now have to take into account the influences of both the incoming edges as well as the outgoing ones, since we want to represent both *forward* and *backward* propagation of beliefs. The value suggested by the incoming edges (IE_v) and the one suggested by the outgoing ones (OE_v) are considered separately.

$$IE_v := \begin{cases} 1 & \text{if } |S_1^v| > |S_{-1}^v| \\ -1 & \text{if } |S_1^v| < |S_{-1}^v| \\ H(v) & \text{otherwise.} \end{cases} \qquad OE_v := \begin{cases} 1 & \text{if } |T_1^v| > |T_{-1}^v| \\ -1 & \text{if } |T_1^v| < |T_{-1}^v| \\ H(v) & \text{otherwise.} \end{cases}$$

Their combination gives the $\Psi(H)$-value of v defined by the following table:

$IE_v \backslash OE_v$	-1	0	1
-1	-1	-1	0
0	-1	0	1
1	0	1	1

With this definition of Ψ, the next theorem can be easily proved.

Theorem 2. *Ψ satisfies the three fact postulates and the three agent postulates.*

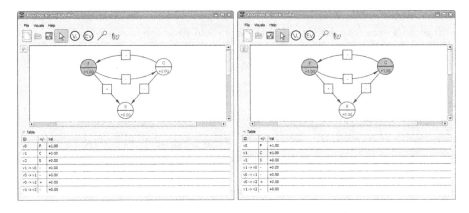

Fig. 1. Initial opinions

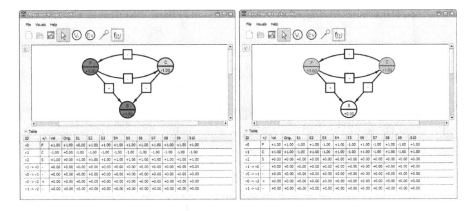

Fig. 2. Final opinions

2.4 Assertion Network Toolkit

As mentioned in the introduction, looking for the adequate iteration function Ψ is largely an empirical task. We can claim that the definition given just now is a plausible one since it satisfies all the postulates, but still more complicated examples are to be checked to validate the claim that this particular definition reflects our intuitive interpretation. The *Assertion Network Toolkit* (ANT), presented in [6], allows us to play around with the functions and values.

As an example of its use, consider the communication situation described at the beginning of this section. The iteration function Ψ defined in the earlier subsection is the one currently implemented in the ANT. Figure 1 shows two screenshots with difference in the values of the initial hypothesis. Figure 2 shows the corresponding final values after the iteration process.

In the first case (the left hand side of Figure 1), the observer believes in her friend because of the friend's first hand experience of what is happening outside the office; besides that, she does not have any initial opinion about her colleague or the discussed fact. In this setting, the initial hypothesis H_0 assigns a value of 1 to the vertex representing the friend $(H_0(F) = 1)$ and a value of 0 to the others $(H_0(C) = H_0(S) = 0)$. In the second case (the right hand side of Figure 1), the observer has an equally high initial opinion about her friend as well as her colleague. The initial hypothesis H_0 assigns a value of 1 to both her friend and colleague $(H_0(C) = H_0(F) = 1)$, but 0 to the mentioned fact $(H_0(S) = 0)$. We let the program iterate the function several times, getting the screenshoots of Figure 2 and the sequence of values of the tables below.

	H_0	H_1	H_2	H_3 $\cdots$
F	1	1	1	1 $\cdots$
C	0	-1	-1	-1 $\cdots$
S	0	1	1	1 $\cdots$

	H_0	H_1	H_2	H_3 $\cdots$
F	1	-1	1	-1 $\cdots$
C	1	-1	1	-1 $\cdots$
S	0	0	0	0 $\cdots$

In the first case, all the vertices reach stable values (in just two steps); in the second case, only the vertex representing S gets a stable value: that of *"no opinion"* of the observer (the values of F and C oscillate). The readers will definitely consent to the fact that in both these cases, the final belief values completely agree with our intuitions.

3   Expressing Belief Networks

This section provides a logical language to express the behavior of the Assertion Network Model. The network focuses on the observer's point of view, so we define a language that takes her perspective. The atomic propositions are expressions indicating the state of belief the observer has about agents or facts portrayed in the network, and then we build more complex formulas using the standard logical connectives. This language does not describe the graph (we cannot express things like *"agent i has a positive opinion about p"*), but it describes the observer's beliefs about the represented situation; this will serve our purpose here. For readers interested in a more expressive language, we refer to [12].

In the language we provide a way to talk about the most important part of the model: the update of beliefs carried out by the iteration function. We introduce the syntactic operator $\bigcirc$ to represent the iteration function: it allows us to talk about what happens with the observer's beliefs after one step of revision and merging of beliefs. Formulas of the form $\bigcirc\varphi$ are read as *"after one iteration of the function, φ is the case"*. This operator describes the way the beliefs of the reasoning agent propagate through the network after a single iteration step.

Finally, we are also interested in the outcome of the whole process. Such a process reaches an end whenever the beliefs of the observer become *stable*, that is, whenever they reach a stage from which further iterations of the function will not change them anymore (which is not always the case). We introduce the syntactic operator $\circledast$; it represents the stable stage reached by the network (whenever it exists) and allows us to talk about what happens with the observer's belief at the end of the process (if it ever ends). Formulas of the form $\circledast\varphi$ are read as *"after the whole process, φ is the case"*.

3.1   A Language Expressing the Observer's Beliefs

Given a set of *agents* **A** and a set of *propositions* **P**, the *Language of Beliefs $\mathcal{LB}$* is given by:

$$\varphi := \mathsf{B}\gamma \mid \mathsf{N}\gamma \mid \mathsf{D}\gamma \mid \neg\varphi \mid \varphi \vee \psi$$

with $\gamma \in \mathbf{A} \cup \mathbf{P}$. Formulas of the form $\mathsf{B}\gamma$ indicates *"the observer believes in γ"*, while $\mathsf{N}\gamma$ indicates *"the observer does not have any opinion about γ"* and $\mathsf{D}\gamma$ indicates *"the observer disbelieves in γ"*.

To avoid any confusion that may arise due to the use of the traditional intensional operators in an extensional language, we make the following remarks.

- Formulas in $\mathcal{LB}$ express exclusively *the observer's* beliefs.
- The language $\mathcal{LB}$ *is not a modal language.* Its atomic propositions $\mathsf{B}\gamma$, $\mathsf{N}\gamma$ and $\mathsf{D}\gamma$ have special meanings, but they are still atomic propositions.
- Usually, the truth values of atomic propositions are not related in any way. Here, the semantics will be defined in a way that the truth values of some of them are related: formulas like $\mathsf{B}\gamma \wedge \mathsf{D}\gamma$, for example, will never be true.

Formulas of $\mathcal{LB}$ are interpreted in Assertion Network Models by assuming a map that uniquely identifies each vertex of the model with an agent or a fact in $\mathbf{A} \cup \mathbf{P}$. The map should satisfy our requirement: facts have to be mapped to terminal vertices.

Let $M = (\mathcal{G}, \Psi)$ be an Assertion Network Model, with $\mathcal{G} = (\mathcal{V}, \mathcal{E}, \ell)$. An *interpretation I* is a partial injective function $I : \mathbf{A} \cup \mathbf{P} \to \mathcal{V}$ such that, for each $p \in \mathbf{P}$, we have $I(p) \in \mathcal{T}_{\mathcal{G}}$, when it is defined. Given I and an initial hypothesis H, the truth definition of formulas of $\mathcal{LB}$ in M is given by

$$
\begin{array}{llll}
M, I, H \models \mathsf{B}\gamma & \text{iff} & H(I(\gamma)) = 1 \\
M, I, H \models \mathsf{N}\gamma & \text{iff} & H(I(\gamma)) = 0 \\
M, I, H \models \mathsf{D}\gamma & \text{iff} & H(I(\gamma)) = -1 \\
M, I, H \models \neg\varphi & \text{iff} & M, I, H \not\models \varphi \\
M, I, H \models \varphi \vee \psi & \text{iff} & M, I, H \models \varphi \text{ or } M, I, H \models \psi
\end{array}
$$

Thus, the formula $\mathsf{B}\gamma$ (resp. $\mathsf{N}\gamma$, $\mathsf{D}\gamma$) is true in the model M under the interpretation I if and only if the H-value of the graph component to which γ is mapped is equal to 1 (resp. 0, -1).

3.2   A Language Expressing Belief Flow

The language $\mathcal{LB}$ is static, in the sense that it does not express how beliefs change as a result of the belief propagation. Here, we extend the language with two dynamic operators that allows us to talk about the model after one iteration step ($\bigcirc$) and also after it reaches a stable situation ($\circledast$). The full language of the *Logic of Belief Flow $\mathcal{LBF}$*, is given by:

$$\varphi := \mathsf{B}\gamma \mid \mathsf{N}\gamma \mid \mathsf{D}\gamma \mid \neg\varphi \mid \varphi \vee \psi \mid \bigcirc\varphi \mid \circledast\varphi$$

with $\gamma \in \mathbf{A} \cup \mathbf{P}$. Formulas of the form $\bigcirc\varphi$ express *"after the observer once considers the information she has, φ is the case"*; formulas of the form $\circledast\varphi$ express *"after the observer considers all the information she has, φ is the case"*.

While the operator $\bigcirc$ represents one step in the iteration process, the operator $\circledast$ represents stable positions. The first one gets truth value by using the iteration function Ψ; the second one looks for iterations that do not change values from some moment on.

$$M, I, H \models \bigcirc\varphi \qquad \text{iff} \qquad M, I, \Psi(H) \models \varphi$$
$$M, I, H \models \circledast\varphi \qquad \text{iff} \qquad \exists n \in \omega \text{ such that } M, I, \Psi^i(H) \models \varphi \text{ for all } i \geq n.$$

To close this section, we give examples of formulas that hold in the Assertion Network Model corresponding to the example described in § 2 and whose iterated values are shown in tables of page 131. Formally, we have

- $\mathcal{V} := \{\mathsf{F}, \mathsf{C}, \mathsf{S}\}$; $\quad \mathcal{E} := \{\langle\mathsf{F}, \mathsf{C}\rangle, \langle\mathsf{C}, \mathsf{F}\rangle, \langle\mathsf{F}, \mathsf{S}\rangle, \langle\mathsf{C}, \mathsf{S}\rangle\}$,
- $\ell\langle\mathsf{F}, \mathsf{S}\rangle = \text{``+''}$; $\quad \ell\langle\mathsf{F}, \mathsf{C}\rangle = \ell\langle\mathsf{C}, \mathsf{F}\rangle = \ell\langle\mathsf{C}, \mathsf{S}\rangle = \text{``−''}$.

and Ψ as defined before. The initial hypothesis H is given by

$$H(\mathsf{F}) = 1 \qquad\qquad H(\mathsf{C}) = 0 \qquad\qquad H(\mathsf{S}) = 0$$

From the values shown in the corresponding table, we have that the following formulas hold in M, I, H:

- $\mathsf{BF} \wedge \mathsf{NC} \wedge \mathsf{NS}$
- $\bigcirc(\mathsf{BF} \wedge \mathsf{DC} \wedge \mathsf{BS})$
- $\bigcirc\bigcirc(\mathsf{BF} \wedge \mathsf{DC} \wedge \mathsf{BS})$
- $\circledast(\mathsf{BF} \wedge \mathsf{DC} \wedge \mathsf{BS})$

Considering some variations of the initial hypothesis, ANT shows us that the following formulas also hold.

- $(\mathsf{BF} \wedge \mathsf{BS}) \rightarrow \circledast(\mathsf{BF} \wedge \mathsf{DC} \wedge \mathsf{BS})$
  If the observer initially believes in F and S, then her initial belief about C is irrelevant.
- $(\mathsf{BF} \wedge \mathsf{BC} \wedge \mathsf{NS}) \rightarrow ((\bigcirc^k\mathsf{BF} \rightarrow \bigcirc^{k+1}\mathsf{DF}) \wedge (\bigcirc^k\mathsf{DF} \rightarrow \bigcirc^{k+1}\mathsf{BF})) \quad (k \geq 0)$
  If she initially believes in F and C without having an opinion about S, then her beliefs about F will oscillate ($\bigcirc^0\varphi := \varphi$ and $\bigcirc^{k+1}\varphi := \bigcirc\bigcirc^k \varphi$).
- $(\mathsf{BF} \wedge \mathsf{BC} \wedge \mathsf{NS}) \rightarrow \neg \circledast (\mathsf{BF} \vee \mathsf{NF} \vee \mathsf{DF})$
  Therefore, there is no stable value for F.
- $(\mathsf{BF} \wedge \mathsf{BC} \wedge \mathsf{NS}) \rightarrow \circledast\mathsf{NS}$
  But there is a stable value (viz. 0) for S.

Evidently, the last three formulas express the observer's opinions in the second example we dealt with in Section 2.4. Finally, we also have some validities which provide some insights towards the complete axiomatization of the proposed logic, which we leave for future work:

- $\mathsf{B}\gamma \rightarrow (\neg\mathsf{N}\gamma \wedge \neg\mathsf{D}\gamma)$
- $\mathsf{D}\gamma \rightarrow (\neg\mathsf{N}\gamma \wedge \neg\mathsf{B}\gamma)$
- $\mathsf{N}\gamma \rightarrow (\neg\mathsf{B}\gamma \wedge \neg\mathsf{D}\gamma)$
- $\bigcirc(\varphi \wedge \psi) \leftrightarrow (\bigcirc\varphi \wedge \bigcirc\psi)$
- $\circledast(\varphi \wedge \psi) \leftrightarrow (\circledast\varphi \wedge \circledast\psi)$
- $\circledast\varphi \rightarrow \circledast \bigcirc \varphi$

4   Other Models and Logics: A Comparison

An extensive amount of work has been done in formalizing and modelling the revising/merging of beliefs/information. Here, we provide a discussion to compare our approach with a few of the existing ones.

4.1   Different Approaches for Revising/Merging

The classical work on belief revision, the *AGM approach* ([13]), introduces postulates that an operator performing revision should satisfy in order to be considered rational. Several other frameworks have been proposed; particularly related with our proposal are those focused on *iterated* revision, like [14] and [15]. The field has extended to incorporate the more general branch of *belief merging*, focussed on situations where both the current and the incoming information have the same priority and the same structure ([16,17,18]).

Our approach lies on the revision side, with the agents' opinions and the observer's beliefs being represented in a different way. Nevertheless, we do not consider simple revision, but *revision by merging*, since the observer revises her beliefs against the merged opinions of all the agents involved, very much in the spirit of [19]. Also, the main novelty of our work is that it considers agents that have opinions not only about the discussed facts, but also about themselves.

The dynamic logic framework provides a natural way to express changes in information. Various logics have been proposed, like dynamic epistemic logic (*DEL*; [20,21]) and dynamic doxastic logic (*DDL*; [22]). In [23] the author looks into *DEL* and *AGM* belief revision, providing a joint perspective. While *DDL* captures the *AGM* postulates for belief revision in a logical language, *DEL* talks about concrete information update procedures that change models/situations.

In contrast, $\mathcal{LBF}$ focuses on introspection of a reasoning agent regarding the transition of her belief states in a communication situation. Belief states are expressed in a propositional language, and their transition is captured by the dynamic modal operators $\bigcirc$ and $\circledast$. Note how *DDL* expresses agents' beliefs after a certain revision process that occur in her doxastic state, while *DEL* provides a framework for dealing with *hard* information (changing the knowledge state) as well as *soft* information (affecting beliefs). $\mathcal{LBF}$ is proposed to capture the process of continuing change in the opinions/beliefs that goes on in the observer's mind in the described situations.

On the other side of the spectrum, and closer to the Assertion Network semantics, there are approaches based on interconnected networks, where the results of the process may sometime corroborate with the stability concepts, and in some other cases, have quite different approaches, e.g. the probabilistic one. To mention a few, in [24,25], a *Neural-Logic Belief Network* (*NLBN*, a neuro-symbolic network) is defined which can be used to model common sense reasoning, providing a way for representing changes in the agent's belief attitudes. In [26], the authors propose a distributed approach to belief revision, where numerical values as probability measures have been incorporated in the models to represent degrees of uncertainty, and computations are performed using Dempster rule and Bayesian conditioning.

We should also mention *Bayesian Belief Nets* (*BBN*; [27]) in this regard. They are directed acyclic graphs, with nodes representing variables and the edges representing their causal relationship. The value of a variable is given by a conditional probability table, based on the causal relationship calculated with Bayes' rule. Based on these tables, *BBN* can be used in decision making, where both inductive as well as deductive reasoning can be performed.

Let us compare those approaches with the model of § 2. The novelty lies in the semantics derived from stability as used in the revision theory of truth [5,4]. In *NLBN*, only forward propagation is considered and the representation is restricted to propositions, while our model considers backward propagation and represents agents as well. Similar is the case of *BBN*, though in some sense their probabilistic approach can be used in a greater variety of domains. The work of [26] is closer to ours, though with subtle but important differences, the most notable among them being our very centralized approach.

Different from connectionist approaches, logical ones have the advantage of providing a better understanding of the underlying process. On the other hand, networks and the stability concept are natural representations of the interconnected information and the discussion process that leads to agreements. In [19], the authors propose a combination: conciliation via iterated belief merging. Beliefs of several agents are merged, and then each one of them revises her own beliefs with respect to the result of the merging. The process is repeated until a fixed point is reached; the conciliation operator is defined with respect to it.

As in our work, they look for *stable* situations, where further interaction between the diverse components will not modify the current status. Somewhat similar to our approach, they use a two-stage iterative process: merging and then revising. But, once again, in this work as well as in similar such, the basic focus lies on different agents' belief sets with no mention of belief/trust over other agents, where the novelty of our work lies.

4.2   Small Steps

The idea of focusing on the small steps of a process is not new. It has been a proposed solution for the so called *logical omniscience* problem, about unrealistic assumptions on the agents' reasoning power.

In [28,29], Duc proposes a dynamic epistemic logic to reason about agents that are neither logically omniscient nor logically ignorant. The main idea is to represent the knowledge of an agent as a set of formulas, and to allow her to improve her information set as time goes by. Instead of representing agents that know everything from the very beginning, this approach focuses on the step-by-step process that leads to that outcome. Our work shares this concept: we focus on the small steps in belief revision/merging process. In some cases, the small steps will lead to stable values, indicating that the (possibly inconsistent) initial information and the observer's initial beliefs can be merged. In others, the values will oscillate, indicating that they cannot find a way to live together.

4.3   Trust

One of the main features of the Assertion Networks is that it allows us to represent not only opinions about facts, but also opinions about agents. This can be interpreted as the observer's *trust*, allowing us to represent asymmetries in the way the agents' opinions will influence the observer's beliefs. Several works have analyzed the notion of *trust* in multi-agent systems.

In [30], Liau proposes a modal logic with three operators: B_i (*"i believes* φ*"*), I_{ij} (*"j informs i about* φ*"*) and T_{ij} (*"i trust j about* φ*"*). Beliefs and information are normal modal operators, so an agent's beliefs are closed under logical consequence, and once she acquires some information from another agent, she also acquires all its logical consequences. Trust, on the other hand, is given by an operator with neighborhoods semantics, so trusting another agent about φ does not make an agent to trust her about the logical consequences of φ.

In [31], the authors extend Liau's work by introducing *topics* and *questions*. As they observe, Liau's work explains the consequence of trust, but does not explain where trust comes from. The notion of *topic* allows to create trust of agent i on agent j about fact ψ whenever i trusts j about a fact φ that shares the same topic with ψ (*topic-based trust transfer*). The notion of *question* allows to create trust or distrust from the answer of some question (*question-based trust derivation* and *question-based distrust derivation*).

In our proposal, the notion of belief in an agent, different from the notion of trust of the described works, is not relative to a particular statement (as formulas of the form $T_{ij}\varphi$ express), but relative to the agent itself. Also, since facts are represented independently from each other, beliefs of the observer are not closed under any inference relation. Moreover, the observer's initial beliefs about the facts and the agents are not necessarily related: the agent can initially believe in p without believing in agents having a positive opinion about p.

The described approaches work on a static level, without considering *dynamics* of the system. Even exchanges of information and questions are semantically represented as properties of the model, and not as actions that modifies it. The main focus of our approach is the *dynamic* process through which all the involved participants interact, updating the model and influencing themselves while trying to reach an agreement.

5   Conclusion and Intentions

In this work, we propose a model of belief propagation based on the methodology of the revision theory of truth. A dynamic language is developed for expressing the belief flow in the model in terms of an external observer's introspection process. We have compared the model and the language with some of the existing frameworks for modelling communication situations.

In our framework, the next-stage belief value of a node is given in terms of the current beliefs about the incoming and outgoing nodes (forward and backward propagation). Our postulates state the behaviour of the iteration function in completely biased cases. Some further avenues of investigation are as follows.

Different iteration functions. In more general situations, there is no unique way to define the iteration function. A *majority-based* one may represent an observer that follows the majority, a *confident* one can represent an agent that gives more weight to her current beliefs and a *credulous* one can represent observers that give more precedence to others' opinions. It will be interesting to formalize these different policies.

Opinionated edges. We can consider beliefs not only about facts and agents, but also about the opinions. We can think of situations where an agent is an expert in some subject but not in some other. Thus in some cases it is more natural to have different degrees of beliefs in the agent's different opinions.

Extending value set. We have considered a three-valued belief-degree set Λ here, but it can be easily extended to any finite valued one, so as to express more possible epistemic states of the observer. The model will get closer to the actual real life situations.

Comparing expressivity. In the presented language, formulas of the form $\circledast\varphi$ express stable values, related with fixed points in some sense. It would be interesting to make a study about the expressiveness of the language compared with fixpoint logics, like the modal μ-calculus.

Acknowledgements. We gratefully acknowledge Erik Scorelle for working on *ANT* with the modified definitions and helping in with the screenshots. We also thank Benedikt Löwe for the initial discussions that provided important pointers towards the definition of the model, and for going through a preliminary draft of this paper, providing insightful comments. Finally, we thank the editors and anonymous referees for their useful suggestions and comments. The second author acknowledges a scholarship by **CONACyT** (# 167693) from México.

References

1. Bolander, T.: Self-reference and logic. Phi. News 1, 9–44 (2002)
2. Gaifman, H.: Operational pointer semantics: Solution to self-referential puzzles I. In: Vardi, M. (ed.) Proceedings of TARK 1988, pp. 43–59 (1988)
3. Gaifman, H.: Pointers to truth. Journal of Philosophy 89, 223–261 (1992)
4. Gupta, A., Belnap, N.D.: The Revision Theory of Truth. The MIT Press, Cambridge (1993)
5. Herzberger, H.G.: Naive semantics and the liar paradox. The Journal of Philosophy 79, 479–497 (1982)
6. Ghosh, S., Löwe, B., Scorelle, E.: Belief flow in assertion networks. In: Priss, U., Polovina, S., Hill, R. (eds.) ICCS 2007. LNCS (LNAI), vol. 4604, pp. 401–414. Springer, Heidelberg (2007)
7. Balkenius, C., Gärdenfors, P.: Nonmonotonic inferences in neural networks. In: Allen, J.A., Fikes, R., Sandewall, E. (eds.) Proceedings of KR 1991, pp. 32–39 (1991)
8. Blutner, R., Doherty, P.D.: Nonmonotonic logic and neural networks, http://citeseer.ist.psu.edu/160749.html

9. d'Avila Garcez, A., Broda, K., Gabbay, D.: Symbolic knowledge extraction from trained neural networks: A sound approach. Artificial Intelligence 125(1–2), 155–207 (2001)

10. Leitgeb, H.: Interpreted dynamical systems and qualitative laws: from neural networks to evolutionary systems. Synthese 146(1-2), 189–202 (2005)

11. Löwe, B.: Revision forever! In: Schärfe, H., Hitzler, P., Øhrstrøm, P. (eds.) ICCS 2006. LNCS (LNAI), vol. 4068, pp. 22–36. Springer, Heidelberg (2006)

12. Ghosh, S., Velázquez-Quesada, F.R.: Merging information, working paper

13. Alchourrón, C., Gärdenfors, P., Makinson, D.: On the logic of theory change. The Journal of Symbolic Logic 50, 510–530 (1985)

14. Darwiche, A., Pearl, J.: On the logic of iterated belief revision. In: Fagin, R. (ed.) Proceedings of TARK 1994, pp. 5–23. Morgan Kaufmann, San Francisco (1994)

15. Jin, Y., Thielscher, M.: Iterated belief revision, revised. Artificial Intelligence 171(1), 1–18 (2007)

16. Konieczny, S.: Sur la logique du changement: révision et fusion de bases de connaissance. PhD thesis, Laboratoire d'Informatique Fondamentale de Lille (1999)

17. Konieczny, S., Pino-Pérez, R.: On the logic of merging. In: Proceedigns of KR 1998, pp. 488–498 (1998)

18. Konieczny, S., Pino-Pérez, R.: Merging information under constraints: a logical framework. Journal of Logic and Computation 12(5), 773–808 (2002)

19. Gauwin, O., Konieczny, S., Marquis, P.: Conciliation through iterated belief merging. Journal of Logic and Computation 17(5), 909–937 (2007)

20. Gerbrandy, J.: Bisimulations on Planet Kripke. PhD thesis, Institute for Logic, Language and Computation (University of Amsterdam) (1999)

21. Plaza, J.A.: Logics of public communications. In: Emrich, M.L., Pfeifer, M.S., Hadzikadic, M., Ras, Z.W. (eds.) Proceedings of ISMIS 1989, pp. 201–216 (1989)

22. Segerberg, K.: The basic dynamic doxastic logic of AGM. In: Williams, M., Rott, H. (eds.) Frontiers in Belief Revision, pp. 57–84. Kluwer, Dordrecht (2001)

23. van Benthem, J.: Dynamic logic for belief revision. Journal of Applied Non-Classical Logic 17(2), 129–155 (2007)

24. Low, B., Foo, N.: Towards a network for representing beliefs. In: Proceedings of the 2nd International Computer Science Conference, pp. 85–91 (1992)

25. Low, B., Foo, N.: A network formalism for commonsense reasoning. In: Proceedings of the Sixteenth Australian Computer Science Conference, pp. 425–434 (1993)

26. Dragoni, A., Giorgini, P.: Distributed belief revision. Autonomous Agents and Multi-Agent Systems 6(2), 115–143 (2003)

27. Williamson, J.: Bayesian nets and causality, Philosophical and computational foundations. OUP (2005)

28. Duc, H.N.: Logical omniscience vs. logical ignorance on a dilemma of epistemic logic. In: Pinto-Ferreira, C., Mamede, N.J. (eds.) EPIA 1995. LNCS, vol. 990, pp. 237–248. Springer, Heidelberg (1995)

29. Duc, H.N.: Reasoning about rational, but not logically omniscient, agents. Journal of Logic and Computation 7(5), 633–648 (1997)

30. Liau, C.J.: Belief, information acquisition, and trust in multi-agent systems: a modal logic formulation. Artificial Intelligence 149(1), 31–60 (2003)

31. Dastani, M., Herzig, A., Hulstijn, J., van der Torre, L.W.N.: Inferring trust. In: Leite, J., Torroni, P. (eds.) CLIMA 2004. LNCS, vol. 3487, pp. 144–160. Springer, Heidelberg (2005)

The Computational Complexity of Quantified Reciprocals

Jakub Szymanik*

Institute for Logic, Language and Computation, University of Amsterdam
Valckenierstraat 65, 1018 XE Amsterdam, The Netherlands
Institute of Philosophy, University of Warsaw
j.szymanik@uva.nl

Abstract. We study the computational complexity of reciprocal sentences with quantified antecedents. We observe a computational dichotomy between different interpretations of reciprocity, and shed some light on the status of the so-called Strong Meaning Hypothesis.

Keywords: Reciprocal expressions, computational complexity, generalized quantifiers, Strong Meaning Hypothesis.

1 Introduction

The English reciprocal expressions *each other* and *one another* are common elements of everyday English. Therefore, it is not surprising that they are extensively studied in the formal semantics of natural language (see e.g. [1]). There are two main approaches to reciprocals in the literature. The long trend of analyzing reciprocals as anaphoric noun phrases with the addition of plural semantics culminates in [2]. A different trend — recently represented in [3] — is to analyze reciprocals as polyadic quantifiers.

In this paper we study the computational complexity of reciprocal sentences with quantified antecedents. We put ourselves in the second tradition and treat reciprocal sentences as examples of a natural language semantic construction that can be analyzed in terms of so-called polyadic lifts of simple generalized quantifiers. We propose new relevant lifts and focus on their computational complexity. From this perspective we also investigate the cognitive status of the so-called Strong Meaning Hypothesis proposed in [4].

1.1 Basic Examples

We start by recalling examples of reciprocal sentences, versions of which can be found in English corpora (see [4]). Let us first consider the sentences (1)–(3).

---

* I would like to thank Johan van Benthem, Nina Gierasimczuk, Theo Janssen, Marcin Mostowski, Jouko Väänänen, Dag Westerståhl, and Yoad Winter for many comments and inspiration. The author was supported by a Marie Curie Early Stage Research fellowship in the project GloRiClass (MEST-CT-2005-020841).

P. Bosch, D. Gabelaia, and J. Lang (Eds.): TbiLLC 2007, LNAI 5422, pp. 139–152, 2009.
© Springer-Verlag Berlin Heidelberg 2009

(1) At least 4 members of parliament refer to each other indirectly.
(2) Most Boston pitchers sat alongside each other.
(3) Some Pirates were staring at each other in surprise.

The possible interpretations of reciprocity exhibit a wide range of variations. For example, sentence (1) implies that there is a subset of parliament members of cardinality at least 4 such that each parliament member in that subset refers to some statement of each of the other parliament members in that subset. However, the reciprocals in the sentences (2) and (3) have different meanings. Sentence (2) entails that each pitcher from the set containing most of the pitchers is directly or indirectly in the relation of sitting alongside with each of the other pitchers from that set. Sentence (3) says that there was a group of pirates such that every pirate belonging to the group stared at some other pirate from the group. Typical models satisfying (1)–(3) are illustrated at Figure 1. Following [4] we will call the illustrated reciprocal meanings *strong*, *intermediate*, and *weak*, respectively.

Fig. 1. On the left, a model satisfying sentence (1). This is so-called *strong reciprocity*. Each element is related to each of the other elements. In the middle, a model satisfying sentence (2) in a context with at most 9 pitchers. This is *intermediate reciprocity*. Each element in the witness set of the quantifier Most is related to each other element in that set by a chain of relations. On the right, a model satisfying sentence (3), so-called *weak reciprocity*. For each element there exists a different related element.

In general according to [4] there are 2 parameters characterizing variations of reciprocity. The first one relates to how the scope relation R should cover the domain A (in our case restricted by a quantifier in antecedent). We have 3 possibilities:

FUL. Each pair of elements from A participates in R directly.
LIN. Each pair of elements from A participates in R directly or indirectly.
TOT. Each element in A participates in the relation R with at least one other element.

The second parameter determines whether the relation R between individuals in A is the extension of the reciprocal's scope (R), or is obtained from the extension by ignoring the direction in which the scope relation holds ($R^\vee = R \cup R^{-1}$).

By combining these 2 parameters we got 6 possible meanings for reciprocals. We encountered already 3 of them: strong reciprocity ($\text{FUL}(R)$), intermediate reciprocity ($\text{LIN}(R)$), and weak reciprocity ($\text{TOT}(R)$). There are 3 new logical possibilities: strong alternative reciprocity ($\text{FUL}(R^\vee)$), intermediate alternative reciprocity (LIN($R^\vee$)), and weak alternative reciprocity (TOT($R^\vee$)). Among alternative reciprocal interpretations two are linguistically attested: intermediate alternative reciprocity exhibited by sentence (4) and weak alternative reciprocity occurring in sentence (5)(See Figure 2).

(4) Most stones are arranged on top of each other.
(5) All planks were stacked atop of each other.

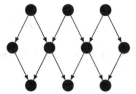 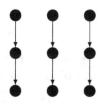

Fig. 2. On the left a model, satisfying sentence (4), so-called *intermediate alternative reciprocity*. Ignoring the direction of arrows, every element in the witness set of the quantifier Most is connected directly or indirectly. On the right a model satisfying sentence (5), so-called *weak alternative reciprocity*. Each element participates with some other element in the relation as the first or as the second argument, but not necessarily in both roles.

Notice also that under certain properties of the relation some of the possible definitions become equivalent. For example, if the relation in question is symmetric, then obviously alternative versions reduce to their "normal" counterparts.

1.2 Strong Meaning Hypothesis

In an attempt to explain variations in the literal meaning of the reciprocal expressions the so-called *Strong Meaning Hypothesis* (SMH) was proposed in [4]. According to this principle, the reading associated with the reciprocal in a given sentence is the strongest available reading which is consistent with relevant information supplied by the context. In [3] a considerably simpler system in which reciprocal meanings are derived directly from semantic restrictions using SMH was suggested. Our results show that the various meanings assigned to reciprocals with quantified antecedents differ drastically in their computational complexity. This fact can be treated as suggesting some improvements for the shifts between possible meanings of reciprocal sentences which are predicted by SMH. We elaborate on this possibility in the last section of the paper before we reach the conclusions.

2 Reciprocal Expressions as Quantifiers

2.1 Generalized Quantifiers

As this paper analyzes reciprocity in the framework of the theory of generalized quantifiers, we start by recalling the definition of a generalized quantifier (see [5], [6]).

A *generalized quantifier* Q of type $(n_1, \ldots, n_k)$ is a class of structures of the form $\mathbb{M} = (M, R_1, \ldots, R_k)$, where M is the universe and R_i is a subset of M^{n_i}. Additionally, Q is closed under isomorphism. Syntactically a quantifier Q of type $(n_1, \ldots, n_k)$ binds $m = n_1 + \ldots + n_k$ first-order variables, and k formulae. If for all i: $n_i \leq 1$, then we say that quantifier is *monadic*, otherwise we call it *polyadic*.

In other words, Q is a functional relation associating with each model $\mathbb{M}$ a relation between relations on M. Hence, if we fix a model $\mathbb{M}$ we have the following equivalence:

$$(M, R_1{}^M, \ldots, R_k{}^M) \in \mathsf{Q} \iff \mathsf{Q}_M(R_1, \ldots, R_k), \text{where } R_i{}^M \subseteq M^{n_i}.$$

As an example consider the quantifier Most of type $(1, 1)$. It corresponds to the following class of finite models:

$$\mathsf{Most} = \{(M, A^M, B^M) : card(A^M \cap B^M) > card(A^M - B^M)\}.$$

In a given model $\mathbb{M}$ the statement $\mathsf{Most}_M(A, B)$ says that $card(A^M \cap B^M) > card(A^M - B^M)$.

Generalized quantifiers were introduced to linguistics in [7].

2.2   Reciprocals as Polyadic Quantifiers

Monadic generalized quantifiers provide the most straightforward way to define the semantics of noun phrases in natural language (see [8]). Sentences with reciprocal expressions transform such monadic quantifiers into polyadic ones. We will analyze reciprocal expressions in that spirit by defining appropriate lifts on monadic quantifiers. These lifts are definable in existential second-order logic. For the sake of simplicity we will restrict ourselves to reciprocal sentences with right monotone increasing quantifiers in antecedents. We say that a quantifier Q is monotone increasing in its right argument, if $Q_M(A, B)$ and $B \subseteq B' \subseteq M$, then $Q_M(A, B')$. Below defined lifts can be extended to cover also sentences with decreasing and non-monotone quantifiers, for example by following the strategy of bounded composition in [4] or using determiner fitting operator proposed in [9].

In order to define the meaning of the strong reciprocity we make use of the well-know operation on quantifiers called *Ramseyfication*. Let Q be a right monotone increasing quantifier of type $(1, 1)$, we define:

$$\mathsf{Rams}(\mathsf{Q})(A, R) \iff \exists X \subseteq A[\mathsf{Q}(A, X) \wedge \forall x, y \in X (x \neq y \Rightarrow R(x, y))].$$

The result of such a lift is called a *Ramsey quantifier*. In the same way we can also easily account for the alternative strong reciprocity:

$$\mathsf{Rams}^{\vee}(\mathsf{Q})(A, R) \iff \exists X \subseteq A[\mathsf{Q}(A, X) \wedge \forall x, y \in X (x \neq y \Rightarrow (R(x, y) \vee R(y, x)))].$$

Rams is defined analogously for unary quantifiers as for type $(1, 1)$, just replace condition $\mathsf{Q}(A, X)$ by $\mathsf{Q}(X)$ in the definition.

In an analogous way we define other lifts to express intermediate and weak reciprocity and their alternative versions. For intermediate reciprocity we have the following:

$$\mathsf{Ram_I}(\mathsf{Q})(A, R) \iff \exists X \subseteq A[\mathsf{Q}(A, X) \land \forall x, y \in X$$
$$(x \neq y \Rightarrow \exists \text{ sequence } z_1, \dots, z_\ell \in X \text{ such that}$$
$$z_1 = x \land R(z_1, z_2) \land \dots \land R(z_{\ell-1}, z_\ell) \land z_\ell = y)].$$

The alternative version is defined naturally. In other words these conditions guarantee that X is connected with respect to R or $R^\vee$. Anyway, graph connectedness is not elementary expressible, we need a universal monadic second-order formula. Hence from the definability point of view $\mathsf{Ram_I}$ ($\mathsf{Ram_I}^\vee$) seems more complicated than $\mathsf{Ram_S}$ ($\mathsf{Ram_S}^\vee$). However, as we will see in the next chapter, this is not always the case when a computational complexity perspective is taken into account.

For weak reciprocity we take the following lift and its alternative version:

$$\mathsf{Ram_W}(\mathsf{Q})(A, R) \iff \exists X \subseteq A[\mathsf{Q}(A, X) \land \forall x \in X \exists y \in X(x \neq y \land R(x, y))].$$

All these lifts produce polyadic quantifiers of type $(1, 2)$. We will call the values of these lifts (alternative) strong, (alternative) intermediate and (alternative) weak reciprocity, respectively.

The linguistic application of these lifts is straightforward. For example, formulae (6)–(10) give the readings to sentences (1)–(5).

(6) $\mathsf{Ram_S}$(At least 4)(MP, Refer-indirectly).
(7) $\mathsf{Ram_I}$(Most)(Pitcher, Sit-next-to).
(8) $\mathsf{Ram_W}$(Some)(Pirate, Staring-at).
(9) $\mathsf{Ram_I}^\vee$(Most)(Stones, Arranged-on-top-of).
(10) $\mathsf{Ram_W}^\vee$(All)(Planks, Stack-atop-of).

2.3   The Computational Complexity of Quantifiers

By the complexity of a quantifier Q we mean the computational complexity (see e.g. [10]) of the corresponding class of finite models. For example, consider a quantifier Q of type $(1, 2)$. In that case Q is a class of finite models of the following form $\mathbb{M} = (M, A^M, R^M)$. We are now given a model $\mathbb{M}$ of that form and a quantifier Q. We can assume that the universe M consists of natural numbers: $M = \{1, \dots, m\}$, A^M is a subset of M and R^M is a binary relation over M. Our computational problem is to decide whether $\mathbb{M} \in \mathsf{Q}$. Equivalently, does $\mathbb{M} \models \mathsf{Q}(A, R)$?

Generalized quantifiers in finite models — from the point of view of computational complexity — were considered for the first time in [11], where the following terminology was introduced. We say that a quantifier Q is *NP-hard* if the corresponding class of finite models is NP-hard. Q is *mighty* (NP-complete) if the corresponding class belongs to NP and is NP-hard.

It was observed in [12] that some natural language quantifiers when assuming their branching interpretation are mighty. More results of this type can be found in [13]. Essentially all of the proofs of NP–completeness for branching quantifiers are based on a kind of Ramsey property which is expressible by means of branching. The main application of branching quantifiers in linguistics is within the study of sentences like:

(11) Some relative of each villager and some relative of each townsman hate each other.

(12) Most villagers and most townsmen hate each other.

However, all these NP-complete natural language constructions are ambiguous. Their reading varies between easy and difficult interpretations. Moreover, such sentences can hardly be found in natural language corpora (see [13]). One of the goals of this paper is to present mighty natural language quantifiers which occur frequently in everyday English.

3   Complexity of the Ramseyfication

We will restrict ourselves to finite models. We identify models of the form $\mathbb{M} = (M, A^M, R^M)$, where $A^M \subseteq M$ and $R^M \subseteq M^2$, with colored graphs. Remember that we are considering only monotone increasing quantifiers. Hence, in graph-theoretical terms we can say that $\mathbb{M} \models \mathsf{Rams}(Q)(A, R)$ if and only if there is a complete subgraph in A^M with respect to R^M of a size bounded below by the quantifier Q. R^M is the extension of a reciprocal relation R. If R is symmetric then we are obviously dealing with undirected graphs. In such cases Rams and $\mathsf{Rams}^\vee$ are equivalent. Otherwise, if the reciprocal relation R is not symmetric, our models become directed graphs. In the following two subsections we will restrict ourselves to undirected graphs and prove that some strong reciprocal quantified sentences are then NP-complete. As undirected graphs are special case of directed graphs then general problems for them also have to be NP-complete.

3.1   Simple Observations

Counting Quantifiers. To decide whether in some model $\mathbb{M}$ sentence $\mathsf{Rams}(\mathsf{At\ least\ k})(A, R)$ is true we have to solve the CLIQUE problem for M and k. A brute force algorithm to find a clique in a graph is to examine each subgraph with at least k vertices and check if it forms a clique. This means that for every fixed k the computational complexity of $\mathsf{Rams}(\mathsf{At\ least\ k})$ is in PTIME. For instance, $\mathsf{Rams}(\mathsf{At\ least\ 5})$ is computable in a polynomial time. Moreover, notice that the strong reciprocal sentence $\mathsf{Rams}(\exists^{\geq k})(A, R)$ is equivalent to the following first-order formula:

$$\exists x_1 \ldots \exists x_k \Big[\bigwedge_{1 \leq i < j \leq k} x_i \neq x_j \wedge \bigwedge_{1 \leq i \leq k} A(x_i) \wedge \bigwedge_{\substack{1 \leq i \leq k \\ 1 \leq j \leq k}} R(x_i, x_j) \Big].$$

However, when we consider natural language semantics from a procedural point of view it is natural to assume that people rather have one quantifier concept At least k, for every natural number k, than the infinite set of concepts At least 1, At least 2, ... It seems reasonable to suppose that we learn one mental algorithm to understand each of the counting quantifiers At least k, At most k, and Exactly k, no matter which natural number k actually is. Mathematically we can account for this idea by introducing counting quantifiers. The counting quantifier $C^{\geq A}$ says that the number of elements satisfying some property in a model $\mathbb{M}$ is greater or equal to the cardinality of set $A \subseteq M$. In other words, the idea here is that determiners like At least k express a relation between number of elements satisfying certain property and cardinality of some prototypical set A. For instance, determiner At least k corresponds to the quantifier $C^{\geq A}$ such that $card(A) = k$. Therefore, determiners At least 1, At least 2, At least 3, ... are interpreted by one counting quantifier $C^{\geq A}$ — just set A has to be chosen differently in every case.[1]

The quantifier $\mathsf{Ram_S}(C^{\geq A})$ expresses the general schema for reciprocal sentences with counting quantifiers in antecedents. Such general pattern defines NP-complete problems

Proposition 1. *The quantifier* $\mathsf{Ram_S}(C^{\geq A})$ *is mighty.*

Proportional Quantifiers. We can give one more general example of strong reciprocal sentences which are NP-complete. Let us consider the following sentences:

(13) Most members of the parliament refer to each other indirectly.
(14) At least one third of the members of the parliament refer to each other indirectly.
(15) At least $q \times 100\%$ of the members of the parliament refer to each other indirectly.

We will call these sentences *the strong reciprocal sentences with proportional quantifiers*. Their general form is given by the sentence schema (15), where q can be interpreted as any rational number between 0 and 1. These sentences say that there is a clique, $Cl \subseteq A$, where A is the set of all parliament members, such that $card(Cl) \geq q \times card(A)$.

For any rational number q between 0 and 1 we say that a set $A \subseteq U$ is q-large if and only if $\frac{card(A)}{card(U)} \geq q$. In this sense q determines a proportional quantifier $\mathsf{R_q}$ of type $(1, 1)$ such that $\mathbb{M} \models \mathsf{R_q}(A, B)$ iff $\frac{card(A^M)}{card(B^M)} \geq q$. The strong reciprocal lift of this quantifier, $\mathsf{Ram_S}(\mathsf{R_q})$, is of type $(1, 2)$ and might be used to express meanings of sentences like (13)–(15). We will call the quantifiers of the form $\mathsf{Ram_S}(\mathsf{R_q})$ *proportional Ramsey quantifiers*. In [16] the following was observed:

Proposition 2. *If q is a rational number between 0 and 1, then the quantifiers* $\mathsf{Ram_S}(\mathsf{R_q})$ *is mighty.*

---

[1] Alternatively we can introduce two-sorted variants of finite structures, augmented by a infinite number sort. Then we can define counting quantifiers in a way that the numeric constants in a quantifier refer to the number domain (see e.g. [14], [15]).

3.2   General Dichotomy

Our examples show that the strong interpretation of some reciprocal sentences is NP-complete. In this section we will describe a class of unary monadic quantifiers for which the strong reciprocal interpretation is PTIME computable.

Following [17] we will identify monotone simple unary quantifiers with number-theoretic functions, $f : \omega \to \omega$, such that for all $n \in \omega$, $f(n) \leq n + 1$. In that setting the quantifier Q_f (corresponding to f) says of a set A that it has at least $f(n)$ elements, where n is the cardinality of the universe. Therefore, given $f : \omega \to \omega$, we define:

$$(Q_f)_M(A) \iff card(A) \geq f(card(M)).$$

Our crucial notion goes back to the paper [18]. We say that a function f (quantifier Q_f) is *bounded* if

$$\exists m \forall n (f(n) < m \vee n - m < f(n)).$$

Otherwise f and the corresponding Q_f are *unbounded*. Typical bounded functions are: $f(n) = 1$ (corresponding to $\exists$) and $f(n) = n$ (corresponding to $\forall$). The first one is bounded from above by 2 as for every n we have $f(n) = 1 < 2$. The second one is bounded below by 1, for every n, $n - 1 < n$. Unbounded functions are for example: $\lceil \frac{n}{2} \rceil$, $\lceil \sqrt{n} \rceil$, $\lceil \log n \rceil$, where $\lceil p \rceil$ is the ceiling function of p. We illustrate the situation in the Figure 3.

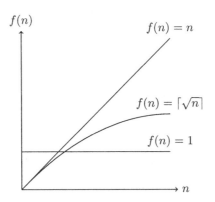

Fig. 3. The functions $f(n) = 1$ and $f(n) = n$ are bounded. The function $\lceil \sqrt{n} \rceil$ is unbounded.

In what follows we will show that the PTIME computable bounded quantifiers of type (1) are closed on the strong reciprocal lift.

Proposition 3. *If a monotone increasing quantifier Q_f is PTIME computable and bounded, then the reciprocal quantifier $\mathsf{Ram_S}(Q_f)$ is PTIME computable.*

Proof. Assume that f is PTIME computable and bounded. Then there exists a number m such that for every n the following disjunction holds ($f(n) < m$ or $n - m < f(n)$).

Let us fix a graph model $\mathbb{G} = (V, E)$, where $card(V) = n$.

In the first case assume that $f(n) < m$. First observe that if there exists a clique of size greater than $f(n)$ then there has to be also a clique of size exactly $f(n)$. Thus to decide whether $\mathbb{G} \in \mathsf{Rams}(Q_f)$ it is enough to check if there is a clique of size $f(n)$ in $\mathbb{G}$. We know that $f(n) < m$. Hence we only need to examine all subgraphs up to m vertices. For each of them we can check in a polynomial time whether it forms a clique. Hence, it is enough to observe that the number of all subgraphs of size between 1 up to m is bounded by the polynomial. In fact it is the case as the number of k-combinations from a set is smaller than the number of permutations with repetitions of lenght k from that set. Therefore, we have:

$$\binom{n}{1} + \binom{n}{2} + \ldots + \binom{n}{m} \le n^1 + n^2 + \ldots + n^m \le m(n^m).$$

Let us consider the second case; assume that $n - m < f(n)$. This time we have to only check large subgraphs, precisely we need to examine all subgraphs containing from n down to $n - m$ vertices. Again, the number of such subgraphs is bounded by the polynomial for fixed m. We use the following well known equality $\binom{n}{n-k} = \binom{n}{k}$ to shows that we have to inspect only polynomial number of subsets:

$$\binom{n}{n} + \binom{n}{n-1} + \ldots + \binom{n}{n-m} = \binom{n}{n} + \binom{n}{1} + \ldots + \binom{n}{m}$$
$$\le 1 + n^1 + n^2 + \ldots + n^m \le m(n^m).$$

Therefore, in every case when f is bounded and computable in a polynomial time we simply run the two above algorithms for every possible case. This model-checking procedure for $\mathsf{Rams}(Q_f)$ simply tests clique property on all subgraphs up to m elements and from n to $n-m$ elements, where m is fixed and independent from the size of a universe. Therefore, it is bounded by a polynomial.

It does not matter whether we consider undirected or directed graphs as in both cases checking whether a given subgraph is complete can be done in polynomial time. Therefore, the result holds also for $\mathsf{Rams}^{\vee}(Q_f)$.

Moreover, notice that the relativization Q_f^{rel} of Q_f is the right monotone type $(1, 1)$ quantifier: $(Q_f^{rel})_M(A, B) \iff card(A \cap B) \ge f(card(A))$. Thus, the restriction is not essential and the result may be easily translated for type $(1, 1)$ quantifiers.

Notice that the property of boundness plays also a crucial role in the definability theory of polyadic lifts. In [18] it has been shown that the Ramseyfication of Q is definable in $FO(Q)$ if and only if Q is bounded. They also obtained similar results for branching and resumption (see [18]).

4   Complexity of the Intermediate and Weak Lifts

Analogously to the case of strong reciprocity we can also express the meanings of intermediate and weak reciprocal lifts in graph-theoretical terms. We say that $\mathbb{M} \models \mathsf{Ram_I}(\mathsf{Q})(A, R)$ if and only if there is a connected subgraph in A^M of a size bounded from below by the quantifier Q. $\mathbb{M} \models \mathsf{Ram_W}(\mathsf{Q})(A, R)$ if and only if there is a subgraph in A^M of a proper size without isolated vertices. All with respect to the relation R^M, either symmetric or asymmetric.

We prove that the class of PTIME quantifiers is closed under the (alternative) intermediate lift and the (alternative) weak lift.

Proposition 4. *If a monotone increasing quantifier* Q *is a PTIME computable quantifier, then the quantifiers* $\mathsf{Ram_I}(\mathsf{Q})$ *and* $\mathsf{Ram_I}^\vee(\mathsf{Q})$ *are PTIME computable.*

Proof. We consider only the case of the quantifier $\mathsf{Ram_I}(\mathsf{Q})$, the proof for the alternative case is analogous. Let $\mathbb{G} = (V, A, E)$ be a directed colored graph-model. To check whether $\mathbb{G} \in \mathsf{Ram_I}(\mathsf{Q})$ compute all connected components of the subgraph determined by A. For example, you can use a breadth-first search algorithm that begins at some node and explores all the connected neighboring vertices. Then for each of those nearest nodes, it explores their unexplored connected neighbor vertices, and so on, until it finds the full connected subgraph. Next, it chooses a node which does not belong to this subgraph and starts searching for the connected subgraph containing it. Since in the worst case this breadth-first search has to go through all paths to all possible vertices, the time complexity of the breadth-first search on the whole $\mathbb{G}$ is $O(card(V) + card(E))$. Moreover, the number of the components in A is bounded by $card(A)$. Having all connected components it is enough to check whether there is a component C of a proper size, i.e. does $\mathsf{Q}(A, C)$ hold for some connected component C. This can be checked in a polynomial time as Q is PTIME computable quantifier. Hence, $\mathsf{Ram_I}(\mathsf{Q})$ is in PTIME.

The next proposition follows immediately.

Proposition 5. *If a monotone increasing quantifier* Q *is a PTIME computable quantifier, then the quantifiers* $\mathsf{Ram_W}(\mathsf{Q})$ *and* $\mathsf{Ram_W}^\vee(\mathsf{Q})$ *are PTIME computable.*

These results show that the intermediate and the weak reciprocal lifts do not increase the complexity of quantifier sentences in such a drastic way as may happen in the case of strong reciprocal lifts. In other words, in many contexts intermediate and weak interpretations are relatively easy as opposed to the strong reciprocal reading.

5   A Complexity Perspective on SMH

In [4] proposed the pragmatic principle, the Strong Meaning Hypothesis, to predict the proper reading of sentences containing reciprocal expressions. According to SMH the reciprocal expression is interpreted as having logically the strongest truth conditions that are consistent with a given context. Therefore, if it is only consistent with specified facts, then a statement containing *each other* will be interpreted as a strong reciprocal sentence. Otherwise, an interpretation will shift toward the logically weaker intermediate or weak readings, depending on a context.

SMH is quite an effective pragmatic principle. We will discuss the shifts SMH predicts from the computational complexity point of view referring to the results provided in the previous sections.

Let us first think about the meaning of a sentence in the intensional way, identifying the meaning of an expression with an algorithm recognizing its denotation in a finite model[2]. Such algorithms can be described by investigating how language users evaluate the truth-value of sentences in various situations. On the cognitive level it means that subjects have to be equipped with mental devices to deal with meanings of expressions. Moreover, it is cognitively plausible to assume that we have one mental device to deal with most instances of the same semantic construction. For example, we believe that there is one mental algorithm to deal with the counting quantifier, At least k, in most possible contexts, no matter what natural number k is. Thus, in the case of logical expressions, like quantifiers, the analogy between meanings and algorithms seems uncontroversial.

However, notice that some sentences, being intractable, are too hard for identifying their truth-value directly by investigating a model. The experience in writing programs suggests that we can claim a sentence to be difficult when it cannot be computed in a polynomial time. Despite the fact that some sentences are sometimes[3] too hard for comprehension, we can find their inferential relations with relatively easier sentences.

According to SMH any reciprocal sentence, if it is possible, should be interpreted as a strong reciprocal sentence. We have shown that the strong interpretation of sentences with quantified antecedents is sometimes intractable but intermediate and weak readings are always easy to comprehend. In other words, it is reasonable to suspect that in some linguistic situations the strong reciprocal interpretation is cognitively much more difficult than the intermediate or the weak interpretation. This prediction makes sense under the assumption that $P \neq NP$ and that the human mind is bounded by computational restrictions. We omit a discussion here and only recall that computational restrictions for cognitive abilities are widely treated in the literature. For example, in philosophy [21], study of reasoning [22], cognitive science [23], linguistics [24], and formal semantics [25]. In [26] the so-called P-Cognition Thesis was explicitly formulated:

---

[2] This approach, going back to [19], exists in the linguistic literature in the different levels of transparency (see e.g.[20]).

[3] The fact that the general problem is hard does not show that all instances normally encountered are hard. It is the matter of empirical studies to provide us with data about computational complexity influence on our everyday linguistic experience. However, we believe that it is reasonable to expect that this happens at least in some situations.

P-Cognition Thesis. *Human cognitive (linguistic) capacities are constrained by polynomial-time computability.*

What happens if a subject is supposed to deal with a sentence too hard for a direct comprehension? One possibility is that the subject will try to establish the truth-value of a sentence indirectly, by shifting to an accessible inferential meaning. That will be, depending on the context, the intermediate or the weak interpretation, both being implied by the strong interpretation.

Summing up, our descriptive complexity perspective on reciprocity shows that it might be not always possible to interpret a reciprocal sentence in the strong way as SMH suggests. If a sentence in question would be intractable under the strong reciprocal interpretation then people will turn to tractable readings, like intermediate and weak. Our observations give a cognitively reasonable argument for some shifts to occur, even though they are not predicted by SMH. For example, SMH assumes that the following sentence should be interpreted as the strong reciprocal statement.

(16) Most parliament members refer to each other indirectly.

However, we know that this sentence is NP-complete. Therefore, if the set of parliament members is large enough then the statement is intractable under the strong interpretation. It gives a perfect reason to switch for a weaker interpretations.

6   Conclusion

By investigating reciprocal expressions in the computational paradigm we found the differences in the complexity between various interpretations of reciprocal sentences with quantified antecedents. In particular, we proved that for PTIME computable quantifiers the intermediate and the weak reciprocal interpretations are PTIME computable. Moreover, if we additionally assume that a quantifier is bounded then also the strong reciprocal interpretation stays in PTIME. Therefore, the semantic distinctions from [4] seem also solid from a computational perspective. Moreover, identifying meanings with algorithms those results allow us to argue in favor of Strong Meaning Hypothesis.

Many questions arise which are to be answered in future work. Here we will mention only a few of them:

(1) Among the reciprocal sentences we found NP-complete constructions. For example, we have shown that the strong reciprocal interpretations of proportional quantifiers are NP-complete. On the other side, we also proved that the strong reciprocal interpretations of bounded quantifiers are in PTIME. We would like to know where the precise border is between those quantifiers for which Ramseyfication is in PTIME and those for which it is NP-complete. Is it the case that for every function f from some class we have a duality theorem, i.e., $\mathsf{Ram}_S(\mathsf{Q}_f)$ is either PTIME computable or NP-complete? Can we prove under some complexity assumptions that PTIME Ramsey quantifiers are exactly bounded Ramsey quantifiers?

(2) There is a vast literature on the definability of polyadic lifts of generalized quantifiers (see e.g. [18]). We introduced some new linguistically relevant lifts, the weak and the intermediate reciprocal lifts. The next step is to study their definability. For example, we would like to know how the definability questions for $\mathsf{Ram_S(Q}_f)$, $\mathsf{Ram_I(Q}_f)$, and $\mathsf{Ram_W(Q}_f)$ depend on the properties of f? Another interesting point is to link our operators with other polyadic lifts, like branching.

(3) What about different complexity measures? For example, how can one repeat our story invoking parametrized or average-case complexity?

(4) Is it well enough justified to identify meanings with algorithms? Broader philosophical discussion on applications of complexity theory to natural language semantics seems inevitable.

(5) Finally, we need to investigate the interplay between cognitive difficulty and computational complexity in more detail. Do the differences in the computational complexity really play an important role in natural language processing as some neuroimaging data suggests (see [27], [28])? For example, we could empirically compare the differences in shifts from the strong interpretation of reciprocal sentences with bounded and proportional quantifiers in antecedents. Our approach predicts that subjects will shift to easier interpretations more frequently in the case of sentences with proportional quantifiers.

References

1. Heim, I., Lasnik, H., May, R.: Reciprocity and plurality. Linguistic Inquiry 22, 63–101 (1991)
2. Beck, S.: The semantics of different: Comparison operator and relational adjective. Linguistics and Philosophy 23, 101–139 (2000)
3. Sabato, S., Winter, Y.: From semantic restrictions to reciprocal meanings. In: Proceedings of FG-MOL 2005. CSLI Publications (2005)
4. Dalrymple, M., Kanazawa, M., Kim, Y., Mchombo, S., Peters, S.: Reciprocal expressions and the concept of reciprocity. Linguistics and Philosophy 21, 159–210 (1998)
5. Mostowski, A.: On a generalization of quantifiers. Fundamenta Mathematicae 44, 12–36 (1957)
6. Lindström, P.: First order predicate logic with generalized quantifiers. Theoria 32, 186–195 (1966)
7. Barwise, J., Cooper, R.: Generalized quantifiers and natural language. Linguistics and Philosophy 4, 159–219 (1981)
8. Peters, S., Westerståhl, D.: Quantifiers in Language and Logic. Clarendon Press, Oxford (2006)
9. Winter, Y.: Flexibility principles in Boolean semantics. The MIT Press, London (2001)
10. Papadimitriou, C.H.: Computational Complexity. Addison-Wesley, Reading (1993)
11. Blass, A., Gurevich, Y.: Henkin quantifiers and complete problems. Annals of Pure and Applied Logic 32, 1–16 (1986)

12. Mostowski, M., Wojtyniak, D.: Computational complexity of the semantics of some natural language constructions. Annals of Pure and Applied Logic 127, 219–227 (2004)
13. Sevenster, M.: Branches of imperfect information: logic, games, and computation. PhD thesis, Universiteit van Amsterdam (2006)
14. Otto, M.: Bounded Variable Logics and Counting, vol. 9. Springer, Heidelberg (1997)
15. Grädel, E., Gurevich, Y.: Metafinite model theory. Information and Computation 140, 26–81 (1998)
16. Mostowski, M., Szymanik, J.: Computational complexity of some Ramsey quantifiers in finite models. The Bulletin of Symbolic Logic 13, 281–282 (2007)
17. Väänänen, J.: Unary quantifiers on finite models. Journal of Logic, Language and Information 6, 275–304 (1997)
18. Hella, L., Väänänen, J., Westerståhl, D.: Definability of polyadic lifts of generalized quantifiers. Journal of Logic, Language and Information 6, 305–335 (1997)
19. Frege, G.: Über Sinn und Bedeutung. Zeitschrift für Philosophie und philosophische Kritik 100, 25–50 (1892)
20. Moschovakis, Y.: A logical calculus of meaning and synonymy. Linguistics and Philosophy 29, 27–89 (2006)
21. Cherniak, C.: Minimal rationality. Mind 90, 161–183 (1981)
22. Levesque, H.J.: Logic and the complexity of reasoning. Journal of Philosophical Logic 17, 355–389 (1988)
23. van Rooij, I.: The tractable cognition thesis. Cognitive Science: A Multidisciplinary Journal 32, 939–984 (2008)
24. Ristad, E.S.: The Language Complexity Game (Artificial Intelligence). The MIT Press, Cambridge (1993)
25. Mostowski, M., Szymanik, J.: Semantic bounds for everyday language. Technical Report ILLC Preprint Series, PP-2006-40, Institute for Logic, Language and Computation, University of Amsterdam (2005) (to appear in Semiotica)
26. Frixione, M.: Tractable competence. Minds and Machines 11, 379–397 (2001)
27. Mcmillan, C.T., Clark, R., Moore, P., Devita, C., Grossman, M.: Neural basis for generalized quantifiers comprehension. Neuropsychologia 43, 1729–1737 (2005)
28. Szymanik, J.: A comment on a neuroimaging study of natural language quantifier comprehension. Neuropsychologia 45, 2158–2160 (2007)

Quantifiers in Japanese

Sumiyo Nishiguchi

Osaka University, Graduate School of Language and Culture, Department of
Language and Information Science
1-8 Machikaneyama, Toyonaka, Osaka 560-0043, Japan
u301192b@ecs.cmc.osaka-u.ac.jp
http://homepage3.nifty.com/sumiyo_nishiguchi/

Abstract. This paper argues that the generalized quantifier theory does
not directly apply to Japanese quantifiers because of the following reasons: (i) the number of noun phrase (NP) arguments is underspecified
and (ii) quantities are often expressed by predicative adjectives. It further claims that the word order changes the interpretation. For example,
non-split quantifiers correspond to definite NPs that are unique in the domain of discourse, while split NPs are wide-scope indefinites. Adjectival
quantifiers are polymorphic, and continuation-based combinatory categorial grammar [1] accounts for different meanings between (non)split
quantifiers.

1 Limitations of the Standard Generalized Quantifier Theory

The generalized quantifier theory in [2, 3] maps the syntactic constituency between a noun and a determiner into a quantifier. However, such a view along
with the relational view on generalized quantifiers, which considers the relation
between two sets [4, 5] cannot directly handle Japanese quantificational words,
which do not necessarily have two arguments. as I show. Moreover, being a
determiner-less language, quantities are often naturally expressed by predicates,
instead of noun phrases (NPs) as in English. Furthermore, a quantificational
phrase and a modified noun demonstrate long-distance dependency as a split
NP or a floating quantifier.

1.1 Predicative Adjectival Quantifiers

In English, quantifiers are normally noun phrases such as *Many people attended*.
However, as [6] observes, numbers and quantities are more naturally expressed
as predicates in Japanese. While English-type quantifiers are possible, as in the
case of (1a), predicative adjectives such as those in (1b) are more natural.

(1) a. Oku-no   nihonjin-wa   A-gata-da.
       many-GEN Japanese-TOP A-type-be
       "Many Japanese are type A."

P. Bosch, D. Gabelaia, and J. Lang (Eds.): TbiLLC 2007, LNAI 5422, pp. 153–164, 2009.
© Springer-Verlag Berlin Heidelberg 2009

    b. Nihonjin-wa   A-gata-ga   oi.
      Japanese-TOP A-type-NOM many
      "Many Japanese are type A."

While weak determiners such as *many*, *few*, and *five* can appear as predicative adjectives, this is not the case with strong determiners like *every* and *most*, in English.[1,2] Japanese, unlike English, has, both weak and strong quantifiers appearing as predicative adjectives (2b).

(2) a. The number of attendants was {many/few/forty/*most/*every}.
      b. Kessekisha-ga {okat/sukunakat/yonju-nin-dat/hotondo-dat/zen-in-dat}
          absentee-NOM many/few/40-CL/most/every-be

          -ta.
          -PAST

          "There were many/few/40/most/all people who were absent."

Since adjectives denote a property or a set of entities, the denotations of *many* and *three* would be sets of entities whose numbers are considered to be many, and three, respectively. [8] proposes the function "BE," which shifts generalized quantifiers such as *an authority* in the (et, t) type into (et) in a predicate position (*Mary considers John competent in semantics and an authority on unicorns*). However, *many* or *three* in the (et) type cannot predicate the relations between two sets. Considering cardinal numbers and the fact that adjectival quantifiers predicate only one argument, the (et) analysis works. However, Japanese quantificational adjectives predicate more than one argument.

1.2 An Underspecified Number of Arguments

Since quantifiers in Japanese—a language without overt determiners—do not correspond to noun phrases as in English, [6] indicates that the NP-quantifier universal in [2] should be rejected.

(3) U1 NP-Quantifier universal:
    "Every language has syntactic constituents (called noun-phrases) whose semantic function is to express generalized quantifiers over the domain of discourse." [2, 177]

Although Japanese generalized quantifiers do not correspond to NPs, [6] claims that quantification in Japanese continues to be based on the relation between two predicates. [9] further proposes that Japanese generalized quantifiers are relational.

---

[1] Weak quantifiers are admitted in there-sentences while strong quantifiers are not [7, 2].

[2] [8] states that *every NP* and *most NP* cannot appear in the complement of *consider*.

  (i) Mary considers that two islands/*every island/*most islands/Utopia.

(4) a. (Tokyo-wa) (gakusei-ga) oi(E)
         Tokyo-TOP dog-NOM   many
         "There are many students in Tokyo."
     b. (hitobito-wa) hotondo(E) (kaetteshimatta).
         people-TOP   most   went home-PAST
         "Most people have left."

This analysis works, provided quantificational words take exactly two arguments. However, in a controversially non-configurational language such as Japanese, the number of arguments is not specified. [10] proposes generating sentences by means of the phrase structure rule presented in (5).

(5) $\overline{X} \to \overline{X}^* \ X$

In an X-bar schema, the head (X) is preceded by any number of complements, including zero. At the sentence level, as I state in (6), any number of NPs may appear, provided there is a predicate—either a verb or an adjective—in the sentence-final position (7)–(9). Therefore, the standard generalized quantifier theory does not apply directly to Japanese quantifiers in (7) and (9).

(6) S → NP* V
     S → NP* AP

1 argument

(7) Shussekisha$_{NP}$-ga {sukunakat/okat}$_{AP}$-ta.
     attendants-NOM   few/many-PAST
     "There were few/many attendants (Lit. The attendants were few/many)."

2 arguments

(8) Nihonjin$_{NP}$-ga A-gata$_{NP}$-ga oi$_{AP}$ (koto).
     Japanese-NOM A-type-NOM many fact
     "Many Japanese are type A."

3 arguments

(9) Gakusei$_{NP}$-ga amerikajin$_{NP}$-ga josei$_{NP}$-ga oi$_{AP}$ (koto).
     student-TOP   American-NOM   female-NOM many fact
     "Many students are female Americans."

1.3 Definite Non-split NP and Indefinite Split NP

Furthermore, we observe that the word order marks the definiteness of quantifier NPs. While English floating quantifiers are limited to universals such as *all* and *each* [11] as in (10a), Japanese floating quantifiers have more variety (11). In addition, English floating quantifiers do not allow long-distance dependencies (10b), whereas a Japanese numeral quantifier and a modified noun can be split by adverbials [12] under certain restrictions (12).

(10) a. The students all came.
      b. *The students yesterday all came.

(11) a. Gakusei-ga   zen-in/mina/3-nin   kita.
         student-NOM all-member/all/3-CL came
         "All/three students came."
      b. Chichioya-wa {hotondo/taigai/daitai} shiawase-da.
         father-TOP   most   happy-be
         "Fathers are mostly happy."
      c. Gakusei-ga rokuwari   kuruma-o mot-teiru (koto).
         student-NOM 60 percent car-ACC   have-PROG fact
         "Sixty percent of the students have a car."

(12) a. NP_{nomi} Adv Q_i V
         Tomodachi-ga (kino)   san-nin kita.
         friend-NOM   yesterday 3-CL   came
         "Three friends of mine came yesterday."
      b. NP_{nom} NP_{acci} Adv Q_i V
         Tomodachi-ga hon-o   (kino)   san-satsu katta.
         friend-NOM   book-ACC yesterday 3-CL   bought
         "A friend of mine bought three books yesterday."
      c. NP_{acci} NP_{nom} Adv Q_i V
         Hon-o   tomodachi-ga (kino)   san-satsu katta.
         book-ACC friend-NOM   yesterday 3-CL   bought
         "Three friends of mine came yesterday."
      d. *NP_{acc} NP_{nomi} (Adv) Q_i V
         *Hon-o   tomodachi-ga (kino)   san-nin katta.
         book-ACC friend-NOM   yesterday 3-CL   bought
         "A friend of mine bought three books yesterday."
      e. *NP_{nomi} NP_{acc} (Adv) Q_i V
         *Tomodachi-ga hon-o   (kino)   san-nin katta.
         friend-NOM   book-ACC yesterday 3-CL   bought
         "Three friends of mine bought a book yesterday."

[13] discusses the NP split of the definite superlative in Hungarian. The NP split is allowed with a comparative indefinite reading, but not with the absolute definite reading of the superlative.

(13) [$_{Leftdisl}$ zöld ló-val]   [$_{FOCUS}$ itt] találkoztam a   legszebb-el
         green   horse-with here   met-I   the prettiest-with
         'I met a prettier green horse here than anywhere else'
         "*As for green horses, it was here that I met the prettiest of them, i.e., the prettiest green horse that there is."

In Japanese, the use of a non-split quantifier phrase (QP) presupposes a unique set of entities, and thus corresponds to a definite description. On the other hand, the referents of a postnominal quantifier are not presupposed so that split quantifiers correspond to indefinites.

(14) a. # 2-to-no zo-ga   hashit-te, hoka-no   zo-wa   suwat-teiru.
2-CL-GEN elephant-NOM run-and   other-GEN elephant-TOP sit-PROG
[exhaustive]

"The two elephants are running and other elephants are sitting."
b. Zo-ga   2-to hashit-te, hoka-no   zo-wa   suwat-teiru.
elephant-NOM 2-CL run-and   other-GEN elephant-TOP sit-PROG
[non-exhaustive]

"Two elephants are running and other elephants are sitting."

(15) a. # 3-nin-no gakusei-ga   kino   hataraita. Mo   hutari-mo hataraita.
3-CL-GEN   student-NOM yesterday worked   more 2-CL-also worked
[exhaustive]

"The three students worked yesterday. Two others worked, too."
b. Gakusei-ga   kino   3-nin hataraita. Mo   hutari-mo hataraita.
student-NOM yesterday 3-CL   worked   more 2-CL-also worked
[non-exhaustive]

"Three students worked yesterday. Two others worked, too."

(16) a. # 2-to-no midori-no uma-ni   at-te,   mata 3-to-ni   atta.
2-CL-GEN green-GEN horse-DAT met-and again 3-CL-DAT met
[exhaustive]

"I met the two green horses and met three more, too."
b. midori-no uma 2-to-ni   at-te,   mata 3-to-ni   atta.
green-GEN horse 2-CL-DAT met-and again 3-CL-DAT met
[non-exhaustive]

"I met two green horses and met three more, too."

In the sentences in (14a), (15a), and (16a), prenominal quantifier phrases such as *2-to-no zo* "two elephants" and *3-nin-no gakusei* "three students" have exhaustive interpretations, leaving no scope for other students or elephants to be mentioned in the following sentences. In other words, prenominal quantifier phrases refer to a unique set of entities that are discourse-given. *2-to-no zo* "elephants" and *3-nin-no gakusei* "three students" each corresponds to definite NPs—*the two elephants* and *the three students*—in which the number of students or elephants is limited. On the contrary, in the sentences in (14b), (15b), and (16b), the postnominal quantifier phases, e.g., *zo-ga 2-to* "two elephants" and *gakusei-ga 3-nin* "three students," are not so exhaustive, as a result of which other elephants and students can be mentioned in the sentences that follow.

(17) a. Asa-kara   3-nin-no gakusei-to   hanashi-ta-ga   nokori-no 3-nin-to-wa
        morning-since 3-CL-GEN student-with speak-PAST-but rest-GEN 3-CL-with-TOP
        hanasa-nakat-ta.
        speak-NEG-PAST
        "I spoke with three students in the morning but I did not speak with
        the (remaining) other three."

    b. #Asa-kara   gakusei 3-nin-to   hanashi-ta-ga   nokori-no 3-nin-to-wa
        morning-since student 3-CL-with speak-PAST-but rest-GEN 3-CL-with-TOP
        hanasa-nakat-ta.
        speak-NEG-PAST
        "I spoke with three students in the morning but I did not speak with
        the (remaining) other three."

In (16a), the prenominal QP *3-nin-no gakusei* "three students" is not exhaustive since the following sentence predicates the rest of the students in the same group. However, even though the total number of students is more than three, the entire set of students is unique. On the other hand, the use of a floating (split) QP phrase does not presuppose the uniqueness of entities; as a result of which, the following sentences cannot mention the rest of students in the group. Therefore, the split QP corresponds to indefinite *two NP* in (16b), while the non-split QP corresponds to definite *the two NP* in (16a).[3]

(18) a. $\exists X.[\text{elephant'}(X) \wedge |X| = 2 \wedge \forall y.[\text{elephant'}(y) \rightarrow y \sqsubseteq X] \wedge \text{ran'}(X)]$
      b. $\exists X.[\text{elephant'}(X) \wedge |X| = 2 \wedge \text{ran'}(X)]$

(19) a. $\exists X.[\text{student'}(X) \wedge [|X| = 3] \wedge \forall y.[\text{student'}(y) \rightarrow y \sqsubseteq X] \wedge \text{worked'}(X)]$
      b. $\exists X.[\text{student'}(X) \wedge [|X| = 3] \wedge \text{worked'}(X)]$

Note that split NPs are scope insensitive and always take a wider scope over a bare NP. It has been pointed out that a split NP allows a distributive reading but not a collective one [15, 16, among others]. In (20a), three students may either bake a cake together (a cake > three students) or bake three cakes each (three students > a cake). On the other hand, (20b) only allows one cake per student (three students > a cake). (20b) shows that both split and non-split quantifiers in the predicate position allow only collective readings.

(20) a. 3-nin-no gakusei-ga   keeki-o   tsukutta. [√collective, √distributive]
        3-CL-GEN student-NOM cake-ACC made
        "The three students made a cake."
      b. Gakusei-ga   3-nin keeki-o   tsukutta. [*collective, √distributive]
        student-NOM 3-CL cake-ACC made
        "Three students made a cake (each)."

---

[3] See discussions on the uniqueness effects of the English definite NPs in [14].

(21) a. {3-biki-no neko-ga/Neko-ga 3-biki} 2-hiki-no nezumi-o   tabeta.
         3-CL-GEN cat-NOM/cat-NOM 3-CL   2-CL-GEN mouse-ACC ate
         [√collective, *distributive]

         "(The) three cat ate two mice."
     b. {3-biki-no neko-ga/Neko-ga 3-biki} nezumi-o   2-hiki tabeta.
         3-CL-GEN cat-NOM/cat-NOM 3-CL   mouse-ACC 2-CL   ate
         [√collective, *distributive]

         "(The) three cats ate two mice."

In order to force a narrower reading on a split QP, a distributivity marker
zutsu "each" is necessary [17].

To sum up, the aforementioned QPs have the following characteristics:

(22) a. non-split QP: definite with uniqueness presuppositions and maximality
         condition (exhaustive)
     b. split QP: wide scope indefinite (non-exhaustive)
     c. *zutsu* "each" QP: distributive phrase[4]

2   Solution

2.1   Flexible-Type Approach to Adjectival Quantifiers

CCG. The underspecified number of arguments suggests a polymorphic type for
adjectival quantifiers (et^n, t) that can be either (et), $(et,(et,t))$, or $((et,(et,(et))),t)$.
Proportional *many* would have the following lexical entry:

(23) $[\![many]\!]_{((e \to t)^n \to t)}$
      $= \lambda P_1, P_2, ..., P_n.|P_1 \cap P_2 \cap, ..., \cap P_n| \geq |P_n| \cdot c$

A quantificational word in such a flexible type can take any number of arguments. We also adopt the N-ary Function Application (NFA) [22, 40] for inter-
preting flat structures. Let us add the NFA to the basic rules in the Combinatory
Categorial Grammar (CCG) [23, 24].

---

[4] Even though Japanese lacks determiners, [18] assumes that Japanese NPs have D or
something equivalent in terms of the function. In harmony with Fukui's analysis, [19]
proposes a null determiner of type $(et, (et, t))$, which combines with a bare NP of type
(et). If this is valid, the null determiner corresponds to an indefinite determiner. [20]
assumes a null determiner for a bare NP and shows that the Hungarian split NP takes
a narrower scope than any other kind of scope-bearing element. Alternatively, we
might assume a contextually determined choice function f [21] that maps a nominal
property into an individual or plural individuals.
(ii) a. Gakusei-ga   kita.
         student-NOM came
         "A student came."
     b. $[\![student]\!] = f_{(et,e)} \exists x. f(\lambda x. student'(x))$

(24) a. N-ary Function Application
$$[\![_{X^n}X^oAA'A"...]\!]^g=$$
$$[\![X^0]\!]^g([\![A_n]\!]^g)([\![A_{n-1}]\!]^g)...([\![A_1]\!]^g),$$
where, $A_1, A_2, ..., A_{n-1}, A_n$ is the order of $A, A', A"...$on X^0's argument-list

b. N-ary Function Application
A_1: a,...,A_n:z A_1,...,$A_n \setminus$ B:f $\Rightarrow$ B: f((a),...,(z)) $(^n <)$

1 argument

(25) Shussekisha-wa sanju-nin-dat-ta.
attendant-TOP 30-CL-be-PAST
"The number of attendants was thirty."

$$\cfrac{\cfrac{shussekisha-wa}{N:\lambda x.attendant'(x)}\text{Lex} \quad \cfrac{sanju-nin-dat-ta}{N \setminus S: \lambda P.|P|=30}\text{Lex}}{S:|\lambda x.attendent'(x)|=30}<$$

2 arguments

(26) Gakusei-wa amerika-jin-ga oi.
student-TOP American-NOM many
"There are many Americans among students."

$$\cfrac{\cfrac{gakusei-wa}{N:\lambda x.student'(x)}\text{Lex} \quad \cfrac{amerikajin-ga}{N:\lambda y.American'(y)}\text{Lex} \quad \cfrac{oi}{N\setminus(N\setminus S):\lambda P,Q.|P\cap Q|\geq|Q|\cdot c}\text{Lex}}{S:|\lambda x.[student'(x)\wedge American'(x)]|\geq|\lambda x.student'(x)|\cdot c}_n<$$

3 arguments

(27) Gakusei-wa amerikajin-ga josei-ga   oi.
student-TOP American-NOM woman-NOM many
"Many students are female Americans."

$$\cfrac{\cfrac{gakusei-wa}{N:\lambda x.student'(x)}\text{Lex} \; \cfrac{amerikajin-ga}{N:\lambda y.American'(y)}\text{Lex} \; \cfrac{josei-ga}{N:\lambda z.female'(z)}\text{Lex} \; \cfrac{oi}{N\setminus(N\setminus(N\setminus S)):\lambda P,Q,R.|P\cap Q\cap R|\geq|R|\cdot c}\text{Lex}}{S:|\lambda x.[student'(x)\wedge American'(x)\wedge female'(x)]|\geq|\lambda x.student'(x)|\cdot c}_n<$$

2.2 Definiteness by Word Order

Problem. Regardless of how we categorize numerals and bare NPs, assigning identical categories to each lexical item does not explain the differences between FQs and non-FQs.

(28)

$$\cfrac{\cfrac{\text{cat-NOM}}{\text{NP}}\text{Lex} \quad \cfrac{\text{3-CL}}{\text{NP}\setminus \text{NP}}\text{Lex}}{\cfrac{\text{NP}}{\cfrac{}{S}}<} \quad \cfrac{\text{came}}{\text{NP}\setminus \text{S}}\text{Lex}<$$

(29)

$$\cfrac{\cfrac{\text{3-CL-GEN}}{\text{NP/NP}}\text{Lex} \quad \cfrac{\text{cat-GEN}}{\text{NP}}\text{Lex}}{\cfrac{\text{NP}}{\cfrac{}{S}}>} \quad \cfrac{\text{came}}{\text{NP}\setminus\text{S}}\text{Lex}<$$

CPS Translation. The differences between FQs and non-FQs imply that word order contributes to meaning. In other words, the meaning of (non)-FQs is sensitive to word order, and the order of evaluation affects interpretations. The (in)definiteness appears to be the result of the left-to-right evaluation, and definite interpretation is the result of processing a prenominal numeral first.

In Continuation Passing Style (CPS), every function takes the extra function k, to which some continuation can apply. CPS transform introduces continuation parameters. A continuation parameter is introduced though λ-abstraction [25, 26, 27, 28].

The CPS translation $\underline{M}$ of a $\lambda\mu$-term M is:

(30) a. $\underline{x} = \lambda k.kx$;
       b. $\underline{M\,N} = \lambda k.\underline{M}(\lambda m.\underline{N}(\lambda n.k(mn)))$

CPS transform of the lexical items

(31) a. $[\![gakusei]\!]$
          NP: $student'$
          $= \lambda k.k(student')$;
       b. $[\![5-nin]\!]$
          N: $\lambda x.[\![x]\!] = 5]$
          $= \overline{\lambda k.k}(\lambda x.[\![x]\!] = 5])$;
       c. $[\![kita]\!]$
          NP$\backslash$ S: $\lambda k.k(\lambda x.came'(x))$;

Syntactic combination

(32) a. $[\![gakusei\_5-nin]\!]$
          $= \underline{NP}QP$
          $= \lambda k.\underline{NP}(\lambda m.QP(\lambda n.k(mn)))$
          $= \lambda k.(\lambda l.l(student'))$
          $(\lambda m.\lambda o.o(\lambda x.[\![x]\!] = 5])$
          $(\lambda n.k(mn)))$
       b. $[\![5-nin-no\_gakusei]\!]$
          $= QP\underline{NP}$
          $= \overline{\lambda k.QP}(\lambda n.\underline{NP}(\lambda m.k(mn))$
          $= \lambda k.\overline{(\lambda l.l}(\lambda x.[\![x]\!] = 5]))$
          $(\lambda n.(\lambda o.o(student'))$
          $(\lambda m.k(mn)))$

Since floating numerals such as *five, many, most, every, each,* and *all* also appear as predicative adjectives, they are assigned type (e, t) here. In the absence of continuations, (non)-FQs would receive the same interpretations. Due to scopal interactions, differences between the interpretations of FQs and non-FQs are predicted. In (32a), a common noun, *student*, has higher scope than *five*. The reverse holds true for (32b).

Let us define a raising rule into a continuized type and a combination rule in the Combinatory Categorial Grammar (CCG) [29, 1, 23, 24]:

(33) a. Functional Application
  A/B: f B: a $\Rightarrow$ A: f(a) (>)
  A: a A\B: f $\Rightarrow$ B: f(a) (<)
 b. Type Raising into a Continuatized Type
  A: $a \Rightarrow$ B/(A\B): $\lambda k.k(a)$ (T)
 c. Syntactic Composition
  C/((A\B)\C): $\lambda k.k(f)$
  C/(A\C): $\lambda m.m(g)$
  $\Rightarrow$ C/(B\C):
  $\lambda k.f(\lambda m.g(\lambda n.k(mn)))$
 d. C/(A\C): $\lambda m.m(g)$
  C/((A\B)\C): $\lambda k.k(f)$
  $\Rightarrow$ C/(B\C):
  $\lambda k.g(\lambda n.f(\lambda m.k(mn)))$

The type raising rule into a continuized type (33a) enables any type of syntactic category to be lifted into higher order.

(34)

gakusei-ga	3-nin	kita
NP:student' Lex	AP:$\lambda y.[\,|y|=3]$ Lex	NP\S:$\lambda y.$came'(y) Lex
B/(NP\B):$\lambda k.k$(student') T	B/(AP\B):$\lambda m.m(\lambda y.|y|=3)$ T	B/((NP\S)\B) T
B/(S\B):$\lambda k.(\lambda l.l$(student'))	$(\lambda m.(\lambda o.o(\lambda x.[\,|x|=3])(\lambda n.k(mn))))$	
	B/(S\B)	

(35)

3-nin-no	gakusei-ga	kita
AP:$\lambda x.[\,|x|=3]$ Lex	NP:student' Lex	NP\S:$\lambda y.$ came'(y) Lex
B/(AP\B):$\lambda m.m(\lambda y.|y|=3)$ T	B/(NP\B):$\lambda k.k$(student') T	B/((NP\S)\B) T
B/(S\B):$\lambda k.(\lambda l.l(\lambda x.[\,|x|=3]))$	$(\lambda n.(\lambda o.o$(student'))$(\lambda m.k(mn)))$	
	B/(S\B)	

The non-exhaustive interpretation of postnominal QPs results from the narrower scope of the numeral while exhaustive interpretation results from the wide scope of the numeral.

3 Conclusion

In Japanese, quantities are expressed by predicative adjectives and split and non-split quantifiers in Japanese. Since the number of arguments is underspecified, we need a polymorphic type for adjectival quantifiers. The word order sets apart the definiteness of quantifiers, which is explainable by the left to right evaluation of a bare noun and a numeral phrase in the continuized type.

References

[1] Shan, C.C., Barker, C.: Explaining crossover and superiority as left-to-right evaluation. Linguistics and Philosophy, 91–134 (2006)
[2] Barwise, J., Cooper, R.: Generalized quantifiers and natural language. Linguistics and Philosophy, 159–219 (1981)

[3] Keenan, E.L., Stavi, J.: A semantic characterization of natural language determiners. Linguistics and Philosophy 9, 253–326 (1986)

[4] Zwarts, F.: Determiners: a relational perspective. In: Studies in Model-Theoretic Semantics, Foris, Dordrecht, pp. 37–62 (1983)

[5] van Benthem, J.: Essays in logical semantics. Reidel, Dordrecht (1986)

[6] Imani, M.: On quantificaiton in japanese. English Linguistics 7, 87–104 (1990)

[7] Milsark, G.: Toward an explanation of certain peculiarities of the existential construction of english. Linguistic Analysis 3, 1–29 (1977)

[8] Partee, B.: Noun phrase interpretation and type-shifting principles. In: Studies in Discourse Representation Theory and the Theory of Generalized Quantifiers, pp. 115–144. Reidel, Dordrecht (1986)

[9] Ogata, N.: Japanese particles and generalized quantifiers. In: Proceedings of the 4th Summer Conference 1990 Tokyo Linguistics Forum, pp. 115–127 (1991)

[10] Hale, K.L.: Remarks on japanese phrase structure: Comments on the papers on japanese syntax. In: MIT working papers in Linguistics, vol. 2, pp. 185–203 (1980)

[11] Sportiche, D.: A theory of floating quantifiers and its corollaries for constituent structure. Linguistic Inquiry, 425–449 (1988)

[12] Miyagawa, S.: Syntax and Semantics: Structure and Case Marking in Japanese, vol. 22. Academic Press, San Diego (1989)

[13] Szabolcsi, A.: Comparative superlatives. In: MITWPL, vol. 8 (1986)

[14] Roberts, C.: Uniqueness in definite noun phrases. Linguistics and Philosophy 26, 287–350 (2003)

[15] Terada, M.: Incorporation and Argument Structure in Japanese. PhD thesis, University of Massachusetts, Amherst (1990)

[16] Nakanishi, K.: Event quantification and distributivity. In: Event Structures in Linguistic Form and Interpretation. Mouton de Gruyter, Berlin (forthcoming)

[17] Choe, J.W.: Anti-Quantifiers and a Theory of Distributivity. PhD thesis, University of Massachusetts, Amherst (1987)

[18] Fukui, N.: The principles-and-parameters approach: a comparative syntax of english and japanese. In: Approaches to Language Typology, pp. 327–372. Clarendon Press, Oxford (1995)

[19] Nishiguchi, S.: Logical properties of japanese kakari zyosi. In: Osaka University Working Papers in English Linguistics, vol. 7, pp. 115–133 (2002)

[20] Szabolcsi, A.: Focussing properties, or the trap of first order. Theoretical Linguistics 10, 125–146 (1983)

[21] Kratzer, A.: Scope or pseudoscope? are there wide-scope indefinites (1997), http://semanticsarchive.net/

[22] Büring, D.: Binding Theory. Cambridge University Press, Cambridge (2005)

[23] Steedman, M.: The Syntactic Process. MIT Press, Cambridge (2000)

[24] Szabolcsi, A.: Bound variables in syntax (are there any?). In: Proceedings of the 6th Amsterdam Colloquium, pp. 331–353 (1987)

[25] Plotkin, G.D.: Call-by-name, call-by-value and the λ-calculus. Theoretical Computer Science 1, 125–159 (1975)

[26] Parigot, M.: $\lambda\mu$-calculus: an algorithmic interpretation of classical natural deduction. In: Voronkov, A. (ed.) LPAR 1992. LNCS (LNAI), vol. 624, pp. 190–201. Springer, Heidelberg (1992)

[27] de Groote, P.: A cps-translation of the $\lambda\mu$-calculus. In: Tison, S. (ed.) CAAP 1994. LNCS, vol. 787, pp. 85–99. Springer, Heidelberg (1994)

[28] Barker, C.: Continuations in natural language. In: Thielecke, H. (ed.) Proceedings of the Fourth ACM SIGPLAN Continuations Workshop (CW 2004), pp. 1–11 (2004)

[29] Barker, C.: Continuations and the nature of quantification. Natural Language Semantics 10, 211–242 (2002)

Exceptional Scope as Discourse Reference to Quantificational Dependencies

Adrian Brasoveanu and Donka F. Farkas*

University of California Santa Cruz
abrsvn@gmail.com, farkas@ucsc.edu

Abstract. The paper proposes a novel solution to the problem of exceptional scope (ES) of (in)definites, exemplified by the widest and intermediate scope readings of the sentence *Every student of mine read every poem that a famous Romanian poet wrote*. We propose that the ES readings have two sources: (*i*) discourse anaphora to particular sets of entities and quantificational dependencies between these entities that restrict the domain of quantification of the two universal determiners and the indefinite article; (*ii*) non-local accommodation of the discourse referent that restricts the quantificational domain of the indefinite article. Our account, formulated within a compositional dynamic system couched in classical type logic, relies on two independently motivated assumptions: (*a*) the discourse context stores not only (sets of) individuals, but also quantificational dependencies between them, and (*b*) quantifier domains are always contextually restricted. Under this analysis, (in)definites are unambiguous and there is no need for special choice-functional variables to derive exceptional scope readings.

Keywords: Exceptional scope, dependent indefinites, anaphora, quantification, dynamic plural logic, compositional DRT, classical type logic.

1 The Problem and the Basic Proposal

The paper proposes a novel solution to the problem of exceptional scope (ES) of (in)definites (first noticed in Farkas (1981) [7]), a problem that is still open despite the many insightful attempts in the literature to solve it. The ES cases we focus on here are the widest and the intermediate scope readings of (1), given below in first order translations:

(1) Every student of mine read every poem that a famous Romanian poet wrote.

(2) Narrowest scope (NS) indefinite:
$\forall x(stud.o.m(x) \rightarrow \forall y(poem(y) \land \exists z(r.poet(z) \land write(z,y)) \rightarrow read(x,y)))$

(3) a. Intermediate scope (IS) indefinite: $\forall x(stud.o.m(x) \rightarrow \exists z(r.poet(z) \land \forall y(poem(y) \land write(z,y) \rightarrow read(x,y))))$

---

* We are grateful to Pranav Anand, Sam Cumming and the audience of the Rutgers Semantics Workshop (October 5-6, 2007) for comments and discussion. The usual disclaimers apply.

P. Bosch, D. Gabelaia, and J. Lang (Eds.): TbiLLC 2007, LNAI 5422, pp. 165–179, 2009.

b. Context for the IS reading: It has been established that every student chose a poet and read every poem written by him.

(4) a. Widest scope (WS) indefinite: $\exists z(r.poet(z) \land \forall x(stud.o.m(x) \to \forall y(poem(y) \land write(z, y) \to read(x, y))))$

b. Context for the WS reading: It has been established that every student chose a poet – the same poet – and read every poem written by him.

The availability of the ES readings is crucially dependent on the discourse context relative to which sentence (1) is interpreted – or the discourse context that can be accommodated based on the utterance context. The importance of the discourse context is shown by the fact that the IS reading is the only available reading when (1) is interpreted in the context given in (3b). Similarly, the WS reading is the only available one in the context given in (4b).

Starting from this observation, we propose that ES readings arise in the presence of anaphoric links between quantificational domains and dependencies. Such anaphoric links are supported by previous discourse or are created online.

For example, we derive the ES readings if the two *every* determiners and the indefinite article in (1) elaborate on the sets of individuals and the correlations between them assumed in the contexts given in (3b) and (4b) – as shown in (5), (6) and (7) below (the superscripts and subscripts indicate the antecedent-anaphor relations).

The IS interpretation arises because of the presence in the input discourse context of a function pairing students and poets that rules out the possibility of covariation between poets and poems. The WS reading arises because the domain restrictor for the indefinite is constant, thus making covariation impossible. In present terms, this means that the value of the discourse referent (dref) r'', the domain restrictor of the indefinite, is constant. We use drefs r, r', r'' etc. for domain restricting drefs, but this is just a mnemonic device – these drefs have the same status as any other dref for individuals, i.e., they can be introduced by quantifiers and indefinites and retrieved by subsequent pronouns, definites and quantifiers.

Finally, the NS reading arises by default, when there are no special contextual restrictions on the indefinite article and the *every* determiners.

(5) Intermediate scope (IS) context:
Every^r student chose a$^{r''}$ poet and read every$^{r'}$ poem written by him$_{r''}$.

(6) Widest scope (WS) context:
Every^r student chose a$^{r''}$ poet – the$_{r''}$ same$_{r''}$ poet – and read every$^{r'}$ poem written by him$_{r''}$.

(7) Anaphora to previously introduced quantificational dependencies:
Every$^{u \sqsubseteq r}$ student of mine read every$^{u' \sqsubseteq r'}$ poem that a$^{u'' \sqsubseteq r''}$ famous Romanian poet wrote.

Unlike the tradition inaugurated in Fodor & Sag (1982) [13] and varied upon in Reinhart (1997) [23] and Kratzer (1998) [18], we take (in)definites to be unambiguous. Moreover, we do not need special choice-functional variables (as in Winter (1997) [26]). Our proposal builds on the insight in Schwarzschild (2002)

[25] concerning the crucial role of contextual restrictions in the genesis of ES readings without, however, relying on the singleton quantifier domain restriction that Schwarzschild (2002) [25] makes use of. We follow Farkas (1997a) [8] in treating ES readings as being the result of the *interaction* between the indefinite and the other quantifiers present in its sentence, but we do not resort to assignment indices on determiners. Our account relies on two independently motivated assumptions: (*i*) the discourse context stores not only (sets of) individuals that are mentioned in discourse, but also dependencies between them (as motivated in van den Berg (1996) [3], Nouwen (2003) [22], Brasoveanu (2007) [4] and references therein), and (*ii*) quantifier domains are contextually restricted.

We assume that the restrictor drefs r, r', r'' etc. can be non-locally introduced in certain cases. This is what is responsible for exceptional wide scope in downward-entailing contexts, exemplified by (8) below based on Chierchia (2001) [5] (p. 60, (16)). We can derive the correct truth conditions for this sentence, provided in (9) below, if we represent it as shown in (10). Note that the first-order formula in (9) is in fact truth-conditionally equivalent to the $\neg(\forall x(ling(x)$ $\ldots \exists z(prob(z) \ldots \forall y(sol(y) \ldots))))$ reading of sentence (8).

The crucial point is the accommodation of the dref r'' that provides the domain restrictor for the indefinite *some*$^{u'' \sqsubseteq r''}$ *problem* intermediately between the two universal quantifiers *every*^{u} *linguist* and *every*$^{u'}$ *solution*. We assume that such restrictor drefs, when they occur on indefinites as opposed to other types of DPs, can be freely accommodated at any point in the structure where presuppositions in general can be accommodated (see Beaver & Zeevat (2007) [2] for a recent discussion of presupposition accommodation).

(8) Not every^u linguist studied every$^{u'}$ solution that some$^{u'' \sqsubseteq r''}$ problem might have.

(9) The most salient reading of (8):
$\exists x(ling(x) \wedge \forall z(prob(z) \rightarrow \exists y(sol(y) \wedge m.have(z,y) \wedge \neg study(x,y))))$

(10) Not every^u linguist [--accommodate the restrictor r'' here--] studied every$^{u'}$ solution that some$^{u'' \sqsubseteq r''}$ problem might have.

Introducing the restrictor dref r'' that restricts the indefinite *some*$^{u''}$ *problem* at the location indicated in (10) above ensures that this indefinite may covary with the values of the dref u contributed by the universal *every* *linguist*, but not with the values of the dref u' contributed by *every* *solution* (see (34) below for the formal account).

The accommodation of the restrictor dref is an extreme case of the proposed account of ES as anaphora to quantificational dependencies: the anaphoric dependency here is created intra-sententially via accommodation. Downward-entailing contexts seem to favor this kind of restrictor dref resolution because it results in the strongest reading.[1]

The same kind of restrictor accommodation is involved in deriving ES readings in upward-entailing contexts like (1) above in the absence of contextually

---

[1] We assume throughout the paper that natural language universal quantifiers come with an existential commitment with respect to their domain.

provided anaphoric dependencies. Thus, if we accommodate the restrictor dref r'' in the position shown in (1) below, we derive the IS reading for sentence (1) without the need for the discourse contexts in (3b) and (4b).

(11) Every^u student of mine [--accommodate the restrictor r'' here--] read every$^{u'}$ poem that a$^{u'' \sqsubseteq r''}$ famous Romanian poet wrote.

Accommodating the restrictor dref for the indefinite between the two universal quantifiers does the work of the intermediate existential closure of choice-function variables in Reinhart (1997) [23] and Winter (1997) [26]. The present proposal is crucially different from these accounts in that it does not need choice-function variables / drefs. Nor do we need a special storage mechanism as Abusch (1994) [1], an indexing mechanism as Farkas (1997a) [8], or a special presupposition for specific indefinites as Geurts (2007) [15]. What we need instead is a freely available accommodation procedure for the drefs that restrict indefinites.

The two options for restricting indefinites in our account, namely by anaphorically retrieving the restrictor drefs or, alternatively, by accommodating them, correspond to the contextual analysis of exceptional scope in Kratzer (1998) [18] and the 'free existential closure' analyses in Reinhart (1997) [23] and Winter (1997) [26] respectively.

The account is independently motivated by the fact that definites and generalized quantifiers (e.g., universals) exhibit the same kind of anaphora to quantificational dependencies via their restrictor drefs, as the examples in (12) and (13) below show. Let us consider them in turn. The sentence-initial quantifier in (12b) is restricted by the domain of quantification contributed by the universal *every^r student* in (12a). Moreover, the definite *the$^{u'' \sqsubseteq r''}$ French poet* in (12b) takes exceptional intermediate scope between the two quantifiers in (12b) precisely because it is anaphoric to, i.e., restricted by, the dref r'' introduced by the indefinite *two$^{r''}$ poets* in (12a). That is, *the$^{u'' \sqsubseteq r''}$ French poet* is a *dependent* definite that, in addition, takes exceptional wide scope. The simpler example in (13) shows that we can also have dependent universals: the domain of quantification of the quantifier *every$^{u' \sqsubseteq r'}$ paper* in (13b) covaries with the quantifier *no/every$^{u \sqsubseteq r}$ graduate student* because the most salient interpretation of (13b) is that no/every graduate student read every paper that s/he was assigned. This interpretation is an immediate consequence of the present account, which takes the two quantifiers in (13b) to be anaphoric to the quantificational dependency introduced by the previous sentence (13a).

(12) a. Every^r student was assigned two$^{r''}$ poets, a Romanian and a French one.
   b. No/Every$^{u \sqsubseteq r}$ Romanian student read every^u poem that the$^{u'' \sqsubseteq r''}$ French poet ever wrote.

(13) a. Every^r student was assigned several$^{r'}$ papers to read.
   b. No/Every$^{u \sqsubseteq r}$ graduate student read every$^{u' \sqsubseteq r'}$ paper.

Although all determiners are anaphoric to the quantifier domains and quantificational dependencies stored by their restrictor drefs, they do not exhibit the same kind of behavior relative to (exceptional) scope. This follows from the fact that determiners differ with respect to the constraints they place on their restrictor drefs. Indefinite determiners are the most liberal: they place no constraints on their restrictor dref, which can be contextually retrieved or freely accommodated (see Farkas (2007a) [11]). In contrast, definites and universal determiners cannot accommodate their restrictor drefs. Consequently, either they are contextually unrestricted or they have to anaphorically retrieve their restrictors.

Cross-linguistically, however, we encounter special kinds of indefinites that place additional constraints on their restrictor sets, e.g., the dependent indefinites in Hungarian and Romanian discussed in Farkas (1997b) [9] and Farkas (2002) [10]. Such indefinites must covary with a quantifier in the same clause, i.e., they introduce values that are distinct relative to distinct values of a variable bound by a quantifier. The last section of the paper shows that these covariation requirements can be formulated as anaphoric constraints relating the restrictor dref of the dependent indefinite and the dref introduced by the quantifier.

2   Exceptional Scope as Anaphora to Dependencies

The account is formulated within the Plural Compositional DRT (PCDRT) system in Brasoveanu (2007) [4], which extends Compositional DRT (Muskens 1996 [21]) with plural information states. Following van den Berg (1996) [3], PCDRT models plural info states as sets of variable assignments, which can be represented as matrices with assignments (sequences) as rows. Plural info states enable us to account for anaphora to both individuals and dependencies between them: as shown in the matrix below, individuals are stored columnwise and dependencies are stored rowwise.[2]

Info State I	...	u	u'	u''	...
i_1	...	α_1 (i.e., ui_1)	β_1 (i.e., $u'i_1$)	γ_1 (i.e., $u''i_1$)	...
i_2	...	α_2 (i.e., ui_2)	β_2 (i.e., $u'i_2$)	γ_2 (i.e., $u''i_2$)	...
i_3	...	α_3 (i.e., ui_3)	β_3 (i.e., $u'i_3$)	γ_3 (i.e., $u''i_3$)	...
...	...	...	...	...	...

Quantifier domains (sets) are stored columnwise: $\{\alpha_1, \alpha_2, \alpha_3, \dots\}$, $\{\beta_1, \beta_2, \beta_3, \dots\}$ etc.

Quantifier dependencies (relations) are stored rowwise: $\{\langle\alpha_1, \beta_1\rangle, \langle\alpha_2, \beta_2\rangle, \langle\alpha_3, \beta_3\rangle, \dots\}$ etc.

We formalize the analysis in a Dynamic Ty2 logic, i.e., in a version of the Logic of Change introduced by Muskens (1996) [21], which reformulates dynamic semantics (Kamp 1981 [17], Heim 1982 [16]) in Gallin's Ty2 (Gallin 1975 [14]). We have three basic types: type t (truth values), type e (individuals; variables: x, x' etc.) and type s ('variable assignments'; variables: i, j etc.).[3]

---

[2] Mixed weak & strong donkey sentences and quantificational and modal subordination discourses provide independent empirical motivation for a semantics based on plural info states – see Brasoveanu (2007) [4] for more discussion.

[3] A suitable set of axioms ensures that the entities of type s behave as variable assignments; see Muskens (1996) [21] for more details.

A dref for individuals u is a function of type se from assignments i_s to individuals x_e (the subscripts on terms indicate their type). Intuitively, the individual $u_{se}(i_s)$ is the individual that the assignment i assigns to the dref u. Thus, we model drefs in much the same way as individual concepts are modeled in Montague semantics. A dynamic info state I is a set of variable assignments (type st). An individual dref u stores a set of individuals with respect to an info state I, abbreviated as $uI := \{u_{se}(i_s) : i_s \in I_{st}\}$, i.e., uI is the image of the set of assignments I under the function u.

A sentence is interpreted as a Discourse Representation Structure (DRS), which is a relation of type $(st)((st)t)$ between an input state I_{st} and an output state J_{st}, as shown in (14) below. A DRS requires: (i) the input state I to differ from the output state J at most with respect to the **new drefs** and (ii) all the **conditions** to be satisfied relative to the output state J. For example, the DRS $[u, u' \mid student\{u\}, poem\{u'\}, read\{u, u'\}]$ abbreviates the term $\lambda I_{st}.\lambda J_{st}.\ I[u, u']J \wedge student\{u\}J \wedge poem\{u'\}J \wedge read\{u, u'\}J$.[4] Conditions denote sets of information states and are interpreted *distributively* relative to an info state, e.g., $read\{u, u'\}$ is basically the term $\lambda I_{st}.\ I \neq \emptyset \wedge \forall i_s \in I(read(ui, u'i))$ of type $(st)t$ (see the exact definition of such conditions in the Appendix).

(14) $[\textbf{new drefs} \mid \textbf{conditions}] := \lambda I_{st}.\lambda J_{st}.\ I[\textbf{new drefs}]J \wedge \textbf{conditions}J$

Given the underlying type logic, we achieve compositionality at subclausal level in the usual Montagovian way.

More precisely, the compositional aspect of interpretation in an extensional Fregean/Montagovian framework is largely determined by the types for the (extensions of the) 'saturated' expressions, i.e., names and sentences. Abbreviate them as **e** and **t**. An extensional static logic identifies **e** with e and **t** with t. The denotation of the noun *poem* is of type **et**, i.e., et: *poem* $\rightsquigarrow \lambda x_e.\ poem_{et}(x)$. The determiner *every* is of type $(\textbf{et})((\textbf{et})\textbf{t})$, i.e., $(et)((et)t)$.

PCDRT assigns the following dynamic types to the 'meta-types' **e** and **t**: **t** abbreviates $(st)((st)t)$, i.e., a sentence is interpreted as a DRS, and **e** abbreviates se, i.e., a name is interpreted as a dref. The denotation of the noun *poem* is still of type **et** – as shown in (15) below. The determiners *every* and *a* are still of type $(\textbf{et})((\textbf{et})\textbf{t})$, as shown in (16) and (17); their translations make use of the maximization and distributivity operators $\textbf{max}^u(\dots)$ and $_u(\dots)$ defined in the Appendix. Maximization stores all and only the individuals that satisfy some property P, while distributivity ensures that *each* stored individual satisfies property P and is associated with whatever dependencies P introduces. Crucially, these operators enable us to extract and store the sets of individuals involved in the interpretation of quantifiers, indefinites etc., as well as their associated dependencies. The compositionally obtained update contributed by (1) is provided in (20) below (see (18), (19) and (20) for some of the intermediate translations[5]).

---

[4] See the Appendix for the definition of dref introduction (a.k.a. random assignment).

[5] The update and the intermediate translations are simplified in inessential ways.

(15) *poem* $\rightsquigarrow \lambda v_{\mathbf{e}}.\,[poem_{et}\{v\}]$ (i.e., $\lambda v_{\mathbf{e}}.\lambda I_{st}.\lambda J_{st}.\,I = J \wedge poem_{et}\{v\}J$)

(16) *every*$^{u \sqsubseteq r} \rightsquigarrow \lambda P_{\mathbf{et}}.\lambda P'_{\mathbf{et}}.\,\mathbf{max}^{u \sqsubseteq r}(_u(P(u)));\,_u(P'(u))$

(17) $a^{u'' \sqsubseteq r''} \rightsquigarrow \lambda P_{\mathbf{et}}.\lambda P'_{\mathbf{et}}.\,[u'' \mid u'' \sqsubseteq r'', \mathbf{singleton}\{u''\}];\,_{u''}(P(u''); P'(u''))$

(18) *every*$^{u \sqsubseteq r}$ *student of mine* $\rightsquigarrow \lambda P_{\mathbf{et}}.\,\mathbf{max}^{u \sqsubseteq r}([stud.o.m\{u\}]);\,_u(P(u))$

(19) $a^{u'' \sqsubseteq r''}$ *Romanian poet* $\rightsquigarrow$
$\qquad \lambda P_{\mathbf{et}}.\,[u'' \mid u'' \sqsubseteq r'', \mathbf{singleton}\{u''\}, r.poet\{u''\}];\,_{u''}(P(u''))$

(20) *read* $\rightsquigarrow \lambda Q_{(et)t}.\lambda v_{\mathbf{e}}.\,Q(\lambda v'_{\mathbf{e}}.\,[read\{v, v'\}])$

(21) *every*$^{u \sqsubseteq r}$ *student of mine read every*$^{u' \sqsubseteq r'}$ *poem that a*$^{u'' \sqsubseteq r''}$ *Romanian*
$\qquad$ *poet wrote* $\rightsquigarrow \mathbf{max}^{u \sqsubseteq r}([stud.o.m\{u\}]);\,_u(\mathbf{max}^{u' \sqsubseteq r'}([poem\{u'\}];$
$\qquad _{u'}([u'' \mid u'' \sqsubseteq r'', \mathbf{singleton}\{u''\}, r.poet\{u''\}, write\{u'', u'\}])));\,[read\{u, u'\}]$

(22)

(23)

The update in (20) can be paraphrased as follows (see the matrix-based representation in (22) above): first, we introduce the dref u and store in it all the speaker's students among the previously introduced r-individuals (as required by $\mathbf{max}^{u \sqsubseteq r}$). Then, relative to each u-student (as required by the distributivity operator $_u(\ldots)$), we introduce the set of all poems (among the r'-entities) written by a Romanian poet and store these poems in dref u', while storing the corresponding poets in dref u''. Finally, we test that each u-student read each of the corresponding u'-poems. The output info state obtained after updating with (20) stores the set of all r-students in dref u, the set of all r'-poems written by a Romanian poet in u' and the corresponding r''-Romanian poets in u''.

The update in (20) yields the NS indefinite reading if there are no special constraints on the restrictor drefs r, r' and r''. If the discourse context places particular constraints on these drefs, as the contexts in (5) and (6) above do, the update in (20) yields different truth conditions, namely the truth conditions associated with the IS and WS readings.

Consider the context in (5) first, represented in (24) below. As (24) shows, the context in (5) stores a functional dependency associating each r-student with one r''-poet. Consequently, the update in (20) above will retrieve this functional dependency and elaborate on it, thereby yielding the IS indefinite reading.

(24) The context for the IS indefinite reading:

r	r'	r''
$stud_1$	$poem_1$	$poet_1$
$stud_1$	$poem_2$	$poet_1$
...	...	...
$stud_2$	$poem_m$	$poet_2$
$stud_2$	$poem_{m+1}$	$poet_2$
...	...	...
$stud_3$	$poem_n$	$poet_3$
$stud_3$	$poem_{n+1}$	$poet_3$
...	...	...

Similarly, the context in (6) is represented in (25) below: the plural info state stores the same r''-poet relative to every r-student. When the update in (20) anaphorically retrieves and elaborates on this *contextually* singleton indefinite (i.e., singleton in the plural info state, but not necessarily relative to the entire model), we obtain the WS indefinite reading.

(25) The context for the WS indefinite reading:

r	r'	r''
$stud_1$	$poem_1$	$poet_1$
$stud_1$	$poem_2$	$poet_1$
...	...	...
$stud_2$	$poem_m$	$poet_1$
$stud_2$	$poem_{m+1}$	$poet_1$
...	...	...
$stud_3$	$poem_n$	$poet_1$
$stud_3$	$poem_{n+1}$	$poet_1$
...	...	...

The formal account of examples like (12) above in which definites take exceptional scope is entirely parallel.

3 Exceptional Scope in Downward-Entailing Contexts

The PCDRT account of exceptional scope as anaphora to quantificational dependencies generalizes to exceptional scope in downward-entailing contexts. Chierchia (2001) [5] draws attention to these contexts and to the problem they pose for the 'free choice-/Skolem-function' approaches to scope in Kratzer (1998) [18] and Matthewson (1999) [20]. To see what the problem is, consider sentence (26) below. Its most salient reading, provided in (27), has the indefinite $some^{u''\sqsubseteq r''}$ taking exceptional scope intermediately between the two universal quantifiers.

(26) Every$^{u\sqsubseteq r}$ linguist that studied every$^{u'}$ solution that some$^{u''\sqsubseteq r''}$ problem might have has become famous.

(27) The most salient reading of (26): $\forall x(ling(x) \wedge \exists z(prob(z) \wedge$
$\forall y(sol(y) \wedge m.have(z, y) \rightarrow study(x, y))) \rightarrow b.f(x))$

(28) $\forall x(ling(x) \wedge \forall y(sol(y) \wedge m.have(\boldsymbol{f}(prob), y) \rightarrow study(x, y)) \rightarrow b.f(x))$

(29) $\forall x(ling(x) \wedge \exists \boldsymbol{f}(\forall y(sol(y) \wedge m.have(\boldsymbol{f}(prob), y) \rightarrow study(x, y))) \rightarrow b.f(x))$

As Chierchia (2001) [5] observes, 'free choice-function variable' approaches like Kratzer (1998) [18] represent sentence (26) as shown in (28) above ('top-level existential closure' approaches like Matthewson (1999) [20] derive a representation that, for our current purposes, is virtually identical), while the 'intermediate existential closure' approaches in Reinhart (1997) [23] and Winter (1997) [26] represent it as shown in (29).

If we assume together with Chierchia (2001) [5] that any choice function can in principle be assigned to a free choice-function variable (but see Kratzer (2003) [19] for an argument against this assumption), then the former kind of approaches derive truth conditions that are too weak: (28) is verified by any problem for which some linguist didn't study every solution – this makes the antecedent false and the whole formula in (28) true (see also the argument in Schwarz (2001) [24] that 'free choice-function variable' approaches undergenerate).

The latter kind of approaches derive the correct truth conditions, but allowing for such intermediate-level existential closure of choice-function variables nullifies much of the initial motivation for them, namely that they enable us to give the indefinite exceptional scope (semantically), while syntactically leaving it *in situ*. If this kind of existential closure is needed, allowing for non-local existential closure of individual-level variables as in Abusch (1994) [1] (which obviates the need for choice functions) might prove to be the more parsimonious choice.

In contrast, our account proceeds as before: in a context like (30) below that provides a suitable dependency between the restrictor drefs r and r'', the representation of sentence (26), given in (31), derives the intuitively correct truth conditions.

(30) Context for the most salient reading of (26):
It has been established that every scientist has a favorite problem that she studied systematically. And being systematic is enough to bring one fame in linguistics. So: every$^{u\sqsubseteq r}$ linguist that studied every$^{u'}$ solution that some$^{u''\sqsubseteq r''}$ problem might have has become famous.

(31) $\mathbf{max}^{u\sqsubseteq r}([ling\{u\}];\ _u(\mathbf{max}^{u'}([sol\{u'\}];\ [u'' \mid u'' \sqsubseteq r'', \mathbf{singleton}\{u''\},$
$prob\{u''\}];\ [m.have\{u'', u'\}]));\ [study\{u, u'\}]);\ [b.f\{u\}]$

The analysis of the ES example in (26) does not face the same problems as choice-/Skolem-function analyses because the determiner *every* is not analyzed in terms of material implication,[6] but as dynamically conjoining the restrictor

---

[6] The 'material implication' problem is not specific to choice-/Skolem-function analyses; see, for example, Abusch (1994) [1] for an early discussion.

and nuclear scope DRSs (which, crucially, update plural info states). This analysis also generalizes to other kinds of downward entailing contexts besides the restrictor of *every*. Consider, for example, the 'wide-scope negation' sentence in (32) below (repeated from (8) above), also from Chierchia (2001) [5]. We can derive the correct truth conditions for this sentence, provided in (33) below, if we represent it as shown in (34). The crucial point is the accommodation of the dref r'' (which restricts the indefinite *some*$^{u''\sqsubseteq r''}$ *problem*) intermediately between the two universal quantifiers *every*^{u} *linguist* and *every*$^{u'}$ *solution*.

(32) **Not every**^{u} **linguist studied every**$^{u'}$ **solution that some**$^{u''\sqsubseteq r''}$ **problem might have.**

(33) The most salient reading of (32):
$\exists x(ling(x) \wedge \forall z(prob(z) \rightarrow \exists y(sol(y) \wedge m.have(z,y) \wedge \neg study(x,y))))$

(34) $[\sim(\mathbf{max}^{u}([ling\{u\}]); [r'']; {}_{u}(\mathbf{max}^{u'}([sol\{u'\}]; [u'' \mid u'' \sqsubseteq r'', \mathbf{singleton}\{u''\}, prob\{u''\}, m.have\{u'', u'\}])); [study\{u, u'\}])]$

(35) Negation requires that no update of the following form is possible:

We can think of this accommodation-based account of intermediate ES under negation as an extreme case of the proposed account of ES as anaphora to quantificational dependencies. The accommodation strategy also generalizes to examples of ES in upward-entailing contexts like the very first example we considered, i.e., example (1) above. The analysis of this example in terms of restrictor accommodation obviates the need for the discourse contexts given in (3b) and (4b). As the representations for the intermediate ES reading in (36) and (37) below show, the crucial feature is that the restrictor dref r'' is accommodated between the two universal quantifiers.

(36) Every^u student of mine [--accommodate r'' here--] read every$^{u'}$ poem that a$^{u''\sqsubseteq r''}$ famous Romanian poet wrote.

(37) $\mathbf{max}^u([stud.o.m\{u\}]); [r'']; {}_u(\mathbf{max}^{u'}([poem\{u'\}];$
${}_{u'}([u''\,|\,u''\sqsubseteq r'', r.poet\{u''\}, write\{u'', u'\}]))); [read\{u, u'\}]$

What we achieve by accommodating the restrictor dref for the indefinite between the two universal quantifiers is done by intermediate existential closure of choice-function variables in Reinhart (1997) [23] and Winter (1997) [26], by a special storage mechanism in Abusch (1994) [1], by assignment-function indexation in Farkas (1997a) [8] and by a special presupposition associated with specific indefinites postulated in Geurts (2007) [15].

The assumption that indefinite-restricting drefs can be freely accommodated enables us to avoid the undergeneration problems raised by Chierchia (2001) [5] and Schwarz (2001) [24] for 'free choice-function variable' approaches.[7]

4   Dependent Indefinites

The type of indefinites we discuss here were first discussed in Farkas (1997b) [9] where it was noted that in Hungarian, the indefinite determiner, as well as cardinal numerals may reduplicate, in which case the DP must be interpreted as covarying with an individual or situation variable bound by a quantifier within the same clause (see also Farkas (2002) [10]). In Farkas (2007b) [12], it is shown that the same effect is obtained in Romanian by having the item *cîte* precede an indefinite or numeral. In present terms, the item *cîte* introduces a new dref u', the values of which must covary with the values of another dref u introduced by a quantificational element scoping over it.

For example, in (38) below, at least two of the students we are quantifying over must have read distinct articles – otherwise, the particle *cîte* is infelicitous. We capture this property by taking the particle *cîte* to place a constraint on the dref r' that restricts the domain of the narrow-scope indefinite *un*$^{u'\sqsubseteq r'}$ *articol*. In particular, *cîte* requires the values of r' to covary with the values of the dref u introduced by the wide-scope universal *fiecare*^{u} *student* – enforced by means of the condition $r' \div u$. This condition requires that, for at least two different students x and x', the corresponding papers have to be distinct (see the appendix for the exact definition). This is informally shown in (38) and the relevant translations are provided in (40) and (41). In (40), underlining indicates presuppositional status.

(38) Fiecare^u student a citit cîte un$^{u'\sqsubseteq r'}$ articol.
     'Every student read CÎTE a paper.'

---

[7] The extent to which the overgeneration problems mentioned in Chierchia (2001) [5] and Schwarz (2001) [24] are relevant for our account is left for future research.

(39) Fiecare^u student [--accommodate r' here and require covariation
with u--] a citit cîte un$^{u'\sqsubseteq r'}$ articol.

(40) $c\hat{\imath}te^{r'\div u}$ $un^{u'\sqsubseteq r'}$ $\rightsquigarrow$
$\lambda P_{\mathbf{et}}.\lambda P'_{\mathbf{et}}.\underline{[r'\,|\,r'\div u]};\,[u'\,|\,u'\sqsubseteq r',\mathbf{singleton}\{u'\}];\,P(u');\,P'(u'))$

(41) (38) $\rightsquigarrow \mathbf{max}^u([student\{u\}]);\,[r'\,|\,r'\div u];$
$_u([u'\,|\,u'\sqsubseteq r',\mathbf{singleton}\{u'\},paper\{u'\},read\{u,u'\}])$

Thus, the particle *cîte* is anaphoric to an individual (or event) dref and the
restrictor dref r' of the indefinite is required to store different (sets of) values
relative to the values of the anaphorically retrieved dref. It is therefore not
surprising that we get weak crossover (WCO) effects with *cîte* in Romanian,
just like we get them with pronouns:

(42) #Cîte$_u$ un student urăşte pe fiecare^u profesor.
'CÎTE A student hates every professor.'

(43) #Mama lui$_u$ iubeşte pe fiecare^u băiat.
'His mother loves every boy.'

And, just as direct object clitic-doubling (i.e., the clitic *îl* in this particular
case) waives WCO effects with pronouns, it waives them with the particle *cîte*:

(44) Cîte$_u$ un student îl urăşte pe fiecare^u profesor.

(45) Mama lui$_u$ îl iubeşte pe fiecare^u băiat.

The crucial requirement contributed by *cîte* is that of covariation. A further restriction involves the nature of the dref that *cîte* must covary with: as
shown in previous work, *cîte* indefinites may only covary with individual or
situation/event drefs but not with worlds. In this view, the core property of dependency is covariation and the parameters of cross-linguistic variation involve
the presence or absence of the covariation requirement, and, in the case of its
presence, the possibility of further restrictions concerning the nature of the 'boss'
dref, the item that induces the covariation.

5   Conclusion

The readings of sentence (1) differ with respect to whether the indefinite covaries
with another DP or not, and if it does, which of the two *every*-DPs it covaries
with. Traditionally, this sort of (in)dependence was the result of the structural
relation between the existential quantifier contributed by the indefinite and the
two universal quantifiers contributed by the two *every*-DPs. *In situ* analyses
employed implicit arguments present in the interpretation of the indefinite (as
arguments of a choice function or as implicit arguments in the restrictor) that
could be left free (WS reading) or that could be bound by the first universal (IS
reading) or the second (NS reading).

Our account dispenses with bound implicit arguments in favor of independently needed contextually introduced and stored dependencies. The essence of
our approach concerns the way restrictors are interpreted. Non-local scope is the

result of contextual anaphoric dependencies or of restrictor accommodation. We suggest that the freedom with which restrictors accommodate is connected to the fact that they are not in the part of the sentence that is asserted. The process of non-locally accommodating restrictor drefs is constrained: on the one hand, it is possible only for indefinite determiners, but not for definite or generalized determiners, and, on the other hand, it is constrained even for indefinites, e.g., as Endriss (2006) [6] argues, such indefinites need to have a topical status.

The approach proposed here leads us to expect that particular determiners may vary with respect to their sensitivity to the presence of interpretational dependencies. 'Ordinary' indefinites, such as $a(n)$, are indifferent to this issue, which is why (1) is three-way ambiguous. We take 'special' indefinite determiners, such as *cîte* in Romanian and *egy-egy* in Hungarian, to require the presence of a particular type of interpretational dependency encoded as an anaphoric constraint on the dref that restricts the quantificational domain of the indefinite. This suggests that a crucial parameter in the semantic typology of DPs is the issue of variation vs. constancy of the values that a DP quantifies over relative to the values quantified over by other DPs – a parameter that our formal system is well equipped to handle.

References

1. Abusch, D.: The Scope of Indefinites. Natural Language Semantics 2.2, 83–135 (1994)
2. Beaver, D., Zeevat, H.: Accommodation. In: Ramchand, G., Reiss, C. (eds.) Oxford Handbook of Linguistic Interfaces, Oxford University Press, Oxford (to appear, 2007)
3. van den Berg, M.: Some Aspects of the Internal Structure of Discourse. PhD dissertation, University of Amsterdam (1996)
4. Brasoveanu, A.: Structured Nominal and Modal Reference. PhD dissertation, Rutgers University (2007)
5. Chierchia, G.: A puzzle about Indefinites. In: Cecchetto, C., et al. (eds.) Semantic Interfaces: Reference, Anaphora and Aspect, pp. 51–89. CSLI, Stanford (2001)
6. Endriss, C.: Quantificational Topics - A Scopal Treatment of Exceptional Wide Scope Phenomena. PhD dissertation, Universität Potsdam (2006)
7. Farkas, D.F.: Quantifier Scope and Syntactic Islands. In: Hendrik, R., et al. (eds.) Proceedings of CLS 7, pp. 59–66. CLC, Cornell University (1981)
8. Farkas, D.F.: Evaluation Indices and Scope. In: Szabolcsi, A. (ed.) Ways of Scope Taking, pp. 183–215. Kluwer, Dordrecht (1997a)
9. Farkas, D.F.: Dependent Indefinites. In: Corblin, F., et al. (eds.) Empirical Issues in Formal Syntax and Semantics, Peter Lang, pp. 243–267 (1997b)
10. Farkas, D.F.: Varieties of Indefinites. In: Jackson, B. (ed.) Proceedings of SALT XII, pp. 59–84. CLC, Cornell University (2002)
11. Farkas, D.F.: The Unmarked Determiner. In: Vogeleer Aloushkova, S., Tasmowski de Rijk, L. (eds.) Non-definites and Plurality, pp. 81–107. John Benjamins, Amsterdam (2007a)
12. Farkas, D.F.: Free Choice in Romanian. In: Drawing the Boundaries of Meaning: Neo-Gricean Studies in Pragmatics and Semantics in Honor of Laurence R. Horn, pp. 71–95. John Benjamins, Amsterdam (2007b)
13. Fodor, J.D., Sag, I.: Referential and Quantificational Indefinites. Linguistics and Philosophy 5, 355–398 (1982)

14. Gallin, D.: Intensional and Higher-Order Modal Logic with Applications to Montague Semantics. North-Holland Mathematics Studies (1975)
15. Geurts, B.: Specific Indefinites, Presupposition and Scope. In: Bäuerle, R., Reyle, U., Zimmermann, T.E. (eds.) Presuppositions and Discourse, Elsevier, Oxford (to appear, 2007)
16. Heim, I.: The Semantics of Definite and Indefinite Noun Phrases. PhD dissertation, UMass Amherst (1982)
17. Kamp, H.: A theory of truth and semantic representation. In: Groenendijk, J., Janssen, T., Stokhof, M. (eds.) Formal Methods in the Study of Language. Part 1, Mathematical Center, Amsterdam, pp. 277–322 (1981)
18. Kratzer, A.: Scope or Pseudo-Scope: Are There Wide-Scope Indefinites? In: Rothstein, S. (ed.) Events in Grammar, pp. 163–196. Kluwer, Dordrecht (1998)
19. Kratzer, A.: A Note on Choice Functions in Context. Ms (2003)
20. Matthewson, L.: On the Interpretation of Wide-Scope Indefinites. Natural Language Semantics 7.1, 79–134 (1999)
21. Muskens, R.: Combining Montague Semantics and Discourse Representation. Linguistics and Philosophy 19, 143–186 (1996)
22. Nouwen, R.: Plural Pronominal Anaphora in Context. PhD dissertation, University of Utrecht (2003)
23. Reinhart, T.: Quantifier Scope: How Labor is Divided between QR and Choice Functions. Linguistics and Philosophy 20, 335–397 (1997)
24. Schwarz, B.: Two Kinds of Long-Distance Indefinites. Ms (2001)
25. Schwarzschild, R.: Singleton Indefinites. Journal of Semantics 19.3, 289–314 (2002)
26. Winter, Y.: Choice Functions and the Scopal Semantics of Indefinites. Linguistics and Philosophy 20, 399–467 (1997)

Appendix: The Formal System

The Basic Dynamic System

(1) $R\{u_1, \ldots, u_n\} := \lambda I_{st}.\ I_{u_1 \neq \#, \ldots, u_n \neq \#} \neq \emptyset \land \forall i_s \in I_{u_1 \neq \#, \ldots, u_n \neq \#}(R(u_1 i, \ldots, u_n i))$, where $I_{u_1 \neq \#, \ldots, u_n \neq \#} := \{i_s \in I : u_1 i \neq \# \land \ldots \land u_n i \neq \#\}$ and $\#$ is the universal falsifier, i.e., the exception individual that falsifies any relation R.

(2) $\mathbf{singleton}\{u\} := \lambda I_{st}.\ |u I_{u \neq \#}| = 1$, where $uI := \{ui : i_s \in I\}$

(3) $\mathbf{2}\{u\} := \lambda I_{st}.\ |u I_{u \neq \#}| = 2$

(4) $r' \div u := \lambda I_{st}.\ I_{u=\#} \subseteq I_{r'=\#} \land \exists x_e \in u I_{u \neq \#} \exists x'_e \in u I_{u \neq \#}(r' I_{u=x} \neq \{\#\} \land r' I_{u=x'} \neq \{\#\} \land x \neq x' \land r' I_{u=x} \cap r' I_{u=x'} = \emptyset)$

(5) $D; D' := \lambda I_{st}.\lambda J_{st}.\ \exists H_{st}(DIH \land D'HJ)$, where D, D' are DRSs (type $\mathbf{t}$).

(6) $\sim D := \lambda I_{st}.\ I \neq \emptyset \land \forall H_{st} \neq \emptyset(H \subseteq I \rightarrow \neg \exists K_{st}(DHK))$

(7) $[R\{u_1, \ldots, u_n\}] := \lambda I_{st}.\lambda J_{st}.\ I = J \land R\{u_1, \ldots, u_n\}J$

(8) $[Condition_1, \ldots, Condition_m] := [Condition_1]; \ldots ; [Condition_m]$

(9) $[u] := \lambda I_{st}.\lambda J_{st}.\ \forall i_s \in I(\exists j_s \in J(i[u]j)) \land \forall j_s \in J(\exists i_s \in I(i[u]j))$

(10) $[u_1, \ldots, u_n] := [u_1]; \ldots ; [u_n]$

(11) $[u_1, \ldots, u_n \mid Condition_1, \ldots, Condition_m] :=$
     $[u_1, \ldots, u_n]; [Condition_1, \ldots, Condition_m]$

(12) A DRS D of type $\mathbf{t}$ is *true* with respect to an input info state I_{st} iff $\exists J_{st}(DIJ)$.

The default input discourse context stores no anaphoric information. This empty discourse context is modeled as the singleton plural info state $\{i_\#\}$, the only member of which is the exception variable assignment $i_\#$ that assigns the exception individual $\#$ (i.e., the universal falsifier) to all drefs.

Structured Inclusion, Maximization and Distributivity

(13) $u \sqsubseteq r := \lambda I_{st}.\ (u \Subset r)I \wedge \forall i_s \in I(ri \in uI_{u \neq \#} \rightarrow ri = ui)$,
    where $u \Subset r := \lambda I_{st}.\ \forall i_s \in I(ui = ri \vee ui = \#).$[8]

(14) $\mathbf{max}^u(D) := \lambda I_{st}.\lambda J_{st}.\ ([u]; D)IJ \wedge \forall K_{st}(([u]; D)IK \rightarrow uK_{u \neq \#} \subseteq uJ_{u \neq \#})$

(15) $\mathbf{max}^{u \sqsubseteq r}(D) := \mathbf{max}^u([u \sqsubseteq r]; D)$

(16) $\mathbf{dist}_u(D) := \lambda I_{st}.\lambda J_{st}.\ uI = uJ \wedge \forall x_e \in uI(DI_{u=x}J_{u=x})$,
    where $I_{u=x} = \{i_s \in I : ui = x\}$.

(17) $_u(D) := \lambda I_{st}.\lambda J_{st}.\ I_{u=\#} = J_{u=\#} \wedge I_{u \neq \#} \neq \emptyset \wedge \mathbf{dist}_u(D)I_{u \neq \#}J_{u \neq \#}$

Translations for Basic Expressions

(18) $\boldsymbol{poem} \rightsquigarrow \lambda v_e.\ [poem_{et}\{v\}]$

(19) $\boldsymbol{every}^{u \sqsubseteq r}$ (anaphoric to r) $\rightsquigarrow \lambda P_{et}.\lambda P'_{et}.\ \mathbf{max}^{u \sqsubseteq r}(_u(P(u)));\ _u(P'(u))$

(20) $\boldsymbol{every}^u$ (unrestricted) $\rightsquigarrow \lambda P_{et}.\lambda P'_{et}.\ \mathbf{max}^u(_u(P(u)));\ _u(P'(u))$

(21) $\boldsymbol{a}^{u \sqsubseteq r}$ (r can be freely accommodated) $\rightsquigarrow$
    $\lambda P_{et}.\lambda P'_{et}.\ [r];\ [u \mid u \sqsubseteq r, \mathbf{singleton}\{u\}];\ _u(P(u);\ P'(u))$

(22) $\boldsymbol{two}^{u \sqsubseteq r}$ (r can be freely accommodated) $\rightsquigarrow$
    $\lambda P_{et}.\lambda P'_{et}.\ [r];\ [u \mid u \sqsubseteq r, \mathbf{2}\{u\}];\ _u(P(u);\ P'(u))$

(23) $\boldsymbol{he}_u \rightsquigarrow \lambda P_{et}.\ [\mathbf{singleton}\{u\}];\ P(u)$

(24) $\boldsymbol{the}^{\mathbf{sg}:u \sqsubseteq r}$ (anaphoric to r) $\rightsquigarrow$
    $\lambda P_{et}.\lambda P'_{et}.\ \mathbf{max}^{u \sqsubseteq r}(P(u));\ [\mathbf{singleton}\{u\}];\ P'(u)$

(25) $\boldsymbol{the}^{\mathbf{sg}:u}$ (unrestricted/unique) $\rightsquigarrow$
    $\lambda P_{et}.\lambda P'_{et}.\ \mathbf{max}^u(P(u));\ [\mathbf{singleton}\{u\}];\ P'(u)$

(26) $\boldsymbol{they}_u \rightsquigarrow \lambda P_{et}.\ P(u)$

(27) $\boldsymbol{the}^{\mathbf{pl}:u \sqsubseteq r}$ (anaphoric to r) $\rightsquigarrow \lambda P_{et}.\lambda P'_{et}.\ \mathbf{max}^{u \sqsubseteq r}(P(u));\ P'(u)$

(28) $\boldsymbol{the}^{\mathbf{pl}:u}$ (unrestricted/maximal) $\rightsquigarrow \lambda P_{et}.\lambda P'_{et}.\ \mathbf{max}^u(P(u));\ P'(u)$

(29) $\boldsymbol{c\hat{\imath}te}^{r' \div u}\ \boldsymbol{un}^{u' \sqsubseteq r'}$ (anaphoric to u) $\rightsquigarrow$
    $\lambda P_{et}.\lambda P'_{et}.\ [r' \mid r' \div u];\ [u' \mid u' \sqsubseteq r', \mathbf{singleton}\{u'\}];\ _{u'}(P(u');\ P'(u'))$

---

[8] The definition of structured inclusion, where we go from a superset r to a subset u by discarding cells in a matrix / plural info state (thereby ensuring that the subset dref preserves the dependencies associated with the superset dref) uses the exception individual $\#$ to 'tag' the discarded cells.

Satisfaction and Friendliness Relations within Classical Logic: Proof-Theoretic Approach

Alexei Y. Muravitsky

Louisiana Scholars' College,
Northwestern State University
Natchitoches, LA 71497, USA
alexeim@nsula.edu

Abstract. We present the logical friendliness relation in a proof-theoretic fashion as sequent system $\boldsymbol{F}$. Then, the completeness theorem is proved. On the way to this theorem, we characterize the notion of satisfiability with respect to the classical two-valued semantics, in a proof-theoretic manner as system $\boldsymbol{S}$, so that the latter becomes part of the definition of system $\boldsymbol{F}$. Also, we obtain the strong compactness property for friendliness as a corollary of our completeness theorem.

Keywords: Classical Logic, logical friendliness, satisfiability, sequent system.

Mathematical Subject Classification (2000). Primary 03B05; Secondary 03B99, 03F99.

1 Introduction

David Makinson introduced in [4] the relation of logical friendliness, $\Gamma \mathrel{|\!\approx} \alpha$, as a binary relation in the ordinary propositional language between sets of formulas and formulas (see definition below), grounding it on the 2-valued semantics for classical propositional logic. The revised and extended version of [4] appeared later as [5], [6], and [7].[1]

Makison has made interesting observations for logical friendliness, among them, in [7], Section 1.5, are "closure properties", which can be interpreted as deduction rules for friendliness. However, the rules mentioned in [7], do not form a complete system. The question about "an axiomatic characterization of friendliness" is raised in Section 4 of [7]. In the present paper, we give one possible answer to this question, though the work had been completed before [7] became available to the author.[2]

A "characterization" mentioned in the previous paragraph, is presented in Section 4 in the form of a Gentzen-style system. It is standard in style, with

---

[1] All three last publications are identical in content. Referring to it, we chose [7] as the most accessible.

[2] I am grateful to the anonymous referee who drew my attention to the existence of the papers [5], [6] and [7].

P. Bosch, D. Gabelaia, and J. Lang (Eds.): TbiLLC 2007, LNAI 5422, pp. 180–192, 2009.

one rather unusual feature: it uses the classical deducibility relation in side-conditions.[3] This feature is not unprecedented. For instance, Łukasiewicz's calculus for refutable formulas employs this idea. (See, e.g., [3] or [10], pp. 46–47.[4]) Actually, we adopt it to define first system S (Section 3) for deriving all satisfiable formulas. Then system S is incorporated into system F (Section 4) that determines relation $\Gamma \Vdash \alpha$, which turns to be equivalent to $\Gamma|\approx \alpha$ (completeness). Thus, in definition of F, we use both classical deducibility and deducibility in S.

The reader is advised that we use symbol $\Vdash$ in two different meanings — for deducibility in S and for deducibility in F. The first usage stands for the deducibility in S of a unary sequent $\Vdash \alpha$. The second usage denotes the deducibility in F of a binary sequent $\Gamma \Vdash \alpha$. Confusion might occur if in the last sequent $\Gamma = \emptyset$. A possible confusion will be eliminated in Corollary 4.5.1. (See also Remark 4.3.)

In [7] Makinson proved strong compactness for friendliness: If $\Gamma|\approx \alpha$, then there is a finite set Γ_0 such that for any Λ with $\Gamma_0 \subseteq \Lambda \subseteq \Gamma$, $\Lambda|\approx \alpha$. Proving this property first for the deducibility relation $\Vdash$, we then obtain strong compactness for friendliness as a corollary of our completeness theorem (Theorem 4.8).

We want to note that in [4], Makinson presented a weaker variant of compactness for friendliness: If $\Gamma|\approx \alpha$, then there is a finite set Γ_0 such that $\Gamma_0|\approx \alpha$; moreover, Γ_0 is nonempty whenever Γ is nonempty. In [4], Section 3.1, Makinson raises the question, 'Can compactness for friendliness be given a constructive proof?' This question was dropped in [7]. The reason of doing this might be the following. Proving strong compactness, he used classical compactness more extensively, while in [4] he acted more directly. The point of Makinson's above-mentioned question is how to constructively obtain Γ_0. Our proof-theoretic approach sheds light on the problem, and we address it in Section 5.

We have one more issue to address before turning to the technical part of the paper. Since our axiomatization of friendliness (system F, which includes three cut rules (Rules 3*–5* below), does not enjoy the subformula property (see Remark 4.2), there seems to be little sense in pursuing cut elimination for F. Nonetheless, we make some comments on the cut elimination issue in Section 5.

2   Preliminaries

We limit ourselves with the propositional language based on the infinite set Var of propositional variables (i.e. $Var = \{p_1, \ldots, p_n, \ldots\}$) and the sentential connectives: $\wedge$ (*conjunction*), $\vee$ (*disjunction*), $\rightarrow$ (*implication*), $\neg$ (*negation*), and $\top$ (*truth*). In the sequel, unspecified formulas are denoted by α, β, γ. Γ, Δ, Λ will represent sets of formulas. We use the term a *formula occurrence*

---

[3] Makinson's "closure properties" also involve the classical deducibility. However, one of his "properties" includes premises $\Gamma \vdash \Delta$ (meaning that $\Gamma \vdash \alpha$, for each $\alpha \in \Delta$) and $\Delta \vdash \Gamma$, which leads to a higher level of deducibility, when rules with infinitely many premises of the form $\Gamma \vdash \alpha$ are allowed.

[4] In literature Łukasiewicz's method is known as rejection. (Cf. [10].)

in the sense of [9]. Thus, more precisely, Γ, Δ, Λ will also stand for sets of formula occurrences. This lets us avoid formulation of structural rules when we define system $\boldsymbol{F}$ (Section 4). We use the notation $E(\alpha)$, $E(\Gamma)$ and the like to denote the set of variables contained in α and Γ, respectively. If Γ is finite, we write $\wedge\Gamma$ for $\wedge\{\alpha \mid \alpha \in \Gamma\}$. As usual, $\wedge\{\alpha\} = \alpha$ and $\wedge\emptyset = \top$. When it is convenient, we write 'Γ, α' instead of '$\Gamma \cup \{\alpha\}$' and the like. Thus, we can note that $E(\Gamma) \cup E(\alpha) = E(\Gamma, \alpha)$.

We recall that a *literal* is a variable or the negation of a variable. We denote a literal by p^*, which can be either p or $\neg p$. If $A = p^* \wedge \ldots \wedge q^*$ is a conjunction of literals, we will denote by $L(A)$ the set $\{p^*, \ldots, q^*\}$. For any literal p^*, we will also be using $\boldsymbol{i}(p^*)$ to denote $p \rightarrow p$, if $p^* = p$, and $\neg\neg(p \rightarrow p)$, if $p^* = \neg p$. Thus, $\boldsymbol{i}(p^*)$ is always a classical tautology.

The classical deduction, symbolically $\Gamma \vdash \alpha$, is defined as usual; see, e.g., [1], [2], [8], or [11] where the classical deducibility is defined in sequent form.[5] Our own system of deduction here resembles that of [11]. We use $\Gamma \vdash \alpha$ in the definition of system $\boldsymbol{F}$ below as a binary predicate and α in the definition of system $\boldsymbol{S}$ below as a unary predicate. The reader is advised that the rule of substitution is not postulated for $\vdash$. In contrast, in systems $\boldsymbol{S}$ and $\boldsymbol{F}$ below the rule of (reverse) substitution is one of the postulated rules of inference.

Let a set $\{p_{i_1}, \ldots, p_{i_n}\}$ of variables be a subset (maybe, proper) of $E(\alpha)$. We denote by $\alpha[p_{i_1} \backslash \beta_1, \ldots, p_{i_n} \backslash \beta_n]$ the result of (simultaneous) *substitution* of the formulas $\beta_1, \ldots, \beta_n$ for the variables $p_{i_1}, \ldots, p_{i_n}$, respectively. If a substitution $\boldsymbol{s}$ applies to α, we denote the resulting formula by $\boldsymbol{s}(\alpha)$.

A *valuation* v is a mapping from the set of propositional variables into the set $\{\boldsymbol{0}, \boldsymbol{1}\}$ where $\boldsymbol{0}$ and $\boldsymbol{1}$ are regarded as truth values *false* and *true*, respectively. In a usual way, each valuation is extended to a homomorphism from the set of formulas into $\{\boldsymbol{0}, \boldsymbol{1}\}$ with respect to the classical logic truth tables. A set of formulas Γ is *satisfiable* if there is a valuation v such that $v(\Gamma) = \boldsymbol{1}$, for any formula $\alpha \in \Gamma$, in symbols $v(\Gamma) = \boldsymbol{1}$, in which case we say that v *validates* Γ. Formula α is called a *contradiction* if $v(\alpha) = \boldsymbol{0}$ for any valuation v, and is a *tautology* if $v(\alpha) = \boldsymbol{1}$ for any valuation v. If a formula is neither a contradiction nor a tautology, it is called *satisfiable*.

A *partial valuation agreed with* a set Γ is a mapping from $E(\Gamma)$ into $\{\boldsymbol{0}, \boldsymbol{1}\}$. Each partial valuation agreed with Γ is assumed to be extended up to a homomorphism from the formulas built up from $E(\Gamma)$ into $\{\boldsymbol{0}, \boldsymbol{1}\}$. By $E(v)$ we denote the domain of v. In this paper, all valuations are regarded as partial. Ordinary (or full) valuations of the classical semantics are regarded as partial with the domain $\boldsymbol{Var}$. Thus, if a partial valuation v is agreed with Γ, then $E(v) = E(\Gamma)$.

A partial valuation w is called an *extension* of a valuation v and, equivalently, v is a *restriction* of w, symbolically $w \geq v$ or $v \leq w$, if $E(v) \subseteq E(w)$ and $w(p) = v(p)$ for all $p \in E(v)$.

---

[5] Since neither of [1], [2], [8], or [11] uses $\top$ as an independent connective, the axiom $\Gamma \vdash \top$ should be added to our classical system for the derivability relation $\Gamma \vdash \alpha$.

We observe the following properties.

Proposition 2.1. *Let v be agreed with Γ and validate Γ, i.e. $v(\Gamma) = 1$. Suppose for some partial valuation $v' \geq v$, $v'(\Gamma, \alpha) = 1$. Then there is a valuation v'' which is an extension of v and restriction of v' and also both $E(v'') = E(\Gamma, \alpha)$ and $v''(\Gamma, \alpha) = 1$ hold.*

Proof is obvious.

Proposition 2.2. *Let three valuations v, v', and v'' satisfy the conditions: $v \leq v'$ and $v \leq v''$. If $E(v') \cap E(v'') \subseteq E(v)$ then there is a common extension v^* of v' and v'', defined on $E(v^*) = E(v') \cup E(v'')$.*

Proof. We define v^* on the set $E(v') \cup E(v'')$ as follows:

$$v^*(p) = \begin{cases} v'(p), & \text{if } p \in E(v') \setminus E(v''); \\ v''(p) & \text{if } p \in E(v'') \setminus E(v'); \\ v(p) & \text{if } p \in E(v') \cap E(v''). \end{cases}$$

For *classical consequence relation*, $\Gamma \models \alpha$, if a (partial) valuation v validates Γ, then any of its extension to $E(\Gamma, \alpha)$ validates α. Also, it is well known that the relations $\Gamma \models \alpha$ and $\Gamma \vdash \alpha$ are equivalent — the property known as *generalized completeness* (of the classical propositional logic). This property is a consequence of the property known as *compactness* (of this logic), which can be spelled out in terms of $\models$ as follows: $\Gamma \models \alpha$ implies that there is a finite $\Gamma_0 \subseteq \Gamma$ such that $\Gamma_0 \models \alpha$. (Cf., e.g., [1], Corollary 1.2.13). In the sequel, we will refer to it as the *classical compactness*. Since the relation $\models$ is monotone, we can assume that Γ_0 above is nonempty. We will be using the relations $\Gamma \models \alpha$ and $\Gamma \vdash \alpha$ interchangeably.

In the sequel, we will need the following observation which is obvious.

Proposition 2.3. *Let v be a valuation that validates a set Γ, that is, $v(\Gamma) = 1$. If $\Gamma \vdash \alpha$ then any extension v' of v with $E(\alpha) \subseteq E(v')$ validates α.*

Following [4], we say that Γ is *friendly* to α, in symbols $\Gamma \approx \alpha$, if any (partial) valuation v with $v(\Gamma) = 1$ and $E(v) = E(\Gamma)$ can be extended to a valuation v' with $v'(\alpha) = 1$ (and thus agreed with $\Gamma \cup \{\alpha\}$, i.e., $E(v') = E(\Gamma, \alpha)$). It will be convenient to remember that the valuation v' validates the whole set $\Gamma \cup \{\alpha\}$; i.e. $v'(\Gamma, \alpha) = 1$. It is clear that when $\Gamma = \emptyset$, the friendliness $\emptyset \approx \alpha$ simply means that α is satisfiable. We denote the *satisfiability predicate* by $\approx \alpha$.

3   Satisfaction

System $\mathbf{S}$ derives *unary sequents* $\Vdash \alpha$, where α can be any formula. As we will see, this system is an adequate axiomatization of the satisfiability predicate $\approx \alpha$. In Section 4, this system will be incorporated as part of definition of derivability in system $\mathbf{F}$.

The axioms and deduction rules of S are:

I Axioms:

1. $\Vdash p$, where p is a variable.
2. $\Vdash \top$.

II Deduction rules:

1^+. Soundness with respect to the classical deduction:
$$\frac{\Vdash \alpha \text{ and } \vdash \alpha \to \beta}{\Vdash \beta}.$$

2^+. Reverse Substitution:
$$\frac{\Vdash s(\alpha)}{\Vdash \alpha}.$$

Deduction, or *derivation*, is defined as usual through the notion of a deduction tree. (See [9].) If a sequent $\Vdash \alpha$ is derivable in S, we simply write '$\Vdash \alpha$'.

Proposition 3.1. *If $\vdash \alpha$ then $\Vdash \alpha$.*

Proof. Indeed, since $\top \to \alpha$ and $\Vdash \top$ (Axiom 2), we derive $\Vdash \alpha$ by Rule 1^+.

Theorem 3.2. *(soundness) If $\Vdash \alpha$ then $\approx \alpha$.*

Proof. by induction on the length of derivation of α.

For the completeness theorem (Theorem 3.4) we need the following

Lemma 3.3. *For any nonempty set $\{p^*, \ldots, q^*\}$ of pairwise distinct literals, $\Vdash p^* \wedge \ldots \wedge q^*$.*

Proof. We prove by induction of the literals in $\{p^*, \ldots, q^*\}$. First of all, $\Vdash p$ is an axiom. Further, since $\vdash p \to \neg\neg p$ and $\Vdash p$, we have, by Rule 1^*, that $\Vdash \neg\neg p$. Then we apply substitution (Rule 2^+) to get $\Vdash \neg p$.

Next, assuming $\Vdash \alpha$, we prove that $\Vdash \alpha \wedge q$ and $\Vdash \alpha \wedge \neg q$, providing that $q \notin E(\alpha)$.

Indeed, from $\vdash \alpha \to \alpha \wedge (q \to q)$ and $\vdash \alpha \to \alpha \wedge \neg\neg(q \to q)$ we derive $\Vdash \alpha \wedge (q \to q)$ and $\Vdash \alpha \wedge \neg\neg(q \to q)$ by using Rule 1^+. Then, we apply substitution (Rule 2^+) to the former and to the latter.

Theorem 3.4. *(completeness) If $\approx \alpha$ then $\Vdash \alpha$.*

Proof. If $E(\alpha) = \emptyset$, then α is deductively equivalent to $\top$. Then we apply Axiom 2 and Rule 1^+.

Now we assume that $E(\alpha) = \{p, \ldots, q\}$. Suppose for a valuation v, $v(\alpha) = 1$. Let $p^*, \ldots, q^*$ bè literals of the variables in $E(\alpha)$ so that $v(p^*) = \ldots = v(q^*) = 1$. According to Kalmar's Lemma (cf. [2], § 29, Lemma 13, or [8], Lemma 1.13), $\vdash p^* \wedge \ldots \wedge q^* \to \alpha..$ Then we use Lemma 3.3 and Rule 1^+.

4 Friendliness

We are about to define system $\boldsymbol{F}$, which serves as an axiomatization of friendliness $\Gamma \not\approx \alpha$.

System $\boldsymbol{F}$ derives *binary* sequents $\Gamma \Vdash \alpha$, where Γ is a set of formulas (possibly empty or infinite) and α is any formula. We prove that the derivability of $\Gamma \Vdash \alpha$ and $\emptyset \Vdash \alpha$ in $\boldsymbol{F}$ is adequate for the relation $\Gamma |\approx \alpha$ and the predicate $|\approx \alpha$, respectively. (See some comments on this in Remark 4.3.)

The axioms and deduction rules of $\boldsymbol{F}$ are:

I Axioms:

$1°$. $\Gamma \Vdash \top$.
$2°$. $\Gamma \Vdash \alpha$, when $E(\alpha) \cap E(\Gamma) = \emptyset$ and $\Vdash \alpha$ is derivable in $\boldsymbol{S}$.
$3°$. $\Gamma \Vdash \wedge\Delta$ and Δ is finite.
$4°$. $\Gamma \Vdash \alpha$ whenever $\Gamma \vdash \alpha$. (*Soundness with respect to the classical logic.*)

Thus, as it is seen from Axioms $1°$ and $4°$, system $\boldsymbol{S}$ and the classical logic are included in system $\boldsymbol{F}$.

We omit structural rules, since Γ, Δ and the like are regarded as multisets (possibly infinite).

II Deduction rules:

1^*. $\vee$-introduction in antecedent:
$$\frac{\Gamma, \alpha \Vdash \gamma \text{ and } \Delta, \beta \Vdash \gamma}{\Gamma \cup \Delta, \alpha \vee \beta \Vdash \gamma}, \text{ providing that } E(\Gamma, \alpha) = E(\Delta, \beta).$$
2^*. Reverse substitution:
$$\frac{\Gamma \Vdash s(\alpha)}{\Gamma \Vdash \alpha}, \text{ where } s(\alpha) = \alpha[p_{i_1} \backslash \beta_1, \ldots, p_{i_n} \backslash \beta_n] \text{ and } E(\Gamma) \cap \{p_{i_1}, \ldots, p_{i_n}\} = \emptyset.$$
3^*. Cut:
$$\frac{\Gamma \Vdash \alpha \text{ and } \alpha \Vdash \beta}{\Gamma \Vdash \beta}, \text{ providing that either } E(\Gamma) \subseteq E(\alpha) \text{ or } E(\Gamma) \cap E(\beta) \subseteq E(\alpha) \subseteq$$
$E(\Gamma)$.
4^*. Deductive replacement in antecedent:
$$\frac{\Gamma, \alpha \Vdash \beta \text{ and } \gamma \Vdash \alpha}{\Gamma, \gamma \Vdash \beta}, \text{ providing that } E(\gamma) \subseteq E(\Gamma, \alpha).$$
5^*. Deductive replacement in consequent:
$$\frac{\Gamma \Vdash \alpha \text{ and } \alpha \vdash \beta}{\Gamma \Vdash \beta}.$$

Derivation of a sequent $\Gamma \Vdash \alpha$ in system $\boldsymbol{F}$ is defined in a usual fashion through the notion of a deduction tree. (See [9].) If a sequent $\Gamma \Vdash \alpha$ is derivable in $\boldsymbol{F}$, we will say that $\Gamma \Vdash \alpha$ is true or write simply '$\Gamma \Vdash \alpha$'.

Remark 4.1. Axioms $1°$–$4°$ above are not independent. Axiom $1°$ is an instant of Axiom $4°$. Also, it is clear that Axiom $3°$ is derived from of Axiom $4°$, using some properties of $\vdash$. However, Axiom $4°$ can be derived from Axioms $1°$ and $3°$ by using Rule 5^*. Axiom $2°$ follows from Axiom $4°$ by using Rule 2^*. Thus it is possible to axiomatize $\boldsymbol{F}$ with one axiom, Axiom $4°$.

Remark 4.2. The *subformula property* in the sense that in any deduction of a sequent $\Gamma \Vdash \alpha$, only subformulas of Γ and α occur, in general does not hold as the following derivation (without cut) shows.

$$\frac{\Vdash q \text{ (axiom in } \boldsymbol{S}) \vdash q \to (p \to q)}{\Vdash p \to q} \text{ (deduction in } \boldsymbol{S})$$

$$\frac{\emptyset \Vdash p \to q \text{ (axiom in } \boldsymbol{F}) \; p \to q \vdash \neg p \vee q}{\emptyset \Vdash \neg p \vee q} \text{ (Rule 5}^*)$$

Remark 4.3. Axiom 2° indicates that system $\boldsymbol{S}$ is part of system $\boldsymbol{F}$. Thus, strictly speaking, we should distinguish derivability of a sequent $\Vdash \alpha$ in $\boldsymbol{S}$ and that of $\emptyset \Vdash \alpha$ in $\boldsymbol{F}$. However, Corollary 4.5.1 shows that these two conditions of derivability are equivalent.

The next observation will be used in Theorem 4.6.

Proposition 4.4. *If* $E(\alpha) \cap E(\beta) = \emptyset$ *and* β *is not a contradiction, then* $\alpha \Vdash \beta$.

Proof. Since $|\approx \beta$, by virtue of Theorem 3.4, we have $\Vdash \beta$. Then, in view of Axiom 2°, we have $\alpha \Vdash \beta$.

Theorem 4.5. *(soundness) If* $\Gamma \Vdash \alpha$ *then* $\Gamma \approx \alpha$.

Proof. We have to go over Axioms 1°–4° and Rules 1*–5*. So, proving by induction on the length of derivation, we have to consider the following cases.

Case: Axioms 1°–4°. For Axiom 1°; we notice that $\Gamma \approx \top$ is obviously true.

For Axiom 2°; if the sequent $\Vdash \alpha$ is derivable in $\boldsymbol{S}$, then, by virtue of Theorem 3.2, α is satisfiable. Hence $\Gamma \approx \alpha$, when $E(\alpha) \cap E(\Gamma) = \emptyset$.

For Axiom 3°; if $\Delta \subseteq \Gamma$ and Δ is finite, then $\Gamma \approx$ $wedge\Delta$ is obviously true.

For Axiom 4°; if $\Gamma \vdash \alpha$, then, in view of Proposition 2.3, $\Gamma \approx \alpha$.

Case: Rule 1*. Assume that $\Gamma, \alpha \approx \gamma$ and $\Delta, \beta \approx \gamma$, where $E(\Gamma, \alpha) = E(\Delta, \beta)$. Now if a valuation v, validates $\Gamma \cap \Delta \cap \{\alpha \vee \beta\}$ then either for some $v' \leq v$, $v'(\Gamma, \alpha) = 1$ or for some $v'' \leq v$, $v''(\Delta, \beta) = 1$. According to one of the premises, whichever is true, there is an extension $v^* \geq v'$ or $v^* \geq v'$ such that $v^*(\Gamma \cap \Delta \cap \{\alpha \vee \beta\} \cap \{\gamma\}) = 1$. We notice that $E(v') = E(v'') = E(v)$. Thus v^* is an extension of v.

Case: Rule 2*. Obvious.

Case: Rule 3* (cut). Suppose a valuation v validates Γ, that is, $v(\Gamma) = 1$. Then, according to the first premise, there is $v' \geq v$ such that $v'(\Gamma, \alpha) = 1$. If v'' is the restriction of v' with $E(v'') = E(\alpha)$, then, according to the second premise, there is an extension $v^* \geq v''$ such that $E(v^*) = E(\alpha, \beta)$ and $v^*(\alpha, \beta) = 1$.

Now assume first that $E(\Gamma) \subseteq E(\alpha)$. It is clear that $v'' = v'$ and hence $v^* \geq v$. Also, $v^*(\Gamma, \alpha, \beta) = 1$. And we use Proposition 2.1 to get an extension of v that validates $\Gamma \cup \{\beta\}$.

Next assume that $E(\Gamma) \cap E(\beta) \subseteq E(\alpha) \subseteq E(\Gamma)$. It implies that $v = v'$. Then $v'' \leq v$ and $v'' \leq v^*$. We notice that $E(v'') = E(\alpha)$, $E(v) = E(\Gamma)$, $E(v^*) = E(\alpha, \beta) = E(\alpha) \cup E(\beta)$. It is clear that $E(v) \cap E(v^*) \subseteq E(v'')$. By virtue of Proposition 2.2, there is a common extension v^{**} of v and v^*, defined on $E(v) \cup E(v^*)$. Thus $E(v^{**}) = E(\Gamma, \beta)$ and $v^{**}(\Gamma, \beta) = \mathbf{1}$.

Case: Rule 4*. Suppose a valuation v validates Γ and γ. Since $\gamma \vdash \alpha$, according to Proposition 2.3, v can be partially extended to v', which validates α and is agreed with $\Gamma \cup \{\gamma, \alpha\}$. Since $E(\gamma) \subseteq E(\Gamma, \alpha)$, $E(v') = E(\Gamma, \alpha)$. Thus, by premise, v' can be extended to $v'\prime$ so that $v'\prime(\Gamma, \alpha, \beta) = \mathbf{1}$ and $E(v'') = E(\Gamma, \alpha, \beta)$. By virtue of Proposition 2.1, there is a restriction v^* of v'' to $E(\Gamma, \gamma, \beta)$, which validates $\Gamma \cup \{\gamma, \beta\}$.

Case: Rule 5*. Suppose a valuation v validates $\Gamma \cup \{\alpha\}$ and is agreed with this set. Then there is an extension $v' \geq v$ such that $E(v') = E(\Gamma, \alpha)$ and $v'(\Gamma, \alpha) = \mathbf{1}$. Then, by virtue of Proposition 2.3, any extension $v'' \geq v$ such that $E(\beta) \subseteq E(v'')$ validates the set $\Gamma \cup \{\alpha, \beta\}$. Obviously, there is a restriction of v'', which is an extension of v, that validates $\Gamma \cup \{\beta\}$.

Corollary 4.5.1. *A sequent $\Vdash \alpha$ is derived in $\mathbf{S}$ if and only if the sequent $\emptyset \Vdash \alpha$ is derived in $\mathbf{F}$.*

Proof. If $\alpha = \top$, the statement is obvious. So assume that $\alpha \neq \top$. The left-to-right implication is true because of Axiom 2°.

Now, if $\emptyset \Vdash \alpha$ is derived in $\mathbf{F}$, then, in view of Theorem 4.5, $\approx \alpha$; that is, α is satisfiable. By virtue of Theorem 3.4, the sequent $\Vdash \alpha$ is derivable in $\mathbf{S}$.

The following lemma is needed to prove the theorem on fine compactness below (Theorem 4.7).

Lemma 4.6. *For a formula α and a set $\{p, \ldots, q\}$ of distinct variables, if $E(\alpha) \cap \{p, \ldots, q\} = \emptyset$ then $\alpha \Vdash p^* \wedge \ldots \wedge q^*$ and $\alpha \Vdash \alpha \wedge p^* \wedge \ldots \wedge q^*$.*

Proof. Indeed, by virtue of Axiom 4°, $\alpha \Vdash \boldsymbol{i}(p^*) \wedge \ldots \wedge \boldsymbol{i}(q^*)$ and $\alpha \Vdash \alpha \wedge \boldsymbol{i}(p^*) \wedge \ldots \wedge \boldsymbol{i}(q^*)$, since $\alpha \vdash \boldsymbol{i}(p^*) \wedge \ldots \wedge \boldsymbol{i}(q^*)$ and $\alpha \vdash \alpha \wedge \boldsymbol{i}(p^*) \wedge \ldots \wedge \boldsymbol{i}(q^*)$. Then we use substitution (Rule 2*).

Theorem 4.7. *(finite completeness) Let Γ be finite. If $\Gamma \not\approx \alpha$ then $\Gamma \Vdash \alpha$.*

Proof. If $\Gamma = \emptyset$ the conclusion follows straightforward from Axiom 2°.

Next we assume that $\Gamma \neq \emptyset$ and let $\gamma = \wedge \Gamma$. It is obvious that $\Gamma \not\approx \alpha$ is equivalent to $\gamma \not\approx \alpha$. We are going to prove that $\gamma \Vdash \alpha$. Then, since $\Gamma \Vdash \gamma$ (by Axiom 3°), we use cut (Rule 3*) to conclude that $\Gamma \Vdash \alpha$. So, we assume that $\gamma \Vdash \alpha$ and start proving that $\gamma \Vdash \alpha$.

If γ is a contradiction, then we obtain $\gamma \Vdash \alpha$ by Axiom 4°. Also, we arrive at this conclusion when α is contradiction. Thus we proceed with the assumption that neither γ nor α is a contradiction.

If $E(\alpha) \cap E(\gamma) = \emptyset$, then, by Proposition 4.4, $\gamma \Vdash \alpha$. So we assume that $E(\alpha) \cap E(\gamma) \neq \emptyset$. If $E(\alpha) \subseteq E(\gamma)$ then $\gamma \not\approx \alpha$ simply means that $\gamma \vDash \alpha$, that is, $\gamma \vdash \alpha$ and, hence, by Axiom 4°, $\Vdash \alpha$.

Next we consider the case when $E(\alpha) \not\subseteq E(\gamma)$, that is, α contains variables which do not occur in γ. If γ contains no variable then $\gamma \Vdash \alpha$, by Theorem 3.4 and Axiom 2°. Thus we proceed with the assumption that both γ and α contain variables.

Let P_γ and P_α be the normal disjunctive forms of γ and α, respectively. For a particular valuation v that validates γ, only one conjunction group of P_γ, say A, can take $\mathbf{1}$. Because of the premise, $\gamma \not\approx \alpha$, there is a valuation $v' \geq v$ that validates α. However, only one conjunction group, say $A' \wedge B$, of P_α can take $\neq$ in v'. Here $E(A') \subseteq E(\alpha) \cap E(\gamma)$. Since $v' \geq v$, $L(A') \subseteq L(A)$ and, hence, $A \vdash A'$. Therefore, by Axiom $4°$, $A \Vdash A'$. Also, by virtue of Lemma 4.6, $A' \Vdash A' \wedge B$. Noticing that $E(A') \subseteq E(A)$ and $E(A) \subseteq E(A' \wedge B) = E(A')$, by cut (Rule 3^*), we get $A \Vdash A' \wedge B$.

Now we apply Axiom $4°$ to get $A \Vdash P_\alpha$ and conclude with application of Rule 1^* (possibly more than one time) that $P_\gamma \Vdash P_\alpha$. Finally, we have $\gamma \vdash P_\gamma$, $P_\gamma \Vdash P_\alpha$ and $P_\alpha \vdash \alpha$, where $E(\gamma) = E(P_\gamma)$. The first two imply, by Rule 4^*, that $\gamma \Vdash P_\alpha$. The latter and $P \vdash \alpha$ imply, by Rule 5^*, that $\gamma \Vdash \alpha$.

Theorem 4.8. *(completeness) If $\Gamma \not\approx \alpha$ then $\Gamma \Vdash \alpha$.*

Proof. We assume that Γ is infinite, for the finite case is covered in Theorem 4.7. Also, we assume that α is not *tru*, because otherwise we simply use Axiom $1°$.

If Γ is not satisfiable then, according to classical compactness (cf., e.g., [1], Corollary 1.2.13), there is a finite nonempty set $\Gamma_0 \subseteq \Gamma$, which is not satisfiable. Then, obviously, $\Gamma \Vdash \wedge \Gamma_0$ (Axiom 3) and $\wedge \Gamma_0 \vdash \alpha$. Applying Rule 5^*, we obtain $\Gamma \Vdash \alpha$.

Now we assume that Γ is satisfiable. Then α is also satisfiable. We denote $\Delta = E(\Gamma) \cap E(\alpha)$. If $\Delta = \emptyset$ then, by Theorem 3.4 and Axiom $2°$, we derive $\Gamma \Vdash \alpha$. If $\Delta \neq \emptyset$ then for any valuation v, we define:

$$\Delta(v) = \{p \mid p \in \Delta, v(p) = \mathbf{1}\} \cup \{\neg p \mid p \in \Delta, v(p) = \mathbf{0}\}.$$

(In particular, if $E(v) \cap \Delta = \emptyset$, then $\Delta(v) = \emptyset$.)

First we observe that there is a finite number of the $\Delta(v)$ sets. Therefore, both sets $\{\Delta(v) \mid v(\Sigma) = \mathbf{1}$ and $\Sigma \subseteq \Gamma\}$ and $\{\Delta(v) \mid v(\Gamma) = \mathbf{1}$ and $E(v) = E(\Gamma)\}$ are finite. Also, neither of these two sets is empty, since Γ is satisfiable. We will identify the last set as $\{\Delta(v_i) \mid 1 \leq i \leq k\}$, for some designated valuations v_i with $v_i(\Gamma) = \mathbf{1}$ and $E(v_i) = E(\Gamma)$, which are pairwise distinct. In the sequel, we will be using the notation

$$\Delta_i = \Delta(v_i) = \{p \mid p \in \Delta, v_i(p) = \mathbf{1}\} \cup \{\neg p \mid p \in \Delta, v_i(p) = \mathbf{0}\}, \quad 1 \leq i \leq k.$$

Next we observe that

$$v(\wedge \Delta(v)) = \mathbf{1}. \tag{1}$$

In particular,

$$v_i(\wedge \Delta_i) = \mathbf{1}; \text{ in addition, for } j \neq i, v_i(\wedge \Delta_j) = \mathbf{0}. \tag{2}$$

Next we prove the following statement:

$$(\wedge \Delta_1) \vee \ldots \vee (\wedge \Delta_k) \not\approx \alpha. \tag{3}$$

We note that $E((\wedge\Delta_1) \vee \ldots \vee (\wedge\Delta_k)) = E(\Delta_1) \cup \ldots \cup E(\Delta_k) = \Delta$, because each $E(\Delta_i) = \Delta$. Assume that a valuation v validates $(\wedge\Delta_1) \vee \ldots \vee (\wedge\Delta_k)$ with $E(v) = \Delta$. Then v validates Δ_i, for some i. Using (2), we see that v is a restriction of v_i. Since v_i is agreed with $E(\Gamma)$ and validates Γ, there is, by premise, $w \geq v_i$ with $w(\Gamma, \alpha) = 1$. Then, by Proposition 2.1, we can take the restriction w' of w to $E(\Delta, \alpha)$, which is an extension of v. Thus (3) is proven.

We define

$$\Gamma^* = \{\Sigma \mid \Sigma \subseteq \Gamma, \ \Sigma \text{ is finite and } \Delta \subseteq E(\Sigma)\}.$$

One can notice that Γ^* is a *join*-semilattice. Next we define for any $\Sigma \in \Gamma^*$,

$$\varphi(\Sigma) = \{\Delta(v) \mid E(v) = E(\Sigma), v(\Sigma) = 1\}.$$

We note that each $\varphi(\Sigma)$ is nonempty, because Γ is satisfiable, and finite, being a subset of a finite set. Also, the set $\{\varphi(\Sigma) \mid \Sigma \in \Gamma^*\}$ is nonempty and finite, because it is a subset of the set of the set of all $\Delta(v)$. Next we define

$$[\Gamma^*] = (\{\varphi(\Sigma) \mid \Sigma \in \Gamma^*\}, \subseteq)$$

and notice that $[\Gamma^*]$ is a finite partially ordered set. Thus $[\Gamma^*]$ has minimal elements. It is not hard to observe that

$$\Sigma_1 \subseteq \Sigma_2 \Rightarrow \varphi(\Sigma_2) \subseteq \varphi(\Sigma_1).$$

The last property and the fact that Γ^* is a *join*-semilattice imply that for some $\Sigma_0 \in \Gamma^*$, $\varphi(\Sigma_0)$ is a least element in $[\Gamma^*]$.

Next we define for $\Sigma \in \Gamma^*$,

$$\varphi^*(\Sigma) = \vee\{\wedge\Delta(v) \mid \Delta(v) \in \varphi(\Sigma)\}.$$

We note that for any $\Sigma \in \Gamma^*$, $E(\varphi^*(\Sigma)) = \Delta$. From the last definition, with help of (1), we obtain the following.

For any $\Sigma \in \Gamma^*$, $\wedge\Sigma \approx \varphi^*(\Sigma)$; in particular, $\wedge\Sigma_0 \approx \varphi^*(\Sigma_0)$. $\qquad$ (4)

Next we prove the key statement:

$$\varphi^*(\Sigma_0) \vdash (\wedge\Delta_1) \vee \ldots \vee (\wedge\Delta_k). \qquad (5)$$

Actually, we will prove that $\varphi(\Sigma_0) = \{\Delta_1, \ldots, \Delta_k\}$. First we show that that for any $\Sigma \in \Gamma^*$, $\{\Delta_1, \ldots, \Delta_k\} \subseteq \varphi(\Sigma)$. Indeed, let $\Sigma \in \Gamma^*$. Let us take any v_i. The valuation v_i validates Γ and, hence, also validates Σ. We remind that $\Delta \subseteq E(\Sigma)$. Now if v is the restriction of v_i to $E(\Sigma)$, then $\Delta(v) = \Delta_i$. However, $\Delta(v) \in \varphi(\Sigma)$. Thus $\Delta_i \in \varphi(\Sigma)$.

Next, for contradiction, we assume that for any $\Sigma \in \Gamma^*$, $\{\Delta_1, \ldots, \Delta_k\} \subset \varphi(\Sigma)$. In particular, $\{\Delta_1, \ldots, \Delta_k\} \subset \varphi(\Sigma_0)$. In other words, there is a valuation v, which validates Σ_0 and is agreed with $E(\Sigma_0)$; moreover, $\Delta(v)$ belongs to all $\varphi(\Sigma)$ and differs from all Δ_i. For us only two last properties are important.

Because then for any $\Sigma \in \Gamma^*$, $\Sigma \nvdash (\wedge \Delta_1) \vee \ldots \vee (\wedge \Delta_k)$. Indeed, given $\Sigma \in \Gamma^*$, there is a valuation w with $E(w) = E(\Sigma)$ and $w(\Sigma) = \mathbf{1}$ such that $\Delta(v) = \Delta(w)$. The last equality implies that $\Delta(w)$ differs from all Δ_i, which means that w refutes $(\wedge \Delta_1) \vee \ldots \vee (\wedge \Delta_k)$. On the other hand, it is clear that $\Gamma \vdash (\wedge \Delta_1) \vee \ldots \vee (\wedge \Delta_k)$. By the classical compactness and monotonicity of $\vdash$, there is $\Sigma_1 \in \Gamma^*$ such that $\Sigma_1 \vdash (\wedge \Delta_1) \vee \ldots \vee (\wedge \Delta_k)$. A contradiction.

Collecting our findings, we obtain the following:

1) $\Gamma \Vdash \wedge \Sigma_0$, by Axiom 3°;
2) $\Sigma_0 \Vdash \varphi^*(\Sigma_0)$, from (4) by Theorem 4.7;
3) $\varphi^*(\Sigma_0) \vdash (\wedge \Delta_1) \vee \ldots \vee (\Delta_k)$, (5);
4) $(\wedge \Delta_1) \vee \ldots \vee (\wedge \Delta_k) \Vdash \alpha$, from (3) by Theorem 4.7.

To complete the proof first we we apply Rule 5* to 2) and 3) above to derive $\wedge \Sigma_0 \Vdash (\wedge \Delta_1) \vee \ldots \vee (\Delta_k)$. Then, we use cut (Rule 3*) twice to conclude that $\Gamma \Vdash \alpha$.

Corollary 4.8.1. *(strong compactness for $\Vdash$)* Let $\Gamma \Vdash \alpha$. Then there is a finite set $\Gamma_0 \subseteq \Gamma$ such that for any Λ with $\Gamma_0 \subseteq \Lambda \subseteq \Gamma$, $\Lambda \Vdash \alpha$.

Proof. We will use the notation of Theorem 4.8. Suppose first that Γ is inconsistent. Then, by the classical compactness, there is a finite inconsistent $\Gamma_0 \subseteq \Gamma$ such that, whenever $\Gamma_0 \subseteq \Lambda \subseteq \Gamma$, Λ is also inconsistent. Therefore, $\Lambda \approx \alpha$. And we apply Theorem 4.8 to get $\Lambda \Vdash \alpha$.

Now assume that Γ is consistent, that is, satisfiable. Then α must also be satisfiable. If $\Delta = \emptyset$, then for any $\Lambda \subseteq \Gamma$, $\Lambda \approx \alpha$ because $E(\Lambda) \cap E(\alpha) \subseteq \Delta = \emptyset$. Again by Theorem 4.8, we get $\Lambda \Vdash \alpha$.

Now assume that Γ is consistent and $\Delta \neq \emptyset$. According to (5) above, $\wedge \Sigma_0 \vdash \alpha$. Now if $\Sigma_0 \subseteq \Lambda$, then, by virtue of Axiom 3°, we have $\Lambda \Vdash \wedge \Sigma_0$. The last sequent and $\wedge \Sigma_0 \Vdash (\wedge \Delta_1) \vee \ldots \vee (\wedge \Delta_k)$ above derive, by cut (Rule 5*), the sequent $\Lambda \Vdash (\wedge \Delta_1) \vee \ldots \vee (\wedge \Delta_k)$. Then we apply cut again to the last sequent and $(\wedge \Delta_1) \vee \ldots \vee (\wedge \Delta_k) \Vdash \alpha$ to conclude $\Lambda \Vdash \alpha$.

Corollary 4.8.2. *(strong compactness for $\approx$)* Let $\Gamma \approx \alpha$. Then there is a finite set $\Gamma_0 \subseteq \Gamma$ such that for any Λ with $\Gamma_0 \subseteq \Lambda \subseteq \Gamma$, $\Lambda \approx \alpha$.[6]

Proof is straightforward from Corollary 4.8.1 and Theorem 4.8.

5   Discussion

Makinson raised the question (see Introduction): Can a finite set $\Gamma_0 \subseteq \Gamma$ in strong compactness for logical friendliness be found in a constructive way? Strictly speaking, the answer depends on to which extent a given set Γ is constructive. As the proof of Theorem 4.8 shows, if Δ above is nonempty, what we have to do is constructively find Σ_0. If $\Delta = \emptyset$, one can take any nonempty subset of Γ as Γ_0, providing that α in the premise $\Gamma \approx \alpha$ is satisfiable. Of course, this

---

[6] The property of strong compactness for $\approx$ was proved first semantically in [7].

works if we are successful in determining, whether Γ is satisfiable. And if it is not, we have to be able to spot a finite unsatisfiable subset of Γ. This is where the main difficulty may lie.

Another topic for discussion can be the cut elimination property. Strictly speaking, we have three cut rules, namely Rules 3*–5*. I believe that neither of them can be eliminated. My supporting argument of this conjecture regarding Rule 5* is as follows. Let us define $Cn(\Gamma) = \{\alpha \mid \Gamma \vdash \alpha\}$ and $Cn_F(\Gamma) = \{\alpha \mid \Gamma \Vdash \alpha\}$. Then the following properties correspond to Axiom 4° and Rule 5*, respectively:

1) For all $\alpha \in Cn(\Gamma)$, $Cn(\alpha) \subseteq Cn_F(\Gamma)$;
2) For all $\alpha \in Cn_F(\Gamma)$, $Cn(\alpha) \subseteq Cn_F(\Gamma)$.

We note that among the deduction rules of F, only Rule 5* has no restriction on variables and all axioms of F are derivable from Axiom 4° (cf. Remark 4.1). Thus, in the light of the question, we focus on possible interconnection between 1) and 2). It is hardly plausible that 1) might imply 2).

Another argument in favor of the conjecture is that the sequent $\neg\neg p \to p \Vdash \neg p \lor p$ can be proven in F either by using only Rule 4* or by using only Rule 5* and in both cases without Rule 3*. Also, one can prove that this sequent cannot be derived without using either Rule 4* or Rule 5*.

I do not have other supporting arguments for my conjecture regarding Rules 3*–5*. However, if I am right, then deleting some or all of the cut rules from the definition of F, we obtain a system that is still stronger than the classical system and remains to be nonmonotone. The last follows, e.g., from this: the sequent $p \Vdash q$ is an instance of Axiom 2°, but $p, \neg q \Vdash q$ is not true and hence, in view of Theorem 4.7, is not derivable even in F. Then, again if my conjecture is true, we would have another nonmonotone consequence-like operator, weaker than Cn. [7]

The final remark. One of the ways to investigate cut elimination for F is the Makinson's characterization of friendliness by the conditions 1–3 in [7], p. 7 (or in [5], p. 201). Since his condition 1 remains true if we delete all of the cut rules from F, we can delete some of them and see, whether the conditions 2–3 remain true. If at least one of them does not, then F is sensitive to the elimination of those cut rules.

References

1. Chang, C.C., Keisler, H.J.: Model Theory. Studies in Logic and Foundations of Mathematics, vol. 73. Elsevier Pub. Com., Amsterdam (1973)
2. Kleene, S.C.: Introduction to Metamathematics. D. Van Nostrand Company, Inc., New York (1952)
3. Łukasiewicz, J.: Aristotle's Syllogistic from the Standpoint of Modern Formal Logic, Oxford (1952)

---

[7] I call Cn_F "consequence-like" operator, because one can prove that Cn_F is not a consequence operator in the sense of Tarski, though it satisfies some of the properties of such an operator. On the other hand, there is a close relation between operator Cn_F and satisfiable sets.

4. Makinson, D.: Logical Friendliness and Sympathy. In: Beziau, J.-Y. (ed.) Logica Universalis, pp. 195–224. Birkhäuser Verlag (2005)
5. Makinson, D.: Logical Friendliness and Sympathy. In: Beziau, J.-Y. (ed.) Logica Universalis, 2nd edn., pp. 191–205. Birkhäuser Verlag (2007)
6. Makinson, D.: Friendliness for Logicians. In: We Will Show Them! Essays in Honor of Dov Gabbay, vol. 2, pp. 259–292. College Publications (2005)
7. Makinson, D.: Friendliness and Sympathy in Logic,
   http://david.makinson.googlepages.com
8. Mendelson, E.: Introduction to Mathematical Logic, 4th edn. Chapman & Hall, Boca Raton (1997)
9. Prawitz, D.: Natural Deduction, Almqvist & Wiksell (1965) (New publication: Prawitz, D.: Natural Deduction: a proof-theoretical study. Dover Publications (2006))
10. Prior, A.N.: Formal Logic. Clarendon Press, Oxford (1963)
11. Troelstra, A.S., Schwichtenberg, H.: Basic Proof Theory, 2nd edn. Cambridge University Press, Cambridge (2000)

Identification through Inductive Verification

Application to Monotone Quantifiers

Nina Gierasimczuk*

Institute for Logic, Language, and Computation, University of Amsterdam
Institute of Philosophy, University of Warsaw
n.gierasimczuk@uva.nl

Abstract. In this paper we are concerned with some general properties
of scientific hypotheses. We investigate the relationship between the situation when the task is to verify a given hypothesis, and when a scientist
has to pick a correct hypothesis from an arbitrary class of alternatives.
Both these procedures are based on induction. We understand hypothe-
ses as generalized quantifiers of types $\langle 1 \rangle$ or $\langle 1, 1 \rangle$. Some of their formal
features, like monotonicity, appear to be of great relevance. We first fo-
cus on monotonicity, extendability and persistence of quantifiers. They
are investigated in context of epistemological verifiability of scientific hypotheses. In the second part we show that some of these properties imply
learnability. As a result two strong paradigms are joined: the paradigm
of computational epistemology (see e.g. [6,5]), which goes back to the notion of identification in the limit as formulated in [4], and the paradigm
of investigating natural language determiners in terms of generalized
quantifiers in finite models (see e.g.[1]).

Keywords: Identification in the limit, induction, monadic quantifiers,
monotonicity, semantics learning, verification.

1 Introduction

The 'identification in the limit' model [4] has found numerous applications in
language learning analysis — for the most part in the acquisition of syntax. In
contrast the model has been underappreciated in the investigations concerning
learning of semantics.

On the other hand, in philosophy of science Gold's paradigm has been used
to account for inductive reasoning and the process of approaching the correct
theory about the world. In this domain various semantic properties of hypotheses
are of great importance [6,8].

In the present paper we abstract from the distinction between learning and
scientific inquiry. We hope that with this generality our results are relevant for
both subjects. Our aim is to analyze semantic properties of inductive verifiability
[6] and consider its connection with identification. The first section is devoted to

---

* The author is the receiver of a Foundation for Polish Science Award for Young
Researchers (START Programme 2008).

P. Bosch, D. Gabelaia, and J. Lang (Eds.): TbiLLC 2007, LNAI 5422, pp. 193–205, 2009.

two kinds of verifiability. The introduction of those notions is illustrated with the example of verifiability of monadic quantifiers in section 2. Next we present the basics about identification in the limit. In the culminating chapter 3 we compare the two notions. We conclude with theorems showing that with some restrictions certain types of verification imply identification.

2   Verification

The idea of verification, except for its obvious connections with semantics, is also very important in philosophy of science, where verifying and falsifying seem to be fundamental procedures for establishing an adequate theory and making predictions about the actual world. The semantic procedure of verification consists essentially in what follows:

Verification task. Given model $\mathcal{M}$ and a sentence φ, answer the question whether $\mathcal{M} \models \varphi$.

Let us start with analyzing restrictions we should make on the verification task to be able to proceed with our considerations.

First of all, for the sake of generality we consider the universe of $\mathcal{M}$ to be infinite. This allows us to talk about infinite procedures being successful in the limit. It is also very important to restrict our attention to computably enumerable structures. The reason is that we are interested in elements of the model being presented one by one — such an inductive procedure essentially requires that it is possible to enumerate them. In connection with this we also require that a presentation of a given model does not include repetitions. This restriction is made to simplify the procedure of counting elements without introducing any additional markers. We also have to say something about φ — the sentence involved in the verification task. We assume that φ has the form of a quantifier sentence, which does not distinguish between isomorphic models. In other words, we assume that hypotheses of our framework are purely about cardinalities or relations between cardinalities, and not about the 'nature' of individual objects.

With the above-explained restrictions in mind, let us now move to define a formal framework of inductive verifiability.

Definition 1. *Let us consider a model* $\mathcal{M} = (\mathsf{M}, B)$, *where* M *is an infinite, computably enumerable set, and* $B \subseteq \mathsf{M}$ *is some computable unary predicate. Let us assume that* λ *is an enumeration of the elements of* M, *without repetitions.*

By 'environment of $\mathcal{M}$', ε, *we mean an infinite binary sequence such that: if* $\lambda_n = x$, *then* $\varepsilon_n = \chi_B(x)$, *where* χ_B *is the characteristic function of* B.

We will use the following notation:

- $\varepsilon | n$ is the finite initial segment of ε through position $n - 1$ (i.e.: a sequence $\varepsilon_0, \varepsilon_1, \ldots, \varepsilon_{n-1}$);
- SEQ denotes a set of all finite initial segments of all environments;
- $set(\varepsilon)$ is a set of elements that occur in ε;

- h will refer to a hypothesis (i.e.: a logical formula), H is a class of hypotheses;
- C is a correctness relation between hypotheses and streams of data. $C(\varepsilon, h)$ is satisfied iff h is correct with respect to ε, i.e., h is true in the model represented by ε;
- α is an assessment method — total map from hypotheses and finite data sequences to conjectures, $\alpha : H \times SEQ \rightarrow \{0, 1, !\}$.

  Conjectures are outputs of α; their meaning is the following:

  1 — corresponds to the judgement that the hypothesis is true on the initial "up to now" segment of data;

  0 — means that the hypothesis is judged to be false on the initial "up to now" segment of data;

  ! — appears as an announcement that there will be now mind change about the statement following in the next step (we also refer to it as the *eureka* sign).

2.1 Verification with Certainty

The first type of verification we want to discuss is verification with certainty. It holds when the process of verification is finished after a finite number of steps. We mean 'finished' in the sense that there is a point in the procedure at which the assessment method, α, *decides* that the hypothesis, h, is true and that it can stop computing right there, because h being false is no longer an option. In such a case we can informally say that α is 'sure' or 'certain' about the answer. This is where the name 'verification with certainty' comes from.

Formally, we will require that the step when certainty comes into the picture is marked with the *eureka* symbol '!' and the actual content of this certainty — the hypothesis being true or false — is '1' or '0', respectively, answered in the next step.

Let us first introduce the general notion of producing an answer with certainty.

Definition 2. *We say that α produces b with certainty on (h, ε) iff there is an n such that:*

1. *$\alpha(h, \varepsilon|n) = !$, and*
2. *$\alpha(h, \varepsilon|n + 1) = b$,*
3. *for each $m < n$, $\alpha(h, \varepsilon|m) \neq !$.*

This definition makes all values after $n + 1$ irrelevant.

Verification and falsification with certainty are defined as an adequate production of 0 or 1 with certainty, respectively.

Definition 3. *We say that α verifies h with certainty on ε (with respect to C) iff α produces 1 with certainty on $(h, \varepsilon) \Leftrightarrow C(\varepsilon, h)$. Definition of refutation with certainty is analogous.*

Definition 4. *We say that h is verifiable with certainty (with respect to C) iff there is an α, which for each ε verifies h on ε with certainty $\Leftrightarrow h$ is true on ε.*

Verification with certainty satisfies the condition of positive introspection of knowledge, i.e., as soon as α answers '!' on h, it 'knows' the logical value of h. Such a situation does not occur in verification in the limit, which is defined below.

2.2   Verification in the Limit

Verification in the limit is much weaker than verification with certainty. In order to define it we exclude the *eureka* sign '!' from the set of possible answers. We restrict the power of the verification procedure α in such a way that it can give only two answers:

1 — corresponds to the fact that the hypothesis is judged to be true on the initial "up to now" segment of data;

0 — the hypothesis is judged to be false on the initial "up to now" segment of data.

As in the previous case, this type of verification consists in giving partial answers to finite initial segments of the environment. This time however the procedure is endless. We are dealing here with an infinite sequence of answers. We say that a procedure verifies a hypothesis in the limit if and only if there is a step in the procedure where the answer is 1 and it stays that way for the rest of the computation.

Definition 5. *We say that α verifies a hypothesis, h, in the limit iff:*

$$\exists n \forall m > n \ \alpha(h, \varepsilon|m) = 1.$$

Definition 6. *We say that h is verifiable in the limit iff there is an α, which for each ε verifies h in the limit on ε iff h is true on ε.*

In the general case of verification in the limit the fact of verification is not 'visible' to α. Whether a hypothesis has been verified can be judged only from a global perspective. Limiting verification corresponds to the scientific strategy of claiming adequacy of some 'up to now' correct hypothesis as long as possible. There is no guarantee however that in the light of future data it will not be rejected. When dealing with verifiability in the limit a scientist has to remain alert all the time.

3   Application: Verification of Monotone Quantifiers

The restriction made in the previous section, that hypotheses of our framework are purely about cardinalities or relations between cardinalities, and not about the 'nature' of individual objects leads us to treat hypotheses as generalized quantifiers. Informally speaking a given hypothesis can be identified with the class of models in which it is true. The same works for quantifiers. Even if intuitively quantifiers are formal counterparts of (natural language) determiners, we have a theory of generalized quantifiers which instructs us to reduce a quantifier simply to the class of models in which this quantifier is true. So, running the risk of being charged with philosophical insensitivity, we will use the notions of quantifiers and hypotheses interchangeably.

In order to talk about the properties we are interested in we have to provide the relational definition of generalized quantifier.

Definition 7. *A generalized quantifier Q of type $t = (n_1, \ldots, n_k)$ is a functor assigning to every set M a k-ary relation Q_M between relations on M such that if $(R_1, \ldots, R_k) \in Q_M$ then R_i is an n_i-ary relation on M, for $i = 1, \ldots, k$.*

It is quite prevalent in the philosophical literature to link notions of verifiability (with certainty) and falsifiability (with certainty) to the existential and universal quantifier, respectively. In fact, as we are going to see, this intuitive correspondence includes a broader class with quantifiers of some special monotonicity properties. We will discuss this connection below.

3.1   Quantifiers of Type $\langle 1 \rangle$

Let us now focus on properties of generalized quantifiers of type $\langle 1 \rangle$. First we define what it means for a quantifier to be monotone increasing and extendable.

Definition 8
(MON↑) *We say that a quantifier Q_M of type $\langle 1 \rangle$ is monotone increasing iff the following holds: if $A \subseteq A' \subseteq M$, then $Q_M(A)$ implies $Q_M(A')$.*
(EXT) *A quantifier Q of type $\langle 1 \rangle$ satisfies EXT iff for all models $\mathcal{M}$ and $\mathcal{M}'$, with the universes M and M', respectively: $A \subseteq M \subseteq M'$ implies $Q_M(A) \implies Q_{M'}(A)$.*

In other words, monotonicity guarantees that extending the predicate does not change the logical value of the quantifier from true to false. On the other hand extension ensures that adding new elements to the complement of A does not make a true quantifier false.

Comparison of the notions of verifiability with certainty and monotonicity allows us to state the following proposition:

Proposition 1. *Let Q be a MON↑ and EXT quantifier of type $\langle 1 \rangle$. There exists a model $\mathcal{M} = (M, A)$ with finite $A \subseteq M$ such that $Q_M(A)$ iff Q is verifiable with certainty on computably enumerable models.*

Proof. ($\Rightarrow$) Let us first assume that Q of type $\langle 1 \rangle$ is MON↑ and EXT, and that there exists a model $\mathcal{M} = (M, A)$ with finite $A \subseteq M$ such that $Q_M(A)$. We use the characteristic function of A, χ_A, to get an infinite sequence, ε_A, of 0's and 1's representing $\mathcal{M}$. ε_A is an environment of $\mathcal{M}$. We run the α procedure on ε_A and $Q(A)$. Step by step, while being fed, α constructs a model $\mathcal{M}' = (M', A')$. This happens in the following way.

First we take $n := 0$, $M' := \emptyset$, $A' := \emptyset$.

α reads ε_n: if $\varepsilon_n = 1$, then $|A'| := |A'| + 1$; else $|\bar{A}'| := |\bar{A}'| + 1$. α checks if $Q_{M'}(A')$: if it holds, α answers '!' and 1 to the rest of ε_A; otherwise it answers 0 and moves to $n := n + 1$.

The procedure α verifies $Q_M(A)$ with certainty. This is because $Q(A)$ is true in $\mathcal{M}$, and from the assumption, there is a finite cardinality of A' which satisfies $Q(A')$. From MON↑ and EXT, we know that as soon as α reaches this cardinality there is no possibility that $Q(A)$ changes its logical value at an extension A', $\bar{A}'$ in $\mathcal{M}'$.

($\Leftarrow$) Let us assume that $\mathcal{M} \models Q(A)$, and that there is a procedure α which verifies with certainty on ε_A. Therefore, there is a point, n, at which α answers ! and then 1. Then we know that $Q(A')$, where $|A'|$ is equal to the number of 1s in $\varepsilon_A|n$ and $|\bar{A}'|$ is equal to the number of 0s in $\varepsilon_A|n$. What remains of ε is not relevant for the logical value of $Q(A')$. This means that if $A' \subseteq A''$ then $Q_{M'}(A'')$ and if $M' \subseteq M''$ then $Q_{M''}(A')$. This is the same as saying that Q is MON$\uparrow$ and EXT.

Having this in mind we can also consider which type $\langle 1 \rangle$ quantifiers correspond to the notion of falsifiability with certainty. The answer is as follows:

Proposition 2. *Let* Q *be a quantifier of type* $\langle 1 \rangle$. Q *is verifiable with certainty iff* $\neg Q$ *is falsifiable with certainty.*

Proof. ($\Rightarrow$) First assume that Q is verifiable with certainty. That is: there is a procedure α such that for every model $\mathcal{M}$ if $\mathcal{M} \models Q(A)$, then α verifies $Q(A)$ with certainty. We now construct a procedure α' such that it falsifies $\neg Q$ with certainty.

$$\alpha'(\varepsilon_A|n) = \begin{cases} 1 & \text{if } \alpha(\varepsilon_A|n) = 0, \\ 0 & \text{if } \alpha(\varepsilon_A|n) = 1, \\ ! & \text{if } \alpha(\varepsilon_A|n) = \, !. \end{cases}$$

Since $\neg Q$ is a complement of Q, this procedure falsifies $\neg Q$ on A iff $\neg Q$ is false in $\mathcal{M}$. ($\Leftarrow$) The other direction works the same way.

3.2   Quantifiers of Type $\langle 1, 1 \rangle$

In the linguistic context it is common to investigate quantifiers of type $\langle 1, 1 \rangle$. It is often assumed (see e.g. [10]) that all natural language determiners correspond to so-called CE-quantifiers. CE-quantifiers satisfy three requirements: isomorphism closure (ISOM), extension and conservativity (CONS). (EXT) for quantifiers of type $\langle 1, 1 \rangle$ is a natural extension of the definition for type $\langle 1 \rangle$. Below we define (CONS).

Definition 9. *We call a quantifier* Q *of type* $\langle 1, 1 \rangle$ *conservative iff:*

(CONS) $\forall A, B \subseteq M$: $Q_M(A, B) \iff Q_M(A, A \cap B)$.

CE-quantifiers then have the property that their logical value depends only on the cardinality of the two constituents, $A - B$ and $A \cap B$, in the model. The part of B falling outside of the scope of A does not influence the logical value of a CE-quantifier. For the rest of the present section we will restrict ourselves to CE-quantifiers.

We will also need a notion of left-side monotonicity, which is usually called 'persistence'.

Definition 10. *We call a quantifier* Q *of type* $\langle 1, 1 \rangle$ *persistent iff:*

(PER) *If* $A \subseteq A' \subseteq M$ *and* $B \subseteq M$, *then* $Q_M(A, B) \Rightarrow Q_M(A', B)$.

Persistence guarantees that adding new elements to both important constituents $A - B$ and $A \cap B$ does not change the logical value of the quantifier from true to false.

We claim the following:

Proposition 3. *Let* Q *be a* PER CE-*quantifier of type* $\langle 1, 1 \rangle$. *There exists a model* $\mathcal{M} = (M, A, B)$ *such that* $A \cap B$ *is finite and* $Q_M(A, B)$ *iff it is verifiable with certainty.*

Proof. The proof is analogous to the proof of Proposition 1. We simply focus on two constituents of the model: $A - B$ and $A \cap B$, and treat them as $\bar{A}$ and A (respectively) in the proof of Proposition 1.

Proposition 4. *Let* Q *be a* CE-*quantifier of type* $\langle 1, 1 \rangle$. $\neg$Q *is falsifiable with certainty iff* Q *is verifiable with certainty.*

Proof. Analogous to the the proof of Proposition 2.

4   Identifiability through Verification

Historically speaking, philosophical analysis of the scientific discovery process led to skepticism. It has been claimed that its creative content cannot be accounted for by any scientific means, in particular by no mathematical or algorithmic model [2]. The natural situation of discovery is indeed so complex and non-uniform that it seems impossible to capture it in an adequate formalism. However, some approximations, which to a certain extent idealize the process, are not only makable, but also already existing and are ready to use. The framework of identification in the limit proposed in [4] started a long line of mathematical investigation of the process of language learning. At first sight scientific discovery and learning might seem distant from each other. In the present paper we assume the adequacy of the identification model for scientific inquiry analysis (for similar approaches see [6,7]).

Intuitively, the verification procedure (discussed in the previous section) is a part of scientific discovery. The latter can be seen as a compilation of assuming hypotheses, checking their logical value on data, and changing them to another hypothesis, if needed. In the present section we will introduce the identification formalism and present some ideas and facts about its correspondence to verification.

4.1   Identification

The identification in the limit approach [4] gives a mathematical reconstruction of the process of inductive inference. The task consists in guessing a correct hypothesis on the basis of an inductively given, infinite sequence of data about the world.

The framework includes: a class of hypotheses H, an infinite sequence of data about the world ε, a learning function f (a scientist).

We will explain the general idea of identification in the limit in terms of a simple game between a Scientist and Nature. First, some class of hypotheses, H, is chosen. It is known by both players. Then Nature chooses a single hypothesis, h, from H, to correctly describe the actual world. After that Nature starts giving out atomic information about the world. She does this in an inductive way. Each time the Scientist gets a piece of information, he guesses a hypothesis from the previously defined class on the basis of the sequence of data given so far. Identification in the limit is successful, if the guesses of the Scientist after some finite time stabilize on the correct answer.

Let us now specify the elements of the framework. By hypotheses we again mean quantified formulae, with a logical (closed under isomorphism) quantifier of type $\langle 1 \rangle$ or CE-quantifier of type $\langle 1, 1 \rangle$ (see e.g. [10]). The reason for this is the same as in the case of verification — that we want order- and intension-independent hypotheses, and a clear and relevant binary representation of models. The above-mentioned encoding of models serves as a basis for environments. The learning function, also referred to as the 'scientist', is defined as $f : SEQ \to H$.

Definition 11 (Identification in the limit)
We say that a learning function, f:

1. *identifies $h \in H$ on ε for $\mathcal{M} \models h$ in the limit iff for cofinitely many n, $f(\varepsilon|n) = h$;*
2. *identifies $h \in H$ in the limit iff it identifies h in the limit on every ε for every $\mathcal{M}$, such that $\mathcal{M} \models h$;*
3. *identifies H in the limit iff it identifies in the limit every $h \in H$.*

We can analogously define the much stronger notion of identifiability with certainty. The difference is that in this case the learning function 'knows' when it has identified the correct hypothesis.

Definition 12 (Identification with certainty)
We say that a learning function, f:

1. *identifies $h \in H$ with certainty on ε for $\mathcal{M} \models h$ iff for some n, $f(\varepsilon|n) =!$ and $f(\varepsilon|n+1) = h$;*
2. *identifies $h \in H$ with certainty iff it identifies h with certainty on every ε for every $\mathcal{M} \models h$;*
3. *identifies H with certainty iff it identifies with certainty every $h \in H$.*

4.2   Comparing Verification and Identification

In the present section we will state two theorems. They show a connection between identifiability and verifiability.

Certainty Setting. Let us take a class of hypotheses, H, and the sequence, ε, of data about the actual world. Assume that H contains only mutually disjoint hypotheses verifiable with certainty, i.e., for every $h \in H$ there is a procedure α, which verifies h with certainty iff it is true in the actual world.

Theorem 1. *Every such computably enumerable class H is identifiable with certainty.*

Proof. Assume that H is a computably enumerable class of mutually disjoint hypotheses verifiable with certainty. We define a procedure **Id-Cert** which identifies with certainty every hypothesis from the class H. An example of a run of the procedure is presented in Figure 1.

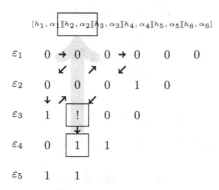

Fig. 1. Identifiability with certainty

Since H is computably enumerable we can assume existence of a sequence $(h)_n$ which enumerates H. Each h_n is associated with its verification with certainty procedure α_n. **Id-Cert** works in the following way: it first checks $\alpha_1(h_1, \varepsilon_1)$ (the value of the first hypothesis on the first piece of data), then it proceeds according to the diagonal enumeration of $\alpha_n(h_n, \varepsilon_m)$ until it meets '!'. Then it performs a check for $\alpha_n(h_n, \varepsilon_{m+1})$. If $\alpha_n(h_n, \varepsilon_{m+1}) = 1$, then **Id-Cert** stops and answers h_n. Otherwise it moves back to $\alpha_n(h_n, \varepsilon_m)$ and continues to perform the diagonal procedure.

By assumption every $h \in H$ is verifiable with certainty. Therefore if h_n, for some n, is true on ε, then α_n will eventually produce '!'. And since **Id-Cert** performs a diagonal search it does not miss any answer. Hence, **Id-Cert** identifies every $h \in H$ with certainty, so H is identifiable with certainty.

Let us again take a class of hypotheses, H, and the sequence, ε, of data about the actual world. Assume that H contains only hypotheses verifiable with certainty, but this time let us drop the assumption of H being a class of mutually disjoint hypotheses. Then we can prove what follows.

Theorem 2. *Every such computably enumerable class H is identifiable in the limit.*

Proof. The proof is very similar to the proof of the previous theorem. We use
the same diagonal method. This time however identification does not stop on the
first '!' it encounters. Let us assume that '!' happens for ε_n. Instead, it answers
the relevant h: the hypothesis which was first recognized to be verified with
certainty; then it goes on with the diagonal search looking for a hypothesis, h',
which reveals '!' for some ε_m, where $m < n$. If it meets such an h' it keeps
answering it as long as no other 'better fitting' hypothesis is found. An example
of a run of the procedure is presented in Figure 2.

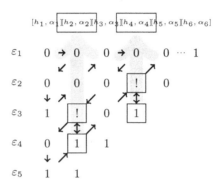

Fig. 2. Identifiability with certainty

By assumption every $h \in H$ is verifiable with certainty. Therefore if h_n,
for some n, is true on ε, then α_n will eventually produce '!'. And since this
identification performs a diagonal search it does not miss any answer. Hence
every $h \in H$ is identified in the limit, so H is identifiable in the limit.

Limiting Setting. Let us again take a computably enumerable class of mutually disjoint hypotheses, H, and a sequence, ε, of data about the actual world.
But this time let us agree that H consists of hypotheses that are verifiable in the
limit, i.e., for every $h \in H$ there is a procedure α which verifies h in the limit iff
h it is true.

Theorem 3. *Every such computably enumerable class H is identifiable in the
limit.*

Proof. Assume that H is a computably enumerable class of mutually disjoint
hypotheses that are verifiable in the limit. This means that for every $h_n \in H$
there is a procedure α_n which verifies h in the limit if and only if h is true. We
are now going to define a procedure **Id-Lim** which identifies every hypothesis
from the class H. An example of a run of the **Id-Lim** is presented in Figure 3.

Since H is computably enumerable we can assume the existence of the sequence $(h)_n$ enumerating the hypotheses from H. Each of them is associated
with its verification in the limit procedure α_n.

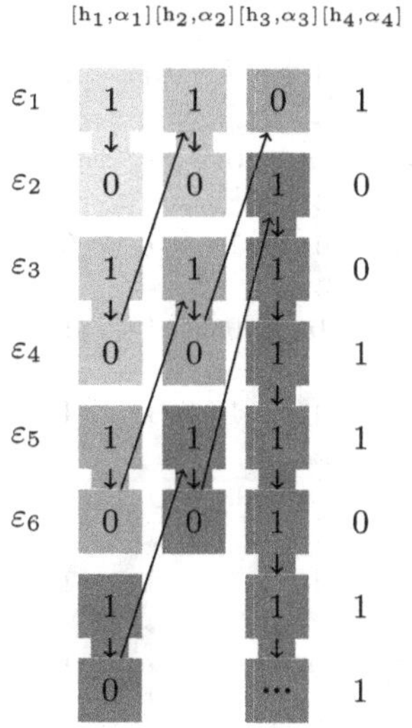

$[h_1,\alpha_1]\,[h_2,\alpha_2]\,[h_3,\alpha_3]\,[h_4,\alpha_4]$

Fig. 3. Id-Lim identifiability

The algorithm **Id-Lim** first performs a single check for $\{h_1\}$:

If $\alpha_1(h_1,\varepsilon|1) = 1$, then **Id-Lim** outputs h_1 and moves to $\alpha_1(h_1,\varepsilon|2)$. The answer is repeated until there is an n such that $\alpha_1(h_1,\varepsilon|n) = 0$. In this case it starts the test for $\{h_1,h_2\}$, i.e., starting from $\varepsilon|n+1$ it looks for another 0 in the column (h_1,α_1) answering h_1 as long as α_1 answers 1. When 0 is visited **Id-Lim** moves to $\alpha_2(h_2,\varepsilon_1)$ and performs a single check for h_2. In such manner we try to check $\{h_1\}$, $\{h_1,h_2\}$, $\{h_1,h_2,h_3\}$, ... In the picture each of those tests is marked with different shade of grey.

Procedure **Id-Lim** never stops. It is successful if after some point its guesses are still the same and correct with respect to ε.

Why does **Id-Lim** work? One can easily observe that **Id-Lim** runs through every finite sequence of 1s. Visiting a point in which $\alpha_n(h_n,\varepsilon_m) = 1$, it answers h_n. If there is a true hypothesis in H, **Id-Lim** will eventually enter an infinite sequence of 1s (in column (h_m,α_m), say), since H consists of hypotheses verifiable in the limit. Once it enters this sequence there is no way out — **Id-Lim** will indefinitely answer h_m. Therefore **Id-Lim** identifies every $h \in H$ in the limit, and hence H is identifiable in the limit.

In case **Id-Lim** identifies some h_n the procedure needs to remember a finite but not predetermined number of points in ε. We would like to have an algorithm which does not run back and forth on the environment. The answer to this is procedure which is introduced below. Let us call it **Id-Lim***. For this procedure it is enough to remember only one point, namely the position in which the procedure finds itself at each moment.

Id-Lim* uses essentially the same idea of column-ruled searching for strings of 1s. It also consecutively performs it for $\{h_1\}$, $\{h_1,h_2\}$, $\{h_1,h_2,h_3\}$, ... The difference is that when it eventually leaves one column, starting a test for a new

$[h_1,\alpha_1]\,[h_2,\alpha_2]\,[h_3,\alpha_3]\,[h_4,\alpha_4]$

	$[h_1,\alpha_1]$	$[h_2,\alpha_2]$	$[h_3,\alpha_3]$	$[h_4,\alpha_4]$
ε_1	1	1	0	1
ε_2	0	0	1	0
ε_3	1	1	1	0
ε_4	0 → 0		1	1
ε_5	1	1	1	1
ε_6	0 → 0 → 1			0
	1		1	1
	0		...	1

Fig. 4. Id-Lim* identifiability

hypothesis, it does not go back to ε_1. Instead, it simply moves to the value in the next column but in the same row.

The difference between **Id-Lim** and **Id-Lim*** is mainly in the use of ε. With **Id-Lim*** it is enough to run through ε once without going back. In case of **Id-Lim** every time we fail on some hypothesis and enter a new one, previously not visited, it has to start reading ε from the beginning. **Id-Lim*** also identifies H. It simply leaves out the truth values of hypotheses on some already visited initial segment of ε.

5   Conclusion

The approach presented in this paper can be seen as an attempt to find some general semantic correlates of identification. Inductive verification can be treated as a condition for and a part of the identification process. This fact contributes to the general problem of semantics learning and to modeling the process of scientific inquiry.

Some attempts to approach the problem of learning of semantic constructions are already present in the literature [9,3]. What is the connection with this framework? The present approach has much to do with the more general idea of model-theoretic learning [8,7], but it is also related to the work of H.-J. Tiede [9]. In his, slightly different, framework he shows that the class of first-order definable persistent quantifiers of type $\langle 1,1 \rangle$ is identifiable in the limit. This result is consistent with our considerations. In fact, for the same class of quantifiers we show that it is verifiable with certainty, and that each class containing solely verifiable with certainty structures is identifiable in the limit.

Intuitively there are at least two main parts of human semantic competence. One of them is responsible for producing grammatically correct (syntax domain) or true (semantics domain) hypotheses. The second is a natural correlate of model-checking, i.e., the competence of deciding whether a sentence is true or false in the actual world. The results presented in this paper show how the latter can be embedded in the identification (learning or discovering) process. In this light verification can be seen as a pillar of learning abilities.

References

1. van Benthem, J.: Essays in Logical Semantics. D. Reidel, Dordrecht (1986)
2. Feyerabend, P.: Against Method. Verso Press, London (1975)
3. Gierasimczuk, N.: The Problem of Learning the Semantics of Quantifiers. In: ten Cate, B.D., Zeevat, H.W. (eds.) TbiLLC 2005. LNCS, vol. 4363, pp. 117–126. Springer, Heidelberg (2007)
4. Gold, E.M.: Language Identification in the Limit. Information and Control 10, 447–474 (1967)
5. Jain, S., Osherson, D., Royer, J.S., Sharma, A.: Systems that Learn. MIT Press, Chicago (1999)
6. Kelly, K.: The Logic of Reliable Inquiry. Oxford University Press, Oxford (1996)
7. Martin, E., Osherson, D.: Elements of Scientific Inquiry. Cambridge (1998)
8. Osherson, D., de Jongh, D., Martin, E., Weinstein, S.: Formal Learning Theory. In: van Benthem, J., Ter Meulen, A. (eds.) Handbook of Logic and Language. MIT Press, Cambridge (1997)
9. Tiede, H.-J.: Identifiability in the Limit of Context-Free Generalized Quantifiers. Journal of Language and Computation 1, 93–102 (1999)
10. Väänänen, J.: On the Expressive Power of Monotone Natural Language Quantifiers over Finite Models. Journal of Philosophical Logic 31, 327–358 (2002)

Enlarging the Diversity of Valency Instantiation Patterns and Its Implications

Igor Boguslavsky

Universidad Politécnica de Madrid/ IITP RAS
Campus de Montegancedo, 28660 Boadilla del Monte, Madrid
Igor.Boguslavsky@upm.es

Abstract. In the prototypical case, arguments (=actants) are directly subordinated to their predicates and occupy positions of the subject and direct or indirect object. Valency slots filled in this way are called active. In non-prototypical cases, arguments can syntactically subordinate their predicate (passive valency slots) and even have no immediate syntactic link with it (discontinuous valency slots). These types of valency slots are mostly characteristic of adjectives, adverbs and nouns. A number of linguistic concepts are related, directly or indirectly, to the notion of actant. However, usually only prototypical – active – valency instantiation is taken into account. If one includes into consideration passive and discontinuous valency slot filling, the area of actant-related phenomena expands greatly. We discuss some of these phenomena and show that the notions of *diathesis* and *conversion* require broader generalization.

Keywords: Argument, actant, valency, valency slot filling, scope, diathesis, converse term.

1 Predicate-Argument Structure as the Semantic Glue

We will approach our subject from the position of Moscow Semantic School (MSS). Here we cannot systematically compare the theory and practice of MSS and Formal Semantics (FS). We will only dwell on some similarities and differences that directly bear on our topic.

The main similarity lies in the recognition of the fact that it is the argument structure of the sentence that plays the role of the "semantic glue" which combines the meanings of words together. FS took in this revolutionary idea in the beginning of the 70ies directly from R. Montague [1:21]. To do justice, it should be mentioned that starting with the famous 8th issue of "Machine translation and applied linguistics" (1964), which initiated the Meaning – Text approach in the Soviet Union, and numerous subsequent publications on the Explanatory Combinatorial Dictionary it was explicitly claimed that the semantic definition of many words contains valency slots for the arguments. In the semantic definition, these slots are represented by variables. To construct the semantic structure of the sentence, one has to identify the actants with the help of the Government Pattern (≈ Subcategorization Frame) and substitute them for the variables.

P. Bosch, D. Gabelaia, and J. Lang (Eds.): TbiLLC 2007, LNAI 5422, pp. 206–220, 2009.

The differences between the MSS and FS approaches are more numerous. They consist, mostly, in the aim, object and tools of semantic analysis. For MSS, the meaning definition of each linguistic unit is of primary importance and should be carried out in maximum detail (cf. [2]). This definition is formulated in a natural language: it may be simplified and standardized, but must be sufficient for capturing subtle semantic distinctions. Rules of meaning amalgamation are devised to closely interact with semantic definition of words.

FS does not make it its aim to semantically define all meaningful units of language. This task is relegated to the lexicon, while FS is more interested in the mechanisms of meaning amalgamation than in the meanings as such. For meaning representation, it uses a logical metalanguage which is less suitable for describing the spectrum of linguistically relevant meanings. On the other hand, this metalanguage is much more convenient for describing logical properties of natural languages than the semantic language of MSS.

However, one cannot describe the way lexical meanings are put together without disposing of the detailed semantic definition of each word. We proceed from the assumption that if word A semantically affects word B, then B should contain a meaning component for A to act upon. To give one example, the Longman Dictionary of Contemporary English defines *accent* as 'the way someone pronounces the words of a language, showing which country or which part of a country they come from'. According to this definition, *southern accent* is interpreted as the way somebody pronounces the words of a language, showing that the speaker is from the South. However, this definition does not explain the combinability of this word with intensifiers: *strong <heavy, pronounced, slight> accent.* It does not contain any quantifiable component that is affected by these adjectives. What do these adjectives intensify? When we say that somebody *speaks English with a HEAVY <SLIGHT> Essex accent* we mean that his pronunciation of English words (a) is typical for people from Essex and (b) is VERY <SLIGHTLY> different from the standard. This is a good reason for revising the definition of *accent* and including the component 'different' in this definition:

(1) *X has an A accent (in B)* = 'the way X pronounces the words of language B is different from the way speakers of B usually pronounce them and typical for speakers of language, group, or locality A'.

Further, MSS differs from FS in that the former does not share the latter's claim of parallelism between syntactic and semantic structures. Sure, it is convenient if they are parallel. However, when the linguistic data resist this requirement, MSS takes the side of the data.

Another difference between MSS and FS is related to the grounds for postulating arguments. For MSS, the starting point is the semantic analysis of the situation denoted by the given word. Analytical semantic definition of this word is constructed according to certain requirements. In this respect, all types of words – verbs, nouns, adjectives, adverbs, prepositions, etc. – are on equal footing and obey the same principles of description.

For a word to have a certain valency it is necessary, though insufficient, that a situation denoted by this word should contain a corresponding participant in the intuitively obvious way. From this point of view, not nearly all generalized quantifiers are eligible for having a valency filled by a verbal phrase. Noun phrases *twenty students* and *many of the students* both form a sentence when combined with a one-place verb (e.g. *were late for the exam*) and therefore are generalized quantifiers. However, only in the second case (*many of*) are we prepared to postulate a semantic valency filled by a verbal phrase.

Finally, deciding on the set of valency slots is only the beginning. Besides that, one needs to exhaustively describe all the ways these slots can be filled, and NOT ONLY CANONICAL ones. We lay special emphasis on describing the whole spectrum of possible syntactic realization of arguments, because non-canonical valency filling significantly complicates the task of detecting arguments and joining them with predicates. To illustrate this point, we refer the reader to our examples below and to [3], where valencies of Russian words *bol'shinstvo* 'most of, majority' and *men'shinstvo* 'minority' are discussed in detail. This aspect should be also relevant for FS, since one cannot combine meanings without having full information on possible syntactic positions of arguments, their morpho-syntactic form and other restrictions. However, as far as we know, descriptions made within FS are mostly based on canonical valency filling patterns and are therefore simplified, however sophisticated their formal apparatus may be.

2 Valency Slot Filling

Let us assume that we have a good dictionary which contains definitions of all meaningful linguistic units. What should we do in order to combine the meanings of these units to obtain the semantic structure of the sentence?

The main mechanism of meaning amalgamation is instantiation of valency slots. To combine meanings of words, we basically need to perform two main operations:

- for each predicate, find its actants (i.e. words or their meaning components filling valency slots of this predicate);
- substitute the actants for the variables in the semantic definition of the predicate.

In the MSS approach to valencies, a set of valency slots of a word is determined by its semantic definition. An obligatory participant of the situation denoted by the word opens a valency slot if this participant is expressed together with this word in a regular way (see more on valency slots and actants in [4,5]). It is often believed that valencies are primarily needed for the description of government properties of words. It is this task that motivates the creation of numerous valency dictionaries. We would like to put a different emphasis: valencies are mainly needed for uniting meanings of words to form the semantic structure of the sentence. As mentioned above, valency slot filling can be considered as semantic glue which connects meanings of words. We proceed from the assumption that if there is a syntagmatic semantic link between two words, then in most cases one of them fills a valency slot of the other. Or, more precisely, the meaning of one of these words contains a predicate whose argument forms part of the meaning of the second one (cf. example (1) above).

There are three types of valency slots: active, passive, and discontinous ones [6]. This distinction is formulated in terms of the position the argument has with respect to its predicate in the DEPENDENCY SYNTACTIC STRUCTURE[1]. An ACTIVE valency slot of

---

[1] We cannot dwell here on how dependency links are established and refer the reader to [7].

predicate L is filled with sentence elements which are syntactically subordinated to L. A PASSIVE valency slot is filled with elements that syntactically subordinate L. The elements that fill a DISCONTINOUS valency slot do not have any direct syntactic link with L. Active valency slots are well fit for assuring slot filling. First of all, this fact manifests itself in that each valency slot has its own set of surface realizations. If a word has several valency slots, their means of realization, as a rule, clearly contrast. Different semantic actants are marked by different means – cases, prepositions, conjunctions.

However, this is not a 100%-true rule. Sometimes, different valency slots of the same predicate can be filled in the same way. The best known example are the genitive subjects and objects of nouns: *amor patris, invitation of the president*. Cf. also prepositionless first and second complements of the type *Give Mary a book*; *Answer the question* vs. *answer nothing*. A rarer example is provided by Russian words *dostatochno* 'sufficient' and *neobxodimo* 'necessary' that can fill both valency slots by means of the same conjunction *chtoby* 'in order to/that'.

(2a) *Čtoby Q, dostatočno, čtoby P* 'for Q it is sufficient if P'

(2b) *Čtoby vse vzletelo na vozdux, dostatočno, čtoby kto-nibud' podnes spičku*
    lit. 'that everything blows up sufficient that anyone strikes a match'
    'it is sufficient to strike a match and everything will blow up'

In this case, though, the identity of the conjunction is made up for by the word order distinction:

(2c) **Čtoby kto-nibud' podnes spičku dostatočno čtoby vse vzletelo na vozdux*
    lit. 'that anyone strikes a match sufficient that everything blows up'

Curiously enough, in case of *dostatochno* 'sufficient' (but not *neobxodimo* 'necessary') valency slot P can be filled with the coordinating conjunction – a phenomenon known in English too: cf. the translation of example (2b):

(2d) *Dostatočno, čtoby kto-nibud' podnes spičku, i vse vzletit na vozdux*
    'it is sufficient to strike a match and everything will blow up'

Even if different valency slots of the same word are marked by the same lexical or grammatic means, the language thus tends to find a way to discriminate between these slots.

3 Filling Active Valency Slots

Let us start with a canonical pattern of valency filling which is obviously the filling of active valency slots. MSS uses a powerful tool for doing that – the Government Pattern (GP). It consists of two correspondences: the correspondence between Semantic Actants of word L (SemA(L)) and its Deep Syntactic Actants (DSyntA(L)), which is called diathesis of L,[2] and the correspondence between Deep and Surface Syntactic Actants (SSyntA(L)). Given the Government Pattern of L and the Surface Syntactic Structure of the sentence, it is easy to find all Semantic Actants.

---

[2] Cf. [8] and [9], where a wider concept of diathesis is adopted.

One of the complications that may arise here is the fact that the correspondence between SemAs and DSyntAs is not unique. A word may have more than one diathesis. A SemA of a word may appear in various syntactic positions and, accordingly, correspond to various DSyntAs. The multiplicity of diatheses attracted much attention, mostly in connection with the category of voice, which is defined as a morphologically marked modification of the basic diathesis that does not affect the propositional meaning (the latest presentation of this approach to voice can be found in [10]). However, alternating diatheses do not necessarily involve voice distinctions. For example:

(3a) *The workers loaded the ship with salt.*

(3b) *The workers loaded salt on the ship.*

In cases like this, one has to postulate two GPs. However, despite the multiplicity of GPs, in practice it is nearly always possible to find out which of the GPs is realized in the sentence. Fragment "*LOAD* + DirObj" alone is not sufficient to determine for sure which valency slot it fills. However, if the form of the indirect complement is taken into account (*with* + NP vs. *on* + NP) the diathesis is determined uniquely. Thus, there is a one-to-one correspondence between SemAs and DSyntAs within the diathesis alternation. It is in the nature of things that the actants are marked in the syntactic structure in an unambiguous way, and each SemA corresponds, as a rule, to a unique syntactic position. An attempt to extend this observation to passive and discontinuous valency slots reveals interesting surprises. The data presented below (section 5) show that this one-to-one correspondence can be violated in a number of ways. However, before that we will have to give a short overview of syntactic positions which are occupied by the arguments filling passive and discontinuous slots (section 4). In section 6 we discuss lexicalized diathetic differences, and in section 7 we will draw some conclusions.

4 Passive and Discontinuous Valency Slots

For each class of predicates there exists a prototypical syntactic position of their actants and a number of non-prototypical positions. The prototypical position is the one occupied by the actant of a monovalent predicate. If a verb has only one valency slot, an actant that fills it will most probably be a subject (*John sleeps*). For nouns, the prototypical position is that of a genitive complement (as in Russian *nachalo koncerta* 'the beginning of the concert'). For predicates with passive valency slots, the prototypical position of the actant is that of the subordinating word: a noun, in case of adjectives (*interesting book*), and a verb, in case of adverbs (*run fast*).

If a predicate has more than one valency slot, other actants occupy other, less prototypical positions. Which are they? Leaving aside directly subordinated actants accounted for by the government pattern, there are three positions which a non-first actant may occupy: that of a subordinating verb, a dependent of the subordinating verb, and a dependent of the subordinating noun.

4.1 Subordinating Verb

An important class of words which have a valency slot filled by a subordinating verb are quantifiers (*all, every, each, some, many of, most, majority, minority,* etc.). These words have at least two valency slots. One of them is filled by a noun phrase directly connected to the quantifier, and the other by a subordinating verbal phrase. For example, the words *most* and *majority* denote a certain part of a whole R that consists of elements having property P and is larger than the part of R that does not share this property.

(4) *Most people* [R] *<the majority of the people* [R]*> haven't taken* [P] *any steps to prepare for a natural disaster.*

This sentence means that the group of people who haven't taken any steps to prepare for natural disasters is larger that the group of people who have. Those who doubt that *most* has valency P may note that the phrase *most people* (as opposed to phrases like *five people*) does not mean anything unless a property is specified which is shared by all members of this group.

4.2 Dependent of the Subordinating Verb

This type of valency slot is typical of adverbs (or adverbials). For example, *by habit* has two valency slots inherited from the underlying predicate 'habit': X – "the person who has a habit" and P – "what X does by habit". Valency P is filled by a subordinating verb, and X by its subject. Therefore, if we introduce this adverbial in sentences which denote the same situation but use verbs with different subjects, synonymy disappears. In (5a) it is John who has a habit, and in (5b) it is Mary:

(5a) *By habit, John* [X] *borrowed* [P] *some money from Mary.*

(5b) *By habit, Mary* [X] *lent* [P] *John some money.*

4.3 Dependent of the Subordinating Noun

The possessive adjective *my* in (6) is syntactically linked to the noun, but semantically is an actant of *favorite: X's favorite Y* is the Y which X likes more than other Y-s:

(6) *my* [X] *favorite color* [Y].

Although filling this valency with a possessive adjective or a noun in the possessive case (*John's favorite color*) is more frequent, it can also be filled by a prepositional phrase:

(7) *a favorite spot* [Y] *for picnickers* [X]

The Russian equivalent of *favorite – izljublennyj –* does not dispose of this possibility and only fills this valency with a possessive:

(8) *moj izljublennyj marshrut* 'my favorite route'.

5 Different Actants – One Syntactic Position, One Actant – Different Positions

Now we have prepared everything to show that one syntactic position can correspond to more than one valency of the word and one valency can correspond to multiple syntactic positions.

5.1 *Majority / Minority*: Active and Passive Filling of the Same Valency

As mentioned above, *majority* belongs to the class of quantifiers. One of its valencies denotes a whole R of which a part is extracted, and another valency corresponds to a property P, which distinguishes the extracted part from the rest of R. Prototypically, R is expressed by an *of*-phrase, and P – by the subordinating verb. Cf. (9a) where the whole class of the opponents of war is divided into two parts by the property of voting against the prime-minister. In (9b) the interpretation of the *of*-phrase is totally different. The opponents of war do not form a set a larger part of which has a certain property (voting against the prime-minister), as it is in (9a). Here, being a war opponent is itself a property that divides the society into a larger and a smaller part. That is, the *of*-phrase fills valency slot P. The same is true for the interpretation of *minority of supporters*.

(9a) <u>*A majority of the opponents of war*</u> [R] *is voting* [P] *against the prime-minister.*

(9b) *The war in Chechnya is splitting the society into* <u>*the majority of its opponents*</u> [P] *and* <u>*the minority of supporters*</u> [P]

Example (10) demonstrates another case of filling valency slot P of *majority/minority* by a subordinated phrase. Here, P is filled by a modifying adjective.

(10) <u>*The rural minority <majority>*</u> *of the population is not happy with the new law.*

5.2 *Strogij* 'strict': Prototypical and Non-prototypical Filling of the Same Valency

In Russian, there is a class of adjectives denoting an emotional attitude or a type of behaviour which have a valency slot for an addressee: *strogij* 'strict', *blagoželatel'nyj* 'benevolent', *snisxoditel'nyj* 'indulgent', *dobryj* 'kind', *zabotlivyj* 'careful', *trebovatel'nyj* 'exacting', *vygodnyj* 'advantageous', etc.

(11) *Stjuarty strogi k svoim detjam* 'the Stuarts are strict with their children'

When this slot is not filled, the sentence obviously bears no information as to who the beneficiary is:

(12a) *Stjuart ochen' strog* 'Stuart is very strict'.

(12b) *strogaja dama* 'a strict lady'

Rather, these phrases should be understood in the universal sense: the strictness applies to everybody. However, in the context of relational nouns, which denote a person who is in a certain relationship to other people, the interpretation of this valency slot changes:

(13) *strogaja mama* 'a strict mother', *ljubjaščie ucheniki* 'affectionate pupils', *trebovatel'nyj načal'nik* 'an exacting boss', *uslužlivyj sosed* 'an obliging neighbor'.

The addressee of adjectives is determined quite definitely: It is a person (or persons) with whom a person denoted by the modified noun is in the corresponding relation. A strict mother is strict with her children, affectionate pupils love their teacher, an exacting boss demands something from his subordinates.

Here we are dealing with a curious type of the syntax-semantics correspondence. In Syntactic Structure, the beneficiary valency slot of the adjective is not filled, just as the valency slot of the noun. However, in SemS these slots are not empty but co-indexed, i.e. filled by the same variable:

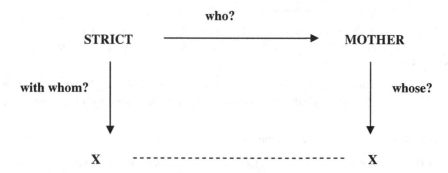

These examples show that a valency slot of some adjectives can be realized in more than one way: Prototypically, by a subordinate prepositional phrase, as in (11), and non-prototypically – by a variable, co-indexed with a variable corresponding to a valency slot of its other SemA, as in (13).

5.3 *Tščetno* 'in vain': Different Semantic Roles of the Subordinating Verb

The Russian adverb *tščetno* 'in vain' denotes a failed try. Its meaning can be defined as follows:

(14) *tščetno(X,P,Q)* = 'X doing P and trying to cause Q to take place, Q did not begin to take place'

(15) *Ona tščetno staralas' skryt' smuščenie* 'she was vainly trying to conceal her embarrassment'

The situation denoted by the adverb has three participants: X, the subject of the attempt, Q, the goal he wanted to achieve, and P, the action he is performing in order to achieve Q. None of these participants opens an active valency slot. The only syntactic link of the adverb is with the verb. The subject X of the attempt is expressed by the subject of this verb. As for two other participants, P and Q, the situation is more tangled. In trying to find them, it is helpful to bear in mind that understanding a sentence with *tščetno* 'vainly' implies being able to specify what the goal of the subject was that he failed to achieve.

There are two classes of sentences. In the first class, the verb subordinating *tščetno* duplicates the 'trying' component of its meaning.

First, let us look at the component 'try to achieve Q'. Its two parts ('try to achieve something' and 'Q') can be verbalized it two different ways. They can be expressed separately, as a combination of an attempt verb and its complement:

(16) *On tščetno staralsja najti ključi* 'he was vainly trying to find [Q] the keys' ($\Rightarrow$ 'he failed to find the keys'),

or both can be included in the meaning of one verb:

(17) *On tščetno iskal ključi* 'he was vainly looking for the keys'; *look for* = 'try to find [Q]' ($\Rightarrow$ 'he failed to find the keys').

In both cases, the main component of the meaning of the verb is 'try'.

Similarly, the components of combination 'doing P, try to' can be expressed separately:

(18) *On tščetno staralsja privleč'* [Q] *nashe vnimanie krikami* [P] 'he tried in vain to attract [Q] our attention shouting [P]' ($\Rightarrow$ 'he failed to attract our attention'),

or within one verb, maybe together with Q:

(19) *On tščetno ubezhdal ee vyjti za nego zamuzh* 'he was vainly trying-to-persuade her to marry him' = 'he was vainly trying to make her decide [Q] to marry him by giving her reasons why she should do it [P]' ($\Rightarrow$ 'he failed to make her decide to marry him').

In the second class of *tščetno*-sentences, the subordinating verb has nothing to do with trying to achieve Q. It only denotes ACTIONS P which the subject is carrying out:

(20) *On tščetno časami brodil* [P] *pod ee oknami* 'he was vainly strolling for hours under her windows' (not: 'he failed to stroll under her windows', but: 'he failed to achieve something for the sake of which he was strolling under her windows', e.g. he wanted to see her in the window but she did not appear).

(21) *On tščetno trjas* [P] *zamok* 'he was vainly shaking the lock' (not: 'he failed to shake the lock', but 'he failed to achieve what he wanted to', e.g. he wanted to open the lock but it would not open.

5.4 *Edinstvennyj* 'only': Different Semantic Roles of the Modified Noun

The adjective *edinstvennyj* 'only' claims that in a certain set or area R there exists object Q with property P, and in R there are no other objects with this property. All three valency slots are filled in sentences like (22):

(22) *Ivan – edinstvennyj Nobelevskij laureat, kotoryj rabotaet v nashem institute* 'Ivan is the only Nobel Prize winner who works at our institute'

Here: Q = 'Ivan'; R = 'Nobel Prize winner'; P = 'x works at out institute'.

Sentence (22) can be glossed like this: among the Nobel Prize winners there is nobody except Ivan who works at our institute. Prototypically, valency slot Q is expressed by the subject of the copula, R – by the subordinating noun and P – by a restrictive modifier of the subordinating noun. Cf. also noun phrase (23) in which only slots R and P are filled:

(23) *edinstvennaja priličnaja gostinica* 'the only decent hotel' = 'among the hotels there is none except this one that is decent'.

It suffices to slightly change the structure of sentence (22) and the distribution of words among the valency slots changes:

(24) *Ivan – edinstvennyj Nobelevskij laureat v nashem institute* 'Ivan is the only Nobel Prize winner at our institute'

Here: Q = 'Ivan'; R = 'our institute'; P = 'x is a Nobel prize winner'. The most natural interpretation of (24) is: among the staff of our institute there is nobody except Ivan who is a Nobel Prize winner. The change of actants is due to the difference in Syntactic Structures. Restrictive modifiers of the governing noun (cf. *kotoryj rabotaet v nashem institute* 'who works in our institute') play the role of P, while locative adjuncts (*v nashem institute* 'at our institute') fill slot R.

Sentences (22) and (24) show that in certain syntactic conditions the modified noun can fill two different slots of *edinstvennyj – R* and P. It is remarkable that if the modifier is detached by punctuation marks, third possibility is added: the modified noun fills slot Q.

(25) *Eto lekarstvo* [R]*, edinstvennoe po-nastojaščemu effektivnoe* [P]*, pojavilos' v prodaže sovsem nedavno*
lit. 'this medicine [R], only really effective, appeared on sale quite recently'
'this medicine [R], the only one to be really effective [P], came into the market quite recently' = 'this medicine came into the market quite recently, and among all the medicines there is no other one that is really effective'

(26) *Gostinica* [P]*, edinstvennaja v gorode* [R]*, byla zabita do otkaza*
lit. 'the hotel, only in the town, was filled to capacity'
'the only hotel in the town was filled to capacity'

(27) *Končilas' groza* [Q]*, edinstvennoe v mire* [R]*, chego bojalsja* [P] *xrabryj pjos*
lit. 'the thunderstorm was over, only in the world [R] that frightened [P] this fearless dog'
'the thunderstorm [Q] was over, the only thing in the world [R] that frightened [P] this fearless dog' = 'there is nothing in the world different from the thunderstorm that frightened this fearless dog'

These examples should not induce an idea that everything is possible and the valency slots are filled without any regularity. This is not the case. Let us show briefly that the actantial properties of *edinstvennyj* in (22) – (27) are determined by very general properties of Russian syntax.

1. There is no insurmountable barrier between P and R. Logically, but not linguistically, they can transform into one another. The same extralinguistic situation can be presented differently in terms of the distribution of meaning between P and R. *The only lawyer* [P] *among my friends* [R] is equivalent to *my only friend* [P] *among the lawyers* [R].

2. There is a natural link between the copulative, modificative, and detached modificative constructions:

> (28) *Father was tired ~ tired father ~ Father, tired and sleepy, (did not pay attention to anything)* [= Father, who was tired and sleepy,...]

3. The modified noun fills slot *R*, if it has a restrictive modifier, and slot *P* otherwise (see (22) – (24) above).
4. The detached modification can have two sources: It can either correlate with the modificative construction or with the copulative one (cf. Step 2). Since it is a variety of the modification in general, the modified noun can be both *R* and *P* (cf. Step 3).
5. Since the detached modification can correlate with the copulative construction (cf. 2 above), the modified noun can behave as the subject of the copulative and fills slot *Q* (cf. (22). In (27) *groza, edinstvennoe chego bojalsja...* is not derived from **edinstvennaja groza* 'the only thunderstorm' but from *Groza byla edinstvennoj veščju, kotoroj...* 'the thunderstorm was the only thing that...'.

5.5 *Besplatno* 'for free': Different Semantic Roles of the VP Dependent

The valencies of the verb *to pay* are clearly opposed: *X* = "who pays?", *Y* = "how much?", *Z* = "to whom?", and *W* = "for what?" What happens to these valency slots when 'pay' forms part of the meaning of adverbs?

> (29) *Pensionery xodjat v muzej besplatno.* 'pensioners visit the museum for free'

In (29), valency slot *Y* of 'pay' is filled inside the adverb meaning: Nothing is paid. *W* is realized by the subordinating verb: It is the visits to museums that should (or should not) be paid for. The subject of this verb fills slot *X*, and *Z* is not expressed. It is essential for our discussion that the subject of the verb can also express *Z*:

> (30) *My rassylaem pis'ma besplatno* 'we send out letters for free'

The position of the subject corresponds to any of these two slots. If anybody is doing something for free, he does not pay for it or does not receive payment. It is only the real-world knowledge that can give the clue as to who is expected to pay; Cf. *I did it for free.* The remaining participant, which is not expressed by the subject, is not bound by any restrictions. It can either coincide with one of the actants of the verb (cf. (31-32)), or have nothing to do with its actants (cf. (29)).

> (31) *My* [Z] *rabotaem u nix* [X] *besplatno* 'we [Z] work for them [X] for free' (they do not pay to us)

> (32) *Nam* [X] *prisylajut Ø* [Z] *objavlenija besplatno* '(they) [Z] send us [X] announcements for free' (we do not pay to them)

6 Conversives

If the category of voice can be considered as a grammaticalized diathesis shift, conversion is its lexicalization. It is not for nothing that the passive voice is the major means of expressing conversive relations [11]. Conversive terms are those which denote identical or very similar situations but differ in syntactic positions of their arguments. Typical examples of conversives are *buy – sell, own – belong, rent1 (He rents this house to us) – rent2 (We rent this house from him)*. Besides verbs, the conversive relation is also admitted for nouns and adjectives that attach one of the actants by means of the copula verb: *John is my son's <u>teacher</u> – My son is John's <u>pupil</u>, Five is <u>more</u> than three – Three is <u>less</u> than five*. It is easy to show that if passive and discontinuous valency slots are taken into account, the variety of syntactic positions of the actants involved in the conversive relation is significantly greater. Let us give some examples.

6.1 *Vse* 'All' vs. *Vseobshchij* 'General' and *Total'nyj* 'Total'

Let us compare some Russian adjectives with the meaning close to the universal quantifier: *vse* 'all', *vseobschij* 'general', and *total'nyj* 'total'. All of them denote a situation in which action *P* extends over all the elements of set *R*. However, there exists an important difference as to how the actants are distributed between the prototypical and non-prototypical syntactic positions and which non-prototypical position is selected in each case.

In sentences (33a,b) and (34a,b) the position of the modified noun is prototypical but it corresponds to different valencies. In both of the (a)-sentences it is valency *R*, and in (b)-sentences it is valency *P*. As far as the non-prototypical position for the second valency is concerned, it is also different. In (a)-sentences it is the position of the dominating verb, and in (b)-sentences it is the position of a dependent of the dominating noun.

(33a) *Ozhidaetsja, chto <u>vse</u> dela* [R] *budut peresmotreny* [P].
    'it is expected that <u>all</u> the cases [R] will be reconsidered [P]'

(33b) *Ozhidaetsja <u>vseobshchij</u> peresmotr* [P] *del* [R].
    'a <u>general</u> reconsideration [P] of cases [R] is expected'

(34a) *<u>Ves'</u> bagazh* [R] *proverjaetsja* [P].
    '<u>all</u> luggage [R] is checked [P]'

(34b) *Proizvoditsja <u>total'naja</u> proverka* [P] *bagazha* [R].
    'a total checkup [P] of luggage is carried out [R]'

These sentences are another example of phenomena discussed in 4.3 above. Moreover, they also show that the adjectives *vse* 'all', *vseobshchij* 'general', and *total'nyj* 'total' are conversives, since they denote the same situation but differ in the syntactic position of their actants.

6.2 *Vse* 'All': Adjective vs. Noun

The Russian sentence (35) has two readings depending on the interpretation of *vse* 'all', which can be both an adjective and a noun, and on the position of the zero copula.

(35) *Zaxozhu, a v komnate vse moi druzhki.*
    lit. 'I come in and in the room all my friends'

(35a) ...*v komnate (byli) vse* (adj) *moi druzhki* ('in the room were all my friends') = 'all who are my friends were in the room'; R = 'my friends'; P = 'were in the room'.

(35b) ...*v komnate vse* (noun) *(byli) moi druzhki* ('in the room all were my friends') ≈ 'all who were in the room were my friends'; R = '(those) in the room'; P = 'my friends'.

Under interpretation (35a) the sentence means that every one of my friends was in the room, while (35b) means that there were no outsiders in the room. Accordingly, the syntactic structures are different. In (35a) the copula verb subordinates the noun phrase (*vse moi druzhki* 'all my friends') and in (35b) noun *vse* 'all' is the subject of the copula.

6.3 *Vse* 'All' vs. *Tol'ko* 'Only'

The relation between *all* and *only* has been largely discussed in Formal Semantics. In the context of this paper, the interesting point is that they are converse:

(36) *Zdes' lezhat* [P] *vse moi dokumenty* [R].
lit. 'here are [P] all my documents [R]' = 'everything which is a document of mine is here'

(37) *Zdes' lezhat* [R] *tol'ko moi dokumenty* [P].

lit. 'here are [R] only my documents [P]' = 'everything which is here is a document of mine'

6.4 *Redko* 'Seldom' vs. *Nemnogie* 'Few'

As was noticed as far back as in the Seventies, quantifying adverbs are sometimes synonymous to adnominal quantifiers: Cf. *often – many, seldom – few, always – all*, etc. ([12], [13: 351], and many others). For example:

(38a) *Lingvisty redko obladajut matematicheskimi sposobnostjami.*
'linguists seldom possess ability in mathematics'

(38b) *Nemnogie lingvisty obladajut matematicheskimi sposobnostjami.*
'few linguists possess ability in mathematics'

Taking into consideration the difference in syntactic position between the members of these pairs, it is more appropriate to call them conversives and not synonyms.

7 Conclusion: Generalization of Diathesis and Conversion

Active valencies, first of all valencies of the verbs, represent the canonical type of valency filling. These valencies presuppose that the expressions which fill them are syntactically subordinated to the predicate. If these valencies are complemented with other valency types (passive and discontinuous ones), additional syntactic positions for the actants have to be taken into account: The subordinating word, its dependent, and its governor.

Due to this extension of the typology of valency types, some conventional concepts turn out to be too narrow and require generalization. In this paper we have considered two such concepts whose extension directly depends on the extension of the concept of valency. These are *diathesis* and *conversion*.

If we take into account not only active valency slots but also passive and discontinuous ones, we will find that the inventory of syntactic positions taken by valency filling elements is significantly larger than the positions of Deep Syntactic Actants (DSyntAs). Let us call any fragment of Deep Syntactic Structure which corresponds to a Semantic Actant (SemA) of L a Deep Syntactic Scope (DSyntSc(L)) [14]. Then, DSyntAs are a particular case of DSyntScs. Non-trivial scopes are described by special Scope Rules, which can be considered as a generalization of Government Patterns.

We showed that SemAs do not always correspond to the same DSyntScs. It may easily happen that a SemA corresponds to more than one DSyntScs, or one DSyntSc serves more than one SemA. In this sense, the absence of one-to-one correspondence between SemAs and DSyntScs is a more general case than the absence of one-to-one correspondence between SemAs and DSyntAs. However, as opposed to the diathesis modification, the difference in DSyntSc is not marked formally, with the help of inflectional or derivational means, which makes these phenomena more difficult to observe and to investigate.

Another important difference between the cases discussed in this paper and traditional cases of non-uniqueness of verbal diathesis consists in the following. If a verb has more than one diathesis, one of them is primary and all the rest are derived. A sentence with the primary diathesis can often be transformed into a sentence with a derived diathesis without significant meaning distortion. Lexical units described in section 5 above do not permit such variation. Non-uniqueness does not necessarily imply the liability to variation.

The concept of the conversive as well as that of the diathesis refers to the syntactic positions of the actants. As shown in section 6, these positions should be selected out of a larger inventory than is customary.

The extension of the area covered by the concepts of diathesis and conversion is a direct consequence of accepting the idea that besides active valences there exist passive and discontinuous ones. All together they form a vast and varied class of phenomena integrated by a concept of valency as a universal mechanism that ensures the possibility to amalgamate meanings of words into the meaning of the sentence.

References

1. Partee, B.H.: The Development of Formal Semantics in Linguistic Theory. In: Lappin, S. (ed.) The Handbook of Contemporary Semantic Theory. Blackwell, Oxford (1996)
2. Apresjan, J.D.: Otechestvennaja teoreticheskaja semantika v konce XX stoletija (in Russian). Izv. AN, serija lit. i jazyka (4) (1999)
3. Boguslavsky, I.: Valentnosti kvantornyx slov (in Russian). In: Logicheskij analiz jazyka, pp. 139–165. Indrik, Moscow (2005)
4. Mel'čuk, I.: Actants in semantics and syntax I: actants in semantics. Linguistics 42(1), 1–66 (2004a)
5. Mel'čuk, I.: Actants in semantics and syntax II: actants in syntax. Linguistics 42(2), 247–291 (2004b)

6. Boguslavsky, I.: On the Passive and Discontinuous Valency Slots. In: Proceedings of the 1st International Conference on Meaning-Text Theory, Ecole Normale Supérieure. Paris, pp. 129–138 (2003)
7. Mel'čuk, I.: Dependency Syntax: Theory and Practice. State Univ. of New York Press (1988)
8. Paducheva, E.: Diathesis: some extended applications of the term. In: Proceedings of the 1st International Conference on Meaning-Text Theory. École Normale Supérieure, Paris (2003)
9. Partee, B.H.: Diathesis Alternations and NP Semantics. In: East West Encounter: Second International Conference on Meaning – Text Theory. Jazyki slavjanskoj kul'tury, Moscow (2005)
10. Mel'čuk, I.: Aspects of the Theory of Morphology. Mouton de Gruyter, Berlin (2006)
11. Apresjan, J.D.: Leksicheskaja semantika (in Russian). Nauka, Moscow (1974)
12. Lewis, D.: Adverbs of quantification. In: Keenan, E.L. (ed.) Formal Semantics of Natural Language, pp. 3–15. Cambridge University Press, Cambridge (1975)
13. Bulygina, T.V.: Grammaticheskie i semanticheskie kategorii i ix svjazi (in Russian). In: Aspecty semanticheskix issledobanij. Nauka, Moscow (1980)
14. Boguslavsky, I.: Sfera dejstvija leksicheskix edinic (in Russian). Shkola Jazyki russkoj kul'tury, Moscow (1996)

The Modal Formula
(†) $\Box\Diamond p \supset \Box\Diamond\Box\Diamond p$
Is Not First-Order Definable

Ali Karatay*

Bogazici University 34342 Bebek, Istanbul, Turkey

Abstract. The formula (†) above is shown not to be first-order definable. The result is obtained by complicating the construction introduced in [4]. Two motivations are given for why the question of the first-order definability of (†) matters, one from theoretical considerations relating to modal logic, the other from applications of modal logic to philosophy, namely logic of ability. Finally a comparison with a cognate notion in the literature is given.

Keywords: Modal Logic, Ability Logic, First-Order Definability of Modal Formulas, Modal Reduction Principles.

1 Terminology and Notation

By first-order language *corresponding* to a basic modal language we mean a first-order language with identity, whose only non-logical constant is a binary relation symbol 'R'. Let us denote this language by 'L_R'. We call a formula α in the basic modal language *first-order definable* if there is a sentence σ in L_R such that for any Kripke frame $\mathcal{F}$, $\mathcal{F} \Vdash \alpha$ iff $\mathcal{F} \models \sigma$. Equivalently, α is *first-order definable* if the corresponding sentence σ characterizes an elementary class of structures in the sense of model theory.

Following [2], I use the symbol '$\Vdash$' for the semantic relation of satisfiability in modal logic, and the symbol '$\models$' for the semantic relation of satisfiability in first-order logic.

2 Motivation

There are two motivations for examining the definability status of (†). One is theoretical, the other practical—directed towards an application of modal logic to philosophy.

2.1 Theoretical Motivation

The formula (†)$\Box\Diamond p \supset \Box\Diamond\Box\Diamond p$ occupies a central place in the lattice of normal modal systems with all its well known neighbours being famously first-order

---

* I am thankful to the three referees of this paper for their helpful suggestions. The diagrams are drawn by Paul Taylor's Commutative Diagrams macro.

P. Bosch, D. Gabelaia, and J. Lang (Eds.): TbiLLC 2007, LNAI 5422, pp. 221–228, 2009.
© Springer-Verlag Berlin Heidelberg 2009

definable.[1] Indeed, **T**† is properly contained in both **S4** and **B** $(= \mathbf{T} + B)$, and it properly contains **T**:

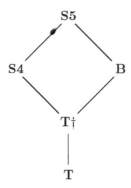

(i) T† is a subsystem of S4. This follows from the fact that iterated modalities in **S4** reduce; in more detail,

1. $\Box\Diamond p \supset \Diamond\Box\Diamond p$, by **T**;
2. $\Box\Box\Diamond p \supset \Box\Diamond\Box\Diamond p$, by **K** and M.P.;
3. $\Box(\Diamond p) \supset \Box\Box(\Diamond p)$, by **S4**;
4. $\Box\Diamond p \supset \Box\Diamond\Box\Diamond p$, by 3., 2. and Hyp. Syll.

(ii) T† is a subsystem of B. Just substitute '$\Box\Diamond p$' for 'p' in '$p \supset \Box\Diamond p$', the axiom (B) of **B**.

Moreover, **T**† is a proper subsystem of **S4** and of **B**. For if **T**† coincides with one of **S4** and **B**, then it can not be a subsystem of the other.

(iii) $\nvdash_{\mathbf{T}}$ †. It is enough to consider the model, where p is assigned $\top$ at w_2 and $\bot$ at w_3:

$$\overset{w_1}{\circlearrowleft} \longrightarrow \overset{w_2}{\circlearrowleft} \longrightarrow \overset{w_3}{\circlearrowleft}$$

Since all the systems **T**, **S4**, and **B** are first-order definable, it is natural to inquire whether **T**† is also first-order definable. (Throughout this paper, I use the locutions such as "the system **T** is first-order definable" in the obvious sense that the proper axiom that distinguishes **T** from **K** is first-order definable.) The main task in this paper is to prove that (†) is not first-order definable.

2.2 Practical Motivation

Another reason that led to the present study is the connection between (†) and the logic of ability. Ability here is the abiliy of doing something reliably. Now the logic of the '*can*' of reliable ability is distinct from that of the '*possible*' of alethic modality. For one example, while in modal logic we have the entailment

$$\vdash_K \Diamond(p \vee q) \rightarrow (\Diamond p \vee \Diamond q),$$

---

[1] The problem that I am going to discuss in this paper was posed to me by Prof. Thomas McKay; in fact, I learned the contents of this section in Prof. McKay's lectures on Modal Logic given in Fall 1987 at Syracuse University.

one may reliably distinguish cubic paintings from others without being reliably able to distinguish Picasso's cubic paintings from those of Braque's; in other words, distributivity fails to hold in the logic of ability. More explicitly, assuming that Picasso and Braque are the only cubist painters, when "p" is the statement, "The painting on the wall is by Picasso," and "q" is "The painting on the wall is by Braque," one may have the ability to reliably assert "p or q," while he is neither able to reliably assert "p" nor able to reliably assert "q."

For another example, that I have once correctly identified a cubic Picasso does not entail that I'll succeed the next time. So, the alethic *'possibility'*, $\Diamond$, in

$$\vdash_T p \to \Diamond p \text{ and in } \vdash_K \Diamond(p \vee q) \to (\Diamond p \vee \Diamond q)$$

does not agree with *'can'* of reliable ability.

What these examples tell us is that a normal modal system does not represent the *'can'* of ability logic. In the late 1980s Professor Mark Brown of Syracuse University, N.Y., examined the logic of ability and some related modalities. Brown has developed a formal system aiming to capture the logic of these modalities and their interrelationships [3]. Brown observed that the *'can'* of ability logic agrees with either of the operators $\Box$ and $\Diamond$ in:

$$\frac{\vdash p \leftrightarrow q}{\vdash \Diamond p \leftrightarrow \Diamond q} \qquad \frac{\vdash p \leftrightarrow q}{\vdash \Box p \leftrightarrow \Box q} \ .$$

But these inference rules are characteristic of classical modal logics. So, non-normal classical modal logics seem to be congenial for the logic of ability. When I can reliably bring about p, I bring it about in one way or another—probably together with a variety of concomitant outcomes. We may understand the phrase "able to reliably bring about p" to mean that there is a cluster of actions each of which brings about p, accompanied collaterally with some or the other of the outcomes $q_1, q_2, q_3, \ldots$. According to Brown, 'can' of ability indicates that there is a way for the agent to make the given statement true (clearly, 'can' of ability is parametric on an agent). Brown symbolizes this notion by: $\Diamond$, so that '$\Diamond A$' says that there is a way for the agent to make A come true. This notion has a dual, $\boxtimes A := \neg \Diamond \neg A$. This means that the agent cannot reliably avoid circumstances where A is false, or briefly, the action of the agent *might lead* to a circumstance in which A is true. This 'might' is in a somewhat negative sense, involving an incapability. Brown has also formalized a positive sense of 'might' within the same systematic approach. According to this, $\Diamond\!\!\!\!\Diamond A$ says that there are ways open to the agent to bring about A, or that the agent *might manage* to bring about a circumstances in which A is true. Dual for this "might" is given by $\Box\!\!\!\Box A$ meaning that in all the relevant ways of action the agent will make A come true.

Now we have the following list of operators in the logic of ability:

'$\Diamond A$' is true at a world w iff there exists an accessible cluster of worlds at every world of which A is true.

'$\boxtimes A$' is true at a world w iff every cluster accessible to w contains a world in which A is true. (This the dual of $\Diamond$.)

'$\Box A$' is true at a world w iff A is true in every world in every cluster accessible to w.

'$\diamondsuit A$' is true at a world w iff in at least one cluster accessible to w there is at least one world at which A is true. (This the dual of $\boxdot$.)

The semantics of reliable ability relates a given world to a cluster of worlds. This suggests that the *minimal models* will be at work for the semantics of the logic of ability, since the accessibility relation R in the minimal model $\langle W, R, V \rangle$ relates a world w not to a world, but to a subset of W. So, the corresponding coalgebra constitutes an hypersystem. This fits well with our observation that classical modal logics are suitable for the logic of ability.

The Formal System $\mathcal{V}$. The formal system $\mathcal{V}$ is a set of sentences closed under the following rules and axioms and the propositional logic inferences:

(**RM $\diamondsuit$**) If $\vdash p \to q$, then $\vdash \diamondsuit p \to \diamondsuit q$
(**RM $\Diamond$**) If $\vdash p \to q$, then $\vdash \Diamond p \to \Diamond q$
(**RN $\boxdot$**) If $\vdash p$, then $\vdash \boxdot p$.

(**C $\diamondsuit$**) $\vdash \diamondsuit (p \vee q) \to (\diamondsuit p \vee \diamondsuit q)$
(**V**) $\vdash \Diamond (p \vee q) \to (\diamondsuit p \vee \Diamond q)$
(**W**) $\vdash \diamondsuit p \to (\boxdot q \to \Diamond q)$

The system $\mathcal{V}$ is sound and complete under the given semantics. Also, there is a translation τ of the formulas of $\mathcal{L}_\mathcal{V}$ into those of $\mathcal{L}_\mathbf{K}$ so that a formula ϕ is valid in $\mathcal{V}$ iff $\tau(\phi)$ is valid in $\mathbf{K}$. In particular, $\tau(\diamondsuit \phi) = \Diamond \Box \tau(\phi)$; and $\tau(\boxtimes \phi) = \Box \Diamond \tau(\phi)$.

An extension of $\mathcal{V}$ that is closed under MP, (**RM $\diamondsuit$**), (**RM $\Diamond$**), (**RN $\boxdot$**) is called a *reliable extension* of $\mathcal{V}$. Some reliable extensions of $\mathcal{V}$ with complete axiomatizations are:

(D $\boxtimes$) $\vdash \boxtimes p \supset \diamondsuit p$ $(\forall \alpha \in W)(\exists K \subseteq W)(\alpha R K)$
(T $\Diamond$) $\vdash p \supset \diamondsuit p$ $(\forall \alpha \in W)(\exists K : \alpha R K)(K \subseteq \{\alpha\})$
(B $\boxdot$) $\vdash p \supset \boxdot \diamondsuit p$ $(\forall \alpha, \beta \in W)((\exists K : \alpha R K)(\beta \in K)$
$\Rightarrow (\exists K' : \beta R K')(\alpha \in K'))$

Note that the characterization of the D-axiom is a generalization of "no dead-ends" condition, the characterization of the T-axiom is a generalization of reflexivity, and the characterization of the B-axiom is a generalization of symmetry. For instance, the last formula says that if a world α is related to a cluster of worlds K that contains a world β, then β is related to a cluster of worlds K' that contains α.

Now, one other conceivable axiom for an extension of $\mathcal{V}$ is:

(**4 $\Diamond$**) $\vdash \Diamond \diamondsuit A \supset \diamondsuit A$.

The method Brown employs for proving that D- T- and B-extensions are completely axiomatizable does not work for this new extension. But note that the schema (**4 $\Diamond$**) is equivalent to $\vdash \boxtimes p \supset \boxtimes \boxtimes p$ and this has a translation into the language of normal logics exactly as (†), so we might expect that a first-order characterization of (†) would shed light for the formulation of an appropriate condition on the models to give a complete axiomatization for the extension $\mathcal{V} + 4\Diamond$. This is the connection we mentioned on page 222 between (†) and the logic of ability.

3   Proof

We prove that (†) is not first-order definable by complicating the construction introduced in [4].

We define a sequence of frames $\mathcal{F}_n = \langle W_n, R_n \rangle$ s.t. $\mathcal{F}_n \models \Box\Diamond p \supset \Box\Diamond\Box\Diamond p$ for all i, $i \geq 1$, but when G is a nonprincipal ultrafilter on N, $\prod \mathcal{F}_n/G \not\models \Box\Diamond p \supset \Box\Diamond\Box\Diamond p$.

Put $W_n = \{w_1\} \cup \{w_2\} \cup \{w_{3,1}, \ldots, w_{3,2n+1}\} \cup \{w_{4,1}, \ldots, w_{4,2n+1}\}$ and define R_n on W_n as follows:

$w_1 R_n w_2$;
$w_1 R_n w_{3,i}$, for $1 \leq i \leq 2n+1$;
$w_2 R_n w_{3,i}$, for $1 \leq i \leq 2n+1$;
$w_{3,1} R_n w_{4,1}$ and $w_{3,1} R_n w_{4,2}$;
$w_{3,i} R_n w_{4,i-1}, w_{3,i} R_n w_{4,i+1}$, for $1 < i < 2n+1$;
$w_{3,2n+1} R_n w_{4,2n}, w_{3,2n+1} R_n w_{4,2n+1}$;
$w_{4,i} R_n w_{4,i}$, for $1 \leq i \leq 2n+1$.

We shall call a world which is denoted by '$w_{i,j}$' an ith-*level world*.

Proposition 1. : $\mathcal{F}_n \models \Box\Diamond p \supset \Box\Diamond\Box\Diamond p$.

Before starting to prove the proposition, it will help to look at a picture of $\mathcal{F}_1$:

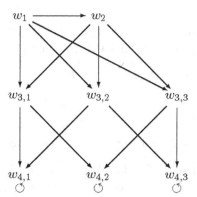

Proof. Suppose a frame $\mathcal{F}_n$ is given. We want to show that for every world w in $\mathcal{F}_n$, under every valuation V, we have $V(\Box\Diamond p \supset \Box\Diamond\Box\Diamond p, w) = T$.

Case of $w_{4,i}$, for $1 \leq i \leq 2n+1$:
Suppose for a valuation V, $V(\Box\Diamond p, w_{4,i}) = T$. Since the 4th-level worlds are R-related just to themselves, we first get $V(\Diamond\Box\Diamond p, w_{4,i}) = T$ and then get $V(\Box\Diamond\Box\Diamond p, w_{4,i}) = T$.

Case of $w_{3,i}$, for $1 < i < 2n + 1$:
Suppose for a valuation V, $V(\Box\Diamond p, w_{3,i}) = T$. Then for all j s.t. $w_{3,i}Rw_{4,j}$, $V(\Diamond p, w_{4,j}) = T$. But since the 4th level worlds are R-related just to themselves, we obtain $V(\Diamond\Box\Diamond p, w_{4,j}) = T$. Hence, $V(\Box\Diamond\Box\Diamond p, w_{3,i}) = T$.

Case of w_2:

$$V(\Box\Diamond p, w_2) = T \Rightarrow V(\Diamond p, w_{3,i}) = T \text{ for all } i$$
$$\Rightarrow \text{ for each } i \text{ there is some } j_i \text{ s.t. } V(p, w_{4,j_i}) = T$$
$$\Rightarrow V(\Diamond p, w_{4,j_i}) = T$$
$$\Rightarrow V(\Box\Diamond p, w_{4,j_i}) = T$$
$$\Rightarrow V(\Diamond\Box\Diamond p, w_{3,i}) = T, \text{ for all } i$$
$$\Rightarrow V(\Box\Diamond\Box\Diamond p, w_2) = T.$$

Case of w_1:
Before examining this case we first note the following

Lemma 2. *For any modal formula φ, for any natural number $n \geq 1$, and for any valuation V,*

(i) if $V(\Diamond\varphi, w_{3,i}) = T$ for all i, $1 \leq i \leq 2n + 1$, then $V(\varphi, w_{4,i}) = T$ in at least $n + 1$ of the 4th-level worlds; and
(ii) if $V(\Box\varphi, w_{3,i}) = F$ for all i, $1 \leq i \leq 2n + 1$, then $V(\varphi, w_{4,i}) = F$ in at least $n + 1$ of the 4th-level worlds.

Proof. Since every 4th-level world is a successor of exactly two 3rd-level worlds, making ϕ true at n 4th-level worlds can make $\Diamond\phi$ true at at most $2n$ 3rd-level worlds. Thus, to make $\Diamond\phi$ true at all $2n + 1$ worlds would require making ϕ true at more than n 4th-level worlds.[2] A dual argument works for the second part of the lemma.   □

Resuming now, in order to prove the case of w_1, we'll show that there is no valuation V s.t. $V(\Box\Diamond p, w_1) = T$ and $V(\Box\Diamond\Box\Diamond p, w_1) = F$. Note that

(1) $V(\Box\Diamond p, w_1) = T \Rightarrow V(\Diamond p, w_{3,i}) = T$ for all i, $1 \leq i \leq 2n + 1$.

On the other hand, $V(\Box\Diamond\Box\Diamond p, w_1) = F$ entails that either $V(\Diamond\Box\Diamond p, w_{3,i}) = F$ for some i, $1 \leq i \leq 2n + 1$ or $V(\Diamond\Box\Diamond p, w_2) = F$.

Subcase 1. $V(\Box\Diamond p, w_1) = T$ and $V(\Diamond\Box\Diamond p, w_{3,i}) = F$ for some i, $1 \leq i \leq 2n + 1$.

$$V(\Diamond\Box\Diamond p, w_{3,i}) = F \text{ for some } i \Rightarrow \text{ for all } j \text{ s.t. } w_{3,i}Rw_{4,j}, V(\Box\Diamond p, w_{4,j}) = F$$
$$\Rightarrow \text{ for all } j \text{ s.t. } w_{3,i}Rw_{4,j}, V(\Diamond p, w_{4,j}) = F$$
$$\Rightarrow \text{ for all } j \text{ s.t. } w_{3,i}Rw_{4,j}, V(p, w_{4,j}) = F$$
$$\Rightarrow V(\Diamond p, w_{3,i}) = F.$$

This contradicts (1) above.

Subcase 2. $V(\Box\Diamond p, w_1) = T$ and $V(\Diamond\Box\Diamond p, w_2) = F$.

---

[2] This elegant argument is suggested to me by one of the unknown referees.

By $V(\Box\Diamond p, w_1) = T$ and (1), $V(\Diamond p, w_{3,i}) = T$ for all i, $1 \le i \le 2n + 1$, and hence by Lemma (i), there are at least $(n + 1)$-many i s.t. $V(p, w_{4,i}) = T$.

On the other hand,

$$V(\Diamond\Box\Diamond p, w_2) = F \Rightarrow V(\Box\Diamond p, w_{3,i}) = F \text{ for all } i,\ 1 \le i \le 2n + 1$$
$$\Rightarrow V(\Diamond p, w_{4,i}) = F \text{ for at least } n + 1\ i \text{ (by Lemma (ii))}$$
$$\Rightarrow V(p, w_{4,i}) = F \text{ for at least } n + 1\ i.$$

Now, on the one hand, we have p True in at least $n + 1$ of the 4th-level worlds, and on the other hand, we have p False in at least $n + 1$ of the 4th-level worlds. Since there are $2n+1$ 4th-level worlds, this means that, under the given valuation p is both T and F in at least one 4th-level world. Contradiction.   □

Proposition 3. *For a free ultrafilter G on N, $\prod \mathcal{F}_n/G \not\models \Box\Diamond p \supset \Box\Diamond\Box\Diamond p$.*

Proof. By considerations similar to those given in Goldblatt's paper the new structure looks as follows:

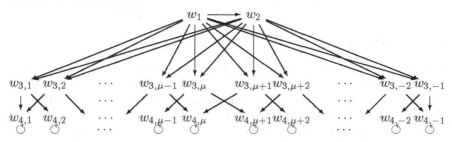

The order type of the 3rd-level (4th-level) worlds is $\omega + (\omega^* + \omega)\theta + \omega^*$, where ω^* is the order type of negative integers (and hence $\omega^* + \omega$ is the order type of integers), θ is some dense linear ordering with no end-points (we don't need to know any further properties of θ in this paper), and, $(\omega^* + \omega)\theta$ is the order type of θ copies of integers. We note that w_1 is the unique element that has an access to every other element in the structure, but that no element in the structure has access to w_1. This property helps us to fix w_1 in the ultraproduct by a first-order formula. w_2 can also be easily fixed by a similar formula. Rest of the structure can be shown to be in the form indicated by the diagram above by arguments following Goldblatt's argument *verbatim* on p. 39 in [4].

Let now V be a valuation on $\prod \mathcal{F}_n/G$, subject to the following (partial) initial conditions:

1. $V(p, w_{3,1}) = T$;
2. $V(p, w_{4,1}) = T$, $V(p, w_{4,2})$ and $V(p, w_{4,3})$ are F and $V(p, w_{4,4})$ and $V(p, w_{4,5})$ are T, and so on throughout the initial segment of type ω of the 4th-level worlds;
3. continuing on the middle segment of type $(\omega^* + \omega)\theta$ with $V(p, w_{4,\mu})$ and $V(p, w_{4,\mu+1})$ as T and $V(p, w_{4,\mu+2})$ and $V(p, w_{4,\mu+3})$ as F, and so on;
4. finally, $V(p, w_{4,-1}) = T$, $V(p, w_{4,-2})$ and $V(p, w_{4,-3})$ are F and $V(p, w_{4,-4})$ and $V(p, w_{4,-5})$ are T, and so on throughout the final segment of type ω^*.

Certainly, there are valuations V with the above assignment of truth values to propositional letters. Thus by (2), and the structure of $\prod \mathcal{F}_n/G$, we have $V(\Diamond p, w_{3,\mu}) = T$ for all places μ in the order type $\omega + (\omega^* + \omega)\theta + \omega^*$, and by (1), we have $V(\Diamond p, w_2) = T$, and these two results yield $V(\Box \Diamond p, w_1) = T$. On the other hand, since under the valuation V the truth value assignment for p at the 4th-level worlds has the pattern

$$TFFTTFFTT \ldots \ldots TTFFTTFFTTFF \ldots \ldots TTFFTTFFT \ ,$$

$V(\Box \Diamond p, w_{3,\mu}) = F$ for each place μ in the order type $\omega + (\omega^* + \omega)\theta + \omega^*$. Hence, $V(\Diamond \Box \Diamond p, w_2) = F$. But then, $V(\Box \Diamond \Box \Diamond p, w_1) = F$, also. Hence $V(\Box \Diamond p \supset \Box \Diamond \Box \Diamond p) = F$ and hence $\prod \mathcal{F}_n/G \not\models \Box \Diamond p \supset \Box \Diamond \Box \Diamond p$.   □

Now, since we have $\{n : \mathcal{F}_n \models \Box \Diamond p \supset \Box \Diamond \Box \Diamond p\} = N \in G$, we have shown that the class of models of the modal formula $\Box \Diamond p \supset \Box \Diamond \Box \Diamond p$ is not closed under ultraproducts. Hence by Corollary 7 in [4], it follows that $\Box \Diamond p \supset \Box \Diamond \Box \Diamond p$ is not first-order definable.

This completes the proof of the main thesis of this paper.

4   Discussion

There is a notion in the literature closely related to our notion of first-order definability, worked out by van Benthem in [1].[3] According to this, given a formula α in the basic modal language, there corresponds a first-order relational property to α if there is a formula $\phi(x)$ with a single free variable x in the language L_R (defined on page 221) such that for any Kripke frame $\mathcal{F}$ and a point w in $\mathcal{F}$, $\mathcal{F}, w \Vdash \alpha$ iff $\mathcal{F} \models \phi[x := w]$. We may call this notion *local first-order definability* and the notion we employed throughout this paper *global first-order definability*. Clearly, when a modal formula is locally first-order definable, this implies that it is also globally first-order definable. Now, Lemma 3, item (3) in [1] indicates that the formula (†) is not locally first-order definable. But since the converse of the above implication is not known to hold, we would not be able to conclude from Lemma 3 in [1] that the formula (†) is not globally first-order definable.

As for the logic of ability, this negative result only shows that we have no immediate way of shedding light on $\mathcal{V} + 4 \Diamond$, but this does not imply that $\mathcal{V} + 4 \Diamond$ has no complete axiomatization.

References

1. van Benthem, J.F.A.K.: Modal Reduction Principles. Journal of Symbolic Logic 41.2, 301–312 (1976)
2. Blackburn, P., de Rijke, M., Venema, Y.: Modal Logic. Cambridge University Press, Cambridge (2001)
3. Brown, M.: On the Logic of Ability. Journal of Philosophical Logic 17, 1–26 (1988)
4. Goldblatt, R.I.: First-Order Definability in Modal Logic. Journal of Symbolic Logic 40.1, 35–40 (1975)

---

[3] I am grateful to an unknown referee of this paper for having informed me of this alternate notion.

Semantic Characterizations of German Question-Embedding Predicates[*]

Kerstin Schwabe[1] and Robert Fittler[2]

[1] Zentrum für Allgemeine Sprachwissenschaft, Schützenstraße 18,
10117 Berlin, Germany
[2] Mathematisches Institut, Freie Universität Berlin, Arnimallee 3
14195 Berlin, Germany
schwabe@zas.gwz-berlin.de, robertfittler@netscape.net

Abstract. The paper investigates the conditions under which German two-place verbs like wissen dass 'know' and bedauern dass 'regret' embed interrogatives. We present a necessary and sufficient condition for a dass-verb to have an ob-form. The corresponding verbs we call objective. An objective verb has a wh-form (F weiß, wer kommt 'F knows who is coming') if it satisfies a further condition stating that it has to be consistent with wissen dass. A non-objective dass-verb does not have an ob-form, but it can have a wh-form if it permits a da- or es-correlate and meets particular consistency conditions which render it factive or cognitive in the presence of the correlate (cf. bedauern 'regret' vs. annehmen 'assume') It turns out that the meaning of the wh-form of non-objective verbs deviates distinctly from the meaning of the wh-form of objective verbs. Unlike other approaches our rules are general and hold without exceptions.

Keywords: Interrogatives, question embedding, axioms, correlates, factivity, cognitivity, consistency, compatibility.

1 Introduction

This paper discusses German simplex predicates which embed declarative or interrogative clauses, cf. (1-5). The paper focuses on only those semantic and syntactic properties which rule the type of the embedding clause. It neglects the syntax and semantics of the embedded clauses as far as possible. The set of verbs we analyse is the union of three partially overlapping syntactic classes of verbs allowing a *dass-* or an *ob-* or a *wh*-form. Below we list the five relevant subsets of {*dass-, ob–, wh–*form} with appropriate examples.

(1)   {*dass-, ob-, wh-*form}
    a.   *Frank weiß/sagt, dass Maria) kommt.*
        Frank knows/says that Maria is coming.
    b.   *Frank weiß/sagt, ob Maria kommt.*
        Frank knows/says whether Maria is coming.

[*] The authors gratefully acknowledge the helpful discussions with Dick de Jongh and Thomas E. Zimmermann as well as the comments of the anonymous reviewers.

P. Bosch, D. Gabelaia, and J. Lang (Eds.): TbiLLC 2007, LNAI 5422, pp. 229–241, 2009.

c.   *Frank weiß/sagt, wer kommt.*
       Frank knows/says who is coming.

(2)   { *dass-, ob-, wh-*form}

a.   **Frank fragt, dass Maria kommt.*
       *Frank asks that Maria is coming.

b.   *Frank fragt, ob Maria kommt.*

c.   *Frank fragt, wer kommt.*

(3)   {*dass-, ob-,* * *wh-*form}

a.   *Frank zweifelt, dass Maria kommt.*
       Frank doubts that Maria is coming.

b.   *Maria zweifelt, ob Frank kommt.*

c.   **Maria zweifelt, wer kommt.*

(4)   {*dass-, *ob-, wh-*form}

a.   *Frank ist überrascht, dass Maria kommt.*
       Frank is surprised that Maria is coming.

b.   **Frank ist überrascht, ob Maria kommt.*

c.   *Frank ist darüber überrascht, wer kommt.*

(5)   {*dass-, *ob-, *wh-*form}

a.   *Maria hofft, dass Frank kommt.*
       Maria hopes that Frank is coming.

b.   **Maria hofft, ob Frank kommt.*

c.   **Maria hofft (darauf), wer kommt.*

Considering the more or less recent literature on question-embedding predicates, which discusses the grammatical rules concerning the embedding behaviour of *dass-*, *ob*, and *wh*-verbs, one notices that it does not give a satisfying answer to the characterization problems we have in mind - for an overview, cf. Dipper (1997) and Krifka (2005).

Karttunen (1977) presents a comprehensive classification of English question- embedding predicates, which is, however, as he remarks, not exhaustive insofar as it lacks, for example, predicates such as *be surprised* and *doubt*. He establishes nine classes of question-embedding verbs which, however, do not reflect coherently the selectional behaviour of their elements.

Groenendijk & Stokhof (1982) argue that verbs such as *know* and *tell* are extensional in that they operate on the denotations of their interrogative or declarative complements, i.e. on "propositions". Verbs like *guess, be certain, ask, be important*, and *depend on* operate on intensions, i.e. on "propositional concepts". Since all extensional and some intensional predicates (cf. *guess, estimate*, and *ask*) select interrogatives, the distinction between extensionality and intensionality is not adequate for our purposes. Like Karttunen, Groenendijk & Stokhof do not discuss predicates like *be surprised, regret* and *doubt*.

Ginzburg & Sag (2000), referring to, among others, Vendler (1980) and Asher (1993), concentrate on the ontology of question-embedding predicates. For them, predicates operating on fact-like or question-like objects embed interrogatives. They regard all embedded interrogatives to be questions. If the predicate operates on facts, the question is coerced into a fact. They include predicates such as *regret*, saying that they are factive, but do not explain why they do not embed *whether*-questions.

Zifonoun et al. (1997) discussing German propositional predicates do not explain why *bestätigen* 'confirm', *bedauern* 'regret', and *sich freuen* 'be glad' can have a *wh*-form.

The account presented in this paper contributes to this issue in providing a comprehensive answer to the question which semantic properties enable propositional predicates to embed yes/no- or constituent questions. In this paper we concentrate on German two-place predicates involving pairs of individual subjects and embedded statements.

2 Basics

The semantic *structures* $\aleph$ modelling the embedded clauses correspond to common first-order predicate structures. They consist *i)* of a set of elements called *subjects* and *ii)* of interpretations of basic *statements* such as *x kommt* 'x comes' or $\sigma(x)$ where x is substitutable by individual constants or elements of $\aleph$ and belongs to a first-order language determined by the context. The language usually includes some names (individual constants) like *Maria*, allowing for statements like *Maria kommt* or $\sigma(Maria)$. For later convenience, let I be the set of individual variables and constants. The more complex statements are built up by the use of the *logical signs* $\neg$, $\wedge$, $\vee$, $\leftarrow$, $\rightarrow$, $\leftrightarrow$, $\forall$, $\exists$. Statements containing no logical signs are called *atomic formulas*. The language might contain the expression $x = y$ in order to permit statements involving numbers. The set of *atomic formulas* will be labelled Σ, while $\Phi(\Sigma)$ is the set of all formulas of the first-order language mentioned so far. The latter just corresponds to the set of embedded clauses. They are subordinated to simplex matrix predicates either by overt complementizers such as *dass* or *ob* or by silent ones as is the case with respect to embedded *wh*-interrogatives – cf. *Maria weiß, dass Frank kommt* 'M knows that F is coming', *Maria fragt, ob Frank kommt* 'M asks whether F is coming' or *Maria sieht, wer kommt* 'M sees who is coming'. More formally, the predicates look like *x verb dass/ob* $\sigma(y)$ or *wh*$(x, verb, \sigma)$. An example containing a quantifier is $\forall x\ A\ verb\ ob\ \sigma(x)$ for *A weiß, wer kommt* 'A knows who is coming'. Notice that we consider first embedding constructions without *correlates*, i.e., we do not discuss *Maria sieht es, wer kommt* 'M sees it who is coming' or *Frank freut sich darüber, dass Pauline kommt* 'F is glad about that P is coming'. Constructions with optional correlates will be introduced in Section 4.2, those with obligatory ones will be considered in a forthcoming paper.

Embedding predicates like *wissen dass/ob* and *fragen ob* constitute a set of new data, say V, the interpretation of which has to be defined on top of the semantic structure $\aleph$. For this purpose, we consider the union

$$\underline{\Sigma} := \Phi(\Sigma) \cup \{x\ verb\ dass/ob\ \tau \mid \tau \in \Phi(\Sigma), x \in I, verb \in V\}$$

to be defined on top of the semantic structure $\aleph$. We consider the union $\underline{\Sigma}$ to be a set of atomic formulas for a new first-order language and extend the previous interpretation of $\Phi(\Sigma)$ on $\aleph$ by determining the validity for the remaining formulas in

$$\{x\ verb\ dass/ob\ \tau \mid \tau \in \Phi(\Sigma), x \in I, verb \in V\} \text{ from } \underline{\Sigma}.$$

We arrive at an enriched type of structure $\aleph$ which we call a *constellation*. The determination of the validity of the new formulas *x verb dass/ob* τ must take into account the intended meaning of the *verb*. For this reason, the *verbs* are subjected to appropriate *semantic axioms*. These in turn will yield the criteria needed to explain which complementizers fit the verb in question, and how they modify the verb meaning. The most basic *verb* here is *wissen dass*.

(6)   **Axiom for wissen dass** 'know'
       Wissen dass is subject to the *axiom of semi-implicativity*.

(7)   **Definition: *semi-implicativity (semi-implicative)*** [1]
       X verb dass $\sigma \rightarrow \sigma$, for all $\sigma \in \Phi(\Sigma)$

The following condition will turn out to be decisive for the question-embedding:

(8)   **Definition: *Witness Existence Condition (WEC)***
       $\exists X$ (X verb dass/ob σ) $\lor$ $\exists X$ (X verb dass/ob $\neg\sigma$), for all $\sigma \in \Phi(\Sigma)$

It expresses that for each σ, there is a "witness X with respect to *verb dass/ob*". It follows that *wissen dass* is compatible with WEC. For a predicate to be *compatible* or *consistent* with some property respectively means that there is a constellation where the predicate satisfies the required property.

If WEC actually holds in $\aleph$ with respect to a semi-implicative *dass*-verb, it follows $\exists A$ (A verb dass σ) $\leftrightarrow \sigma$, for all $\sigma \in \Phi(\Sigma)$.

A structure $\aleph$ with respect to $\Phi(\Sigma)$ can generally be extended into a constellation with respect to *wissen dass* in various ways. One possibility is that all $\alpha \in \aleph$ know all valid σ's. Another one is that just one α knows all valid σ's. In both cases WEC happens to hold with respect to *wissen dass*.

Like *wissen dass*, *beweisen dass* 'prove' is semi-implicative, but unlike *wissen dass*, it is incompatible with WEC. The respective sets of statements {$\exists x$ (x verb dass σ) $\lor$ $\exists x$ (x verb dass $\neg\sigma$) | $\sigma \in \Phi(\Sigma)[\aleph]$} cannot equal $\Phi(\Sigma)[\aleph]$; the set of all statements with parameters from $\aleph$ substituted for the free variables. The reason for this is that *beweisen dass* singles out very special valid statements never being meant to cover all possible valid statements σ without exception. Thus, *beweisen dass* is subject to the axiom *semi-implicative* & $\neg WEC$ – cf. V in the Appendix. The next basic definition we need is:

(9)   **Definition: *anti-semi-implicativity (anti-semi-implicative)***
       A verb dass $\sigma \rightarrow \sigma$, for all $\sigma \in \Phi(\Sigma)$

This property is, for instance, fulfilled by *widerlegen dass* 'refute'. Like *beweisen*, it is incompatible with WEC because of:

(10)   **Axiom for widerlegen dass** 'refute'
       A widerlegt dass $\sigma \leftrightarrow A$ *beweist dass* $\neg\sigma$

---

[1] We claim that *wissen dass* and *bedauern dass* are not factive, in distinction to the usual assumption (cf. for instance Krifka 2005) since σ need not necessarily be valid in a valid expression like *A weiß/bedauert nicht dass* σ 'A does not know/regret that σ'. Imagine an exam situation where a professor when listing some statements the candidate did not know says that the candidate did not know that the "Unfinished" was Schubert's last symphony. Unlike *wissen*, *bedauern* is not even semi-implicative. *A* can regret that σ even if he wrongly believes that σ.

The subsequent, third basic verb *fragen ob* is characterised by the following axiom – cf. (2). The property given in (11) is called *negation-invariance*.

(11) **Axiom for fragen ob 'ask'**
$$A \text{ fragt ob } \sigma \leftrightarrow A \text{ fragt ob } \neg\sigma$$

(12) **Definition: *negation-invariance (negation-invariant)***
$$A \text{ verb dass/ob } \sigma \leftrightarrow A \text{ verb dass/ob } \neg\sigma, \text{ for all } \sigma \in \Phi(\Sigma)$$

Fragen ob is negation-invariant and compatible with WEC. The complementizer *dass* in (12) is motivated by *zweifeln dass* 'doubt' which, as will be shown in Section 3, exhibits negation invariance in some but not all constellations – cf. (3). Another negation-invariant verb is *kontrollieren ob* 'check'. However, it is not compatible with WEC since tautologies and contradictions representing constant truth functions are not meant to be checked with respect to changing truth values.

Wissen, beweisen, widerlegen, kontrollieren, and *fragen* all satisfy:

(13) **Definition: *Witness Independence Condition (WIC)***
If *X verb dass/ob* σ and (*Y verb dass/ob* τ $\vee$ *Y verb dass/ob* $\neg\tau$) and if σ and τ have the same truth value, then *Y verb dass/ob* τ.

Believe, for instance, need not fulfill WIC, even if σ and τ coincide. It is just an exercise to show:

(14) *WIC* $\leftrightarrow$ *semi-implicative* $\vee$ *anti-semi-implicative* $\vee$ *negation-invariant*, the three alternatives excluding each other.

For the purpose of illustration, we show that any negation-invariant verb satisfies WIC: Because of the negation invariance of the verb, the part (*Y verb dass/ob* τ $\vee$ *Y verb dass/ob* $\neg\tau$) of the assumption is already logically equivalent to the assertion *Y verb dass/ob* τ to be proved.

Wissen dass being semi-implicative and *fragen ob* being negation-invariant submit to WIC. *Bedauern dass, glauben dass, denken dass* 'think' and *zweifeln dass* do not always satisfy WIC, they are only compatible with it, i.e. *bedauern dass, glauben dass* and *denken dass* are compatible with semi-implicativity, and *zweifeln dass* is compatible with negation-invariance.

3 Conditions for the *ob*-Form for *dass*-Verbs

What are the precise conditions for a predicate allowing the *dass*-form also to allow the *ob*-form, and how can the *ob*-form be expressed by the *dass*-form? Recall that *dass*-predicates allowing the *ob*-form are *wissen dass, sagen dass,* and *zweifeln dass* – cf. (1b) and (3b). The predicates of the classes (4) and (5) forbid the *ob*-form both (cf. (4-5b)).

(15) **Condition for the ob-Form: Objectivity Condition**
A necessary and sufficient condition for a *dass*-predicate to have an *ob*-form is that it is *objective*. A *dass*- or *ob*-verb is objective if it is simultaneously compatible with WEC and just one of the two main alternatives in WIC, either semi-implicative or negation-invariant, i.e. if it is compatible with WIC & WEC.

This condition entails that a negation-invariant *dass/ob*-verb is objective iff it is compatible *with $\exists X(X$ verb dass/ob $\sigma)$*, for each $\sigma \in \Phi(\Sigma)$. Objective predicates are, for example, *wissen dass,* which is compatible with semi-implicativity & WEC and *fragen ob,* which is compatible with negation-invariance &WEC. The restriction to the two main alternatives in WIC does in fact not exclude any predicates simultaneously compatible with anti-semi-implicativity and WEC, since there are no such predicates in German. *Lesen dass 'read'* and *sagen dass* are ambiguous with respect to semi-implicativity – cf. Ginzburg & Sag's (2000) *resolutive* predicates. The reason for this is that, for instance, *A sagt dass σ* can be true in a constellation where σ is not valid. Being ambiguous with respect to semi-implicativity and incompatible with negation-invariance & WEC, *sagen dass* is simultaneously compatible with just the alternative *semi-implicativity* and with WEC. Thus, it can exhibit the *ob*-form as shown in (1b).
Another ambiguous verb is *zweifeln dass* which is compatible with negation-invariant.[2] If *zweifeln dass* is negation-invariant, the following equivalence holds: *A zweifelt dass σ $\leftrightarrow$ A zweifelt ob σ* – cf. (16). Like *sagen dass, zweifeln dass* is compatible with WIC & WEC and allows the *ob*-form, as we have seen in (3b). Furthermore, it is inconsistent with *wissen dass* – cf. III in the Appendix.
Wissen dass and *fragen ob* always satisfying WIC and, being compatible with WEC, are *inherently objective,* whereas *sagen dass* and *zweifeln dass,* being ambiguous with respect to WIC, but nevertheless compatible with WIC & WEC, are *non-inherently objective.*
The meaning of the *ob*-form of an objective *dass*-predicate can be paraphrased as follows:

(16) **Meaning of the ob-form of an objective dass-verb**
X verb ob σ $\leftrightarrow$ (X verb dass σ $\vee$ X verb dass $\neg\sigma$),
where for any ambiguously semi-implicative *dass*-verb and any particular *X* and σ, the validity of *X verb dass σ $\rightarrow\sigma$* is taken for granted.

Thus, *Maria told us whether Pauline was coming* does not only mean *Maria told us that Pauline was coming or Maria told us that Pauline was not coming,* but even *if Pauline was coming, Maria told us that Pauline was coming and Maria did not tell us that Pauline was not coming* and *if Pauline was not coming, Maria told us that Pauline was not coming and Maria did not tell us that Pauline was coming.*[3]

---

[2] Cf. Fischer's (2003) stronger claim that *Paul zweifelt ob p $\leftrightarrow$ Paul zweifelt dass p und Paul zweifelt, dass $\neg p$.* For Fischer, *zweifeln dass* is inherently negation-invariant, to use our terminology. He justifies Paul's bias towards Paul's belief that $\neg p$ pragmatically.

[3] Cf. Hintikka (1976), Karttunen (1977) and Groenendijk & Stokhof (1982) who argue that *if p and A says whether p, then A says p* and *if $\neg p$ and A says whether p, then A says $\neg p$.*

Unlike *wissen, fragen, zweifeln,* and *sagen,* the predicates *bedauern, beweisen,* and *widerlegen* are not objective. *Bedauern* is incompatible with WEC, since *X bedauert dass σ* only holds for contingent *σ*'s.[4] *Beweisen* and *widerlegen,* being semi-implicative or anti-semi-implicative, respectively, are incompatible with WEC – cf. the remarks on (8). *Annehmen, überrascht sein, glauben,* and *hoffen* are compatible with WIC and with WEC separately, but they are not compatible with WEC and WIC simultaneously, they are not compatible with WIC & WEC. And finally, *kontrollieren* is negation-invariant, but incompatible with WEC – cf. the comment below (12).

4 Verbs and *wh*-Form

4.1 Wh-Form of Objective Predicates

As to objective predicates, they exhibit the *wh*-form if they fulfil the following condition:

(17) **Wh-form Condition for Objective Verbs**
Any objective *verb dass/ob* allows a well-formed *wh*-form *wh(A, verb, σ)* if and only if it is consistent with *wissen dass.*

This condition is met by *wissen, sagen,* and *fragen,* but not by *zweifeln* – cf. (1-2c) vs. (3c).

The meaning of *wh*-forms with predicates such as *wissen, sagen* and *fragen* can be paraphrased as follows:

(18) **Meaning of the wh-form of objective verbs**
$wh(Y, verb, σ) ↔ ∀x (Y \; verb \; ob \; σ(x))$,
i.e. for an objective *dass*-verb
$wh(Y, verb, σ) ↔ ∀x [Y \; verb \; dass \; σ(x) ∨ Y \; verb \; dass \; ¬σ(x)]$,
where $∀x (Y \; verb \; dass \; σ(x) → σ(x))$ is granted in the ambiguously semi- implicative case.

This means in particular that if *Frank says who is coming* is valid, what he says is true.

4.2 *Wh*-Form of Non-objective Predicates

The examples in (19) illustrate *wh*-forms of non-objective verbs.

(19) a. *Frank ist darüber überrascht, wer kommt.*
Frank is *da-cor*   surprised who is coming.
b. *Frank kontrolliert es,   wer kommt.*
Frank checks   *es-cor* who is coming

The explanatory paraphrases of these *wh*-forms deviate distinctly from the paraphrase of *wh*-forms of objective verbs. Unlike the *wh*-forms with *fragen* or *wissen,* the

---

[4] A statement *σ* is contingent if there is a constellation where *σ* is valid and another one where it is invalid.

wh-forms of *überrascht sein* or *kontrollieren* cannot be paraphrased as in (18) i.e. by *for all x, Frank is surprised that x is coming or Frank is surprised that x is not coming* or *for all x, Frank checks whether x is coming,* since these paraphrases do not reflect the intended meaning. The intended meaning of (19) is, for instance, *Frank is surprised at the fact that only women are coming* or *Frank checks whether only women are coming.* That is, the sentence relates to a specific statement or answer μ the choice of which is determined by the context. We call this statement *specification.* (19 a,b) not explicitly exhibiting their specifications *only women are coming* are semantically underdetermined versions of statements such as *Frank is surprised at that only women are coming,* i.e. *A verb da-cor dass μ,* or *Frank checks whether only women are coming,* i.e. *A verb es-cor ob μ.* Other examples are *Frank bedauert es / glaubt es, wer kommt* 'Frank regrets it/believes it who is coming'.

With regard to well-formed *wh*-forms of non-objective verbs, three points turn out to be important. First, the non-objective *dass-* or *ob*-predicate needs an appropriate correlate, either a *da*-correlate (*da*-cor) or an *es*-correlate (*es*-cor), which relates to the contextually given specification. Second, without its correlate, the non-objective predicate has to satisfy particular consistency conditions concerning the embedded clause. And third, without its correlate, the non-objective predicate must not be semi-implicative or anti-semi-implicative. The last point explains why *beweisen dass* or *widerlegen dass* do not have a *wh*-form. The second issue concerns the fact that, for instance, the non-objective predicates *es annehmen dass* 'assume', *es denken dass* 'think', *es/daran glauben dass* 'believe (it/in)' and *es/darauf hoffen dass* 'hope it/for', cannot construe the *wh*-form despite exhibiting a correlate – cf. **Frank nimmt es an, wer kommt* 'Frank assumes es-cor who is coming', **Frank denkt es, wer kommt* 'Frank thinks es-cor who is coming', **Frank glaubt es/daran, wer kommt* 'Frank believes es/da-cor who is coming' and **Frank nimmt hofft es/darauf, wer kommt* 'Frank hopes es/da-cor who is coming'. The reason for their behavior is, as will be shown in (20-24), that *es annehmen dass, es denken dass, es glauben dass,* and *es hoffen dass* do not entail the validity of their embedded statement, and that *daran glauben dass* and *darauf hoffen dass* do not entail that the embedded statement follows from what the subject knows – cf. IV and V in the Appendix.

(20) **Consistency conditions** *to allow the wh-form for non-objective dass/ob-verbs with optional es- or da-correlates*

    a.   For a non-objective *dass*-verb, the *wh*-form with an **es**-cor is well-formed iff

        i.   it is neither semi-implicative nor anti-semi-implicative

    and

        ii.   *A verb dass σ entails σ is consistent*
            or
        iii.   *A verb dass σ entails σ is valid $\vee$*
             σ does not follow from what A knows

    b.   For a non-objective *ob*-verb, the *wh*-form with an *es-cor* is well-formed without any restrictions.

    c.   For a non-objective *dass*-verb, the *wh*-form *with da-cor* is well-formed iff

iv. *A verb dass σ* entails *σ is consistent with what A knows*
or

v. *A verb dass σ* entails *σ is not tautological* ∨
σ follows from what A knows

As shown in IV in the Appendix, *bedauern dass* fulfils *i* and *ii*, *überrascht sein* fulfils *iv*, and *denken* fulfils *v*. However, predicates like *beweisen dass*, *widerlegen dass*, *annehmen dass*, and *hoffen dass*, which do not exhibit the appropriate consistency conditions, do not have a *wh*-form with their correlates – cf. V in the Appendix.

The correlates induce two remarkable modifications of the original meaning of a non-objective, non-negation-invariant *dass*-verb:[5]

(21) **Semantic impact of the es-correlate**
      If *i* and *ii* or *i* and *iii*, then
      a. *A verb es-cor dass σ* means *A verb dass σ & σ is valid*
          and
      b. *A es-cor nicht verb dass σ* means *¬A verb dass σ & σ is valid.*

Any predicate *verb **es-cor** dass* satisfying (21) is called *factive* – cf. e.g. Kiparsky & Kiparsky (1970). Factivity obviously implies semi-implicativity. As to non-objective *ob*-verbs like *kontrollieren* 'check', the *es*-correlate does not change the original meaning of *A verb ob σ* – cf. (19b) and (20b).

(22) **Semantic impact of the da-correlate**
      If *iv* or *v*, then
      a. *A verb da-cor dass σ* means
          A verb dass σ & σ follows from what A knows
          and
      b. *A da-cor nicht verb dass σ* means
          ¬A verb dass σ & σ follows from what A knows.

Any predicate *verb da-cor dass* satisfying (22) is called *cognitive*. Cognitivity obviously implies factivity.

We can summarise the behaviour of non-objective *dass*-verbs with respect to construing their *wh*-form by the following condition:

(23) **Wh-Form Condition for non-Objective Verbs**
      A non-objective *dass/ob*-verb has a well-formed *wh*-form iff it has an *es*- or a *da*-correlate and fulfils the respective consistency statement in (20). This in its turn corresponds to the factivity of the *es-cor verb dass* or the cognitivity of the *da-cor verb dass*, respectively.

As to the meaning of the *wh*-form of a non-objective predicate, it can be summarised as follows:

---

[5] Which correlate type is licensed by which predicate is the subject of Schwabe & Fittler (forthcoming).

(24) ***Meaning of the wh-form of non-objective verbs***

    a.   The *wh*-form *wh*(A, *es-cor*, (not) *pred dass*, σ) means
               A (not) *pred dass* μ & μ is valid;

    b.   The *wh*-form *wh*(A, *da-cor*, (not) *pred dass*, σ) means
               A (not) *pred dass* μ & μ follows from what A knows;
               where μ is the contextually given specification.

5   Conclusion

The main issue of our paper was to describe the precise conditions under which German propositional verbs embed interrogatives. First we investigated predicates not exhibiting their correlates such as *wissen dass* or *zweifeln dass* which embed declaratives, with respect to their ability to embed also *ob*-interrogatives and with respect to their ability to embed *wh*-interrogatives without correlates. Second, we investigated predicates like *überrascht sein dass* or *kontrollieren ob* which do not embed *wh*-interrogatives without correlates, with respect to their ability to embed *wh*-interrogatives with correlates.

I) A *dass*-verb has an *ob*-form if and only if it is *objective*, i.e., if it satisfies the *Objectivity Condition* (15) saying that the verb has to be compatible with WEC and just one of the first two alternatives of WIC simultaneously. WIC actually means that the verb is either semi-implicative or negation-invariant or anti-semi-implicative (13) and WEC demands that for all σ, there exists an *X* with *X verb dass/ob* σ or *X verb dass/ob* ¬σ (8). Since there are no German propositional verbs which are simultaneously compatible with WEC and anti-semi-implicativity, the latter condition is omitted in the Objectivity Condition.

Ambiguous objective verbs such as *sagen dass* and *zweifeln dass* are, like *wissen dass* and *fragen ob*, compatible with WEC. But unlike *wissen dass* and *fragen ob*, they are only compatible with WIC, i.e. they need not satisfy WIC in every constellation. However, they are simultaneously compatible with just the appropriate main alternative of WIC and with WEC. Thus they are objective, although not *inherently objective*.

The distinction between objective and non-objective verbs makes *ad hoc* explanations for the impossibility of the *ob*-form of *dass*-verbs like *bedauern* or *überrascht sein* unnecessary – cf. for instance, d'Avis' (2002) or Abels' (2007) approaches.

II) An objective predicate has a well-formed *wh*-form without correlate if it satisfies the *wh-Form Condition for Objective Verbs* (17) saying that any objective *dass/ob*-predicate has such a well-formed *wh*-form *wh*(A, *verb*, σ) if and only if it is consistent with *wissen dass*. The *wh*-form *wh*(Y, *verb*, σ) means ∀x(Y *verb ob* σ (x)).

III) A non-objective predicate has a well-formed *wh*-form if it obeys the *Wh-Form Condition for non-Objective Verbs* (23). It demands that the wh-form contains a *da*- or an *es*-correlate and that the non-objective *dass*-predicate meets particular consistency conditions (20). Under these conditions, it has turned out that using an *es*- or *da*-correlate modifies the meaning of a non-negation-invariant non-objective *dass*-verb distinctly in that an *es*-correlate makes it *factive* and the *da*-correlate makes it *cognitive* – cf. (23) and (24).

IV) The meaning of the *wh*-form *wh*(Y, *da /es-cor*, *pred dass*, σ) of non-objective predicates is semantically underspecified since its meaning *Y verb da/es-cor dass/ob* μ is determined by a specification μ which is contextually given and not determined by the *wh*-form *wh*(Y, *da /es-cor*, *pred dass*, σ) alone.

References

1. Abels, K.: Deriving selectional properties of 'exclamative' predicates. In: Spaeth, A. (ed.) Interface and interface conditions, pp. 115–140. Mouton de Gruyter, Berlin (2007)
2. d'Avis, F.-J.: On the interpretation of wh-clauses in exclamative environments. Theoretical Linguistics 28/1, 5–32 (2002)
3. Asher, N.: Reference to abstract objects in discourse. Kluwer, Dordrecht (1993)
4. Dipper, S.: Zur Selektion von Fragesatzkomplementen (Arbeitspapiere des SFB 340 Sprachtheoretische Grundlagen der Computerlinguistik 122) (1997)
5. Fischer, M.: Ein Zweifelsfall: zweifeln im Deutschen. Linguistische Berichte 202, 127–169 (2003)
6. Ginzburg, J., Sag, I.A.: Interrogative Investigations: The Form, Mea¬ning, and Use of English Interrogatives. CSLI Publications, Stanford (2000)
7. Groenendijk, J., Stokhof, M.: Semantic Analysis of WH-Complements. Linguistics and Philosophy 5, 175–233 (1982)
8. Groenendijk, J., Stokhof, M.: Questions. In: van Benthem, J., ter Meulen, A. (eds.) Handbook of Logic and Language, pp. 1055–1124. Elsevier and MIT Press, Amsterdam and Cambridge, MA and North Holland, Amsterdam (1997)
9. Hintikka, J.: The semantics of questions and the questions of semantics (vol. 28.4 of Acta Philosophica Fennica. Amsterdam and New Holland) (1976)
10. Karttunen, L.: Syntax and semantics of questions. Linguistics and Philosophy 1, 3–44 (1977)
11. Kiparsky, P., Kiparsky, C.: Fact. In: Bierwisch, M., Heidolph, K.E. (eds.) Progress in Linguistics, pp. 143–173. Mouton, The Hague (1970)
12. Krifka, M.: Syntax und Semantik von Fragen und Antworten. Retrieved August 2007, from Humboldt U Berlin, Institute for Linguistics (2005), http://amor.rz.hu-berlin.de
13. Vendler, Z.: Telling the Facts. In: Searle, J.R., Kiefer, F., Bierwisch, M. (eds.) Speech Act Theory and Pragmatics, pp. 273–290. Reidel, Dordrecht (1980)
14. Zifonun, G., Hoffmann, L., Strecker, B.: Grammatik der deutschen Spra¬che. Walter de Gruyter, Berlin (1997)

Appendix:

Objective predicates:

I **wissen** *dass* 'know'

A:[6] *X weiß dass σ → σ is valid*, i.e. semi-implicative

C: compatible with WIC & WEC, inherently objective, *ob*- and *wh*-form

lesen *dass* 'read'

A: WEC → *lesen dass* is not anti-semi-implicative,

WEC → *lesen dass* is not negation-invariant

C: compatible with semi-implicative, compatible with WIC & WEC, objective, but not inherently objective, *ob*-form, consistent with *wissen dass*, *wh*-form

sagen *dass* 'say' see *lesen dass*

II **fragen** *ob* 'ask'

A: *X fragt ob σ ↔ X fragt ob ¬σ*

C: negation-invariant, compatible with WIC & WEC, inherently objective, consistent with *wissen dass*, *wh*-form

III *zweifeln* *dass* 'doubt'

A: WEC → *zweifeln dass is not (anti-)semi-implicative*,

X zweifelt dass σ → ¬X weiß dass σ

C: compatible with negation-invariant, compatible with WIC & WEC, objective, but not inherently objective, not consistent with *wissen dass*, no *wh*-form

Non-objective predicates:

IV **bedauern** [*es*] *dass* 'regret'

A: *X bedauert dass σ → σ is contingent,*

incompatible with WEC

C: not objective, no *ob*-form, axioms imply factivity in connection with *es*, *wh*-form with *es*

überrascht sein [*darüber*] *dass* 'be surprised'

A: *X ist überrascht dass σ → σ is consistent with what X knows,*

incompatible with WIC & WEC

C: not objective, no *ob*-form, axioms imply cognitivity in connection with *darüber*, *wh*-form with *darüber*

denken [*es/daran*] *dass* 'think'

A: *X denkt dass σ → (σ is not tautological ∨ σ follows from what X knows)*,

incompatible with WIC & WEC

C: not objective, no *ob*-form, axioms imply cognitivity in connection with *daran*, but do not imply factivity in connection with *es*, *wh*-form with *daran*, no *wh*-form with *es*.

---

[6] A = axiom, C = comment.

V annehmen [*es*] *dass* 'assume'

A: *X nimmt an dass σ → σ is not tautological,*
incompatible with WIC & WEC

C: not objective, no *ob*-form, axiom does not imply factivity in connection
with *es*, no *wh*-form with *es*

glauben [*es/daran*] *dass* 'believe'

A: *X glaubt dass → (σ is not tautological ∨ σ is consistent with what X
knows),* incompatible with WIC & WEC

C: not objective, no *ob*-form, axioms do not imply factivity in connection with
es or cognitivity in connection with *daran,* no *wh*-form with *es,* no *wh*-form
with *daran.*

hoffen [*es/darauf*] *dass* 'hope'

A: *X hofft dass σ → (σ is contingent ∨ σ does not follow from what X knows),*
incompatible with WIC & WEC

C: not objective, no *ob*-form, axioms do neither imply factivity nor cognitivity
in connection with *es* or *darauf,* no *wh*-form with *es* or *darauf*

beweisen [*es*] *dass* 'prove'

A: *X beweist dass σ → σ is valid,* i.e. semi-implicative,
incompatible with WEC,

C: not objective, no *ob*-form, no *wh*-form with *es*

widerlegen [*es*] *dass* 'refute'

A: *X widerlegt dass σ → σ is invalid,* i.e. anti-semi-implicative,
incompatible with WEC

C: not objective, no *ob*-form, no *wh*-form with *es*

VI kontrollieren [*es*] *ob* 'check'

A: *X kontrolliert ob σ ↔ X kontrolliert ob ¬σ,* i.e. *negation-invariant*
incompatible with WEC

C: not objective, *es, wh*-form with *es*

Processing Definite Determiners: Formal Semantics Meets Experimental Results

Peter Bosch

Institute of Cognitive Science
University of Osnabrück, D-49069 Osnabrück, Germany
pbosch@uos.de

Abstract. Experiments on the online processing of linguistic utterances provide information about language processing in the first instance, and only indirectly about linguistic knowledge, while it has been linguistic knowledge, and not linguistic processing, that has been the subject matter of theoretical linguistics. So how can such evidence be relevant to theoretical linguistics? Or how can linguistic theory inform a theory of language processing? – This issue is discussed here with respect to the processing and the formal semantics of the English definite determiner. I argue that the meaning of the definite determiner, as it shows up in experiments on online comprehension, can actually be accounted for in an incremental variant of current formal semantics.

Keywords: Definite determiner, domain restrictions, formal semantics, incremental processing, psycholinguistics, eye-tracking.

1 Linguistic Knowledge and Language Processing

Theoretical linguistics investigates the native speaker's implicit *knowledge of the language*. This includes not only phonology, morphology, syntax, and compositional semantics, but also the systematic and equally implicit knowledge the speaker has of *using* linguistic expressions appropriately in a context or situation. Linguistic knowledge in this sense is characterized in abstract algebraic terms, very much as in the theory of formal languages. Questions relating to how linguistic knowledge is *implemented* in human behaviour or in the human brain, on the other hand, are not part of theoretical linguistics, but belong to a theory of linguistic processing, i.e., to neurolinguistics or psycholinguistics.

What, then, is the relation between linguistic knowledge and linguistic processing? I don't think that we have a very good answer yet. But one fairly simple way of relating linguistic knowledge to linguistic processing is in assuming that the linguistic knowledge provides *constraints* on processes of comprehension and production. In some cases, all other things being equal, these constraints may provide for empirical predictions regarding the time course and output of linguistic processing. Linguistic theory thus may inform a theory of language processing, and observations about language processing may inform linguistic theory, i.e., support or disconfirm its predictions.

P. Bosch, D. Gabelaia, and J. Lang (Eds.): TbiLLC 2007, LNAI 5422, pp. 242–256, 2009.

In the following I will look at some experimental results concerning the processing of definite determiners and attempt to relate these results to what theoretical linguistics has to say about the definite determiner. In Section 3, I will discuss a proposal for how current semantic formalism may be used to describe incremental comprehension processes. Also here the issue is the meaning and processing of the definite determiner.

2 Some Findings from Experimental Work: Immediacy, Incrementality, and Crossmodality

In this section I want to review some experimental results about linguistic comprehension and, on the side, as it were, introduce three processing properties that are now widely accepted as properties of human natural language comprehension and that constitute a certain challenge to linguistic theory: immediacy, incrementality, and crossmodality.

By *immediacy* I mean the observation that all information that becomes available to the language processor is in principle used immediately in the comprehension process and thus may show immediate effects. By *incrementality* I mean the observation that information that has already been acquired in the ongoing comprehension process is used to control later processing steps. And by *crossmodality* I mean the observation that linguistic processing happens in tandem with non-linguistic processing steps, which may guide or be guided by the linguistic processing. These ideas about linguistic processing have entered psycholinguists in the 1980s (cf. Marslen-Wilson & Tyler 1980, Garfield 1987, Altmann & Steedman 1988) and are now shared by a broad community of researchers (cf. Trueswell & Tanenhaus 2005, Hagoort & van Berkum 2007).

2.1 Visual World

The experimental work I want to focus on is close to what has become known as the *Visual World* paradigm (Tanenhaus e.a. 1995). Experimental subjects wear a device on their heads that makes a video recording, showing exactly what they are looking at. They listen to spoken instructions or stories and carry out various tasks. The eye-tracking provides evidence of the cognitive activity of subjects that can be correlated with the linguistic input. A methodologically essential point is that eye movement in this set-up is spontaneous and not under the subject's conscious control. Subjects' reflection or intuition on meaning do not interfere.

In a typical Visual World experiment about lexical access for instance (e.g., Allopenna e.a. 1998) participants view a panel with four drawings of simple objects, such as, for instance, a beetle, a beaker, a speaker, and a dolphin, and they listen to instructions as in (1).

(1)   Pick up the {beetle, beaker, speaker, dolphin}.

Participants focus the target object more frequently than its competitors already before the target noun is completed, unless the word is similar to a word that would be the default name for one of the competing objects in the display. For instance., when the instruction uses the word *beetle* and both a beetle and a beaker are present, participants' focussing frequency for both objects is initially similar and the difference starts to show only after the word's offset. In brief: focussing reacts as soon as there is enough information.

We conducted an experiment in a slightly more natural setting, where subjects were not choosing from a small set of separately depicted referents, but where they listened to short stories while they were viewing a picture of a related semi-natural scene (Karabanov e.a. 2007). While subjects heard a story as in (2), they would be shown a picture as in Figure 1.

(2)   Heute ist Markt im Dorf. Die Marktfrau streitet sich mit dem Arbeiter. Sie sagt jetzt gerade, dass er ihr nun das neue Fahrrad zurückgeben soll, das er sich geliehen hat.
'It's market day in the village. The market woman is quibbling with the worker. She's just saying that he should give the new bike back that he has borrowed.'

Subjects' focussing probability for the referents of the referential expressions in the story (full lexical NPs as well as pronouns in our example) regularly started to increase immediately, already while the referential expression was heard, and reached a peak within about one second.

Fig. 1. Display from Karabanov e.a. (2007)

This is not what linguistic theory would make us expect. If we took theoretical linguistic accounts straightforwardly as accounts of processing, what should happen would be rather something like a purely linguistic bottom-up process: lexical access would be performed word by word and the morphological, syntactic, and semantic properties of each lexical item would be retrieved from the mental lexicon. Once the end of a sentence is reached, parsing could start and the string of expressions would be assigned a constituent structure, which would determine, among other things, which expressions may count as referential constituents, so that on the basis of their lexical meaning and anaphoric status subjects could then assign to these expressions referents in the picture. The last step would then be reflected in the focussing frequency for these referents.

What we find experimentally is quite different: subjects process incoming referential expressions immediately with regard to the referential domain, here the visual domain. This also holds for pronouns, which are referentially resolved immediately when they are heard (cf. Eisenband e.a. 2000). This requires not only that the linguistic information is used as soon as it is available, but also that the visual input, and possibly other relevant sources of knowledge, are used immediately in the comprehension process.

The various sources of non-linguistic and contextual knowledge, together with what has already been understood, may occasionally be strong enough to predict referents of expressions that have not yet occurred in the acoustic input – just as in everyday life where we are often able to complete a sentence that somebody else started. In Example (2) for instance we found that the focussing probability for the worker in the display started to increase already at the time the word *streitet* was heard – presumably, because subjects "understand" at this point that the market woman is said to quibble with somebody; and since there is only one other person in the picture, the expected prepositional object expression is likely to refer to him. The German verb *streitet* 'quibbles' is commonly used in constructions like *(sich) mit jemandem (über etwas) streiten* 'to quibble with somebody (over something)', where the verb may either be construed reflexively or not. In either case linguistic knowledge predicts a referential expression for the person to quibble with to occur soon after the verb. The early increase of focussing on the worker would indicate that already when the verb is understood the corresponding interpretation is expected. These observations about anticipation are well supported by earlier experiments by Altmann & Kamide (1999) and Boland (2005).

2.2 Determiner Gender

The example just discussed shows that at least some grammatical and semantic information from the lexicon is used immediately in conjunction with visual information to predict referential interpretations for expressions still to come. But one may wonder if this applies also to more abstract grammatical features, such as gender or number, or definiteness. We will look at an experiment about determiner gender first.

2.2.1 German Determiner Gender
Hartmann (2004) investigated the role of determiner gender in a Visual World experiment. Subjects were viewing displays as in Figure 2 while they heard instructions as in (3).

(3)   Klicken Sie auf {das$_{[neut]}$ gelbe$_{[neut]}$ Hufeisen$_{[neut]}$ / die$_{[fem]}$ gelbe$_{[fem]}$
         Giraffe$_{[fem]}$ / die$_{[fem]}$ gelbe$_{[fem]}$ Rakete$_{[fem]}$ / den$_{[masc]}$ blauen$_{[masc]}$
         Stern$_{[masc]}$ }
         'Click on {the yellow horseshoe / the yellow giraffe / the yellow rocket /
         the blue star}'

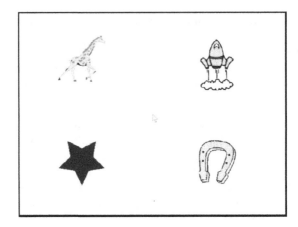

Fig. 2. Display with a yellow giraffe, a yellow rocket, a blue star, and a yellow horseshoe

German nouns come in one of three genders, masculine, feminine, or neuter, which represent a purely formal and semantically unpredictable noun classification, except when the genders correspond to the natural gender of persons. Determiners as well as adjectives agree in gender with their noun heads. Thus in instructions like (3), presented with Figure 2, already the determiner would exclude some of the objects as potential referents for the unfolding Determiner Phrase (DP), and the adjective with the additional information on colour would lead to further exclusions. For the four instructions in (3) the referential options would hypothetically develop as follows:

(a) Klicken Sie auf die$_{[fem]}$ gelbe$_{[fem]}$ Giraffe$_{[fem]}$
   die – excludes star and horseshoe; *gelbe* – leads to no further exclusions; *Giraffe* – estabishes the referent.
(b) Klicken Sie auf die$_{[fem]}$ gelbe$_{[fem]}$ Rakete$_{[fem]}$
   die – excludes star and horseshoe; *gelbe* – leads to no further exclusions; *Rakete* – estabishes the referent.
(c) Klicken Sie auf den$_{[masc]}$ blauen$_{[masc]}$ Stern$_{[masc]}$
   den – excludes all competitors; unique reference is established before the adjective or the noun have occurred
(d) Klicken Sie auf das$_{[neut]}$ gelbe$_{[neut]}$ Hufeisen$_{[neut]}$
   das – excludes all competitors; unique reference is established before the adjective or the noun have occurred

Hartmann's results support this hypothetical selection process. Figure 3 shows the focussing probabilities over time for a condition in which there was one competitor with the same colour and gender as the target, plus two other competitors that are not of the same gender but of the same colour as the target (the graph shows the average focussings for the latter two referents). There is no significant difference in focussing probability for different referents during the hearing of the determiner. This would in fact not even be possible, because it takes about 200 ms to initiate a saccade and the determiners took just under 200 ms. Very soon after the determiner offset, and before the adjective could have had any influence on the saccades, at around 300 ms from the determiner onset (and 100 ms after adjective onset) we can observe a clear increase in focussing frequency for both the target and the gender-congruent referent, not though for the other competitors. The final differentiation, between the target on the one hand, and the gender- and colour-matching competitor on the other, becomes significant in the focussing probabilities only after the noun is recognized, at about 200 ms after the noun onset.

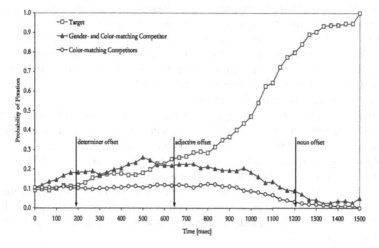

Fig. 3. Focussing probability over time for *den blauen Stern* in view of a display with one gender- and colour-matching competitor (e.g., *den blauen Hut*) and two colour-matching competitors (e.g., *die blaue Rakete, das blaue Hufeisen*)

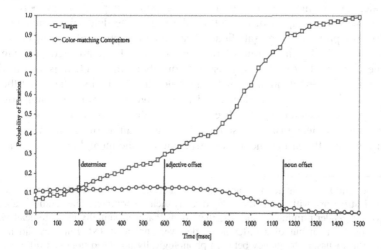

Fig. 4. Focussing probability over time for *den blauen Stern* when the display show no gender-matching competitors (e.g., *die blaue Rakete, das blaue Hufeisen, die blaue Giraffe*)

In a condition where there are no gender-matching competitors (like (c) and (d) above) subjects seem to have decided on the target already at the time of processing the determiner. A difference in focussing frequency shows up around the time of determiner offset Figure 4[1].

2.2.2 Determiner Meaning

What do these experiments tell us about the meaning of the determiner? It may seem odd to link the gender feature to questions of meaning. After all German gender has no semantic content and merely reflects an abstract classification of nouns. But we saw that the determiner may select a referent for the DP already when no other part of the DP is known, and referent selection is a matter of semantics, if anything is. Still, linguistic theory would not attribute a referential function to determiners. What the experiment shows, however, is that – given suitable conditions – determiners can sometimes do the full job that referential expressions do.

This points to a gap in the theory: as long as we cannot say what those "suitable conditions" are, we cannot link our linguistic generalization to our observations. A linguistic theory that bluntly says that determiners are not referential expressions is obviously wrong in view of what we saw in Hartmann's experiment. – What are we to do? Withdraw our statement about referential expressions and determiners?

Let us think about where the gap is that needs to be bridged. Frege models the denotation of the determiner as a partial function, defined for a domain in which the NP denotes a singleton. In a modern formulation from Heim & Kratzer (1998:75,85) this read as in (4):

(4) $\qquad \lambda f : f \in D_{\langle e,t \rangle} \& \exists![xf(x)].\iota y[f(y)=1]_{\langle\langle e,t\rangle,e\rangle}$

In plain English: for any predicate f that denotes a singleton, the unique thing y that is f. The idea of making the definition of the function depend on properties of the domain to which it is applied, i.e., letting the use of the determiner presuppose that these domain properties are satisfied, opens up the option of taking context into account. Accordingly, the notion of referentiality can be relativized to assumptions about the context. In (4) the only assumption about the context is in the domain condition, i.e., that the denotation of f is a singleton. We shall see later that the use of domain conditions can be broadened and may provide one way of doing something about the gap between theory and observation. We shall return to this point.

For the moment let's just suppose that (4) is the meaning of the definite determiner and that it is actually part of the determiner's entry in the mental lexicon. As long as f,

---

[1] Dahan e.a. (2000) investigated the same question as Hartmann for French definite determiners, but used instructions with nouns following directly their determiners, They could establish clear evidence for gender priming by showing that nouns that were initially phonologically identical with the target noun but of a different gender were not activated. But they did not find a difference in focussing frequency between phonologically unrelated nouns of different gender, at least not within the first 200 ms after noun onset. At the time when the difference becomes significant, however, the effect may be attributed either to the preceding determiner or to the noun itself. Hartmann's experiment resolved this indeterminacy by inserting between the determiner and the noun an adjective that adds no disambiguating information but pulls the effect of the determiner and the noun apart.

i.e. the denotation of the nominal, is not known, the determiner thus *could not* have any processing effect. Hartmann's experiment seems to demonstrate the contrary. – But then one of our assumptions may be wrong: who says that the denotation of the following nominal is not known? It is clearly not known from the linguistic input at this time, but utterance comprehension is *crossmodal* and takes in also the visual information. The instruction *Klicken Sie auf...* 'click on...', uttered in view of a display as in Figure 2, limits the choice of referents for the following determiner phrase to four objects, and linguistic experience provides default nouns (i.e. basic level common nouns that are most frequently used for naming the relevant objects) for these objects. For a display as in Figure 2 and an instruction like (c) or (d) only one of these nouns happens to be gender-congruent with the determiner. – So the knowledge active in the processor after hearing the determiner *den* is this:

(i)   an entry in the mental lexicon that makes the noun $Stern_{[masc]}$ the default description for $[\![star]\!]$ instances,

(ii)   the identification of exactly one display object as an instance of $[\![star]\!]$,

(iii) the subsumption of the remaining display objects under concepts with non-gender-congruent default nouns, such as $Giraffe_{[fem]}$, $Rakete_{[fem]}$, and $Hufeisen_{[neut]}$

(iv)   a lexical entry for the denotation $[\![den]\!]$ that also includes gender information: $\lambda f{:}f \in D_{\langle e,t\rangle}\,\&\,\exists!x\ (f(x)\ \&\ g(x,\text{masc}))\ .\ \iota y\ f(y)$ [2]

None of (i) – (iii) is strictly speaking *linguistic knowledge*. (ii) and (iii) represent purely contingent contextual knowledge, and (i) is knowledge about preferences of lexical usage in a language community, i.e., with no change in the semantics of *Stern*, there could still be another noun that German speakers would prefer, or that comes to their minds first, when they recognize the object in the display. So the only piece of linguistic knowledge proper that is involved in the effect of determiner gender on referent identification is the lexical entry in (iv).

There is still a certain complication that comes from the syncretism of German determiner forms. The form *den* in its function as a determiner, is ambiguous between four grammatical words, with any of the following features values: [num:sg; gend:m; case:acc], [num:pl; gend:n; case:dat], [num:pl; gend:m; case:dat], [num:pl; gend:f; case:dat]. In addition we have its use as a demonstrative pronoun and as a relative pronoun; in either case the form is unambiguous: [num:sg; gend:m; case:acc]. Since in the regular understanding of *Klicken Sie auf...* only the accusative would be permitted in the continuation and we are left with a three-way ambiguity between determiner, demonstrative pronoun, and relative pronoun. Since also the relative pronoun is unlikely in this position, the realistic choice is between definite determiner and demonstrative pronoun. Since the features relevant for referent selection are identical in both cases, i.e., [num:sg; gend:m], the ambiguity that is left after applying all constraints that we find in linguistic knowledge does not affect processing.

---

[2] It would be a little sloppy to attribute gender to anything other than a linguistic expression. So let's take *g* as a function that assigns to a thing, x, the gender of the noun that is preferentially used for a description of x. But note that this brings in *linguistic experience*: The function *g* is given not as part of *knowledge of the language* but can be acquired only from linguistic experience.

In the case of the neuter accusative determiner *das* the syncretism is again limited to the ambiguity between the singular determiner, the singular demonstrative and the singular relative pronoun, so that we have the same situation as with *den*.

In the third case, the case of the accusative determiner *die*, the situation seems worse to start with, *die* boosting 12 grammatical words only in its accusative "reading". Nine of these are plural forms, however, and as such they are made less likely by the display properties: there is no plurality of objects in the display, at least not at the conceptual level of basic level common noun denotations. Still, in principle, we could have the unlikely instruction *Klicken Sie auf die Objekte im Bild, eins nach dem anderen* 'click on the objects in the display, one after the other'. Ignoring this option, we are down to the same three-way ambiguity again as already with *den* and *das*.

The point I've been trying to make is simple: in order to explain the observed focussing behaviour we require assumptions about *linguistic knowledge*, in the case at hand morphological, lexical, syntactic, and semantic knowledge, *plus* knowledge from *linguistic experience*, like naming preferences and the knowledge of basic level common nouns, *plus* knowledge of the *reference situation*, here the visual display. The formulation for the determiner denotation in (iii) includes the relevant linguistic knowledge, and with the function *g* it also includes a way of taking linguistic experience for the relevant domain into account. Still: (iii) is a representation of linguistic knowledge and is valid for the determiner *den* in any context, *pace* the ambiguity caused by its syncretism.

3 Definiteness

Let us suppose that our rough model for the role of gender information in the definite determiner, as part of the domain condition of the determiner, is correct in the sense that it helps to isolate the contribution of linguistic knowledge to the effect that Hartmann observed. Would the role of the *definiteness* feature in the determiner condition do an equally useful job in explaining how *this* feature contributes to the processing of definite DPs?

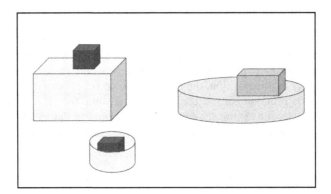

Fig. 5. A large grey block with a red cube on top, a yellow disk with a green block on top, and a red cube inside a round grey box

Suppose subjects are viewing a display as in Figure 5 while they hear an instruction like (5), with a prosody that preserves the structural ambiguity.

(5)   Put the red cube on the block on the disk.

The experiment would include the possibility to manipulate the display, e.g., by mouse action. What do we expect subjects to do? How will their focussing probability develop over the time they listen to the instruction?

3.1 A Problem for Formal Semantics

Let us start from the theory side and attempt a conventional formal semantic derivation for a sentence like (5). There are two alternative constituent structures as in (6) and (7).

(6)   put [the [red cube]] [on [the [block [on [the disk]]]]]
(7)   put [the [red [cube [on [the block]]]]] [on [the disk]]

The two constituent structures would result in formal representations that require the definite determiner function $\lambda f \in D_{<e,t>} \& \exists! x f(x) = 1. \iota y [f(y) = 1]$ to be applied to the function $\lambda z.\text{red\_cube}(z)$ in (6) and to $\lambda z.\text{block}(z)$ in (7), neither of which, with respect to the world depicted in Figure 5, satisfies the domain condition for f: the denotation of *red cube* is not a singleton – the display shows two red cubes – and for (7), there is no singleton denotation for *block* – the display shows at least two blocks. The structure in (6) seems to disqualify also intuitively, as the DP *the red cube* cannot unambiguously be assigned a referent in our display. The alternative DP, *the red cube on the block* in (7), seems intuitively fine and could be assigned an unambiguous referent. Still, also in this case the formal derivation is blocked, because the domain condition is not satisfied.

Supposing that our intuition is supported in an experiment yet to be carried out and subjects choose the interpretation corresponding to (7). How could we capture this theoretically? There are two solutions I am aware of. The first is by Nicholas Haddock (1987) and the second by Cecile Meier (2003).

The core idea of Haddock, applied to our example, is that, although the expression *the block* as such would not be unambiguous in the world of the display, listeners of (5), by the time they have reached the expression *the block*, would also know that the block must be a block on which there is a red cube. If this latter condition is added, the display in Figure 5 yields the needed singleton denotation. Haddock presents his idea in the framework of a constraint satisfaction approach and uses a store for collecting constraints, so that, in collecting constraints for the referent of the entire DP, he has already collected the constraints that the referent must be unique, must be red, a cube, must be on something, and that that something must be described as a singleton. At this point the set of potential referents, given the display, is narrowed down to the disk and the big grey block. The final word, *block*, would provide the last piece of information and the constraint set is satisfied by the red cube on top of the big grey block. – There is a problem however that does not immediately show up when constraints are collected: if the uniqueness constraint on *block* is taken seriously, the singleton reference can only be established, intuitively speaking, by saying that it is the block on top of which there is the red cube. But what red cube?

Well, presumably the one that is on top of the block, etc. – This is not entirely convincing.

The other proposal by Meier (2003) reverts to the idea that not all definites need to be used referentially, but some, in particular embedded definites as in our case *the block*, may be predicational. Meier uses an additional lexical denotation for the predicative use of the determiner that turns a property into a unique property and does not *presuppose* a unique block, but *entails* the existence of such a block. – There are indeed cases that may call for such a move, in particular when the determiner does not involve a specific but rather an arbitrary reference (or, perhaps, is not referential at all), as, e.g., in *She stood by the window* – which is not felicitously continued by *The other window was closed* (cf. Carlson e.a. 2006, Cieschinger 2006). Carlson speaks here of "weak definites", similarly Poesio (1994). In the case at hand, however, I believe that we are concerned with regular definites. Note, in particular, that the reference of *the block* may be resumed anaphorically – which should not be possible if the expression was used as a weak definite: *Pick up the red cube on the block. It must be cleared so that we can put the green block there.*

3.2 Incremental Construction

Although I don't find Haddock's solution fully convincing as it stands, his idea of an incremental construction is also pursued here, albeit with the help of conventional formal semantic representations, as we used them in modelling Hartmann's observations. Let me illustrate the method by walking step by step through an utterance of (5), i.e., *Put the red cube on the block on the disk.*

The lexicon should provide us for *put* with a denotation like (8).

(8) $\lambda x e[\lambda y e \lambda z \langle e,t \rangle.PUT(x,y,z)] \langle e, \langle e, \langle \langle e,t \rangle, t \rangle \rangle \rangle$

Assuming that in view of the experimental context the listener expects an instruction and that *put* is the first word in the instruction, an interpretation as an imperative is reasonable. We will ignore the deontic element here and simply insert the listener, *l*, as the subject:

(9) $[\lambda y_e \lambda z_{\langle e,t \rangle}.PUT(l,y,z)] \langle e, \langle \langle e,t \rangle, t \rangle \rangle$

The next word in the instruction is *the*, with a lexical denotation as in (4), i.e., $\lambda f: f \in D\langle e,t \rangle \& \exists![xf(x)].\iota y[f(y)=1] \langle \langle e,t \rangle, e \rangle$, where $f \in D\langle e,t \rangle \& \exists![xf(x)]$ is a condition on the domain of *f*: the function is defined only for predicates with a singleton denotation. The determiner thus imposes a first constraint on the denotation of the direct object expression, represented in (9) by the variable y. The string *put the* thus leads to the representation in (10). We are not claiming, though, that *put the* in any sense figures as a constituent. (10) represents only an intermediate state of the processor, which shows that the processor expects a predicate denotation to complete the information on the direct object denotation.

(10) $\lambda f: f_{\langle e,t \rangle} \& \exists!x(f(x)). \lambda z.PUT(l,\iota y.f(y),z)_{\langle \langle e,t \rangle, \langle \langle e,t \rangle, t \rangle \rangle}$

The following word, *red*, with the lexical denotation $\lambda g.RED(g)_{\langle \langle e,t \rangle, \langle e,t \rangle \rangle}$ provides such information by a constraint on a predicate g, i.e., a nominal still to come. It is added to the domain condition for f: the denotation of the direct object must not only be unique but must also be a red something.

(11) $\lambda g_{\langle e,t\rangle}\ \lambda f\!:\!f_{\langle e,t\rangle}\&\exists!x(f(x)\&g(x)\&RED(g)).$
$$\lambda z.PUT(l,\iota y.f(y),z))_{\langle\langle e,t\rangle,\langle\langle e,t\rangle,t\rangle\rangle}$$

With the next word, *cube*, with the denotation $\lambda x.CUBE(x)_{\langle e,t\rangle}$, the direct object DP could be completed. The domain of f is now restricted so that f must be of the type $\langle e,t\rangle$ and its denotation must be a singleton red cube.

(12) $\lambda f\!:\!f_{\langle e,t\rangle}\&\exists!x(f(x)\&RED(CUBE(x))).\ \lambda z.PUT(l,\iota y.f(y),z)\ _{\langle\langle e,t\rangle,t\rangle}$

But the display does not offer a unique red cube, there are two. So the DP node cannot be closed and the processor must wait for further information that could help decide between the two red cubes in the display.

The principle is probably clear by now. The representation specifies at each point in the comprehension process the "meaning" of what has already been processed by assigning a denotation to the string *as it is understood in the utterance context*, including all information available. Constituent structure enters only via the semantic type of the intermediate representation, by specifying the denotations still required in order to arrive at a complete constituent. The semantic type of (12), e.g., is $\langle\langle e,t\rangle,t\rangle$. Thus what is still required to complete the instruction is an $\langle e,t\rangle$ type denotation to fill in the third argument slot of the verb *put*. The first argument has already been fixed to the listener by the constant l and the second argument is specified as $\iota y.f(y)$, where f is restricted with respect to its domain: it must be a unique thing that is red and a cube.

The next word, *on*, with the lexical denotation $\lambda x\lambda yON(y,x))_{\langle\langle e\rangle,\langle e,t\rangle\rangle}$, starts a further constraint on the singleton that the processor is looking for by adding to the domain restriction for f and by adding the expectation that the next expression would provide a value for v, i.e., the location of x.

(13) $\lambda v.\lambda f\!:\!f_{\langle e,t\rangle}\&\exists!x(f(x)\&RED(CUBE(x))\&ON(x,v)).$
$$\lambda z.PUT(l,\iota y.f(y),z)_{\langle\langle e\rangle,\langle\langle e,t\rangle,t\rangle\rangle}$$

But this representation as it stands does not make explicit that the value for v must be an entity that has a red cube on it. The latter constraint is inferred from the domain restriction for f, and if our representation is to predict how incoming information is used, the constraint must be added as a restriction on v as in (14).

(14) $\lambda v\!:\!\exists x(RED(CUBE(x))\&ON(x,v).$
$\lambda f\!:\!f_{\langle e,t\rangle}\&\exists!x(f(x)\&RED(CUBE(x))\&ON(x,v)).$
$$\lambda z.PUT(l,\iota y.f(y),z)_{\langle\langle e\rangle,\langle\langle e,t\rangle,t\rangle\rangle}$$

The following determiner, *the*, starts a DP for the position of the prepositional object variable v in (14) and adds a uniqueness constraint for the NP denotation to come. The processor now expects an $\langle e,t\rangle$-type denotation to complete the information on the thing on which there is a red cube.

(15) $\lambda g{:}g_{\langle e,t\rangle}\&\exists!w.g(w)\&\exists x(RED(CUBE(x))\&ON(x,\imath w.g(w)).$

$\qquad \lambda f{:}f_{\langle e,t\rangle}\&\exists!x(f(x)\&RED(CUBE(x))\&ON(x,\imath u.g(u))).$

$\qquad\qquad \lambda z.PUT(l,\imath y.f(y),z)_{\langle\langle e,t\rangle,\langle\langle e,t\rangle,t\rangle\rangle}$

The next word, *block*, completes the DP, and the uniqueness condition on *g* is satisfied by the display: there is exactly one block in the display on which there is a red cube. Thus the processor can move via (16) to (17).

(16) $\lambda f{:}f_{\langle e,t\rangle}\&\exists!x(f(x)\&RED(CUBE(x))\&ON(x,\imath u.\exists v[BLOCK(u)$

$\qquad \&ON(v,u)\&RED(CUBE(v))])\ .\ \lambda z.PUT(l,\imath y.f(y),z)_{\langle\langle e,t\rangle,t\rangle}$

(17) $\lambda z.PUT(l,\imath y.RED(CUBE(y)$

$\qquad \&ON(y,\imath u.\exists v[BLOCK(u)\&ON(v,u)\&(RED(CUBE(v))],z)_{\langle\langle e,t\rangle,t\rangle}$

The trick that has given us a unique block is that the notion that *contextual denotation* for *the block* is not $\imath u.BLOCK(u)$ but rather $\imath u.\exists v[BLOCK(u)\ \&ON(v,u)$ $(RED(CUBE(v))]$. The latter has an unambiguous interpretation in the display, the former would not.

But there is also an alternative model for the unique interpretation of *the block* as follows. When the potential ambiguity of *the red cube* in (5) causes the parser not to close the current DP node, but to attach the following information to the NP, the reference resolution for the DP becomes the current task on the agenda of the comprehension process. Hence the following input must, if possible, be used immediately for this task, thus narrowing the attention to the two red cubes as alternative referents for the DP being built. If this hypothesis is correct, then already with the occurrence of the preposition *on* a decision for one of the two red cubes is preconfigured, and within the domain of attention thus created, the denotation of *the block* is indeed unique.

A Visual World experiment by Chambers e.a. (1998) strongly suggests the latter model. Using a display that included, among other things, either two containers (a can and a bowl) or just one container (a can), subjects heard instructions like *Put the cube inside the can*. In the first condition, focussing frequency for the can started to increase over the focussing frequency of the bowl between 100 and 200 ms after the onset of the noun *can*. In the condition with only the can and no other container, the saccades to the can went up already about 100 ms before the offset of *inside*, i.e., well before the determiner or the noun *can* was heard.

If the latter model is correct, we must take the preposition *on*, and the relation that it denotes, more seriously and allow $\lambda x\lambda yON(y,x))_{\langle\langle e\rangle,\langle e,t\rangle\rangle}$ to impose constraints on its argument domains. $[\![on]\!]$ would require a *location object*, i.e., the value of x (which, together with the relation $[\![on]\!]$ yields a location property) and a *located object*, the value of y. The domain for the block is thus limited to objects suited as *location objects*.

I believe that either model makes sense and that experimental work will have to decide between them. We predict on either model that there will be a significant increase in the focussing frequency for both red cubes, starting with the hearing of the word *red*. If then, starting with the word *on*, the focussing frequency for the red cube in the round box would drop and at the same time focussings would increase for the other red cube on top of the grey block, this would support the second of the above models. If on the other hand the differentiation between the focussings to the two cubes only starts with the word *block*, this would support the first model.

4 What's New, Then?

The modelling of the comprehension process proposed in this paper uses the apparatus of current formal semantics, including lexical entries and constituent structure, without modification. The representations are re-interpreted though as *representations of states of the processor*, and include all relevant information that is cross-modally available. Semantic types are procedurally re-interpreted as representing expectations of the processor. The feature that supports this re-interpretation is the lexically given domain restrictions of the various functions used: knowledge of the context enters as knowledge about the domain of our functions.

The central idea, then, is to change as little as possible in theories of linguistic knowledge and use linguistic knowledge to *constrain the theory of language processing*. Knowledge of the language is thus respected as an object of study in its own right. We don't want to deal with processing matters in the theory of linguistic knowledge, and we don't want to mistake processor properties for properties of language. - This is a strictly modular approach to linguistic processing, but it assumes strong inter-action between modules.

Acknowledgements

The experiments reviewed in this paper were conducted at our institute in Osnabrück, involving work by Nadine Hartmann, Anke Karabanov, Graham Katz, and Peter König. I am very grateful for their cooperation. I am also grateful for the invitation to present these ideas at the 7th International Symposium on Language, Logic and Information, 1-5 October, 2007, in Tbilisi, Georgia, and at the Summer School on Formal Methods in Philosophy and Linguistics, 19.-31.08, 2007 in Tartu, Estonia and for the comments that I received. I also had very helpful comments from Stefan Evert and from two anonymous reviewers for the current volume. I regret that, for mere lack of space, I could not take up, or even acknowledge, all issues raised in these comments.

References

[1] Allopenna, P., Magnuson, J.S., Tanenhaus, M.K.: Tracking the time course of spoken word recognition using eye-movements. Journal of Memory and Language 38, 419–439 (1998)
[2] Altmann, G.T.M., Kamide, Y.: Incremental interpretation at verbs: Restricting the domain of subsequent reference. Cognition 73, 247–264 (1999)
[3] Altmann, G.T.M., Steedman, M.J.: Interaction with context during human sentence processing. Cognition 30, 191–238 (1988)
[4] Boland, J.E.: Visual arguments. Cognition 95, 237–274 (2005)

[5] Chambers, C.G., Tanenhaus, M.K., Eberhard, K.M., Carlson, G.N., Filip, H.: Words and worlds: The construction of context for definite reference. In: Gernsbacher, M.A., Derry, S.J. (eds.) Proc. of the 20th Ann. Conf. of the Cognitive Science Society, pp. 220–225. Erlbaum, Mahwah (1998)

[6] Cieschinger, M.: Constraints on the Contraction of Preposition and Definite Article in German. BSc Thesis, Univ. of Osnabrück, CogSci. (2006), http://www.cogsci.uos.de/~CL/download/BSc_thesis_Cieschinger.pdf

[7] Carlson, G., Sussman, R., Klein, N., Tanenhaus, M.: Weak definite NPs. In: Davis, C., Deal, A.R., Zabbal, Y. (eds.) Proceedings of NELS 36. UMass/Amherst. GLSA/Chicago (2006)

[8] Dahan, D., Swingley, D., Tanenhaus, M.K., Magnuson, J.S.: Linguistic Gender and Spoken-Word Recognition in French. J. Mem. & Lang. 42, 465–480 (2000)

[9] Eisenband, A.J., Brown-Schmidt, S., Trueswell, J.: The Rapid Use of Gender Information. Cognition 76, B13–B26 (2000)

[10] Garfield, J.L. (ed.): Modularity in Knowledge Representation and Natural Language Understanding. MIT Press, Cambridge (1987)

[11] Haddock, N.J.: Incremental interpretation and combinatora categorial grammar. In: Proceedings of IJCAI 1987, vol. 2, pp. 661–663 (1987)

[12] Hagoort, P., van Berkum, J.: Beyond the sentence given. Philosophical Transactions of the Royal Society 362, 801–811 (2007)

[13] Hartmann, N.: Processing Grammatical Gender in German - An Eye-Tracking Study on Spoken-Word Recognition. BSc Thesis. Univ. of Osnabrück, Cognitive Science (2004), http://www.cogsci.uni-osnabrueck.de/~CL/download/Hartmann_GramGender.pdf

[14] Heim, I., Kratzer, A.: Semantics in Generative Grammar. Blackwell, Oxford (1997)

[15] Karabanov, A., Bosch, P., König, P.: Eye Tracking as a Tool to Investigate the Comprehension of Referential Expressions. In: Featherston, S., Sternefeld, W. (eds.) Roots. Linguistics in Search of its Evidential Base, pp. 207–226. Walter de Gruyter, Berlin (2007)

[16] Marslen-Wilson, W.D., Tyler, L.K.: The temporal structure of spoken language understanding. Cognition 8, 1–71 (1980)

[17] Meier, C.: Embedded Definites. In: van Rooy, R. (ed.) Proceedings of the Fourteenth Amsterdam Colloquium, pp. 163–168. ILLC, Amsterdam (2003)

[18] Poesio, M.: Weak Definites. In: Proceedings of the Fourth Conference on Semantic und Linguistic Theory. SALT-4 (1994)

[19] Tanenhaus, M.K., Spivey-Knowlton, M.-J., Eberhard, K.M., Sedivy, J.C.: Integration of visual and linguistic information in spoken language-comprehension. Science 268, 1632–1634 (1995)

[20] Trueswell, J.C., Tanenhaus, M.K. (eds.): Approaches to Studying World-Situated Language Use. MIT Press, Cambridge (2005)

Terminal Sequence Induction via Games

Clemens Kupke*

Imperial College London
180 Queen's Gate
London SW7 2AZ
ckupke@doc.ic.ac.uk

Abstract. In this paper we provide an alternative proof of a fundamental theorem by Worrell stating that the (possibly infinite) behaviour of an F-coalgebra state can be faithfully approximated by the collection of its finite, n-step behaviours, provided that $F : \mathbf{Set} \to \mathbf{Set}$ is a finitary set functor. The novelty of our work lies in our proof technique: our proof uses a certain graph game that generalizes Baltag's F-bisimilarity game. Phrased in terms of games, our main technical result is that behavioural equivalence on F-coalgebras for a finitary set functor F can be captured by a two-player graph game in which at every position a player has only finitely many moves.

1 Introduction

Coalgebras for a set functor $F : \mathbf{Set} \to \mathbf{Set}$ provide an abstract framework for studying various types of transition systems in a uniform way. In particular, coalgebras for the power set functor correspond to Kripke frames. Therefore it is natural to employ modal languages for specifying and for reasoning about coalgebras. For an overview of the theory of coalgebras and its close connection to modal logic the reader is referred to [10, 13].

Central to the theory of coalgebras is the question of when two coalgebra states should be considered to be "behaviourally equivalent". In case we are dealing with F-coalgebras for a weak pullback preserving functor, behavioural equivalence can be nicely characterized using so-called F-bisimulations. In particular, this characterization also allows for a game-theoretic treatment of behavioural equivalence via the F-bisimilarity game. This game has been first introduced by Baltag in [2] and found applications in [14] for the definition of coalgebra automata and the corresponding coalgebraic fixed-point logics.

When studying modal languages for F-coalgebras an important issue to be addressed is the question whether the language under consideration is "expressive", i.e., whether logically equivalent coalgebra states are also behaviourally equivalent. Languages that have a finitary syntax fail in general to be expressive. There are, however, finitary languages that are expressive with respect to F-coalgebras for a "finitary" set functor F (cf. e.g. [12]).

* Supported by NWO under FOCUS/BRICKS grant 642.000.502.

P. Bosch, D. Gabelaia, and J. Lang (Eds.): TbiLLC 2007, LNAI 5422, pp. 257–271, 2009.

One explanation for this expressiveness can be given by looking at a fundamental result of Worrell in [15]. Using the so-called terminal sequence of a functor one can define the n-step behaviour of a state. Worrell's result says that if the functor F under consideration is finitary, the (possibly infinite) behaviour of an F-coalgebra state can be faithfully approximated by the set of its finite n-step behaviours, i.e., two states are behaviourally equivalent iff they have the same n-step behaviour for all $n \in \mathbb{N}$. This fact is usually referred to as "terminal sequence induction" as it enables us to prove behavioural equivalence by induction along the terminal sequence.

Why does Worrell's result explain the existence of expressive languages for coalgebras for a finitary functor? The answer to this question lies in the fact that the n-step behaviour of a state can be often expressed using a single modal formula. Therefore logically equivalent coalgebra states usually also have the same n-step behaviour for all n and thus, if the functor under consideration is finitary, we can conclude by terminal sequence induction that both states are in fact behaviourally equivalent.

In this paper we are demonstrating that Worrell's result can be seen as a consequence of König's Lemma. Our proof uses a variant of the F-bisimilarity game. As noted before, the F-bisimilarity game can be used for characterizing behavioural equivalence of states only under the assumption that the functor F is weak pullback preserving. There are, however, interesting instances of coalgebras for a functor that does not preserve weak pullbacks. For example (monotone) neighbourhood frames correspond to coalgebras for such a functor. In [6] the notion of a "relational equivalence" has been proposed as a generalization of F-bisimulation.

We are going to demonstrate how relational equivalence can be captured using a two-player graph game similar to the F-bisimilarity game. This "F-relational equivalence game" will then be the key tool for our game-theoretic proof of the principle of terminal sequence induction for arbitrary finitary set functors.

2   Preliminaries

2.1   Coalgebras and the Category Set

We assume that the reader is familiar with the basic notions from category theory and with universal coalgebra. Because these notions will play a central role in this paper, we briefly recall the construction of pullbacks and pushouts in **Set**. For the general definition the reader is referred to any textbook on category theory (e.g. [1]).

Definition 1. *Let $f_1 : S_1 \to Q$ and $f_2 : S_2 \to Q$ be functions. The* pullback *of f_1 and f_2 (in **Set**) can be constructed as the triple $(\mathrm{pb}(f_1, f_2), \pi_1, \pi_2)$, where $\mathrm{pb}(f_1, f_2) := \{(s_1, s_2) \in S_1 \times S_2 \mid f_1(s_1) = f_2(s_2)\}$; and $\pi_1 : \mathrm{pb}(f_1, f_2) \to S_1$ and $\pi_2 : \mathrm{pb}(f_1, f_2) \to S_2$ are the projections. Let $Z \subseteq S_1 \times S_2$ be a relation with projections $\pi_1 : Z \to S_1$ and $\pi_2 : Z \to S_2$. We denote by $\equiv_Z$ the smallest equivalence relation on $S_1 + S_2$ that contains Z, and $(S_1 + S_2)/ \equiv_Z$ is the set of*

$\equiv_Z$-*equivalence classes. The* pushout of π_1 and π_2 in **Set** *(which we will also call the pushout of the relation* Z*) can be constructed as the triple* $(po(\pi_1, \pi_2), p_1, p_2)$, *where* $po(\pi_1, \pi_2) := (S_1 + S_2)/_{\equiv_Z}$, *and* $p_1 : S_1 \rightarrow po(\pi_1, \pi_2)$ *and* $p_2 : S_2 \rightarrow po(\pi_1, \pi_2)$ *are the obvious quotient maps.*

Relations that are pullbacks of two functions have a special shape. These relations are what is called "zigzag closed" or "z-closed" (cf. e.g. [11]).

Definition 2. *Let* $Z \subseteq S_1 \times S_2$ *be a relation. We say* Z *is* zigzag closed *if for all* $s_1, s_1' \in S_1$, *for all* $s_2, s_2' \in S_2$ *we have* $(s_1, s_2) \in Z$ & $(s_1', s_2) \in Z$ & $(s_1', s_2') \in Z$ *implies* $(s_1, s_2') \in Z$.

We will later use the fact that pullback relations are zigzag closed.

Lemma 1. *Let* $(Z, \pi_1 : Z \rightarrow S_1, \pi_2 : Z \rightarrow S_2)$ *be the pullback of two functions* $f_1 : S_1 \rightarrow Q$ *and* $f_2 : S_2 \rightarrow Q$. *Then* Z *is zigzag-closed.*

Proof. Let $s_1, s_1' \in S_1$ and $s_2, s_2' \in S_2$ such that $(s_1, s_2), (s_1', s_2), (s_1', s_2') \in Z$. Then $f_1(s_1) = f_2(s_2) = f_1(s_1') = f_2(s_2')$ and therefore $(s_1, s_2') \in Z$ which shows that Z is zigzag closed.

Let us now briefly state the definition of an F-coalgebra.

Definition 3. *Let* $F : $ **Set** $\rightarrow$ **Set** *be a functor. Then an* F-coalgebra *is a pair* $\mathbb{S} = \langle S, \sigma \rangle$ *where* S *is a set (whose elements are referred to as "states") and* $\sigma : S \rightarrow FS$ *is a function. A* pointed F-coalgebra $(\langle S, \sigma \rangle, s)$ *is an* F-coalgebra $\langle S, \sigma \rangle$ *together with a designated point* $s \in S$. *Given two* F-coalgebras, $\langle S_1, \sigma_1 \rangle$ *and* $\langle S_2, \sigma_2 \rangle$, *a function* $f : S_1 \rightarrow S_2$ *is a* coalgebra morphism *if* $F(f) \circ \sigma_1 = \sigma_2 \circ f$.

At places we will focus on so-called *finitary* set functors.

Definition 4. *A set functor* F *is called* finitary *if for all sets* X *and for all* $x \in FX$ *there exists some finite subset* $U_x \subseteq X$ *such that* $x \in Fi[FU_x]$, *where* $i : U_x \rightarrow X$ *denotes the inclusion of* U_x *into* X.

Therefore, if F is finitary, we can choose for any set X and any element $x \in FX$ a finite subset U such that $x \in Fi[FU]$.

Definition 5. *Let* F *be a finitary set functor. Given a set* X *and an element* $x \in FX$, *the* base *of* x *is defined by choosing*

$$\mathsf{B}(x) := U \quad \text{for some non-empty, finite set } U \subseteq_\omega X \text{ such that } x \in Fi[FU]$$

where $i : U \rightarrow X$ *denotes the inclusion map. Given an* F-coalgebra $\mathbb{S} = \langle S, \sigma \rangle$ *and states* $s, s' \in S$ *we write* $\mathsf{B}(s)$ *for* $\mathsf{B}(\sigma(s))$ *and* $\mathsf{B}(s, s')$ *in order to denote* $\mathsf{B}(s) \cup \mathsf{B}(s')$.

Remark 1. It would be nice to avoid the choice in the previous definition. For example one could think of defining the base of x to be the intersection of all U such that $x \in Fi[FU]$. The problem is, however, that arbitrary set functors only preserve *non-empty* finite intersections, which means that with this definition we could not guarantee that $x \in Fi[F\mathsf{B}(x)]$.

The main observation for defining equivalences between coalgebras is that coalgebra morphisms preserve the behaviour of coalgebra states. This basic idea motivates the well-known coalgebraic definition of behavioural equivalence.

Definition 6. *Let $\mathbb{S}_1 = \langle S_1, \sigma_1 \rangle$, $\mathbb{S}_2 = \langle S_2, \sigma_2 \rangle$ be F-coalgebras. Two states $s_1 \in S_1$ and $s_2 \in S_2$ are called* behaviourally equivalent *(Notation: $s_1 \leftrightarrow^b s_2$) if there is an F-coalgebra $\langle Q, \lambda \rangle$ and if there are F-coalgebra morphisms $f_i : \mathbb{S}_i \to \langle Q, \lambda \rangle$ for $i = 1, 2$ such that $f_1(s_1) = f_2(s_2)$.*

There is one shortcoming of behavioural equivalence: in general it is difficult to provide a criterion that makes it easy to verify that two states are behaviourally equivalent. If the functor F under consideration preserves weak pullbacks, behavioural equivalence can be captured by so called "F-bisimulations". These bisimulations can be nicely characterized using relation lifting (cf. e.g. [9]). In order to have a similar characterization of behavioural equivalence also if the functor does not preserve weak pullbacks, the notion of a "relational equivalence" has been introduced in [6].

Definition 7. *Let $\mathbb{S}_1 = \langle S_1, \sigma_1 \rangle$ and $\mathbb{S}_2 = \langle S_2, \sigma_2 \rangle$ be F-coalgebras. Furthermore let $Z \subseteq S_1 \times S_2$ be a relation and let $\langle P, p_1, p_2 \rangle$ be the canonical pushout of Z (cf. Def. 1). Then Z is called a* relational equivalence *between $\mathbb{S}_1$ and $\mathbb{S}_2$ if there exists a coalgebra $\lambda : P \to F(P)$ such that the functions p_1 and p_2 become coalgebra morphisms from $\mathbb{S}_1$ and $\mathbb{S}_2$ to $\langle P, \lambda \rangle$. If two states s_1 and s_2 are related by some relational equivalence we write $s_1 \leftrightarrow^r s_2$.*

The main advantage of relational equivalences is that they can be characterized by some form of relation lifting:

Definition 8. *([6]) Let $\langle S_1, \sigma_1 \rangle$ and $\langle S_2, \sigma_2 \rangle$ be F-coalgebras, let $Z \subseteq S_1 \times S_2$ and let (P, p_1, p_2) be the pushout of Z. We define the* pushout lifting $\hat{F}$ *of Z, by $\hat{F}(Z) := \mathrm{pb}(Fp_1, Fp_2) \subseteq F(S_1) \times F(S_2)$.*

It can easily be shown that the pushout lifting precisely captures relational equivalence between F-coalgebras.

Proposition 1. *Let $\langle S_1, \sigma_1 \rangle$ and $\langle S_2, \sigma_2 \rangle$ be F-coalgebras and $Z \subseteq S_1 \times S_2$ a relation. Z is a relational equivalence iff for all $(s_1, s_2) \in Z$ we have $(\sigma_1(s_1), \sigma_2(s_2)) \in \hat{F}(Z)$.*

The pushout lifting $\hat{F}$ is monotone with respect to the inclusion order.

Lemma 2. *Let $Z \subseteq Z'$ be two relations between S_1 and S_2. The pushout lifting respects the inclusion order, i.e., $\hat{F}Z \subseteq \hat{F}Z'$.*

Given sets S_1, S_2, T_1 and T_2 such that $S_1 \subseteq T_1$ and $S_2 \subseteq T_2$ we can view any given relation $Z \subseteq S_1 \times S_2$ as a relation $Z' \subseteq T_1 \times T_2$. Unfortunately the definition of the pushout lifting is not independent of this, i.e., the lifting of Z can be different from the lifting of Z'. The following lemma establishes a connection between $\hat{F}Z$ and $\hat{F}Z'$.

Lemma 3. *Let S_1, S_2, T_1, T_2 be sets such that $S_1 \subseteq T_1$ and $S_2 \subseteq T_2$ and let $i_1 : S_1 \to T_1$, $i_2 : S_2 \to T_2$ be the inclusion maps. Furthermore let $Z \subseteq S_1 \times S_2$ be a relation and let $Z' \subseteq T_1 \times T_2$ be the same relation considered as a relation between T_1 and T_2. For any elements $s_1 \in FS_1$ and $s_2 \in FS_2$ we have*

$$(s_1, s_2) \in \hat{F}Z \quad implies \quad (Fi_1(s_1), Fi_2(s_2)) \in \hat{F}Z'.$$

Both Lemma 2 and Lemma 3 can be easily proven by looking at the corresponding diagrams. By definition relational equivalent points are also behavioural equivalent. A simple, but interesting observation is that the converse is also true on a coalgebra for an *arbitrary* functor $F : \mathbf{Set} \to \mathbf{Set}$.

Fact 1. *(cf. [6]) Let $\mathbb{S} = \langle S, \nu \rangle$ be an F-coalgebra. We have $s \leftrightarrow^b s'$ iff $s \leftrightarrow^r s'$ for all $s, s' \in S$.*

Remark 2. This fact demonstrates an advantage of relational equivalence when compared to F-bisimilarity: In [5] it is proven that one needs in general to assume that the functor F weakly preserves kernel pairs in order to ensure that on any F-coalgebra, F-bisimilarity and behavioural equivalence coincides.

2.2   Basic Graph Games

Before we move on to the next section we have to introduce some terminology concerning graph games. Two-player infinite graph games, or *graph games* for short, are defined as follows. For a more comprehensive account of these games, the reader is referred to Grädel, Thomas & Wilke [4].

A graph game is played on a *board* B, that is, a set of *positions*. Each position $b \in B$ *belongs* to one of the two *players*, $\exists$ (Éloise) and $\forall$ (Abélard). Formally we write $B = B_\exists \cup B_\forall$, and for each position b we use $P(b)$ to denote the player i such that $b \in B_i$. Furthermore, the board is endowed with a binary relation E (the "edge relation"), so that each position $b \in B$ comes with a set $E[b] \subseteq B$ of *successors*. Formally, we say that the *arena* of the game consists of a directed two-sorted graph $(B_\exists, B_\forall, E)$.

A *match* or *play* of the game consists of the two players moving a pebble around the board, starting from some *initial position* b_0. When the pebble arrives at a position $b \in B$, it is player $P(b)$'s turn to move; (s)he can move the pebble to a new position of their liking, but the choice is restricted to a successor of b. Should $E[b]$ be empty then we say that player $P(b)$ *got stuck* at the position. A *match* or *play* of the game thus constitutes a (finite or infinite) sequence of positions $b_0 b_1 b_2 \ldots$ such that $b_i E b_{i+1}$ (for each i such that b_i and b_{i+1} are defined). A *full play* is either (i) an infinite play or (ii) a finite play in which the last player got stuck. A non-full play is called a *partial* play.

The rules of the game associate a *winner* and (thus) a *loser* for each full play of the game. A finite full play is lost by the player who got stuck; in our paper the winning condition for infinite plays is very basic, because we let $\exists$ win all infinite plays of the game. We call graph games with this simple winning condition *basic graph games*.

A *strategy* for player i is a function mapping partial plays $\beta = b_0 \cdots b_n$ with $P(b_n) = i$ to admissible next positions, that is, to elements of $E[b_n]$. In such a way, a strategy tells i how to play: a play β *conforms to* or is *consistent with* strategy f for i if for every proper initial sequence $b_0 \cdots b_n$ of β with $P(b_n) = i$, we have that $b_{n+1} = f(b_0 \cdots b_n)$. A strategy is *history free* if it only depends on the current position of the match, that is, $f(\beta) = f(\beta')$ whenever β and β' are partial plays with the same last element (which belongs to the appropriate player). A strategy is *winning for player i* from position $b \in B$ if it guarantees i to win any match with initial position b, no matter how the adversary plays — note that this definition also applies to positions b for which $P(b) \neq i$. A position $b \in B$ is called a *winning position* for player i, if i has a winning strategy from position b; the set of winning positions for i in a game $\mathcal{G}$ is denoted as $\mathrm{Win}^i(\mathcal{G})$. Furthermore for $n \in \mathbb{N}$ we define $\mathrm{Win}_n^\exists(\mathcal{G})$ to be the set of those positions at which $\exists$ has a strategy that enables her to not lose the play in less than n rounds, i.e., she only can get stuck after she has made at least n moves.

Fact 2. *Let $\mathcal{G} = (B_\exists, B_\forall, E)$ be a basic graph game. Then*

(1) $\mathcal{G}$ is determined: $B = \mathrm{Win}^\exists(\mathcal{G}) \cup \mathrm{Win}^\forall(\mathcal{G})$.

(2) Each player i has a history-free strategy which is winning from any position in $\mathrm{Win}^i(\mathcal{G})$.

In order to see why this fact holds, note first that our basic graph games can be seen as very simple parity graph games. The fact that parity games are history-free determined was independently proved in Mostowski [8] and Emerson & Jutla [3].

3   Game-Theoretic Characterisation of Relational Equivalence

Relational equivalence can be characterised in terms of pushout lifting as demonstrated in Proposition 1. Using this lifting we now define what we call "relational equivalence game". This game is very similar to Baltag's F-bisimilarity game (cf. [2]). The only difference is that we replace the "standard" relation lifting with the pushout lifting.

Definition 9. *Let F be a set functor and let $\mathbb{S}_1 = \langle S_1, \sigma_1 \rangle$ and $\mathbb{S}_2 = \langle S_2, \sigma_2 \rangle$ be F-coalgebras. We define the arena of the relational equivalence game $\mathcal{G}(\mathbb{S}_1, \mathbb{S}_2)$ to be a bipartite graph $(B_\exists, B_\forall, E)$ where $B_\exists = S_1 \times S_2$, $B_\forall = \mathcal{P}(S_1 \times S_2)$ and the edge relation $E \subseteq (B_\exists \cup B_\forall) \times (B_\forall \cup B_\exists)$ is specified in the following table:*

Position: b	Player	Admissible moves: $E[b]$
$(s_1, s_2) \in S_1 \times S_2$	$\exists$	$\{Z \subseteq S_1 \times S_2 \mid (\sigma_1(s_1), \sigma_2(s_2)) \in \hat{F}Z\}$
$Z \in \mathcal{P}(S_1 \times S_2)$	$\forall$	$\{(s, s') \mid (s, s') \in Z\}$

Here the second column indicates whether a given position b belongs to player $\exists$ or $\forall$, i.e. whether $b \in B_\exists$ or $b \in B_\forall$, and $\hat{F}Z$ is the relation lifting of Z. A match of $\mathcal{G}(\mathbb{S}_1, \mathbb{S}_2)$ starts at some position $b_0 \in B_\exists \cup B_\forall$ and proceeds as follows: at position $b \in B_\exists$ player $\exists$ has to move to a position $b' \in E[b]$ and likewise at position $b \in B_\forall$ player $\forall$ has to move to some $b' \in E[b]$. A player who cannot move ("gets stuck") loses the match and all infinite matches are won by $\exists$.

Let us see that this game captures relational equivalence of states.

Proposition 2. *Let F be a set functor and let $\mathbb{S}_1 = \langle S_1, \sigma_1 \rangle, \mathbb{S}_2 = \langle S_2, \sigma_2 \rangle$ be F-coalgebras. For all coalgebra states $s_1 \in S_1$ and $s_2 \in S_2$ we have $s_1 \leftrightarrow^r s_2$ iff $\exists$ has a winning strategy at position (s_1, s_2) in $\mathcal{G}(\mathbb{S}_1, \mathbb{S}_2)$.*

Proof. We provide a short sketch of the proof. Suppose first that $s_1 \leftrightarrow^r s_2$, i.e., there exists a relation $Z \subseteq S_1 \times S_2$ such that $(s_1, s_2) \in Z$ and such that for all $(s, s') \in Z$ we have $(\sigma_1(s), \sigma_2(s')) \in \hat{F}Z$ (cf. Prop. 1). It is now easy to see that $\exists$ has winning strategy in $\mathcal{G} := \mathcal{G}(\mathbb{S}_1, \mathbb{S}_2)$ at (s_1, s_2): at any position $(s, s') \in Z$ she moves to position Z.

For the converse direction of our claim it suffices to show that the set

$$\text{Win}^\exists(\mathcal{G}) := \{(s, s') \in S_1 \times S_2 \mid \exists \text{ has a winning strategy at } (s, s') \text{ in } \mathcal{G}\}$$

is a relational equivalence. Consider an arbitrary element $(s, s') \in \text{Win}^\exists(\mathcal{G})$. Because $\exists$ has a winning strategy at this position there exists some relation $Z \subseteq S_1 \times S_2$ such that $(\sigma_1(s), \sigma_2(s')) \in \hat{F}Z$ and such that $Z \subseteq \text{Win}^\exists(\mathcal{G})$. Therefore by Lemma 2 we get $(\sigma_1(s), \sigma_2(s')) \in \hat{F}\text{Win}^\exists(\mathcal{G})$. As (s, s') was an arbitrary element of $\text{Win}^\exists(\mathcal{G})$ this implies, according to Prop. 1, that $\text{Win}^\exists(\mathcal{G})$ is a relational equivalence.

If we restrict our attention to one single coalgebra, we obtain a game-theoretic characterization of behavioural equivalence.

Corollary 1. *Let $\mathbb{S} = \langle S, \sigma \rangle$ be an F-coalgebra for some set functor F. Two states $s, s' \in S$ are behaviourally equivalent iff $\exists$ has a winning strategy at position (s, s') in the relational equivalence game $\mathcal{G}(\mathbb{S}, \mathbb{S})$.*

Proof. A direct consequence of Fact 1 and Proposition 2.

The game-theoretic analysis of F-relational equivalence naturally leads to the notion of n-relational equivalence.

Definition 10. *Let $\langle S_1, \sigma_1 \rangle$ and $\langle S_2, \sigma_2 \rangle$ be F-coalgebras. We say that two states $s \in S_1$ and $s' \in S_2$ are n-relational equivalent (notation: $(\langle S_1, \sigma_1 \rangle, s) \leftrightarrow^r_n (\langle S_2, \sigma_2 \rangle, s'))$ if $(s, s') \in \text{Win}^\exists_n(\mathcal{G})$ (cf. page 262).*

4 Terminal Sequence Induction via Games

We will now use the game-theoretic characterisation for giving an alternative proof of a theorem by Worrell sometimes referred to as "terminal sequence induction". Before we can state this theorem we have to introduce the terminal sequence of a functor. As we will be concerned in this section with finitary functors only, we only focus on the "finitary part" of the terminal sequence, i.e. its first ω elements.

Definition 11. *Given a set functor F we define functions $p_i : F^{i+1}1 \to F^i1$ for all $i \in \mathbb{N}$ by putting $p_0 :=!_{F1}$ and $p_{i+1} := Fp_i$. Here 1 denotes the one-element set, $!_S$ denotes the (unique) function from a set S to the one-element set 1 and for a set S we write $F^0 S := S$ and $F^{i+1}S := F(F^iS)$. For all $n \in \mathbb{N}$ elements of the set F^n1 will be called n-step behaviours.*

The terminal sequence plays an important rôle in the theory of coalgebras where it is used in order to compute or approximate the final F-coalgebra. More details about the terminal sequence of a functor we can be found in [15]. We will use the fact that given an F-coalgebra $\langle S, \sigma \rangle$ one can easily define a sequence $\{\sigma_n\}_{n \in \mathbb{N}}$ of functions as depicted in Figure 1.

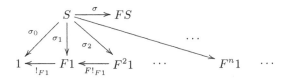

Fig. 1. Terminal sequence and n-step behaviour maps

Definition 12. *Given an F-coalgebra $\mathbb{S} = \langle S, \sigma \rangle$ we define a family of maps $\{\sigma_n : S \to F^n1\}_{n \in \mathbb{N}}$ by putting $\sigma_0(s) :=!_S$ and $\sigma_{i+1}(s) := F\sigma_n \circ \sigma$.*

For each $n \in \mathbb{N}$ the map σ_n maps a state s to its n-step behaviour which can be thought of as the behaviour of a state up-to "depth" n.

Definition 13. *Let F be a set functor and let $\mathbb{S} = \langle S, \sigma \rangle$, $\mathbb{T} = \langle T, \delta \rangle$ be F-coalgebras with projections $\sigma_n : S \to F^n1$, $\delta_n : T \to F^n1$ into the terminal sequence of F for all $n \in \mathbb{N}$. Two states $s \in S$ and $t \in T$ of $\mathbb{S}$ and $\mathbb{T}$ are called n-step equivalent if $\sigma_n(s) = \delta_n(t)$. We write $s \equiv_n t$.*

We have introduced all the necessary terminology for stating Worrell's theorem. Formulated in words it says, that a state s of some F-coalgebra $\langle S, \sigma \rangle$ can be characterized by its n-step behaviours - provided that F is a finitary set functor.

Theorem 3. *([15]) Let $F : \mathbf{Set} \to \mathbf{Set}$ be a finitary set functor and let $\langle S_1, \sigma_1 \rangle$ and $\langle S_2, \sigma_2 \rangle$ be F-coalgebras. Then we have*

$$s \leftrightarrow^b s' \quad \text{iff} \quad s \equiv_n s' \text{ for all } n \in \mathbb{N}.$$

Worrell's proof of this fact consists essentially of showing that the limit $F^\omega1$ of the terminal sequence of F is the carrier of a weakly final F-coalgebra. We are attacking the question from a different angle, using the relational equivalence game.

In order to prove Theorem 3 we are going to prove two equivalences: two coalgebra states are relational equivalent *iff* they are n-relational equivalent for all $n \in \mathbb{N}$ *iff* they have the same n-step behaviour for all $n \in \mathbb{N}$. For the first equivalence we will have to require that the given set functor F is finitary. The key observation is that finitarity of the functor implies that the game board of the relational equivalence games can be assumed to be "finitely branching". To this end we will define a finitely branching version of the relational equivalence game that employs the fact that every element $x \in FS$ has a finite base (cf. Def. 5).

There is one technical problem which complicates our argument. In order to make the game board finitely branching we will need the fact that the pushout lifting commutes with taking restrictions, i.e., ideally we would want that

$$\hat{F}(Z\lceil_{S\times T}) = \hat{F}(Z)\lceil_{FS\times FT} \tag{1}$$

This equation, however, fails to hold in general. Luckily it turns out that we can prove something similar to equation (1) if we consider Z to be an equivalence relation. This is the content of Proposition 3. First we need a small technical lemma which has a straightforward proof.

Lemma 4. *Let S be a set, let $E \subseteq S \times S$ be an equivalence relation on S and let (P, p, p) be the pushout of E. Then E is the kernel of p, i.e., E is the pullback of (P, p, p).*

Proposition 3. *Let S be a set, let $E \subseteq S \times S$ be an equivalence relation and let $S' \subseteq S$ be a non-empty subset of S with inclusion map $i : S' \to S$. For all $s_1, s_2 \in FS'$ we have*

$$((Fi)(s_1), (Fi)(s_2)) \in \hat{F}E \quad \textit{iff} \quad ((Fi)(s_1), (Fi)(s_2)) \in \hat{F}E_{S'},$$

where $E_{S'} \subseteq S \times S$ is the relation on S that corresponds to the relation $E' := E\lceil_{S'\times S'}$. Here $E\lceil_{S'\times S'} \subseteq S' \times S'$ denotes the restriction of E to $S' \times S'$.

Proof. We first show that for all $s_1, s_2 \in FS'$ we have

$$((Fi)(s_1), (Fi)(s_2)) \in \hat{F}E \quad \textit{iff} \quad (s_1, s_2) \in \hat{F}E' \tag{2}$$

The relations E and E' are related in the following way:

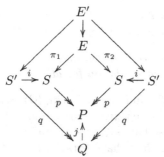

Here $i : S' \to S$ is the inclusion map, (P, p, p) is the pushout of E and (Q, q, q) depicts the pushout of E' (the special shape of these pushouts is due to the fact that both E and E' are equivalence relations). Obviously $(P, p \circ i, p \circ i)$ is a cocone over E' and hence, by the universal property of the pushout (Q, q, q), there exists a unique $j : Q \to P$ such that $p \circ i = j \circ q$. Furthermore it is not difficult to see that j is injective: Suppose $j(x_1) = j(x_2)$ for some $x_1, x_2 \in Q$. There exist $s_1', s_2' \in S'$ such that $q(s_k') = x_k$ for $k \in \{1, 2\}$. Therefore $j(q(s_1')) = j(q(s_2'))$ and thus $p(s_1') = p(i(s_1')) = p(i(s_2')) = p(s_2')$. By Lemma 4 we get $(s_1', s_2') \in E$ which implies by the definition of E' that $(s_1', s_2') \in E'$. Because (Q, q, q) is the pushout of E' we get $q(s_1') = q(s_2')$, i.e., $x_1 = x_2$ as required for the injectivity of j.

We are now ready for proving (2):

$$
\begin{array}{rll}
((Fi)(s_1), (Fi)(s_2)) \in \hat{F}E & \text{iff} & (Fp)(Fi(s_1)) = (Fp)(Fi(s_2)) \\
{\scriptstyle (F \text{ is a functor})} & \text{iff} & (Fj)(Fq(s_1)) = (Fj)(Fq(s_2)) \\
{\scriptstyle (Fj \text{ injective})} & \text{iff} & Fq(s_1) = Fq(s_2) \\
& \text{iff} & (s_1, s_2) \in \hat{F}E'.
\end{array}
$$

Finally let us see why (2) implies our claim: Suppose that $((Fi)(s_1), (Fi)(s_2)) \in \hat{F}E$, then by (2) we have $(s_1, s_2) \in \hat{F}E'$. By Lemma 3 we get $(Fi(s_1), Fi(s_2)) \in \hat{F}E_{S'}$.

For proving the previous proposition we had to assume that the relation E was an equivalence relation. As demonstrated in Proposition 4 below, we can always assume that in a match of the relational equivalence game only equivalence relations occur, provided that we are playing the game on a single coalgebra. Before we are able to prove this proposition we need two technical lemmas concerning the structure of $\exists$'s strategies.

Lemma 5. *Let $\mathbb{S}_1$ and $\mathbb{S}_2$ be F-coalgebras for some set functor F. The following holds:*

1. *for $s_1 \in S_1, s_2 \in S_2$ we have $s_1 \leftrightarrow^r s_2$ iff there exists a relation $Z \subseteq \mathrm{Win}_\exists(\mathcal{G}(\mathbb{S}_1, \mathbb{S}_2))$ such that $(\sigma_1(s_1), \sigma_2(s_2)) \in \hat{F}Z$.*
2. *$s_1 \leftrightarrow_{n+1}^r s_2$ iff there exists $Z \subseteq \leftrightarrow_n^r$ such that $(\sigma_1(s_1), \sigma_2(s_2)) \in \hat{F}Z$.*

Proof. The claims follow immediately from the definitions.

Lemma 6. *Let F be a set functor, let $\mathbb{S} = \langle S, \sigma \rangle$ be an F-coalgebra and let $\mathcal{G} := \mathcal{G}(\mathbb{S}, \mathbb{S})$ be the relational equivalence game on $\mathbb{S}$. The following holds true:*

1. *$\mathrm{Win}^\exists(\mathcal{G})$ is an equivalence relation, and*
2. *$\mathrm{Win}_n^\exists(\mathcal{G})$ is an equivalence relation for all $n \in \mathbb{N}$.*

Proof. Let $W := \mathrm{Win}^\exists(\mathcal{G})$ and $W_n := \mathrm{Win}_n^\exists(\mathcal{G})$. Obviously we have $(s, s) \in W$ for all $s \in S$, i.e., W is reflexive. Furthermore it is easy to see that W is symmetric. Finally assume that $(s_1, s_2) \in W$ and $(s_2, s_3) \in W$. Therefore by the first observation in Lemma 5 we have $(\sigma(s_1), \sigma(s_2)) \in \hat{F}W$ and $(\sigma(s_3), \sigma(s_2)) \in$

$\hat{F}W$. Moreover $(\sigma(s_2), \sigma(s_2)) \in \hat{F}W$. Because $\hat{F}W$ is a pullback we know that it is zigzag-closed (cf. Lemma 1). Hence we obtain $(\sigma(s_1), \sigma(s_3)) \in \hat{F}W$ and thus $(s_1, s_3) \in W$. The second claim of the lemma can be proven analogously.

Proposition 4. *Let F be a set functor, let $\mathbb{S} = \langle S, \sigma \rangle$ be an F-coalgebra and let $\mathcal{G}^\sharp = \mathcal{G}^\sharp(\mathbb{S}, \mathbb{S})$ be the variant of $\mathcal{G} = \mathcal{G}(\mathbb{S}, \mathbb{S})$ in which $\exists$ can only move to equivalence relations, i.e., at all positions $(s, s') \in S \times S$ the set of possible moves of $\exists$ is given by*

$$\{E \subseteq S \times S \mid (\sigma(s), \sigma(s')) \in \hat{F}E \text{ and } E \text{ is an equivalence relation}\}.$$

Then $(s, s') \in \mathrm{Win}^\exists(\mathcal{G}^\sharp)$ iff $(s, s') \in \mathrm{Win}^\exists(\mathcal{G})$. Similarly, we get $(s, s') \in \mathrm{Win}_n^\exists(\mathcal{G}^\sharp)$ iff $(s, s') \in \mathrm{Win}_n^\exists(\mathcal{G})$ for all $n \in \mathbb{N}$.

Proof. Clearly we have $\mathrm{Win}^\exists(\mathcal{G}^\sharp) \subseteq \mathrm{Win}^\exists(\mathcal{G})$. For the converse direction suppose that $(s_1, s_2) \in \mathrm{Win}^\exists(\mathcal{G})$. By Lemma 5 this means that $(\sigma(s_1), \sigma(s_2)) \in \hat{F}\mathrm{Win}^\exists(\mathcal{G})$ and $\mathrm{Win}^\exists(\mathcal{G})$ is an equivalence relation according to Lemma 6. Therefore $\mathrm{Win}^\exists(\mathcal{G})$ is a legitimate move for $\exists$ at position (s_1, s_2) in $\mathcal{G}^\sharp$ and it is not difficult to see that $\exists$ has a winning strategy in $\mathcal{G}^\sharp$ by moving at position (s_1, s_2) to $\mathrm{Win}^\exists(\mathcal{G})$ and by repeating this move at all following positions of the match that are of form (s, s').

For the second half of the claim it is again obvious that $\mathrm{Win}_n^\exists(\mathcal{G}^\sharp) \subseteq \mathrm{Win}_n^\exists(\mathcal{G})$ for all $n \in \mathbb{N}$. The converse inclusion can be proven by induction on n. The case $n = 0$ is trivial. Consider now some $(s_1, s_2) \in \mathrm{Win}_{n+1}^\exists(\mathcal{G})$. Then by the second half of Lemma 5 we have $(\sigma(s_1), \sigma(s_2)) \in \hat{F}\mathrm{Win}_n^\exists(\mathcal{G})$ and by I.H. $\mathrm{Win}_n^\exists(\mathcal{G}) = \mathrm{Win}_n^\exists(\mathcal{G}^\sharp)$. Hence we obtain $(\sigma(s_1), \sigma(s_2)) \in \hat{F}\mathrm{Win}_n^\exists(\mathcal{G}^\sharp)$ which is sufficient for showing that $(\sigma(s_1), \sigma(s_2)) \in \mathrm{Win}_{n+1}^\exists(\mathcal{G}^\sharp)$.

We are now ready to define a finitely branching version of the relational equivalence game on a single coalgebra.

Definition 14. *Let F be a finitary set functor and let $\mathbb{S} = \langle S, \sigma \rangle$ be an F-coalgebra. We define the arena of the* finitary relational equivalence game $\mathcal{G}_\omega(\mathbb{S}, \mathbb{S})$ *to be a bipartite graph $(B_\exists, B_\forall, E)$ where $B_\exists = S \times S$, $B_\forall = \mathcal{P}(S \times S)$ and the edge relation $E \subseteq (B_\exists \cup B_\forall) \times (B_\forall \cup B_\exists)$ is specified in the following table:*

Position: b	Player	Admissible moves: $E[b]$
$(s_1, s_2) \in S \times S$	$\exists$	$\{Z \subseteq S \times S \mid \mathrm{rng}(Z) \subseteq \mathsf{B}(s_1, s_2), \mathrm{dom}(Z) \subseteq \mathsf{B}(s_1, s_2),$ $(\sigma(s_1), \sigma(s_2)) \in \hat{F}Z\}$
$Z \in \mathcal{P}(S \times S)$	$\forall$	$\{(s, s') \mid (s, s') \in Z\}$

where $\mathrm{rng}(Z)$ and $\mathrm{dom}(Z)$ denote the range and the domain of the relation Z, respectively.

Hence the arena of $\mathcal{G}_\omega(\mathbb{S}_1, \mathbb{S}_2)$ differs from the arena of $\mathcal{G}(\mathbb{S}_1, \mathbb{S}_2)$ in the possible moves for $\exists$: at position (s_1, s_2), $\exists$ is only allowed to chose relations that contain states in $\mathsf{B}(s_1, s_2) = \mathsf{B}(\sigma(s_1)) \cup \mathsf{B}(\sigma(s_2))$. It turns out that the simpler game is equivalent to the relational equivalence game from Definition 9.

Proposition 5. *Let F be a finitary set functor and let $\mathbb{S} = \langle S, \sigma \rangle$ be an F-coalgebra. We have* $\mathrm{Win}^{\exists}(\mathcal{G}(\mathbb{S}, \mathbb{S})) = \mathrm{Win}^{\exists}(\mathcal{G}_\omega(\mathbb{S}, \mathbb{S}))$ *and moreover for all $n \in \omega$,* $\mathrm{Win}_n^{\exists}(\mathcal{G}(\mathbb{S}, \mathbb{S})) = \mathrm{Win}_n^{\exists}(\mathcal{G}_\omega(\mathbb{S}, \mathbb{S}))$.

Proof. We only prove the first equality, the proof of the respective equalities for all $n \in \omega$ is analogous. The direction from left to right is trivial, because any strategy of $\exists$ in $\mathcal{G}_\omega = \mathcal{G}_\omega(\mathbb{S}, \mathbb{S})$ is also a strategy for her in $\mathcal{G} = \mathcal{G}(\mathbb{S}, \mathbb{S})$. For the converse direction suppose that $\exists$ has a winning strategy in $\mathcal{G}$ at position (s_1, s_2). By Prop. 4 we can assume w.l.o.g. that $\exists$'s strategy consists of moves to *equivalence relations* only, i.e., at any position $(s, s') \in S \times S$ that is reached during the match $\exists$ will move to an equivalence relation. Let $(s, s') \in S \times S$ and recall from Prop. 3 that for all equivalence relations $Z \subseteq S \times S$ and for all $(x, x') \in F\mathsf{B}(s, s')$ we have

$$(Fi(x), Fi(x')) \in \hat{F}Z \quad \text{iff} \quad (Fi(x), Fi(x')) \in \hat{F}(Z_{\mathsf{B}(s,s')}) \tag{3}$$

where $Z_{\mathsf{B}(s,s')} \subseteq S \times S$ denotes the restriction of Z to $\mathsf{B}(s, s') \times \mathsf{B}(s, s')$ and $i : \mathsf{B}(s, s') \to S$ is the inclusion map. By the definition of $\mathsf{B}(s, s')$ it is clear that there are elements $y, y' \in F\mathsf{B}(s, s')$ such that $Fi(y) = \sigma(s)$ and $Fi(y') = \sigma(s')$. Therefore (3) yields $(\sigma(s), \sigma(s')) \in \hat{F}Z$ iff $(\sigma(s), \sigma(s')) \in \hat{F}(Z_{\mathsf{B}(s,s')})$. As (s, s') and Z were arbitrary it is now easy to see that $\exists$'s winning strategy in $\mathcal{G}$ can be turned into a winning strategy for her in $\mathcal{G}_\omega$ by replacing any of her moves from some pair (s, s') to an equivalence relation Z by a move from (s, s') to $Z_{\mathsf{B}(s,s')}$.

The previous proposition together with Fact 1 and Prop. 2 has as corollary that behavioural equivalence can be captured using the *finitary* game $\mathcal{G}_\omega$.

Corollary 2. *Let $\mathbb{S} = \langle S, \sigma \rangle$ be an F-coalgebra for some finitary set functor F. For all $s, s' \in S$ we have $s \leftrightarrow^b s'$ iff $(s, s') \in \mathrm{Win}^{\exists}(\mathcal{G}_\omega(\mathbb{S}, \mathbb{S}))$.*

We now prove the crucial property of the finitary relational equivalence game: if $\exists$ has for any $n \in \mathbb{N}$ a strategy ensuring that she does not lose the game before making n moves, then she also has a winning strategy.

Proposition 6. *Let F be a finitary set functor and let $\mathbb{S} = \langle S, \sigma \rangle$ be an F-coalgebra. For any pair of states $(s_1, s_2) \in S \times S$ we have $s_1 \leftrightarrow^r s_2$ iff for all $n \in \mathbb{N}$ we have $s_1 \leftrightarrow_n^r s_2$.*

Proof. The direction from left to right is trivial. For the converse direction suppose for a contradiction that for some $s_1 \in S_1$, $s_2 \in S_2$ we have $s_1 \leftrightarrow_n^r s_2$ for all $n \in \mathbb{N}$ and $s_1 \not\leftrightarrow^r s_2$, i.e., $\exists$ does not have a winning strategy in $\mathcal{G}_\omega(\mathbb{S}, \mathbb{S})$ at position (s_1, s_2). Because graph games are positionally determined, $\forall$ has a positional winning strategy $f : \mathcal{P}(S \times S) \to S \times S$ in $\mathcal{G}_\omega(\mathbb{S}, \mathbb{S})$ at position (s_1, s_2). We define a relation $\mathcal{T} \subseteq (S \times S) \times (S \times S)$ by putting

$$((t_1, t_2), (t_1', t_2')) \in \mathcal{T} \quad \text{if} \quad \exists Z \subseteq S \times S, \mathrm{rng}(Z) \subseteq \mathsf{B}(t_1, t_2), \mathrm{dom}(Z) \subseteq \mathsf{B}(t_1, t_2)$$
$$\text{s.t. } (\sigma(t_1), \sigma(t_2)) \in \hat{F}Z \text{ and } f(Z) = (t_1', t_2').$$

Let us prove some properties of $\mathcal{T}$:

1. There is a round of $\mathcal{G}_\omega(\mathbb{S}, \mathbb{S})$ starting at position (t_1, t_2) and ending at position (t_1', t_2') in which $\forall$ plays according to f iff $(t_1, t_2)\mathcal{T}(t_1', t_2')$.
2. There are no $\mathcal{T}$-cycles that are reachable from (s_1, s_2), i.e., $(s_1, s_2)\mathcal{T}^*(t_1, t_2)$ and $(t_1, t_2)\mathcal{T}^+(t_1', t_2')$ imply $t_1 \neq t_1'$ or $t_2 \neq t_2'$, where $\mathcal{T}^*$ and $\mathcal{T}^+$ are the usual notation for the reflexive, transitive closure and the transitive closure, respectively.

The first property follows easily from spelling out the definitions. The second property can be obtained as follows: Suppose for a contradiction that there is a $\mathcal{T}$-cycle from (s_1, s_2), i.e. suppose that $(s_1, s_2)\mathcal{T}^*(t_1, t_2)\mathcal{T}^+(t_1, t_2)$. Then by condition (1) there is a match of $\mathcal{G}_\omega(\mathbb{S}, \mathbb{S})$ in which $\forall$ sticks to his winning strategy and which is of the form $(s_1, s_2)\ldots(t_1, t_2)\ldots(t_1, t_2)$. This means that $\exists$ has a strategy against $\forall$'s strategy f which ensures that starting from position (t_1, t_2) the match will again arrive at position (t_1, t_2). Therefore $\exists$ can win the match by sticking to her strategy: she repeats her strategy such that the match repeatedly reaches position (t_1, t_2) and in this way the match continues for an infinite number of moves. As $\forall$'s strategy was assumed to be winning we arrive at a contradiction, i.e. no $\mathcal{T}$-cycles are reachable from position (s_1, s_2).

Hence we proved that the collection of all pairs that are $\mathcal{T}$-reachable from (s_1, s_2) together with the relation $\mathcal{T}$ form a connected and acyclic graph G that is finitely branching by definition. Paths through G that start at (s_1, s_2) are in one-to-one correspondence with matches of the game $\mathcal{G}_\omega(\mathbb{S}, \mathbb{S})$ that start in (s_1, s_2) and in which $\forall$ plays according to his winning strategy f. By our assumption that $s_1 \leftrightarrow_n^r s_2$ for all $n \in \omega$ and using Prop. 5 we get for all $n \in \omega$ the existence of a $\mathcal{T}$-path through G of length n that starts in (s_1, s_2). An application of König's Lemma yields the existence of an infinite path on G starting at (s_1, s_2). This infinite path corresponds to a match that is won by $\exists$ which contradicts the fact that all paths correspond to matches in which $\forall$ is playing his winning strategy.

What is left in order to prove Worrell's theorem is that we have to establish a connection between our game-theoretic notion of n-relational equivalence and the notion of n-step equivalence (cf. Def. 13).

Proposition 7. *Let F be a set functor and let $\mathbb{S} = \langle S, \sigma \rangle$ be an F-coalgebra. For all $n \in \mathbb{N}$ and all states $s, s' \in S$ of $\mathbb{S}$ we have*

$$s \equiv_n s' \quad iff \quad s \leftrightarrow_n^r s'.$$

Proof. We prove $\equiv_n = \leftrightarrow_n^r$ by induction on n. The base case $n = 0$ is trivial. For the inductive step consider first the following diagram

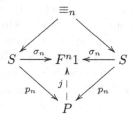

where (P, p_n, p_n) is the pushout of $\equiv_n$. It is easy to see that p_n is surjective and that the map $j : P \to F^n 1$, that exists because of the universal property of the pushout, is injective. Therefore Fj is injective and we obtain

$$F\sigma_n(x) = F\sigma_n(x') \quad \text{iff} \quad Fp_n(x) = Fp_n(x') \quad \text{iff} \quad (x, x') \in \hat{F}(\equiv_n). \quad (4)$$

Suppose now that $s \equiv_{n+1} s'$ for some $s, s' \in S$. We obtain the following chain of equivalences:

$$
\begin{aligned}
s \equiv_{n+1} s' \quad &\Leftrightarrow \quad \sigma_{n+1}(s) = \sigma_{n+1}(s') \\
\text{\scriptsize (Def. of } \sigma_{n+1}) \quad &\Leftrightarrow \quad F\sigma_n(\sigma(s)) = F\sigma_n(\sigma(s')) \overset{(4)}{\Leftrightarrow} Fp_n(\sigma(s)) = Fp_n(\sigma(s')) \\
&\Leftrightarrow \quad (\sigma(s), \sigma(s')) \in \hat{F}(\equiv_n) \quad \overset{\text{(I.H.)}}{\Leftrightarrow} \quad (\sigma(s), \sigma(s')) \in \hat{F}(\leftrightarrow_n^r)
\end{aligned}
$$

The last statement is clearly equivalent to the fact that $(s, s') \in \leftrightarrow_{n+1}^r$ which finishes the proof of the proposition.

We are now able to prove Theorem 3.

Proof. Let $\mathbb{S} = \langle S, \sigma \rangle$ and $\mathbb{T} = \langle T, \tau \rangle$ be F-coalgebras for some finitary set functor F. It is easy to see that for all $s \in S$ and for all $t \in T$ we have $\mathbb{S}, s \leftrightarrow^b \mathbb{T}, t$ implies $\sigma_n(s) = \tau_n(t)$ for all $n \in \mathbb{N}$. For the converse consider the coproduct $\mathbb{S} + \mathbb{T} = \langle S + T, \gamma \rangle$ of $\mathbb{S}$ and $\mathbb{T}$ in the category of F-coalgebras with canonical embeddings $\kappa_1 : S \to S + T$ and $\kappa_2 : T \to S + T$. Consider now $s \in S$ and $t \in T$ such that $\sigma_n(s) = \tau_n(t)$ for all $n \in \mathbb{N}$. Because the canonical embeddings are coalgebra morphisms is it easy to see that $\gamma_n(\kappa_1(s)) = \gamma_n(\kappa_2(t))$ for all $n \in \mathbb{N}$. By Proposition 7 this implies $\kappa_1(s) \leftrightarrow_n^r \kappa_2(t)$ for all $n \in \mathbb{N}$. As F was assumed to be finitary we can apply Proposition 6 and we obtain $\kappa_1(s) \leftrightarrow^r \kappa_2(t)$. The latter implies $\kappa_1(s) \leftrightarrow^b \kappa_2(t)$ (cf. Fact 1). Putting everything together we arrive at $s \leftrightarrow^b \kappa_1(s) \leftrightarrow^b \kappa_2(t) \leftrightarrow^b t$ which implies $s \leftrightarrow^b t$ because $\leftrightarrow^b$ can be easily seen to be transitive using the fact that the category of F-coalgebras has pushouts.

5   Conclusions

The main technical result of this paper is that behavioural equivalence on F-coalgebras can be captured by a game with finitely-branching game board (Corollary 2). We employed this fact in order to obtain a proof of Worrell's theorem using games. Moreover we established a connection between the $(n$-$)$relational equivalence game and the terminal sequence of a set functor that we hope to explore further. It should be mentioned that Worrell's result holds not only for finitary set functors but also for some functors that are not finitary such as the functor $FX = \mathcal{P}_\omega(X)^A$ for some infinite set A. Our hope would be that games offer a good perspective for giving an exact characterization of those set functors, for which the principle of terminal sequence induction holds. Furthermore we would like to investigate the possibility of using the pushout lifting and the relational equivalence game for defining a coalgebraic logic à la Moss ([7]) for F-coalgebras without the assumption that F weakly preserves pullbacks.

References

[1] Adámek, J., Herrlich, H., Strecker, G.E.: Abstract and Concrete Categories, The Joy of Cats. John Wiley and Sons, Inc., Chichester (1990)

[2] Baltag, A.: A logic for coalgebraic simulation. In: Reichel, H. (ed.) Proceedings of the Workshop on Coalgebraic Methods in Computer Science (CMCS). Electronic Notes in Theoretical Computer Science, vol. 33 (2000)

[3] Emerson, E.A., Jutla, C.S.: Tree automata, mu-calculus and determinacy. In: Proceedings of the 32nd IEEE Symposium on Foundations of Computer Science (FoCS 1991), pp. 368–377. IEEE Computer Society Press, Los Alamitos (1991)

[4] Grädel, E., Thomas, W., Wilke, T. (eds.): Automata, Logics, and Infinite Games. LNCS, vol. 2500. Springer, Heidelberg (2002)

[5] Gumm, H.P., Schröder, T.: Types and coalgebraic structure. Algebra universalis 53, 229–252 (2005)

[6] Hansen, H.H., Kupke, C., Pacuit, E.: Bisimulation for Neighbourhood Structures. In: Mossakowski, T., Montanari, U., Haveraaen, M. (eds.) CALCO 2007. LNCS, vol. 4624, pp. 279–293. Springer, Heidelberg (2007)

[7] Moss, L.S.: Coalgebraic Logic. Annals of Pure and Applied Logic 96, 277–317 (1999)

[8] Mostowski, A.: Games with forbidden positions. Technical Report 78, Instytut Matematyki, Uniwersytet Gdański, Poland (1991)

[9] Rutten, J.J.M.M.: Relators and Metric Bisimulation (Extended Abstract). Electronic Notes in Theoretical Computer Science 11, 1–7 (1998)

[10] Rutten, J.J.M.M.: Universal coalgebra: A theory of systems. Theoretical Computer Science 249, 3–80 (2000)

[11] Rutten, J.J.M.M., de Vink, E.P.: Bisimulation for probabilistic transition systems: a coalgebraic approach. Theoretical Computer Science 221(1–2), 271–293 (1999)

[12] Schröder, L.: Expressivity of Coalgebraic Modal Logic: The Limits and Beyond. Theoretical Computer Science 390, 230–247 (2008)

[13] Venema, Y.: Algebras and coalgebras. In: Handbook of Modal Logic, vol. 3, pp. 331–426. Elsevier, Amsterdam (2006)

[14] Venema, Y.: Automata and fixed point logic: a coalgebraic perspective. Information and Computation 204, 637–678 (2006)

[15] Worrell, J.: On the final sequence of a finitary set functor. Theoretical Computer Science 338(1–3), 184–199 (2005)

Dutch Grammar and Processing: A Case Study in TLG

Glyn Morrill[1], Oriol Valentín[2], and Mario Fadda[3]

[1] Universitat Politècnica de Catalunya
morrill@lsi.upc.edu
http://www-lsi.upc.edu/~morrill/
[2] Universitat Pompeu Fabra
oriol.valentin@upf.edu
[3] Universitat Politècnica de Catalunya
mfadda@lsi.upc.edu

Abstract. The aim of this paper is to see *type logical grammar* (TLG) at work on an interesting linguistic case: the incremental processing of Dutch subordinate clause word order, namely the so-called cross-serial dependencies. With the help of proof net machinery adapted for the continuous and discontinuous Lambek calculus we are able to account for the increasing unacceptability of cross-serial dependencies with increasingly multiple embeddings.

Keywords: Discontinuous Lambek calculus, Dutch cross-serial dependencies, proof net complexity metric, Type Logical Grammar.

1 Introduction

In this paper we present a type-logical account of the incremental processing of Dutch cross-serial dependencies.[1] Within the framework of the Lambek Calculus **LC** (Lambek 1958)[4], Morrill (2000)[7] gave a simple metric of complexity of categorial proof nets for **LC** (Roorda (1991)[14]). This metric correctly predicted a variety of performance phenomena such as garden pathing, left to right quantifier scope preference and so on. All these phenomena remained in the terrain of concatenative (continuous) grammar. We know however that natural language goes beyond concatenation. Morrill and Fadda (2008)[9] presents proof nets for basic discontinuous Lambek calculus **BDLC**. Here, an extension of this system called **1-DLC**, which is based on Morrill (2002)[8], is defined. **1-DLC** is more polymorphic than **BDLC**, and includes new unary connectives. With the help of the new connectives we give a simple type-logical analysis of Dutch subordinate clause word order, which includes an account of the complexity of processing of cross-serial dependencies.

---

[1] Work partially funded by the DGICYT project TIN2005–08832–C03–03 (MOISES-BAR).

P. Bosch, D. Gabelaia, and J. Lang (Eds.): TbiLLC 2007, LNAI 5422, pp. 272–286, 2009.
© Springer-Verlag Berlin Heidelberg 2009

In Section 2, the **1-DLC**, an extension of **LC** is presented. In Section 3, proofnets for **1-DLC** are considered. The approach to defining proof nets for **BDLC** is presented and prospects for proof nets for the full fragment **1-DLC** are envisaged. In Section 4 we consider relevant linguistic facts of Dutch. Finally, Section 5 gives a **1-DLC** analysis of the grammar and processing of Dutch in terms of the metric of Morrill (2000)[7] adapted to **1-DLC** proof nets.

2   1-Discontinuous Lambek Calculus, 1-DLC

A *discontinuous prosodic algebra* is a free algebra $(L, +, 0, 1)$ where $(L, +, 0)$ is a monoid and 1 (the *separator*) is a prime (Morrill 2002)[8]; let $\sigma(s)$ be the number of separators in a prosodic object s. This induces the *1-discontinuous prosodic structure* $(L_0, L_1, +, \times, 0, 1)$ where

(1) – $L_0 = \{s \in L \mid \sigma(s) = 0\}$
     – $L_1 = \{s \in L \mid \sigma(s) = 1\} = L_0 1 L_0$
     – $+ : L_i, L_j \rightarrow L_{i+j}, i + j \leq 1$
     – $\times : L_1, L_j \rightarrow L_j, j \leq 1$ is such that $(s_1 + 1 + s_3) \times s_2 = s_1 + s_2 + s_3$

The sets $\mathcal{F}_0$ and $\mathcal{F}_1$ of *1-discontinuous types* of *sort zero* and *one* are defined on the basis of sets $\mathcal{A}_0$ and $\mathcal{A}_1$ of primitive 1-discontinuous types of sort zero and one as follows:[2]

(2) $\mathcal{F}_0 ::= \mathcal{A}_0 \mid \triangleright^{-1}\mathcal{F}_1 \mid \triangleleft^{-1}\mathcal{F}_1 \mid {}^{\wedge}\mathcal{F}_1 \mid \mathcal{F}_0\backslash\mathcal{F}_0 \mid \mathcal{F}_1\backslash\mathcal{F}_1 \mid$
      $\qquad \mathcal{F}_0/\mathcal{F}_0 \mid \mathcal{F}_1/\mathcal{F}_1 \mid \mathcal{F}_0\bullet\mathcal{F}_0 \mid \mathcal{F}_1\downarrow\mathcal{F}_0 \mid \mathcal{F}_1\odot\mathcal{F}_0$
      $\mathcal{F}_1 ::= \mathcal{A}_1 \mid \triangleright\mathcal{F}_0 \mid \triangleleft\mathcal{F}_0 \mid {}^{\vee}\mathcal{F}_0 \mid \mathcal{F}_0\backslash\mathcal{F}_1 \mid \mathcal{F}_1/\mathcal{F}_0 \mid$
      $\qquad \mathcal{F}_0\bullet\mathcal{F}_1 \mid \mathcal{F}_1\bullet\mathcal{F}_0 \mid \mathcal{F}_1\downarrow\mathcal{F}_1 \mid \mathcal{F}_0\uparrow\mathcal{F}_0 \mid \mathcal{F}_1\odot\mathcal{F}_1$

A *prosodic interpretation of 1-discontinuous types* is a function $[[\cdot]]$ mapping each type $\mathcal{A}_i \in \mathcal{F}_i$ into a subset of L_i as shown in Figure 1.[3]
   We give *hypersequent calculus* (not in the sense of A. Avron) for sorted discontinuity (Morrill 1997)[6]. The sets $\mathcal{Q}_0$ and $\mathcal{Q}_1$ of output *figures of sort zero and one* of **1-DLC** are defined as follows (where A_0 denotes an arbitrary type of sort 0, and A_1 an arbitrary type of sort 1):

(3) $\mathcal{Q}_0 ::= A_0$
     $\mathcal{Q}_1 ::= \sqrt[0]{A_1}, [\,], \sqrt[1]{A_1}$

The vectorial notation $\overrightarrow{A}$ refers to the figure of a type A. The sets $\mathcal{O}_0$ and $\mathcal{O}_1$ of input *configurations of sort zero and one of* **1-DLC** are defined as follows:

(4) $\mathcal{O}_0 ::= \Lambda \mid A_0, \mathcal{O}_0 \mid \sqrt[0]{A_1}, \mathcal{O}_0, \sqrt[1]{A_1}, \mathcal{O}_0$
     $\mathcal{O}_1 ::= \mathcal{O}_0, [\,], \mathcal{O}_0 \mid \mathcal{O}_0, \sqrt[0]{A_1}, \mathcal{O}_1, \sqrt[1]{A_1}, \mathcal{O}_0$

---

[2] Sorting for discontinuity was introduced in Morrill and Merenciano (1996)[12].
[3] The first type-logical formulations of discontinuous product, infix and extract were made by M. Moortgat. Bridge and split were introduced in Morrill and Merenciano (1996)[12]. Injections and projections are new here.

$$
\begin{array}{ll}
[[\rhd A]] = \{1{+}s|\ s \in [[A]]\} & \text{right injection} \\
[[\rhd^{-1} B]] = \{s|\ 1{+}s \in [[B]]\} & \text{right projection} \\
[[\lhd A]] = \{s{+}1|\ s \in [[A]]\} & \text{left injection} \\
[[\lhd^{-1} B]] = \{s|\ s{+}1 \in [[B]]\} & \text{left projection} \\
[[\hat{\ }A]] = \{s_1{+}s_2|\ s_1{+}1{+}s_2 \in [[A]]\} & \text{bridge} \\
[[\check{\ }B]] = \{s_1{+}1{+}s_2|\ s \in [[B]]\} & \text{split} \\
[[A{\bullet}B]] = \{s_1{+}s_2|\ s_1 \in [[A]]\ \&\ s_2 \in [[B]]\} & \text{(continuous) product} \\
[[A{\backslash}C]] = \{s_2|\ \forall s_1 \in [[A]], s_1{+}s_2 \in [[C]]\} & \text{under} \\
[[C/B]] = \{s_1|\ \forall s_2 \in [[B]], s_1{+}s_2 \in [[C]]\} & \text{over} \\
[[A{\odot}B]] = \{s_1{+}s_2{+}s_3|\ s_1{+}1{+}s_3 \in [[A]]\ \&\ s_2 \in [[B]]\} & \text{discontinuous product} \\
[[A{\downarrow}C]] = \{s_2|\ \forall s_1{+}1{+}s_3 \in [[A]], s_1{+}s_2{+}s_3 \in [[C]]\} & \text{infix} \\
[[C{\uparrow}B]] = \{s_1{+}1{+}s_3|\ \forall s_2 \in [[B]], s_1{+}s_2{+}s_3 \in [[C]]\} & \text{extract}
\end{array}
$$

Fig. 1. Prosodic interpretation of **1-DLC** types

Note that figures are "singular" configurations. We define the *components* of a configuration as its maximal substrings not containing the metalinguistic separator [ ]. We extend the interpretation of types to include configurations as follows:

$$
\begin{array}{ll}
(5) & [[\Lambda]] = \{0\} \\
& [[[\ ], \Gamma]] = \{1{+}s|\ s \in [[\Gamma]]\} \\
& [[A, \Gamma]] = \{s_1{+}s_2|\ s_1 \in [[A]]\ \&\ s_2 \in [[\Gamma]]\} \\
& [[\sqrt[0]{A}, \Gamma, \sqrt[1]{A}, \Delta]] = \{s_1{+}s_2{+}s_3{+}s_4|\ s_1{+}1{+}s_3 \in [[A]]\ \&\ s_2 \in [[\Gamma]]\ \&\ s_4 \in [[\Delta]]\}
\end{array}
$$

A *hypersequent* $\Gamma \Rightarrow X$ of sort i comprises an input configuration Γ of sort i and an output figure X of sort i; it is *valid* iff $[[\Gamma]] \subseteq [[X]]$ in every prosodic interpretation. The *hypersequent calculus* for **1-DLC** is as shown in Figure 2 where $\Delta(\Gamma)$ means a configuration Δ in which in some distinguished positions the components of Γ appear in order successively though not necessarily continuously.

The calculus of **1-DLC** is sound with respect to the interpretation given, i.e. every theorem is valid, as can be seen by an easy induction on the length of proofs. It also enjoys Cut-elimination, i.e. every theorem has a Cut-free proof, as is essentially proved in Valentín (2006)[16]. As a corollary, **1-DLC** has the sub-formula property, i.e. every theorem has a proof containing only its subformulas. This follows since every rule except Cut has the property that all the types in the premises are either in the conclusion (side formulas) or are the immediate subtypes of the active formula, and Cut itself is eliminable. It also follows that it is decidable whether a **1-DLC** sequent is a theorem, by backward-chaining in the finite Cut-free hypersequent search space.

It is an open question whether **1-DLC** is complete with respect to the interpretation given, i.e. whether every valid sequent is a theorem. Perhaps the reasoning of Pentus (1993)[13] for **LC** can be replicated. For some results (completeness for the continuous and discontinuous implicational fragment, and full completeness with respect to power-set preordered discontinuous prosodic algebras), see Valentín (2006)[16].

$$\overline{\vec{A} \Rightarrow \vec{A}} \; id \qquad \frac{\Gamma \Rightarrow \vec{A} \qquad \Delta(\vec{A}) \Rightarrow \vec{C}}{\Delta(\Gamma) \Rightarrow \vec{C}} \; Cut$$

$$\frac{\Delta(\sqrt[0]{A}, \Gamma, \sqrt[1]{A}) \Rightarrow \vec{C}}{\Delta(\Gamma, \triangleright^{-1}A) \Rightarrow \vec{C}} \triangleright^{-1}L \qquad \frac{[\,], \Gamma \Rightarrow \sqrt[0]{A}, [\,], \sqrt[1]{A}}{\Gamma \Rightarrow \triangleright^{-1}A} \triangleright^{-1}R$$

$$\frac{\Delta(\Gamma, A) \Rightarrow \vec{C}}{\Delta(\sqrt[0]{\triangleright A}, \Gamma, \sqrt[1]{\triangleright A}) \Rightarrow \vec{C}} \triangleright L \qquad \frac{\Gamma \Rightarrow A}{[\,], \Gamma \Rightarrow \sqrt[0]{\triangleright A}, [\,], \sqrt[1]{\triangleright A}} \triangleright R$$

$$\frac{\Delta(\sqrt[0]{A}, \Gamma, \sqrt[1]{A}) \Rightarrow \vec{C}}{\Delta(\triangleleft^{-1}A, \Gamma) \Rightarrow \vec{C}} \triangleleft^{-1}L \qquad \frac{\Gamma, [\,] \Rightarrow \sqrt[0]{A}, [\,], \sqrt[1]{A}}{\Gamma \Rightarrow \triangleleft^{-1}A} \triangleleft^{-1}R$$

$$\frac{\Delta(A, \Gamma) \Rightarrow \vec{C}}{\Delta(\sqrt[0]{\triangleleft A}, \Gamma, \sqrt[1]{\triangleleft A}) \Rightarrow \vec{C}} \triangleleft L \qquad \frac{\Gamma \Rightarrow A}{\Gamma, [\,] \Rightarrow \sqrt[0]{\triangleleft A}, [\,], \sqrt[1]{\triangleleft A}} \triangleleft R$$

$$\frac{\Delta(B) \Rightarrow \vec{C}}{\Delta(\sqrt[0]{\check{} B}, \sqrt[1]{\check{} B}) \Rightarrow \vec{C}} \check{} L \qquad \frac{\Gamma(\Lambda) \Rightarrow B}{\Gamma([\,]) \Rightarrow \sqrt[0]{\check{} B}, [\,], \sqrt[1]{\check{} B}} \check{} R$$

$$\frac{\Delta(\sqrt[0]{A}, \sqrt[1]{A}) \Rightarrow \vec{C}}{\Delta(\hat{} A) \Rightarrow \vec{C}} \hat{} L \qquad \frac{\Gamma([\,]) \Rightarrow \sqrt[0]{A}, [\,], \sqrt[1]{A}}{\Gamma(\Lambda) \Rightarrow \hat{} A} \hat{} R$$

$$\frac{\Gamma \Rightarrow \vec{A} \qquad \Delta(\vec{C}) \Rightarrow \vec{D}}{\Delta(\Gamma, \overrightarrow{A \backslash C}) \Rightarrow \vec{D}} \backslash L \qquad \frac{\vec{A}, \Gamma \Rightarrow \vec{C}}{\Gamma \Rightarrow \overrightarrow{A \backslash C}} \backslash R$$

$$\frac{\Gamma \Rightarrow \vec{B} \qquad \Delta(\vec{C}) \Rightarrow \vec{D}}{\Delta(\overrightarrow{C/B}, \Gamma) \Rightarrow \vec{D}} /L \qquad \frac{\Gamma, \vec{B} \Rightarrow \vec{C}}{\Gamma \Rightarrow \overrightarrow{C/B}} /R$$

$$\frac{\Delta(\vec{A}, \vec{B}) \Rightarrow \vec{D}}{\Delta(\overrightarrow{A \bullet B}) \Rightarrow \vec{D}} \bullet L \qquad \frac{\Gamma_1 \Rightarrow \vec{A} \qquad \Gamma_2 \Rightarrow \vec{B}}{\Gamma_1, \Gamma_2 \Rightarrow \overrightarrow{A \bullet B}} \bullet R$$

$$\frac{\Gamma_1, [\,], \Gamma_2 \Rightarrow \sqrt[0]{A}, [\,], \sqrt[1]{A} \qquad \Delta(\vec{C}) \Rightarrow \vec{D}}{\Delta(\Gamma_1, \overrightarrow{A \downarrow C}, \Gamma_2) \Rightarrow \vec{D}} \downarrow L \qquad \frac{\sqrt[0]{A}, \Gamma, \sqrt[1]{A} \Rightarrow \vec{C}}{\Gamma \Rightarrow \overrightarrow{A \downarrow C}} \downarrow R$$

$$\frac{\Gamma \Rightarrow \vec{B} \qquad \Delta(\vec{C}) \Rightarrow \vec{D}}{\Delta(\sqrt[0]{C \uparrow B}, \Gamma, \sqrt[1]{C \uparrow B}) \Rightarrow \vec{D}} \uparrow L \qquad \frac{\Gamma_1, \vec{B}, \Gamma_2 \Rightarrow \vec{C}}{\Gamma_1, [\,], \Gamma_2 \Rightarrow \overrightarrow{C \uparrow B}} \uparrow R$$

$$\frac{\Delta(\sqrt[0]{A}, \vec{B}, \sqrt[1]{A}) \Rightarrow \vec{C}}{\Delta(\overrightarrow{A \odot B}) \Rightarrow \vec{C}} \odot L \qquad \frac{\Gamma_1, [\,], \Gamma_3 \Rightarrow \sqrt[0]{A}, [\,], \sqrt[1]{A} \qquad \Gamma_2 \Rightarrow \vec{B}}{\Gamma_1, \Gamma_2, \Gamma_3 \Rightarrow \overrightarrow{A \odot B}} \odot R$$

Fig. 2. 1-DLC hypersequent calculus

3 Towards Proof Nets for 1-DLC

Proof nets can be seen as the (parallel) syntactic structures of categorial grammar, for they encode the essence of sequent derivations, so that different proof
nets for a given provable sequent have distinct lambda terms assigned via the
Curry-Howard homomorphism.[4] In this section we present a formulation of proof
nets for the (continuous) **LC** which allows an extension to some discontinuous
connectives (see Morrill and Fadda (2008)[9]).

A *polar type* A^p comprises a type A and a polarity $p = \bullet$ (input) or $\circ$ (output).
We define the *complements* of a polar type as: $\overline{A^\circ} = A^\bullet$ and $\overline{A^\bullet} = A^\circ$. The *logical
links* are as shown in Figure 3.

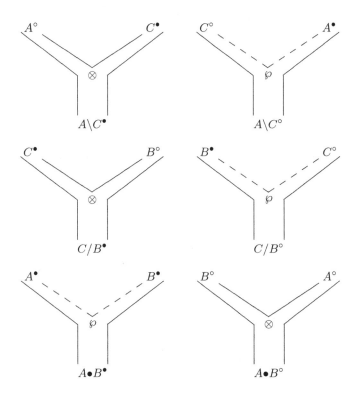

Fig. 3. LC logical links

We refer to lane edges as *parameter edges* and we refer to sequences of dashed
parameter edges as ∀-*segments*. We refer to entire highways seen as single broad
edges as *predicate edges*.

---

[4] As Moot and Piazza (2001)[5] put it, "multiple proof nets for a given theorem differ
for interesting, non-bureaucratic reasons".

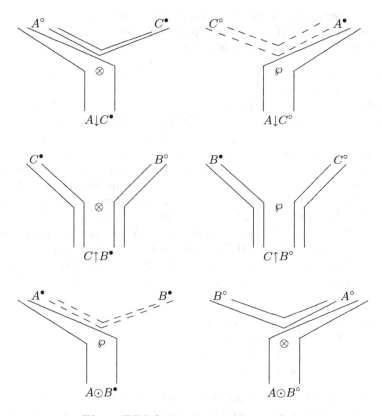

Fig. 4. BDLC discontinuous logical links

A *polar type tree* is the result of unfolding a polar type up to its atomic leaves according to the logical links. A *proof frame* for a sequent $A_0, \ldots, A_n \Rightarrow A$ is the multiset of unfolded polar type trees of $A^\circ, A_1^\bullet, \ldots, A_n^\bullet$. An *axiom link* is as follows, where P is an atomic polar type:

(6)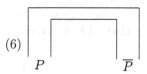

A *proof structure* is a proof frame to which have been added axiom links connecting each leaf to exactly one other complementary leaf. A *proof net* is a proof structure satisfying the following correctness criteria:

(7)   – (*Danos-Regnier acyclicity*) Every predicate edge cycle crosses both premise edges of some $\wp$-link.

– (∀-*correctness*) every parameter edge cycle contains exactly one
∀-segment, and if a parameter path does not form part of a cycle then
it does not contain any ∀-segment.

A **LC** sequent is a theorem if and only if a proof net can be built on its proof
frame. (Morrill and Fadda 2008)[9].

Morrill and Fadda (2008)[9] give proof nets for a subsystem of **1-DLC** called
basic discontinuous Lambek calculus, **BDLC**. Discontinuous proof nets can be
seen as the syntactic structures of discontinuous hypersequent derivations.
BDLC has only functionalities $+ : L_0, L_0 \rightarrow L_0$ and $\times : L_1, L_0 \rightarrow L_0$, and
has no unary connectives. The logical links for the discontinuous connectives of
that subsystem are given in Figure 4. It is an open question how to formulate
proof nets for the **1-DLC** binary connectives and unary connectives. The complication for these latter is that they are akin to units, for which it has been
found difficult to give proof nets in linear logic. A step towards a rigorous formulation of proof nets for **1-DLC**, would be to extend the approach of Moot
and Piazza (2001)[5] and Morrill and Fadda (2008)[9] by translating into first
order linear logic with the theory of equality the unary connectives of **1-DLC**.
Thus, we propose:[5]

– $|{\lhd}A|^{<x,y,u,v>} = |A|^{<x,y>} \otimes u \approx v$
– $|{\lhd^{-1}}A|^{<u,v>} = \forall t \forall l (t \approx l \multimap |A|^{<u,v,t,l>})$
– $|{^{\wedge}}A|^{<u,v>} = \exists x \exists y (|A|^{<u,x,y,v>} \otimes x \approx y)$
– $|{^{\vee}}A|^{<u,x,y,v>} = x \approx y \multimap |A|^{<u,v>}$

The questions which arise are how to formulate proof links for the unary connectives defined in terms of $\approx$, and what are their correctness criteria. We leave
this study for further research. In this paper we use informal proof nets for
1-DLC.

4   Dutch Word Order

Morrill, Fadda and Valentín (2007)[10] gives an account of cross-serial dependencies in discontinuous Lambek calculus without the unary connectives $\lhd, \lhd^{-1}, \rhd,$
$\rhd^{-1}$, which involves lexical assignments of sort 1 to verb raising triggers. Here
we refine the analysis with right projections in such a way that all lexical assignments are of sort 0.

In Dutch, subordinate clauses are verb final:

(8) (... dat) Jan   boeken las
     (... that) J.   books   read
     CP/S   N   N   N\(N\S) ⇒ CP
     '(... that) Jan read books'

---

[5] The embeddings of the other injection and projection are completely similar.

Modals and control verbs, so-called verb raising triggers, appear in a verb final verb cluster with the English word order:[6]

(9) (... dat) Jan boeken kan   lezen
     (... that) J.   books is able   read
     CP/S   N   N $(N\backslash Si)\downarrow(N\backslash S)$ $\triangleright^{-1}(N\backslash(N\backslash Si))$ $\Rightarrow$ CP
     '(... that) Jan is able to read books'

(10) (... dat) Jan boeken wil   kunnen
     (... that) J.   books wants   be able
     CP/S   N   N $(N\backslash Si)\downarrow(N\backslash S)$ $\triangleright^{-1}((N\backslash Si)\downarrow(N\backslash Si))$

     lezen
     read
     $\triangleright^{-1}(N\backslash(N\backslash Si))$ $\Rightarrow$ CP
     '(... that) Jan wants to be able to read books'

When the infinitival complement verbs also take objects, cross-serial dependencies are generated. Calcagno (1995)[1] provides an analysis of cross-serial dependencies which is a close precedent to ours, but in terms of categorial head-wrapping of headed strings, rather than wrapping of separated strings.

(11) (... dat) Jan Cecilia$_1$ Henk$_2$ de   nijlpaarden$_3$
     (... that) J. C.   H.   the   hippos
     CP/S   N   N   N   N/CN CN

     zag$_1$ helpen$_2$ voeren$_3$
     saw   help   feed
     $(N\backslash Si)\downarrow(N\backslash(N\backslash S))$ $\triangleright^{-1}((N\backslash Si)\downarrow(N\backslash(N\backslash Si)))$ $\triangleright^{-1}(N\backslash(N\backslash Si))$ $\Rightarrow$ CP
     '(... that) Jan saw$_1$ Cecilia$_1$ help$_2$ Henk$_2$ feed$_3$ the hippos$_3$'

Main clause yes/no interrogative word order, V1, is derived from subordinate clause word order by fronting the finite verb. We therefore propose a lexical rule mapping (subordinate clause) finite verb types V to $Q/^{\wedge}(S{\uparrow}V)$, cf. Hepple (1990)[2].

(12) Wil   Jan boeken lezen?
     wants   J.   books read
     $Q/^{\wedge}(S{\uparrow}((N\backslash Si)\downarrow(N\backslash S)))$ N   N $\triangleright^{-1}(N\backslash(N\backslash Si))$ $\Rightarrow$ Q
     'Does Jan want to read books?'

Main clause declarative word order, V2, is further derived from V1 by fronting a major constituent. We propose to achieve this by allowing complex distinguished types (cf. Morrill and Gavarró 1992)[11].

(13) Jan wil   boeken lezen.
     J.   wants   books read
     N $Q/^{\wedge}(S{\uparrow}((N\backslash Si)\downarrow(N\backslash S)))$ N $\triangleright^{-1}(N\backslash(N\backslash Si))$ $\Rightarrow$ N$\bullet^{\wedge}(Q{\uparrow}N)$
     'Jan wants to read books.'

---

[6] Note that the atomic type Si is of sort 1.

5   Analyses of Dutch

We are now in a position to account for the following claim on Dutch cross-serial dependencies:

(14) 'An increasing load in processing makes such multiple embeddings increasingly unacceptable.' [Steedman (1985)[15], fn. 29, p.546]

$$
\cfrac{
N \Rightarrow N \qquad
\cfrac{
N \Rightarrow N \qquad
\cfrac{
\cfrac{
\cfrac{
\cfrac{
\cfrac{
\cfrac{
\cfrac{
\sqrt[0]{VPi},[\,],\sqrt[1]{VPi} \Rightarrow \sqrt[0]{VPi},[\,],\sqrt[1]{VPi} \qquad N,VP \Rightarrow S
}{
N \Rightarrow N \qquad N,\sqrt[0]{VPi},VPi{\downarrow}VP,\sqrt[1]{VPi} \Rightarrow S
}\;{\downarrow}L
}{
N,N,\sqrt[0]{N\backslash VPi},VPi{\downarrow}VP,\sqrt[1]{N\backslash VPi} \Rightarrow S
}\;{\backslash}L
}{
N,N,VPi{\downarrow}VP,\triangleright^{-1}(N\backslash VPi) \Rightarrow S
}\;{\triangleright}^{-1}L
}{
N,N,[\,],\triangleright^{-1}(N\backslash VPi) \Rightarrow \sqrt[0]{S{\uparrow}(VPi{\downarrow}VP)},[\,],\sqrt[1]{S{\uparrow}(VPi{\downarrow}VP)}
}\;{\uparrow}R
}{
N,N,\triangleright^{-1}(N\backslash VPi) \Rightarrow {}^{\wedge}(S{\uparrow}(VPi{\downarrow}VP)) \qquad Q \Rightarrow Q
}\;{}^{\wedge}R
}{
Q/{}^{\wedge}(S{\uparrow}(VPi{\downarrow}VP)),N,N,\triangleright^{-1}(N\backslash VPi) \Rightarrow Q
}\;/L
}{
Q/{}^{\wedge}(S{\uparrow}(VPi{\downarrow}VP)),[\,],N,\triangleright^{-1}(N\backslash VPi) \Rightarrow \sqrt[0]{Q{\uparrow}N},[\,],\sqrt[1]{Q{\uparrow}N}
}\;{\uparrow}R
}{
Q/{}^{\wedge}(S{\uparrow}(VPi{\downarrow}VP)),N,\triangleright^{-1}(N\backslash VPi) \Rightarrow {}^{\wedge}(Q{\uparrow}N)
}\;{}^{\wedge}R
}{
N,Q/{}^{\wedge}(S{\uparrow}(VPi{\downarrow}VP)),N,\triangleright^{-1}(N\backslash VPi) \Rightarrow N{\bullet}{}^{\wedge}(Q{\uparrow}N)
}\;{\bullet}R
$$

Fig. 5. Hypersequent derivation of *Jan wil boeken lezen*

The (continuous and discontinuous) proof net machinery defines a simple measure of the incremental complexity[7] of a sentence, which consists of a graph relating word positions and the number of open (unresolved) dependencies at this point. This graph is called the complexity profile (Morrill 2000[7]).

A hypersequent calculus derivation of *Jan wil boeken lezen* is given in Figure 5, where here and henceforth VP abbreviates N\S and VPi abbreviates N\Si. The proof net syntactic structure for *Jan wil boeken lezen* is given in Figure 6. The complexity profile is as follows:

(15)
```
3 | a                        a
2 |       a    a
1 |
0 |                               a
  |_____
    Jan   wil  boeken  lezen
```

A hypersequent calculus derivation of *Marie zegt dat Jan Cecilia Henk de nijlpaarden zag helpen voeren* ('Marie says that Jan saw Cecilia help Henk feed the hippos') is given in Figure 7. An outline of the proof net syntactic structure for this example is given in Figures 8 and 9. We note the marked increase of

---

[7] For some results on complexity of sentences in terms of proof nets, see independent work by M. Johnson (1998)[3].

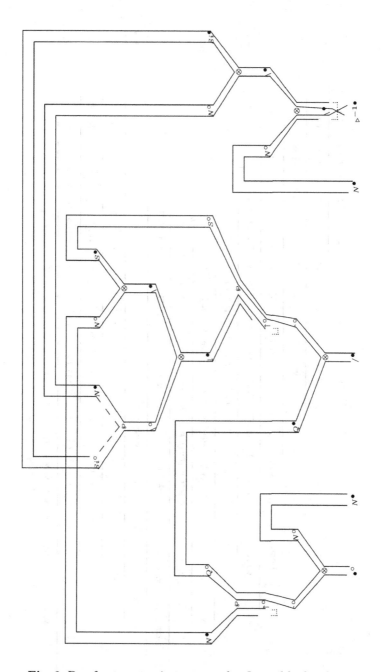

Fig. 6. Proof net syntactic structure for *Jan wil boeken lezen*

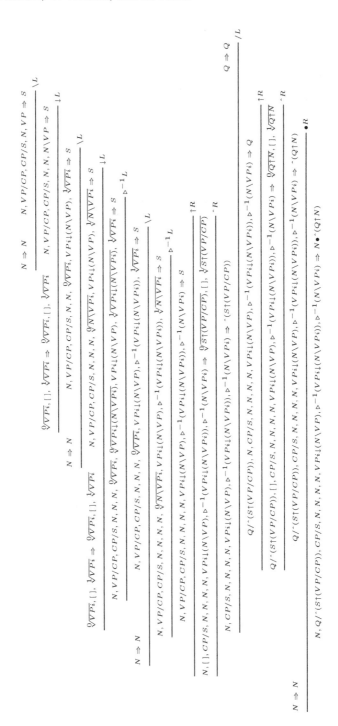

Fig. 7. Hypersequent derivation of *Marie zegt dat Jan Cecilia Henk de nijlpaarden zag helpen voeren*

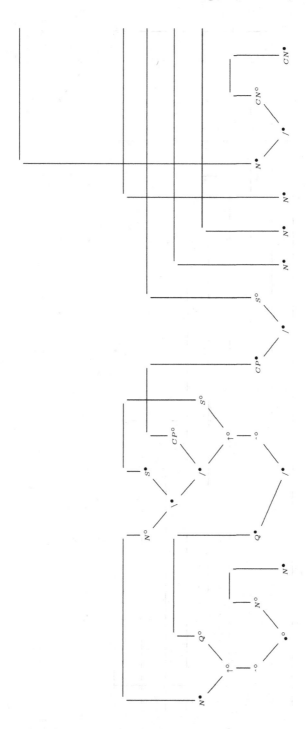

Fig. 8. Syntactic structure for *Marie zegt dat Jan Cecilia Henk de nijlpaarden zag helpen voeren*, part I

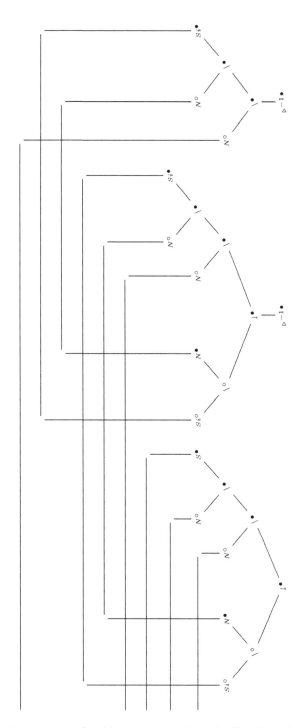

Fig. 9. Syntactic structure for *Marie zegt dat Jan Cecilia Henk de nijlpaarden zag helpen voeren*, part II

complexity between the proof net syntactic structures in Figure 6 and in Figures 8 and 9:

(16)

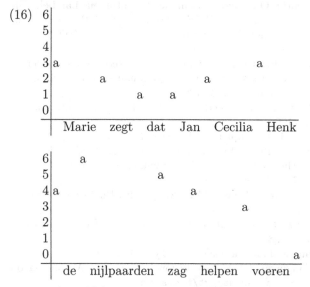

Morrill (2000)[7] observes that when a complexity profile reaches a level of around 7, usually taken to be about the capacity of short term memory, an analysis becomes unacceptable. Here, the number of unresolved dependencies in between *de* and *nijlparden* is 6, a fact which we claim causes the sentence to be near the limit of unacceptability of further nesting of cross-serial dependencies.

References

1. Calcagno, M.: A Sign-Based Extension to the Lambek Calculus for Discontinuous Constituency. Bulletin of the IGPL 3(4), 555–578 (1995)
2. Hepple, M.: The Grammar and Processing of Order and Dependency. PhD thesis, University of Edinburgh (1990)
3. Johnson, M.: Proof nets and the complexity of processing center-embedded constructions. Journal of Logic, Language and Information 7(4), 433–447 (1998)
4. Lambek, J.: The mathematics of sentence structure. American Mathematical Monthly 65, 154–170 (1958); reprinted in: Buszkowski, W., Marciszewski, W., van Benthem, J.: Categorial Grammar. Linguistic & Literary Studies in Eastern Europe, vol. 25, pp. 153–172. John Benjamins, Amsterdam (1958)
5. Moot, R., Piazza, M.: Linguistic applications of first order intuitionistic linear logic. Journal of Logic, Language and Information 10, 211–232 (2001)
6. Morrill, G.: Proof Syntax of Discontinuity. In: Dekker, P., Stokhof, M., Venema, Y. (eds.) Proceedings of the 11th Amsterdam Colloquium, Universiteit van Amsterdam, pp. 235–240. Institute for Logic, Language and Computation, ILLC (1997)
7. Morrill, G.: Incremental Processing and Acceptability. Computational Linguistics 26(3), 319–338 (2000)
8. Morrill, G.: Towards Generalised Discontinuity. In: Jäger, G., Monachesi, P., Penn, G., Wintner, S. (eds.) Proceedings of the 7th Conference on Formal Grammar, Trento, pp. 103–111. ESSLLI (2002)

9. Morrill, G., Fadda, M.: Proof Nets for Basic Discontinuous Lambek Calculus. Logic and Computation 18(2), 239–256 (2008)
10. Morrill, G., Fadda, M., Valentín, O.: Nondeterministic Discontinuous Lambek Calculus. In: Geertzen, J., Thijsse, E., Bunt, H., Schiffrin, A. (eds.) Proceedings of the Seventh International Workshop on Computational Semantics, IWCS-7, pp. 129–141. Tilburg University (2007)
11. Morrill, G., Gavarró, A.: Catalan Clitics. In: Lecomte, A. (ed.) Word Order in Categorial Grammar / L'Ordre des mots dans les grammaires catégorielles, pp. 211–232. Édicions Adosa, Clermont-Ferrand (1992)
12. Morrill, G., Merenciano, J.-M.: Generalising discontinuity. Traitement automatique des langues 37(2), 119–143 (1996)
13. Pentus, M.: Lambek calculus is L-complete. ILLC Report, University of Amsterdam (1993); shortened version published as Language completeness of the Lambek calculus. In: Proceedings of the Ninth Annual IEEE Symposium on Logic in Computer Science, Paris, pp. 487–496 (1994)
14. Roorda, D.: Resource Logics. Proof-theoretical Investigations. PhD thesis, Universiteit van Amsterdam (1991)
15. Steedman, M.: Dependency and Coordination in the Grammar of Dutch and English. Language 61, 523–568 (1985)
16. Valentín, O.: 1-Discontinuous Lambek Calculus: Type Logical Grammar and discontinuity in natural language. DEA dissertation, Universitat Autònoma de Barcelona (2006), http://seneca.uab.es/ggt/tesis.htm

Author Index

Printed in the United States
By Bookmasters